Constitutional Law

Fifth Edition

2019 Supplement

2019 Supplement

Constitutional Law

Fifth Edition

Erwin Chemerinsky
Dean and Jesse H. Choper Distinguished Professor of Law
University of California, Berkeley School of Law

Published by Wolters Kluwer in New York.

Wolters Kluwer Legal & Regulatory U.S. serves customers worldwide with CCH, Aspen Publishers, and Kluwer Law International products. (www.WKLegaledu.com)

To contact Customer Service, e-mail customer.service@wolterskluwer.com, call 1-800-234-1660, fax 1-800-901-9075, or mail correspondence to:

> Wolters Kluwer
> Attn: Order Department
> PO Box 990
> Frederick, MD 21705

Printed in the United States of America.

1 2 3 4 5 6 7 8 9 0

ISBN 978-1-5438-0935-0

SUSTAINABLE FORESTRY INITIATIVE

Certified Chain of Custody
Promoting Sustainable Forestry
www.sfiprogram.org
SFI-01028

About Wolters Kluwer Legal & Regulatory U.S.

Wolters Kluwer Legal & Regulatory U.S. delivers expert content and solutions in the areas of law, corporate compliance, health compliance, reimbursement, and legal education. Its practical solutions help customers successfully navigate the demands of a changing environment to drive their daily activities, enhance decision quality and inspire confident outcomes.

Serving customers worldwide, its legal and regulatory portfolio includes products under the Aspen Publishers, CCH Incorporated, Kluwer Law International, ftwilliam.com and MediRegs names. They are regarded as exceptional and trusted resources for general legal and practice-specific knowledge, compliance and risk management, dynamic workflow solutions, and expert commentary.

Contents

Preface

Since the fifth edition of the casebook was completed, two justices, Antonin Scalia and Anthony Kennedy, have left the Supreme Court. Two new justices, Neil Gorsuch and Brett Kavanaugh, have replaced them. It is a time of important transition for the Court. This Supplement presents the Supreme Court's decisions from October Terms 2016, 2017, and 2018.

Major cases in the Supplement are:

Chapter 1—*Rucho v. Common Cause* (2019)—concerning whether federal courts can hear challenges to partisan gerrymandering.

Chapter 2—*Murphy v. NCAA* (2018)—concerning the Tenth Amendment.

Chapter 3—*Trump v. Hawaii* (2018)—regarding the constitutionality of President Trump's travel ban. *Gundy v. United States* (2019)—concerning the principle that Congress cannot delegate legislative power to agencies. *Lucia v. Securities and Exchange Commission* (2018)—on the distinction between officers of the United States and government employees. I also chose to include *Department of Commerce v. New York* (2019), on the inclusion of a question on citizenship in the census, though the case is primarily about administrative law.

Chapter 4—*Tennessee Wine and Spirits Retailers Association v. Thomas* (2019)—preventing a state from discriminating against out-of-staters in providing licenses to sell alcohol. *South Dakota v. Wayfair* (2018)—regarding the ability of states to require that businesses collect sales tax even if they do not have a physical presence in the state.

Chapter 5—*Timbs v. Indiana* (2019)—holding that the excessive fines clause applies to state and local governments. *Manhattan Community Access Project v. Halleck* (2019)—concerning whether cable public access channels created by the government must comply with the Constitution.

Chapter 6—*Knick v. Township of Scott, Pennsylvania* (2019)—regarding the need to exhaust state procedures before bringing a takings claim. *Murr v. Wisconsin* (2017)—concerning the Takings Clause and how to determine what is the "property."

Chapter 7—*Cooper v. Harris* (2017)—concerning the use of race in drawing election district lines. Also presented is *Pena-Rodriguez v. Colorado* (2017) on race and jury deliberations.

Chapter 8—*Pavan v. Smith* (2017)—regarding the constitutionality of denying a married same-sex couple the ability to list both parents on a child's birth certificate. Also, *Box v. Planned Parenthood of Indiana and Kentucky* (2019), a *per curium* opinion concerning a state law regulating fetal remains.

Chapter 9—five free speech cases are presented: *Matal v. Tam* (2017), *Iancu v. Brunetti* (2019), *NIFLA v. Becerra* (2018), *Packingham v. North Carolina* (2017), and *Expressions Hair Design v. Schneiderman* (2017).

Chapter 10—*Masterpiece Cakeshop v. Colorado Civil Rights Commission* (2019)—concerning whether it violated free exercise of religion for a baker to be held liable for refusing, based on his religion, to design and bake a cake for a same-sex wedding celebration. *Trinity Lutheran, Columbia, Missouri v. Comer* (2017) involved whether the denial of aid to a religious institution infringed free exercise of religion. *American Legion v. American Humanist Association* (2019)—regarding the constitutionality of a large, 40-foot cross on public property.

I will continue to prepare a Supplement each summer and a new edition every four years. I welcome comments and suggestions from users of the casebook and the supplement.

Erwin Chemerinsky
Berkeley, California
July 2019

Constitutional Law

Fifth Edition

2019 Supplement

Chapter 1

The Federal Judicial Power

B. Limits on the Federal Judicial Power

3. Justiciability Limits

c. Ripeness (casebook p. 81)

In *Knick v. Township of Scott, Pennsylvania*, 139 S. Ct. ___ (2019), the Supreme Court held that takings claims are ripe for review when the taking occurs. The Court overruled *Williamson County Regional Planning Commission v. Hamilton Bank*, 473 U.S. 172 (1985), which held that a takings claim is not ripe until there has been exhaustion of state remedies because it cannot be said until then that there has been a taking without just compensation. *Knick* is presented below in Chapter 6, as part of the consideration of the Takings Clause.

e. The Political Question Doctrine (casebook p. 91)

i. The Political Question Doctrine Defined

What is a Political Question? The Issues of Malapportionment and Partisan Gerrymandering

Partisan gerrymandering is where the political party that controls a legislature draws election districts to maximize safe seats for that party. In *Vieth v. Jubelirer* (casebook p. 96), the Court held that such challenges pose a non-justiciable political question. Justice Scalia wrote a plurality opinion for four justices that there were not judicially discoverable or manageable standards for determining when gerrymandering violates the Constitution. Justice Kennedy was the fifth vote for the majority and concluded that there were not standards yet, but left open the possibility for the development of standards in the future.

The issue came back to the Court in 2019, in *Gill v. Whitford,* where a lower court found partisan gerrymandering unconstitutional. But the Supreme Court reversed, holding that the plaintiffs failed to prove that they had standing. The issue returned to the Court in *Rucho v. Common Cause* and the Court held, 5-4, that challenges to partisan gerrymandering pose non-justiciable political questions.

RUCHO v. COMMON CAUSE
139 S. Ct. 2484 (2019)

Chief Justice ROBERTS delivered the opinion of the Court.

Voters and other plaintiffs in North Carolina and Maryland challenged their States' congressional districting maps as unconstitutional partisan gerrymanders. The North Carolina plaintiffs complained that the State's districting plan discriminated against Democrats; the Maryland plaintiffs complained that their State's plan discriminated against Republicans. The plaintiffs alleged that the gerrymandering violated the First Amendment, the Equal Protection Clause of the Fourteenth Amendment, the Elections Clause, and Article I, § 2, of the Constitution. The District Courts in both cases ruled in favor of the plaintiffs, and the defendants appealed directly to this Court.

These cases require us to consider once again whether claims of excessive partisanship in districting are "justiciable"—that is, properly suited for resolution by the federal courts. This Court has not previously struck down a districting plan as an unconstitutional partisan gerrymander, and has struggled without success over the past several decades to discern judicially manageable standards for deciding such claims. The districting plans at issue here are highly partisan, by any measure. The question is whether the courts below appropriately exercised judicial power when they found them unconstitutional as well.

I

The first case involves a challenge to the congressional redistricting plan enacted by the Republican-controlled North Carolina General Assembly in 2016. The Republican legislators leading the redistricting effort instructed their mapmaker to use political data to draw a map that would produce a congressional delegation of ten Republicans and three Democrats. As one of the two Republicans chairing the redistricting committee stated, "I think electing Republicans is better than electing Democrats. So I drew this map to help foster what I think is better for the country." He further explained that the map was drawn with the aim of electing ten Republicans and three Democrats because he did "not believe it [would be] possible to draw a map with 11 Republicans and 2 Democrats." One Democratic state senator objected that entrenching the 10–3 advantage for Republicans was not "fair, reasonable, [or] balanced" because, as recently as 2012, "Democratic congressional candidates had received more votes on a state-wide basis than Republican candidates." The General Assembly was not swayed by that objection and approved the 2016 Plan by a party-line vote.

In November 2016, North Carolina conducted congressional elections using the 2016 Plan, and Republican candidates won 10 of the 13 congressional districts. In the 2018 elections, Republican candidates won nine congressional districts, while Democratic candidates won three. The Republican candidate narrowly prevailed in the remaining district, but the State Board of Elections called a new election after allegations of fraud.

The second case before us is *Lamone v. Benisek*. In 2011, the Maryland Legislature — dominated by Democrats — undertook to redraw the lines of that State's eight congressional districts. The Governor at the time, Democrat Martin O'Malley, led the process. He appointed a redistricting committee to help redraw the map, and asked Congressman Steny Hoyer, who has described himself as a "serial gerrymanderer," to advise the committee. The Governor later testified that his aim was to "use the redistricting process to change the overall composition of Maryland's congressional delegation to 7 Democrats and 1 Republican by flipping" one district. The map was adopted by a party-line vote. It was used in the 2012 election and succeeded in flipping the Sixth District. A Democrat has held the seat ever since.

II

Article III of the Constitution limits federal courts to deciding "Cases" and "Controversies." We have understood that limitation to mean that federal courts can address only questions "historically viewed as capable of resolution through the judicial process." In these cases we are asked to decide an important question of constitutional law. "But before we do so, we must find that the question is presented in a 'case' or 'controversy' that is, in James Madison's words, 'of a Judiciary Nature.'"

Chief Justice Marshall famously wrote that it is "the province and duty of the judicial department to say what the law is." *Marbury v. Madison* (1803). Sometimes, however, "the law is that the judicial department has no business entertaining the claim of unlawfulness — because the question is entrusted to one of the political branches or involves no judicially enforceable rights." *Vieth v. Jubelirer*, (2004) (plurality opinion). In such a case the claim is said to present a "political question" and to be nonjusticiable — outside the courts' competence and therefore beyond the courts' jurisdiction. *Baker v. Carr* (1962). Among the political question cases the Court has identified are those that lack "judicially discoverable and manageable standards for resolving [them]."

Partisan gerrymandering is nothing new. Nor is frustration with it. The practice was known in the Colonies prior to Independence, and the Framers were familiar with it at the time of the drafting and ratification of the Constitution. During the very first congressional elections, George Washington and his Federalist allies accused Patrick Henry of trying to gerrymander Virginia's districts against their candidates — in particular James Madison, who ultimately prevailed over fellow future President James Monroe. In 1812, Governor of Massachusetts and future Vice President Elbridge Gerry notoriously approved congressional districts that the legislature had drawn to aid the Democratic-Republican Party. The moniker "gerrymander" was born when an outraged Federalist newspaper observed that one of the misshapen districts resembled a salamander. "By 1840, the gerrymander was a recognized force in party politics and was generally attempted in all legislation enacted for the formation of election districts. It was generally conceded that each party would attempt to gain power which was not proportionate to its numerical strength."

The Framers addressed the election of Representatives to Congress in the Elections Clause. Art. I, § 4, cl. 1. That provision assigns to state legislatures the power to prescribe the "Times, Places and Manner of holding Elections" for Members of Congress, while giving Congress the power to "make or alter" any such regulations. Congress has regularly exercised its Elections Clause power, including to address partisan gerrymandering. The Apportionment Act of 1842, which required single-member districts for the first time, specified that those districts be "composed of contiguous territory," Congress also used its Elections Clause power in 1870, enacting the first comprehensive federal statute dealing with elections as a way to enforce the Fifteenth Amendment. Starting in the 1950s, Congress enacted a series of laws to protect the right to vote through measures such as the suspension of literacy tests and the prohibition of English-only elections.

The Framers were aware of electoral districting problems and considered what to do about them. They settled on a characteristic approach, assigning the issue to the state legislatures, expressly checked and balanced by the Federal Congress.

Courts have nevertheless been called upon to resolve a variety of questions surrounding districting. Early on, doubts were raised about the competence of the federal courts to resolve those questions.

To hold that legislators cannot take partisan interests into account when drawing district lines would essentially countermand the Framers' decision to entrust districting to political entities. The "central problem" is not determining whether a jurisdiction has engaged in partisan gerrymandering. It is "determining when political gerrymandering has gone too far."

III

In considering whether partisan gerrymandering claims are justiciable, we are mindful of Justice Kennedy's counsel in *Vieth*: Any standard for resolving such claims must be grounded in a "limited and precise rationale" and be "clear, manageable, and politically neutral." An important reason for those careful constraints is that, as a Justice with extensive experience in state and local politics put it, "[t]he opportunity to control the drawing of electoral boundaries through the legislative process of apportionment is a critical and traditional part of politics in the United States." An expansive standard requiring "the correction of all election district lines drawn for partisan reasons would commit federal and state courts to unprecedented intervention in the American political process."

As noted, the question is one of degree: How to "provid[e] a standard for deciding how much partisan dominance is too much." And it is vital in such circumstances that the Court act only in accord with especially clear standards: "With uncertain limits, intervening courts—even when proceeding with best intentions—would risk assuming political, not legal, responsibility for a process that often produces ill will and distrust." If federal courts are to "inject [themselves] into the most heated partisan issues" by adjudicating partisan gerrymandering claims, they must be armed with a standard that can reliably differentiate unconstitutional from "constitutional political gerrymandering."

Partisan gerrymandering claims rest on an instinct that groups with a certain level of political support should enjoy a commensurate level of political power and influence. Explicitly or implicitly, a districting map is alleged to be unconstitutional because it makes it too difficult for one party to translate statewide support into seats in the legislature. But such a claim is based on a "norm that does not exist" in our electoral system—"statewide elections for representatives along party lines."

Partisan gerrymandering claims invariably sound in a desire for proportional representation. As Justice O'Connor put it, such claims are based on "a conviction that the greater the departure from proportionality, the more suspect an apportionment plan becomes.". "Our cases, however, clearly foreclose any claim that the Constitution requires proportional representation or that legislatures in reapportioning must draw district lines to come as near as possible to allocating seats to the contending parties in proportion to what their anticipated statewide vote will be."

The Founders certainly did not think proportional representation was required. For more than 50 years after ratification of the Constitution, many States elected their congressional representatives through at-large or "general ticket" elections. Such States typically sent single-party delegations to Congress. That meant that a party could garner nearly half of the vote statewide and wind up without any seats in the congressional delegation. The Whigs in Alabama suffered that fate in 1840: "their party garnered 43 percent of the statewide vote, yet did not receive a single seat." When Congress required single-member districts in the Apportionment Act of 1842, it was not out of a general sense of fairness, but instead a (mis)calculation by the Whigs that such a change would improve their electoral prospects.

Unable to claim that the Constitution requires proportional representation outright, plaintiffs inevitably ask the courts to make their own political judgment about how much representation particular political parties *deserve*—based on the votes of their supporters—and to rearrange the challenged districts to achieve that end. But federal courts are not equipped to apportion political power as a matter of fairness, nor is there any basis for concluding that they were authorized to do so.

The initial difficulty in settling on a "clear, manageable and politically neutral" test for fairness is that it is not even clear what fairness looks like in this context. There is a large measure of "unfairness" in any winner-take-all system. Fairness may mean a greater number of competitive districts. Such a claim seeks to undo packing and cracking so that supporters of the disadvantaged party have a better shot at electing their preferred candidates. But making as many districts as possible more competitive could be a recipe for disaster for the disadvantaged party. As Justice White has pointed out, "[i]f all or most of the districts are competitive . . . even a narrow statewide preference for either party would produce an overwhelming majority for the winning party in the state legislature."

On the other hand, perhaps the ultimate objective of a "fairer" share of seats in the congressional delegation is most readily achieved by yielding to the gravitational pull of proportionality and engaging in cracking and packing, to ensure each party its "appropriate" share of "safe" seats. Such an approach, however, comes at the expense of competitive districts and of individuals in districts allocated to the opposing party.

Or perhaps fairness should be measured by adherence to "traditional" districting criteria, such as maintaining political subdivisions, keeping communities of interest together, and protecting incumbents. But protecting incumbents, for example, enshrines a particular partisan distribution. And the "natural political geography" of a State—such as the fact that urban electoral districts are often dominated by one political party—can itself lead to inherently packed districts. As Justice Kennedy has explained, traditional criteria such as compactness and contiguity "cannot promise political neutrality when used as the basis for relief. Instead, it seems, a decision under these standards would unavoidably have significant political effect, whether intended or not."

Deciding among just these different visions of fairness (you can imagine many others) poses basic questions that are political, not legal. There are no legal standards discernible in the Constitution for making such judgments, let alone limited and precise standards that are clear, manageable, and politically neutral. Any judicial decision on what is "fair" in this context would be an "unmoored determination" of the sort characteristic of a political question beyond the competence of the federal courts.

And it is only after determining how to define fairness that you can even begin to answer the determinative question: "How much is too much?" At what point does permissible partisanship become unconstitutional? If compliance with traditional districting criteria is the fairness touchstone, for example, how much deviation from those criteria is constitutionally acceptable and how should mapdrawers prioritize competing criteria? Should a court "reverse gerrymander" other parts of a State to counteract "natural" gerrymandering caused, for example, by the urban concentration of one party? If a districting plan protected half of the incumbents but redistricted the rest into head to head races, would that be constitutional? A court would have to rank the relative importance of those traditional criteria and weigh how much deviation from each to allow.

If a court instead focused on the respective number of seats in the legislature, it would have to decide the ideal number of seats for each party and determine at what point deviation from that balance went too far. If a 5–3 allocation corresponds most closely to statewide vote totals, is a 6–2 allocation permissible, given that legislatures have the authority to engage in a certain degree of partisan gerrymandering? Which seats should be packed and which cracked? Or if the goal is as many competitive districts as possible, how close does the split need to be for the district to be considered competitive? Presumably not all districts could qualify, so how to choose?

Even assuming the court knew which version of fairness to be looking for, there are no discernible and manageable standards for deciding whether there has been a violation. The questions are "unguided and ill suited to the development of judicial standards," and "results from one gerrymandering case to the next would likely be disparate and inconsistent."

Appellees contend that if we can adjudicate one-person, one-vote claims, we can also assess partisan gerrymandering claims. But the one-person, one-vote rule is relatively easy to administer as a matter of math. The same cannot be said of partisan gerrymandering claims, because the Constitution supplies no objective measure for assessing whether a districting map treats a political party fairly. It hardly follows from the principle that each person must have an equal say in the election of representatives that a person is entitled to have his political party achieve representation in some way commensurate to its share of statewide support.

More fundamentally, "vote dilution" in the one-person, one-vote cases refers to the idea that each vote must carry equal weight. In other words, each representative must be accountable to (approximately) the same number of constituents. That requirement does not extend to political parties. It does not mean that each party must be influential in proportion to its number of supporters. As we stated unanimously in *Gill*, "this Court is not responsible for vindicating generalized partisan preferences. The Court's constitutionally prescribed role is to vindicate the individual rights of the people appearing before it."

Nor do our racial gerrymandering cases provide an appropriate standard for assessing partisan gerrymandering. "[N]othing in our case law compels the conclusion that racial and political gerrymanders are subject to precisely the same constitutional scrutiny. In fact, our country's long and persistent history of racial discrimination in voting—as well as our Fourteenth Amendment jurisprudence, which always has reserved the strictest scrutiny for discrimination on the basis of race—would seem to compel the opposite conclusion." Unlike partisan gerrymandering claims, a racial gerrymandering claim does not ask for a fair share of political power and influence, with all the justiciability conundrums that entails. It asks instead for the elimination of a racial classification. A partisan gerrymandering claim cannot ask for the elimination of partisanship.

IV

Appellees and the dissent propose a number of "tests" for evaluating partisan gerrymandering claims, but none meets the need for a limited and precise standard that is judicially discernible and manageable. And none provides a solid grounding for judges to take the extraordinary step of reallocating power and influence between political parties.

Even the most sophisticated districting maps cannot reliably account for some of the reasons voters prefer one candidate over another, or why their preferences may change. Voters elect individual candidates in individual districts, and their selections depend on the issues that matter to them, the quality of the candidates, the tone of the candidates' campaigns, the performance of an incumbent, national events or local issues that drive voter turnout, and other considerations. Many voters split their tickets. Others never register with a political party, and vote for candidates from both major parties at different points during their lifetimes. For all of those reasons, asking judges to predict how a particular districting map will perform in future elections risks basing constitutional holdings on unstable ground outside judicial expertise.

The District Courts also found partisan gerrymandering claims justiciable under the First Amendment, coalescing around a basic three-part test: proof of intent to burden individuals based on their voting history or party affiliation; an actual burden on political speech or associational rights; and a causal link between the invidious intent and actual burden.

To begin, there are no restrictions on speech, association, or any other First Amendment activities in the districting plans at issue. The plaintiffs are free to engage in those activities no matter what the effect of a plan may be on their district. The plaintiffs' argument is that partisanship in districting should be regarded as simple discrimination against supporters of the opposing party on the basis of political viewpoint. Under that theory, any level of partisanship in districting would constitute an infringement of their First Amendment rights. But as the Court has explained, "[i]t would be idle . . . to contend that any political consideration taken into account in fashioning a reapportionment plan is sufficient to invalidate it." The First Amendment test simply describes the act of districting for partisan advantage. It provides no standard for determining when partisan activity goes too far.

The dissent proposes using a State's own districting criteria as a neutral baseline from which to measure how extreme a partisan gerrymander is. The dissent would have us line up all the possible maps drawn using those criteria according to the partisan distribution they would produce. Distance from the "median" map would indicate whether a particular districting plan harms supporters of one party to an unconstitutional extent.

As an initial matter, it does not make sense to use criteria that will vary from State to State and year to year as the baseline for determining whether a gerrymander violates the Federal Constitution. The degree of partisan advantage that the Constitution tolerates should not turn on criteria offered by the gerrymanderers themselves. It is easy to imagine how different criteria could move the median map toward different partisan distributions. As a result, the same map could be constitutional or not depending solely on what the mapmakers said they set out to do. That possibility illustrates that the dissent's proposed constitutional test is indeterminate and arbitrary.

Even if we were to accept the dissent's proposed baseline, it would return us to "the original unanswerable question (How much political motivation and effect is too much?)." Would twenty percent away from the median map be okay? Forty percent? Sixty percent? Why or why not? (We appreciate that the dissent finds all the unanswerable questions annoying, but it seems a useful way to make the point.) The dissent's answer says it all: "This much is too much." That is not even trying to articulate a standard or rule.

The dissent argues that there are other instances in law where matters of degree are left to the courts. True enough. But those instances typically involve constitutional or statutory provisions or common law confining and guiding the exercise of judicial discretion.

The North Carolina District Court further concluded that the 2016 Plan violated the Elections Clause and Article I, § 2. We are unconvinced by that novel approach.

Article I, § 2, provides that "[t]he House of Representatives shall be composed of Members chosen every second Year by the People of the several States." The Elections Clause provides that "[t]he Times, Places and Manner of holding Elections for Senators and Representatives, shall be prescribed in each State by the Legislature thereof; but the Congress may at any time by Law make or alter such Regulations, except as to the Places of chusing Senators." Art. I, § 4, cl. 1.

The District Court concluded that the 2016 Plan exceeded the North Carolina General Assembly's Elections Clause authority because, among other reasons, "the Elections Clause did not empower State legislatures to disfavor the interests of supporters of a particular candidate or party in drawing congressional districts." The court further held that partisan gerrymandering infringes the right of "the People" to select their representatives. Before the District Court's decision, no court had reached a similar conclusion. In fact, the plurality in *Vieth* concluded—without objection from any other Justice—that neither § 2 nor § 4 of Article I "provides a judicially enforceable limit on the political considerations that the States and Congress may take into account when districting."

The District Court nevertheless asserted that partisan gerrymanders violate "the core principle of [our] republican government" preserved in Art. I, § 2, "namely, that the voters should choose their representatives, not the other way around." That seems like an objection more properly grounded in the Guarantee Clause of Article IV, § 4, which "guarantee[s] to every State in [the] Union a Republican Form of Government." This Court has several times concluded, however, that the Guarantee Clause does not provide the basis for a justiciable claim.

V

Excessive partisanship in districting leads to results that reasonably seem unjust. But the fact that such gerrymandering is "incompatible with democratic principles," does not mean that the solution lies with the federal judiciary. We conclude that partisan gerrymandering claims present political questions beyond the reach of the federal courts. Federal judges have no license to reallocate political power between the two major political parties, with no plausible grant of authority in the Constitution, and no legal standards to limit and direct their decisions. "[J]udicial action must be governed by *standard*, by *rule*," and must be "principled, rational, and based upon reasoned distinctions" found in the Constitution or laws. Judicial review of partisan gerrymandering does not meet those basic requirements.

What the appellees and dissent seek is an unprecedented expansion of judicial power. We have never struck down a partisan gerrymander as unconstitutional—despite various requests over the past 45 years. The expansion of judicial authority would not be into just any area of controversy, but into one of the most intensely partisan aspects of American political life. That intervention would be unlimited in scope and duration—it would recur over and over again around the country with each new round of districting, for state as well as federal representatives. Consideration of the impact of today's ruling on democratic principles cannot ignore the effect of the unelected and politically unaccountable branch of the Federal Government assuming such an extraordinary and unprecedented role.

Our conclusion does not condone excessive partisan gerrymandering. Nor does our conclusion condemn complaints about districting to echo into a void. The States, for example, are actively addressing the issue on a number of fronts. In 2015, the Supreme Court of Florida struck down that State's congressional districting plan as a violation of the Fair Districts Amendment to the Florida Constitution. The dissent wonders why we can't do the same. The answer is that there is no "Fair Districts Amendment" to the Federal Constitution. Provisions in state statutes and state constitutions can provide standards and guidance for state courts to apply. Indeed, numerous other States are restricting partisan considerations in districting through legislation. One way they are doing so is by placing power to draw electoral districts in the hands of independent commissions. Other States have mandated at least some of the traditional districting criteria for their mapmakers. Some have outright prohibited partisan favoritism in redistricting.

As noted, the Framers gave Congress the power to do something about partisan gerrymandering in the Elections Clause. The first bill introduced in the 116th Congress would require States to create 15-member independent commissions to draw congressional districts and would establish certain redistricting criteria, including protection for communities of interest, and ban partisan gerrymandering. Another example is the Fairness and Independence in Redistricting Act, which was introduced in 2005 and has been reintroduced in every Congress since. We express no view on any of these pending proposals. We simply note that the avenue for reform established by the Framers, and used by Congress in the past, remains open.

No one can accuse this Court of having a crabbed view of the reach of its competence. But we have no commission to allocate political power and influence in the absence of a constitutional directive or legal standards to guide us in the exercise of such authority. "It is emphatically the province and duty of the judicial department to say what the law is." In this rare circumstance, that means our duty is to say "this is not law."

Justice KAGAN, with whom Justice GINSBURG, Justice BREYER, and Justice SOTOMAYOR join, dissenting.

For the first time ever, this Court refuses to remedy a constitutional violation because it thinks the task beyond judicial capabilities. And not just any constitutional violation. The partisan gerrymanders in these cases deprived citizens of the most fundamental of their constitutional rights: the rights to participate equally in the political process, to join with others to advance political beliefs, and to choose their political representatives. In so doing, the partisan gerrymanders here debased and dishonored our democracy, turning upside-down the core American idea that all governmental power derives from the people. These gerrymanders enabled politicians to entrench themselves in office as against voters' preferences. They promoted partisanship above respect for the popular will. They encouraged a politics of polarization and dysfunction. If left unchecked, gerrymanders like the ones here may irreparably damage our system of government.

And checking them is *not* beyond the courts. The majority's abdication comes just when courts across the country, including those below, have coalesced around manageable judicial standards to resolve partisan gerrymandering claims. Those standards satisfy the majority's own benchmarks. They do not require—indeed, they do not permit—courts to rely on their own ideas of electoral fairness, whether proportional representation or any other. And they limit courts to correcting only egregious gerrymanders, so judges do not become omnipresent players in the political process. But yes, the standards used here do allow—as well they should—judicial intervention in the worst-of-the-worst cases of democratic subversion, causing blatant constitutional harms. In other words, they allow courts to undo partisan gerrymanders of the kind we face today from North Carolina and Maryland. In giving such gerrymanders a pass from judicial review, the majority goes tragically wrong.

I

A

Maybe the majority errs in these cases because it pays so little attention to the constitutional harms at their core. After dutifully reciting each case's facts, the majority leaves them forever behind, instead immersing itself in everything that could conceivably go amiss if courts became involved. So it is necessary to fill in the gaps. To recount exactly what politicians in North Carolina and Maryland did to entrench their parties in political office, whatever the electorate might think. And to elaborate on the constitutional injury those politicians wreaked, to our democratic system and to individuals' rights. All that will help in considering whether courts confronting partisan gerrymandering claims are really so hamstrung—so unable to carry out their constitutional duties—as the majority thinks.

The plaintiffs here challenge two congressional districting plans—one adopted by Republicans in North Carolina and the other by Democrats in Maryland—as unconstitutional partisan gerrymanders. As I relate what happened in those two States, ask yourself: Is this how American democracy is supposed to work?

Start with North Carolina. After the 2010 census, the North Carolina General Assembly, with Republican majorities in both its House and its Senate, enacted a new congressional districting plan. That plan governed the two next national elections. In 2012, Republican candidates won 9 of the State's 13 seats in the U.S. House of Representatives, although they received only 49% of the statewide vote. In 2014, Republican candidates increased their total to 10 of the 13 seats, this time based on 55% of the vote. [After a federal court order, new districts were drawn and the person responsible declared:]. "I think electing Republicans is better than electing Democrats. So I drew this map to help foster what I think is better for the country."

You might think that judgment best left to the American people. In 2016, Republican congressional candidates won 10 of North Carolina's 13 seats, with 53% of the statewide vote. Two years later, Republican candidates won 9 of 12 seats though they received only 50% of the vote. (The 13th seat has not yet been filled because fraud tainted the initial election.)

Events in Maryland make for a similarly grisly tale. For 50 years, Maryland's 8-person congressional delegation typically consisted of 2 or 3 Republicans and 5 or 6 Democrats. Maryland's Democrats proved no less successful than North Carolina's Republicans in devising a voter-proof map. In the four elections that followed (from 2012 through 2018), Democrats have never received more than 65% of the statewide congressional vote. Yet in each of those elections, Democrats have won (you guessed it) 7 of 8 House seats—including the once-reliably-Republican Sixth District.

B

Now back to the question I asked before: Is that how American democracy is supposed to work? I have yet to meet the person who thinks so. "Governments," the Declaration of Independence states, "deriv[e] their just Powers from the Consent of the Governed." The Constitution begins: "We the People of the United States." The Gettysburg Address (almost) ends: "[G]overnment of the people, by the people, for the people." If there is a single idea that made our Nation (and that our Nation commended to the world), it is this one: The people are sovereign. The "power," James Madison wrote, "is in the people over the Government, and not in the Government over the people."

Free and fair and periodic elections are the key to that vision. The people get to choose their representatives. And then they get to decide, at regular intervals, whether to keep them. Madison again: "[R]epublican liberty" demands "not only, that all power should be derived from the people; but that those entrusted with it should be kept in dependence on the people." Election day—next year, and two years later, and two years after that—is what links the people to their representatives, and gives the people their sovereign power. That day is the foundation of democratic governance.

And partisan gerrymandering can make it meaningless. At its most extreme—as in North Carolina and Maryland—the practice amounts to "rigging elections." By drawing districts to maximize the power of some voters and minimize the power of others, a party in office at the right time can entrench itself there for a decade or more, no matter what the voters would prefer. Just ask the people of North Carolina and Maryland. The "core principle of republican government," this Court has recognized, is "that the voters should choose their representatives, not the other way around." Partisan gerrymandering turns it the other way around. By that mechanism, politicians can cherry-pick voters to ensure their reelection. And the power becomes, as Madison put it, "in the Government over the people."

The majority disputes none of this. I think it important to underscore that fact: The majority disputes none of what I have said (or will say) about how gerrymanders undermine democracy. Indeed, the majority concedes (really, how could it not?) that gerrymandering is "incompatible with democratic principles."

And therefore what? That recognition would seem to demand a response. The majority offers two ideas that might qualify as such. One is that the political process can deal with the problem—a proposition so dubious on its face that I feel secure in delaying my answer for some time. The other is that political gerrymanders have always been with us. To its credit, the majority does not frame that point as an originalist constitutional argument. After all (as the majority rightly notes), racial and residential gerrymanders were also once with us, but the Court has done something about that fact. The majority's idea instead seems to be that if we have lived with partisan gerrymanders so long, we will survive.

That complacency has no cause. Yes, partisan gerrymandering goes back to the Republic's earliest days. (As does vociferous opposition to it.) But big data and modern technology—of just the kind that the mapmakers in North Carolina and Maryland used—make today's gerrymandering altogether different from the crude linedrawing of the past. Old-time efforts, based on little more than guesses, sometimes led to so-called dummymanders—gerrymanders that went spectacularly wrong. Not likely in today's world. Mapmakers now have access to more granular data about party preference and voting behavior than ever before. County-level voting data has given way to precinct-level or city-block-level data; and increasingly, mapmakers avail themselves of data sets providing wide-ranging information about even individual voters. Just as important, advancements in computing technology have enabled mapmakers to put that information to use with unprecedented efficiency and precision. While bygone mapmakers may have drafted three or four alternative districting plans, today's mapmakers can generate thousands of possibilities at the touch of a key—and then choose the one giving their party maximum advantage (usually while still meeting traditional districting requirements). The effect is to make gerrymanders far more effective and durable than before, insulating politicians against all but the most titanic shifts in the political tides. These are not your grandfather's—let alone the Framers'—gerrymanders.

C

Partisan gerrymandering of the kind before us not only subverts democracy (as if that weren't bad enough). It violates individuals' constitutional rights as well. That statement is not the lonesome cry of a dissenting Justice. This Court has recognized extreme partisan gerrymandering as such a violation for many years.

Partisan gerrymandering operates through vote dilution—the devaluation of one citizen's vote as compared to others. A mapmaker draws district lines to "pack" and "crack" voters likely to support the disfavored party. He packs supermajorities of those voters into a relatively few districts, in numbers far greater than needed for their preferred candidates to prevail. Then he cracks the rest across many more districts, spreading them so thin that their candidates will not be able to win. Whether the person is packed or cracked, his vote carries less weight—has less consequence—than it would under a neutrally drawn (non-partisan) map. In short, the mapmaker has made some votes count for less, because they are likely to go for the other party.

That practice implicates the Fourteenth Amendment's Equal Protection Clause. The Fourteenth Amendment, we long ago recognized, "guarantees the opportunity for equal participation by all voters in the election" of legislators. And that opportunity "can be denied by a debasement or dilution of the weight of a citizen's vote just as effectively as by wholly prohibiting the free exercise of the franchise." Based on that principle, this Court in its one-person-one-vote decisions prohibited creating districts with significantly different populations. A State could not, we explained, thus "dilut[e] the weight of votes because of place of residence." The constitutional injury in a partisan gerrymandering case is much the same, except that the dilution is based on party affiliation. In such a case, too, the districters have set out to reduce the weight of certain citizens' votes, and thereby deprive them of their capacity to "full[y] and effective[ly] participat[e] in the political process[ ]."

And partisan gerrymandering implicates the First Amendment too. That Amendment gives its greatest protection to political beliefs, speech, and association. Yet partisan gerrymanders subject certain voters to "disfavored treatment"—again, counting their votes for less—precisely because of "their voting history [and] their expression of political views." And added to that strictly personal harm is an associational one. Representative democracy is "unimaginable without the ability of citizens to band together in [support of] candidates who espouse their political views." By diluting the votes of certain citizens, the State frustrates their efforts to translate those affiliations into political effectiveness.

Though different Justices have described the constitutional harm in diverse ways, nearly all have agreed on this much: Extreme partisan gerrymandering (as happened in North Carolina and Maryland) violates the Constitution.

II

So the only way to understand the majority's opinion is as follows: In the face of grievous harm to democratic governance and flagrant infringements on individuals' rights—in the face of escalating partisan manipulation whose compatibility with this Nation's values and law no one defends—the majority declines to provide any remedy. For the first time in this Nation's history, the majority declares that it can do nothing about an acknowledged constitutional violation because it has searched high and low and cannot find a workable legal standard to apply.

The majority gives two reasons for thinking that the adjudication of partisan gerrymandering claims is beyond judicial capabilities. First and foremost, the majority says, it cannot find a neutral baseline—one not based on contestable notions of political fairness—from which to measure injury. According to the majority, "[p]artisan gerrymandering claims invariably sound in a desire for proportional representation." But the Constitution does not mandate proportional representation. So, the majority contends, resolving those claims "inevitably" would require courts to decide what is "fair" in the context of districting. They would have "to make their own political judgment about how much representation particular political parties *deserve*" and "to rearrange the challenged districts to achieve that end." And second, the majority argues that even after establishing a baseline, a court would have no way to answer "the determinative question: 'How much is too much?' " No "discernible and manageable" standard is available, the majority claims—and so courts could willy-nilly become embroiled in fixing every districting plan.

I'll give the majority this one—and important—thing: It identifies some dangers everyone should want to avoid. Judges should not be apportioning political power based on their own vision of electoral fairness, whether proportional representation or any other. And judges should not be striking down maps left, right, and center, on the view that every smidgen of politics is a smidgen too much. Respect for state legislative processes — and restraint in the exercise of judicial authority — counsels intervention in only egregious cases.

But in throwing up its hands, the majority misses something under its nose: What it says can't be done *has* been done. Over the past several years, federal courts across the country — including, but not exclusively, in the decisions below — have largely converged on a standard for adjudicating partisan gerrymandering claims (striking down both Democratic and Republican districting plans in the process). And that standard does what the majority says is impossible. The standard does not use any judge-made conception of electoral fairness — either proportional representation or any other; instead, it takes as its baseline a State's *own* criteria of fairness, apart from partisan gain. And by requiring plaintiffs to make difficult showings relating to both purpose and effects, the standard invalidates the most extreme, but only the most extreme, partisan gerrymanders.

Start with the standard the lower courts used. The majority disaggregates the opinions below, distinguishing the one from the other and then chopping up each into "a number of 'tests.'" But in doing so, it fails to convey the decisions' most significant — and common — features. Both courts focused on the harm of vote dilution. And both courts (like others around the country) used basically the same three-part test to decide whether the plaintiffs had made out a vote dilution claim. As many legal standards do, that test has three parts: (1) intent; (2) effects; and (3) causation. First, the plaintiffs challenging a districting plan must prove that state officials' "predominant purpose" in drawing a district's lines was to "entrench [their party] in power" by diluting the votes of citizens favoring its rival. Second, the plaintiffs must establish that the lines drawn in fact have the intended effect by "substantially" diluting their votes. And third, if the plaintiffs make those showings, the State must come up with a legitimate, non-partisan justification to save its map. If you are a lawyer, you know that this test looks utterly ordinary. It is the sort of thing courts work with every day.

The majority's broadest claim, as I've noted, is that this is a price we must pay because judicial oversight of partisan gerrymandering cannot be "politically neutral" or "manageable."

Consider neutrality first. Contrary to the majority's suggestion, the District Courts did not have to — and in fact did not — choose among competing visions of electoral fairness. That is because they did not try to compare the State's actual map to an "ideally fair" one (whether based on proportional representation or some other criterion). Instead, they looked at the difference between what the State did and what the State would have done if politicians hadn't been intent on partisan gain.

The majority's "how much is too much" critique fares no better than its neutrality argument. How about the following for a first-cut answer: This much is too much. By any measure, a map that produces a greater partisan skew than any of 3,000 randomly generated maps (all with the State's political geography and districting criteria built in) reflects "too much" partisanship. Think about what I just said: The absolute worst of 3,001 possible maps. The *only one* that could produce a 10–3 partisan split even as Republicans got a bare majority of the statewide vote. And again: How much is too much? This much is too much: A map that without any evident non-partisan districting reason (to the contrary) shifted the composition of a district from 47% Republicans and 36% Democrats to 33% Republicans and 42% Democrats. A map that in 2011 was responsible for the largest partisan swing of a congressional district in the country. Even the majority acknowledges that "[t]hese cases involve blatant examples of partisanship driving districting decisions." If the majority had done nothing else, it could have set the line here. How much is too much? At the least, any gerrymanders as bad as these.

And if the majority thought that approach too case-specific, it could have used the lower courts' general standard—focusing on "predominant" purpose and "substantial" effects—without fear of indeterminacy. I do not take even the majority to claim that courts are incapable of investigating whether legislators mainly intended to seek partisan advantage.

III

This Court has long understood that it has a special responsibility to remedy violations of constitutional rights resulting from politicians' districting decisions. Over 50 years ago, we committed to providing judicial review in that sphere, recognizing as we established the one-person-one-vote rule that "our oath and our office require no less." Of course, our oath and our office require us to vindicate all constitutional rights. But the need for judicial review is at its most urgent in cases like these. "For here, politicians' incentives conflict with voters' interests, leaving citizens without any political remedy for their constitutional harms." Those harms arise because politicians want to stay in office. No one can look to them for effective relief.

The majority disagrees, concluding its opinion with a paean to congressional bills limiting partisan gerrymanders. "Dozens of [those] bills have been introduced," the majority says. One was "introduced in 2005 and has been reintroduced in every Congress since." And might be reintroduced until the end of time. Because what all these *bills* have in common is that they are not *laws*. The politicians who benefit from partisan gerrymandering are unlikely to change partisan gerrymandering. And because those politicians maintain themselves in office through partisan gerrymandering, the chances for legislative reform are slight.

No worries, the majority says; it has another idea. The majority notes that voters themselves have recently approved ballot initiatives to put power over districting in the hands of independent commissions or other non-partisan actors. Fewer than half the States offer voters an opportunity to put initiatives to direct vote; in all the rest (including North Carolina and Maryland), voters are dependent on legislators to make electoral changes (which for all the reasons already given, they are unlikely to do). And even when voters have a mechanism they can work themselves, legislators often fight their efforts tooth and nail.

The majority's most perplexing "solution" is to look to state courts. But what do those courts know that this Court does not? If they can develop and apply neutral and manageable standards to identify unconstitutional gerrymanders, why couldn't we?

We could have, and we should have. The gerrymanders here — and they are typical of many — violated the constitutional rights of many hundreds of thousands of American citizens. Those voters (Republicans in the one case, Democrats in the other) did not have an equal opportunity to participate in the political process. Their votes counted for far less than they should have because of their partisan affiliation. When faced with such constitutional wrongs, courts must intervene: "It is emphatically the province and duty of the judicial department to say what the law is."

Of all times to abandon the Court's duty to declare the law, this was not the one. The practices challenged in these cases imperil our system of government. Part of the Court's role in that system is to defend its foundations. None is more important than free and fair elections. With respect but deep sadness, I dissent.

Chapter 2

The Federal Legislative Power

C. The Commerce Power

4. 1990s-???: Narrowing of the Commerce Power and Revival of the Tenth Amendment as a Limit on Congress

b. Does the Tenth Amendment Limit Congress's Authority? (casebook p. 217)

In *New York v. United States* (casebook p. 217) and *Printz v. United States* (casebook p. 227), the Court held that Congress cannot "commandeer" state and local governments by forcing them to adopt laws or enforce federal mandates. The Court applied this in *Murphy v. NCAA*.

MURPHY v. NATIONAL COLLEGIATE ATHLETIC ASSOCIATION
138 S. Ct. 1461 (2018)

Justice ALITO delivered the opinion of the Court.

The State of New Jersey wants to legalize sports gambling at casinos and horseracing tracks, but a federal law, the Professional and Amateur Sports Protection Act, generally makes it unlawful for a State to "authorize" sports gambling schemes. We must decide whether this provision is compatible with the system of "dual sovereignty" embodied in the Constitution.

I

Americans have never been of one mind about gambling, and attitudes have swung back and forth. By the end of the 19th century, gambling was largely banned throughout the country, but beginning in the 1920s and 1930s, laws prohibiting gambling were gradually loosened.

New Jersey's experience is illustrative. In 1897, New Jersey adopted a constitutional amendment that barred all gambling in the State. But during the Depression, the State permitted parimutuel betting on horse races as a way of increasing state revenue, and in 1953, churches and other nonprofit organizations were allowed to host bingo games. In 1970, New Jersey became the third State to run a state lottery, and within five years, 10 other States followed suit.

By the 1960s, Atlantic City, "once the most fashionable resort of the Atlantic Coast," had fallen on hard times, and casino gambling came to be seen as a way to revitalize the city. In 1974, a referendum on state-wide legalization failed, but two years later, voters approved a narrower measure allowing casino gambling in Atlantic City alone. At that time, Nevada was the only other State with legal casinos, and thus for a while the Atlantic City casinos had an east coast monopoly. "With 60 million people living within a one-tank car trip away," Atlantic City became "the most popular tourist destination in the United States." But that favorable situation eventually came to an end.

With the enactment of the Indian Gaming Regulatory Act in 1988, casinos opened on Indian land throughout the country. Some were located within driving distance of Atlantic City, and nearby States (and many others) legalized casino gambling. But Nevada remained the only state venue for legal sports gambling in casinos, and sports gambling is immensely popular.

Sports gambling, however, has long had strong opposition. Opponents argue that it is particularly addictive and especially attractive to young people with a strong interest in sports, and in the past gamblers corrupted and seriously damaged the reputation of professional and amateur sports. Apprehensive about the potential effects of sports gambling, professional sports leagues and the National Collegiate Athletic Association (NCAA) long opposed legalization.

By the 1990s, there were signs that the trend that had brought about the legalization of many other forms of gambling might extend to sports gambling, and this sparked federal efforts to stem the tide. Opponents of sports gambling turned to the legislation now before us, the Professional and Amateur Sports Protection Act (PASPA). PASPA's proponents argued that it would protect young people, and one of the bill's sponsors, Senator Bill Bradley of New Jersey, a former college and professional basketball star, stressed that the law was needed to safeguard the integrity of sports.

PASPA's most important provision, part of which is directly at issue in these cases, makes it "unlawful" for a State or any of its subdivisions "to sponsor, operate, advertise, promote, license, or authorize by law or compact . . . a lottery, sweepstakes, or other betting, gambling, or wagering scheme based . . . on" competitive sporting events. § 3702(1). In parallel, § 3702(2) makes it "unlawful" for "a person to sponsor, operate, advertise, or promote" those same gambling schemes—but only if this is done "pursuant to the law or compact of a governmental entity." PASPA does not make sports gambling a federal crime (and thus was not anticipated to impose a significant law enforcement burden on the Federal Government). Instead, PASPA allows the Attorney General, as well as professional and amateur sports organizations, to bring civil actions to enjoin violations.

At the time of PASPA's adoption, a few jurisdictions allowed some form of sports gambling. In Nevada, sports gambling was legal in casinos, and three States hosted sports lotteries or allowed sports pools. PASPA contains "grandfather" provisions allowing these activities to continue. Another provision gave New Jersey the option of legalizing sports gambling in Atlantic City—provided that it did so within one year of the law's effective date.

New Jersey did not take advantage of this special option, but by 2011, with Atlantic City facing stiff competition, the State had a change of heart. New Jersey voters approved an amendment to the State Constitution making it lawful for the legislature to authorize sports gambling, and in 2012 the legislature enacted a law doing just that.

The 2012 Act quickly came under attack. The major professional sports leagues and the NCAA brought an action in federal court against the New Jersey Governor and other state officials (hereinafter New Jersey), seeking to enjoin the new law on the ground that it violated PASPA. [The New Jersey law was struck down].

[T]he New Jersey Legislature enacted the law now before us. The 2014 Act declares that it is not to be interpreted as causing the State to authorize, license, sponsor, operate, advertise, or promote sports gambling. Instead, it is framed as a repealer. Specifically, it repeals the provisions of state law prohibiting sports gambling insofar as they concerned the "placement and acceptance of wagers" on sporting events by persons 21 years of age or older at a horseracing track or a casino or gambling house in Atlantic City. The new law also specified that the repeal was effective only as to wagers on sporting events not involving a New Jersey college team or a collegiate event taking place in the State.

Predictably, the same plaintiffs promptly commenced a new action in federal court. They won in the District Court, and the case was eventually heard by the Third Circuit sitting en banc. The en banc court affirmed, finding that the new law, no less than the old one, violated PASPA by "author[izing]" sports gambling.

II

Before considering the constitutionality of the PASPA provision prohib-iting States from "author[izing]" sports gambling, we first examine its meaning. The parties advance dueling interpretations, and this dispute has an important bearing on the constitutional issue that we must decide. Neither respondents nor the United States, appearing as an *amicus* in sup-port of respondents, contends that the provision at issue would be consti-tutional if petitioners' interpretation is correct. Indeed, the United States expressly concedes that the provision is unconstitutional if it means what petitioners claim.

Petitioners argue that the anti-authorization provision requires States to maintain their existing laws against sports gambling without alteration. One of the accepted meanings of the term "authorize," they point out, is "permit." They therefore contend that any state law that has the effect of permitting sports gambling, including a law totally or partially repealing a prior prohibition, amounts to an authorization.

Respondents interpret the provision more narrowly. They claim that the *primary* definition of "authorize" requires affirmative action. To authorize, they maintain, means "'[t]o empower; to give a right or authority to act; to endow with authority.'" And this, they say, is precisely what the 2014 Act does: It empowers a defined group of entities, and it endows them with the authority to conduct sports gambling operations. Respondents do not take the position that PASPA bans all modifications of old laws against sports gambling, but just how far they think a modification could go is not clear.

In our view, petitioners' interpretation is correct: When a State com-pletely or partially repeals old laws banning sports gambling, it "autho-rize[s]" that activity. This is clear when the state-law landscape at the time of PASPA's enactment is taken into account. At that time, all forms of sports gambling were illegal in the great majority of States, and in that context, the competing definitions offered by the parties lead to the same conclusion. The repeal of a state law banning sports gambling not only "permits" sports gambling (petitioners' favored definition); it also gives those now free to conduct a sports betting operation the "right or author-ity to act"; it "empowers" them (respondents' and the United States's definition).

The concept of state "authorization" makes sense only against a back-drop of prohibition or regulation. A State is not regarded as authorizing everything that it does not prohibit or regulate. No one would use the term in that way. For example, no one would say that a State "autho-rizes" its residents to brush their teeth or eat apples or sing in the shower.

We commonly speak of state authorization only if the activity in question would otherwise be restricted.

III

The anticommandeering doctrine may sound arcane, but it is simply the expression of a fundamental structural decision incorporated into the Constitution, *i.e.*, the decision to withhold from Congress the power to issue orders directly to the States. When the original States declared their independence, they claimed the powers inherent in sovereignty — in the words of the Declaration of Independence, the authority "to do all . . . Acts and Things which Independent States may of right do." The Constitution limited but did not abolish the sovereign powers of the States, which retained "a residuary and inviolable sovereignty." Thus, both the Federal Government and the States wield sovereign powers, and that is why our system of government is said to be one of "dual sovereignty."

The legislative powers granted to Congress are sizable, but they are not unlimited. The Constitution confers on Congress not plenary legislative power but only certain enumerated powers. Therefore, all other legislative power is reserved for the States, as the Tenth Amendment confirms. And conspicuously absent from the list of powers given to Congress is the power to issue direct orders to the governments of the States. The anticommandeering doctrine simply represents the recognition of this limit on congressional authority.

Although the anticommandeering principle is simple and basic, it did not emerge in our cases until relatively recently, when Congress attempted in a few isolated instances to extend its authority in unprecedented ways.

Our opinions in *New York* and *Printz* explained why adherence to the anticommandeering principle is important. Without attempting a complete survey, we mention several reasons that are significant here. First, the rule serves as "one of the Constitution's structural protections of liberty." "The Constitution does not protect the sovereignty of States for the benefit of the States or state governments as abstract political entities." "To the contrary, the Constitution divides authority between federal and state governments for the protection of individuals." "'[A] healthy balance of power between the States and the Federal Government [reduces] the risk of tyranny and abuse from either front.'"

Second, the anticommandeering rule promotes political accountability. When Congress itself regulates, the responsibility for the benefits and burdens of the regulation is apparent. Voters who like or dislike the effects of the regulation know who to credit or blame. By contrast, if a State imposes regulations only because it has been commanded to do so by Congress, responsibility is blurred.

Third, the anticommandeering principle prevents Congress from shifting the costs of regulation to the States. If Congress enacts a law and requires enforcement by the Executive Branch, it must appropriate the funds needed to administer the program. It is pressured to weigh the expected benefits of the program against its costs. But if Congress can compel the States to enact and enforce its program, Congress need not engage in any such analysis.

IV

The PASPA provision at issue here—prohibiting state authorization of sports gambling—violates the anticommandeering rule. That provision unequivocally dictates what a state legislature may and may not do. And this is true under either our interpretation or that advocated by respondents and the United States. In either event, state legislatures are put under the direct control of Congress. It is as if federal officers were installed in state legislative chambers and were armed with the authority to stop legislators from voting on any offending proposals. A more direct affront to state sovereignty is not easy to imagine.

Neither respondents nor the United States contends that Congress can compel a State to enact legislation, but they say that prohibiting a State from enacting new laws is another matter.

This distinction is empty. It was a matter of happenstance that the laws challenged in *New York* and *Printz* commanded "affirmative" action as opposed to imposing a prohibition. The basic principle—that Congress cannot issue direct orders to state legislatures—applies in either event.

Here is an illustration. PASPA includes an exemption for States that permitted sports betting at the time of enactment, § 3704, but suppose Congress did not adopt such an exemption. Suppose Congress ordered States with legalized sports betting to take the affirmative step of criminalizing that activity and ordered the remaining States to retain their laws prohibiting sports betting. There is no good reason why the former would intrude more deeply on state sovereignty than the latter.

V

Respondents and the United States defend the anti-authorization prohibition on the ground that it constitutes a valid preemption provision, but it is no such thing. Preemption is based on the Supremacy Clause, and that Clause is not an independent grant of legislative power to Congress. Instead, it simply provides "a rule of decision." It specifies that federal law is supreme in case of a conflict with state law. Therefore, in order for the PASPA provision to preempt state law, it must satisfy two requirements. First, it must represent the exercise of a power conferred on Congress by the Constitution; pointing to the Supremacy Clause will not do. Second, since the Constitution "confers upon Congress the power to regulate individuals, not States," the PASPA provision at issue must be best read as one that regulates private actors.

In sum, regardless of the language sometimes used by Congress and this Court, every form of preemption is based on a federal law that regulates the conduct of private actors, not the States. Once this is understood, it is clear that the PASPA provision prohibiting state authorization of sports gambling is not a preemption provision because there is no way in which this provision can be understood as a regulation of private actors. It certainly does not confer any federal rights on private actors interested in conducting sports gambling operations. (It does not give them a federal right to engage in sports gambling.) Nor does it impose any federal restrictions on private actors. If a private citizen or company started a sports gambling operation, either with or without state authorization, § 3702(1) would not be violated and would not provide any ground for a civil action by the Attorney General or any other party. Thus, there is simply no way to understand the provision prohibiting state authorization as anything other than a direct command to the States. And that is exactly what the anticommandeering rule does not allow.

[The Court then turned to whether other provisions of the Act should be upheld. The Court concluded:] "We hold that no provision of PASPA is severable from the provision directly at issue in these cases."

The legalization of sports gambling is a controversial subject. Supporters argue that legalization will produce revenue for the States and critically weaken illegal sports betting operations, which are often run by organized crime. Opponents contend that legalizing sports gambling will hook the young on gambling, encourage people of modest means to squander their savings and earnings, and corrupt professional and college sports.

The legalization of sports gambling requires an important policy choice, but the choice is not ours to make. Congress can regulate sports gambling directly, but if it elects not to do so, each State is free to act on its own. Our job is to interpret the law Congress has enacted and decide whether it is consistent with the Constitution. PASPA is not. PASPA "regulate[s] state governments' regulation" of their citizens. The Constitution gives Congress no such power.

[The other opinions focused entirely on the question of severability. Justice Thomas questioned the severability doctrine as developed by the Supreme Court. Justice Breyer concurred and dissented in part, and said that the provisions should be regarded as severable. He stated:]

I agree with Justice Ginsburg that 28 U.S.C. § 3702(2) is severable from the challenged portion of § 3702(1). The challenged part of subsection (1) prohibits a State from "author[izing]" or "licens[ing]" sports gambling schemes; subsection (2) prohibits individuals from "sponsor[ing], operat[ing], advertis[ing], or promot[ing]" sports gambling schemes "pursuant to the law . . . of a governmental entity." As Justice Ginsburg makes clear, the latter section can live comfortably on its own without the first. Why would Congress enact both these provisions? The obvious answer is that Congress wanted to "keep sports gambling from spreading."

[Justice Ginsburg wrote a dissent, joined by Justice Sotomayor, and in part by Justice Breyer. It focused entirely on the severability question and said the rest of the statute, which does not commandeer the states, should be upheld. She concluded:]

In PASPA, shorn of the prohibition on modifying or repealing state law, Congress permissibly exercised its authority to regulate commerce by instructing States and private parties to refrain from operating sports-gambling schemes. On no rational ground can it be concluded that Congress would have preferred no statute at all if it could not prohibit States from authorizing or licensing such schemes. Deleting the alleged "commandeering" directions would free the statute to accomplish just what Congress legitimately sought to achieve: stopping sports-gambling regimes while making it clear that the stoppage is attributable to federal, not state, action. I therefore dissent from the Court's determination to destroy PASPA rather than salvage the statute.

Chapter 3

The Federal Executive Power

A. Inherent Presidential Power (casebook p. 321)

In considering the constitutionality of President Trump's travel ban, the Supreme Court expressed the view that the President has broad powers as to immigration and that only a rational basis test is to be used for restrictions on immigration. Under rational basis review, a court asks only whether there is a conceivable permissible purpose for the government's action; its actual purpose is irrelevant. The Court found national security to be a conceivable permissible purpose, whereas the dissent focused on what it saw as the actual purpose: a ban on Muslims entering the United States.

TRUMP v. HAWAII
138 S. Ct. 2392 (2018)

Chief Justice ROBERTS delivered the opinion of the Court.

Under the Immigration and Nationality Act, foreign nationals seeking entry into the United States undergo a vetting process to ensure that they satisfy the numerous requirements for admission. The Act also vests the President with authority to restrict the entry of aliens whenever he finds that their entry "would be detrimental to the interests of the United States." Relying on that delegation, the President concluded that it was necessary to impose entry restrictions on nationals of countries that do not share adequate information for an informed entry determination, or that otherwise present national security risks. The plaintiffs in this litigation, respondents here, challenged the application of those entry restrictions to certain aliens abroad. We now decide whether the President had authority under the Act to issue the Proclamation, and whether the entry policy violates the Establishment Clause of the First Amendment.

I

Shortly after taking office, President Trump signed Executive Order No. 13769, Protecting the Nation From Foreign Terrorist Entry Into the United States. EO-1 directed the Secretary of Homeland Security to conduct a review to examine the adequacy of information provided by foreign governments about their nationals seeking to enter the United States. Pending that review, the order suspended for 90 days the entry of foreign nationals from seven countries—Iran, Iraq, Libya, Somalia, Sudan, Syria, and Yemen—that had been previously identified by Congress or prior administrations as posing heightened terrorism risks. The District Court for the Western District of Washington entered a temporary restraining order blocking the entry restrictions, and the Court of Appeals for the Ninth Circuit denied the Government's request to stay that order.

In response, the President revoked EO-1, replacing it with Executive Order No. 13780, which again directed a worldwide review. Citing investigative burdens on agencies and the need to diminish the risk that dangerous individuals would enter without adequate vetting, EO-2 also temporarily restricted the entry (with case-by-case waivers) of foreign nationals from six of the countries covered by EO-1: Iran, Libya, Somalia, Sudan, Syria, and Yemen. The order explained that those countries had been selected because each "is a state sponsor of terrorism, has been significantly compromised by terrorist organizations, or contains active conflict zones." The entry restriction was to stay in effect for 90 days, pending completion of the worldwide review.

These interim measures were immediately challenged in court. The District Courts for the Districts of Maryland and Hawaii entered nationwide preliminary injunctions barring enforcement of the entry suspension, and the respective Courts of Appeals upheld those injunctions, albeit on different grounds. The temporary restrictions in EO-2 expired before this Court took any action, and we vacated the lower court decisions as moot.

On September 24, 2017, after completion of the worldwide review, the President issued the Proclamation before us—Proclamation No. 9645, Enhancing Vetting Capabilities and Processes for Detecting Attempted Entry Into the United States by Terrorists or Other Public-Safety Threats. The Proclamation (as its title indicates) sought to improve vetting procedures by identifying ongoing deficiencies in the information needed to assess whether nationals of particular countries present "public safety threats." To further that purpose, the Proclamation placed entry restrictions on the nationals of eight foreign states whose systems for managing and sharing information about their nationals the President deemed inadequate.

Following the 50-day period, the Acting Secretary of Homeland Security concluded that eight countries—Chad, Iran, Iraq, Libya, North Korea, Syria, Venezuela, and Yemen—remained deficient in terms of their risk profile and willingness to provide requested information. The Proclamation further directs DHS to assess on a continuing basis whether entry restrictions should be modified or continued, and to report to the President every 180 days. Upon completion of the first such review period, the President, on the recommendation of the Secretary of Homeland Security, determined that Chad had sufficiently improved its practices, and he accordingly lifted restrictions on its nationals.

[II]

The text of [8 U.S.C.] § 1182(f) states:

> Whenever the President finds that the entry of any aliens or of any class of aliens into the United States would be detrimental to the interests of the United States, he may by proclamation, and for such period as he shall deem necessary, suspend the entry of all aliens or any class of aliens as immigrants or nonimmigrants, or impose on the entry of aliens any restrictions he may deem to be appropriate.

By its terms, § 1182(f) exudes deference to the President in every clause. It entrusts to the President the decisions whether and when to suspend entry ("[w]henever [he] finds that the entry" of aliens "would be detrimental" to the national interest); whose entry to suspend ("all aliens or any class of aliens"); for how long ("for such period as he shall deem necessary"); and on what conditions ("any restrictions he may deem to be appropriate").

The Proclamation falls well within this comprehensive delegation. The sole prerequisite set forth in § 1182(f) is that the President "find[ ]" that the entry of the covered aliens "would be detrimental to the interests of the United States." The President has undoubtedly fulfilled that requirement here.

Plaintiffs' final statutory argument is that the President's entry suspension violates § 1152(a)(1)(A), which provides that "no person shall . . . be discriminated against in the issuance of an immigrant visa because of the person's race, sex, nationality, place of birth, or place of residence." In any event, we reject plaintiffs' interpretation because it ignores the basic distinction between admissibility determinations and visa issuance that runs throughout the INA.

The distinction between admissibility—to which § 1152(a)(1)(A) does not apply—and visa issuance—to which it does—is apparent from the text of the provision, which specifies only that its protections apply to the "issuance" of "immigrant visa[s]," without mentioning admissibility or entry. Had Congress instead intended in § 1152(a)(1)(A) to constrain the President's power to determine who may enter the country, it could easily have chosen language directed to that end.

Common sense and historical practice confirm as much. Section 1152(a)(1)(A) has never been treated as a constraint on the criteria for admissibility in § 1182. Presidents have repeatedly exercised their authority to suspend entry on the basis of nationality.

IV

We now turn to plaintiffs' claim that the Proclamation was issued for the unconstitutional purpose of excluding Muslims.

Our cases recognize that "[t]he clearest command of the Establishment Clause is that one religious denomination cannot be officially preferred over another." Plaintiffs believe that the Proclamation violates this prohibition by singling out Muslims for disfavored treatment. The entry suspension, they contend, operates as a "religious gerrymander," in part because most of the countries covered by the Proclamation have Muslim-majority populations. Relying on Establishment Clause precedents concerning laws and policies applied domestically, plaintiffs allege that the primary purpose of the Proclamation was religious animus and that the President's stated concerns about vetting protocols and national security were but pretexts for discriminating against Muslims.

At the heart of plaintiffs' case is a series of statements by the President and his advisers casting doubt on the official objective of the Proclamation. For example, while a candidate on the campaign trail, the President published a "Statement on Preventing Muslim Immigration" that called for a "total and complete shutdown of Muslims entering the United States until our country's representatives can figure out what is going on." Then-candidate Trump also stated that "Islam hates us" and asserted that the United States was "having problems with Muslims coming into the country." Shortly after being elected, when asked whether violence in Europe had affected his plans to "ban Muslim immigration," the President replied, "You know my plans. All along, I've been proven to be right."

One week after his inauguration, the President issued EO-1. In a television interview, one of the President's campaign advisers explained that when the President "first announced it, he said, 'Muslim ban.' He called me up. He said, 'Put a commission together. Show me the right way to do it legally.'" The adviser said he assembled a group of Members of Congress and lawyers that "focused on, instead of religion, danger. . . . [The order] is based on places where there [is] substantial evidence that people are sending terrorists into our country."

Plaintiffs also note that after issuing EO-2 to replace EO-1, the President expressed regret that his prior order had been "watered down" and called for a "much tougher version" of his "Travel Ban." Shortly before the release of the Proclamation, he stated that the "travel ban . . . should be far larger, tougher, and more specific," but "stupidly that would not be politically correct." More recently, on November 29, 2017, the President retweeted links to three anti-Muslim propaganda videos. In response to questions about those videos, the President's deputy press secretary denied that the President thinks Muslims are a threat to the United States, explaining that "the President has been talking about these security issues for years now, from the campaign trail to the White House" and "has addressed these issues with the travel order that he issued earlier this year and the companion proclamation."

The President of the United States possesses an extraordinary power to speak to his fellow citizens and on their behalf. Our Presidents have frequently used that power to espouse the principles of religious freedom and tolerance on which this Nation was founded.

Plaintiffs argue that this President's words strike at fundamental standards of respect and tolerance, in violation of our constitutional tradition. But the issue before us is not whether to denounce the statements. It is instead the significance of those statements in reviewing a Presidential directive, neutral on its face, addressing a matter within the core of executive responsibility. In doing so, we must consider not only the statements of a particular President, but also the authority of the Presidency itself.

The case before us differs in numerous respects from the conventional Establishment Clause claim. Unlike the typical suit involving religious displays or school prayer, plaintiffs seek to invalidate a national security directive regulating the entry of aliens abroad. Their claim accordingly raises a number of delicate issues regarding the scope of the constitutional right and the manner of proof. The Proclamation, moreover, is facially neutral toward religion. Plaintiffs therefore ask the Court to probe the sincerity of the stated justifications for the policy by reference to extrinsic statements—many of which were made before the President took the oath of office. These various aspects of plaintiffs' challenge inform our standard of review.

For more than a century, this Court has recognized that the admission and exclusion of foreign nationals is a "fundamental sovereign attribute exercised by the Government's political departments largely immune from judicial control." Because decisions in these matters may implicate "relations with foreign powers," or involve "classifications defined in the light of changing political and economic circumstances," such judgments "are frequently of a character more appropriate to either the Legislature or the Executive."

Nonetheless, although foreign nationals seeking admission have no constitutional right to entry, this Court has engaged in a circumscribed judicial inquiry when the denial of a visa allegedly burdens the constitutional rights of a U.S. citizen.

"[J]udicial inquiry into the national-security realm raises concerns for the separation of powers" by intruding on the President's constitutional responsibilities in the area of foreign affairs. For another, "when it comes to collecting evidence and drawing inferences" on questions of national security, "the lack of competence on the part of the courts is marked."

The upshot of our cases in this context is clear: "Any rule of constitutional law that would inhibit the flexibility" of the President "to respond to changing world conditions should be adopted only with the greatest caution," and our inquiry into matters of entry and national security is highly constrained. For our purposes today, we assume that we may look behind the face of the Proclamation to the extent of applying rational basis review. That standard of review considers whether the entry policy is plausibly related to the Government's stated objective to protect the country and improve vetting processes. As a result, we may consider plaintiffs' extrinsic evidence, but will uphold the policy so long as it can reasonably be understood to result from a justification independent of unconstitutional grounds.

Given the standard of review, it should come as no surprise that the Court hardly ever strikes down a policy as illegitimate under rational basis scrutiny. On the few occasions where we have done so, a common thread has been that the laws at issue lack any purpose other than a "bare . . . desire to harm a politically unpopular group."

The Proclamation does not fit this pattern. It cannot be said that it is impossible to "discern a relationship to legitimate state interests" or that the policy is "inexplicable by anything but animus." Indeed, the dissent can only attempt to argue otherwise by refusing to apply anything resembling rational basis review. But because there is persuasive evidence that the entry suspension has a legitimate grounding in national security concerns, quite apart from any religious hostility, we must accept that independent justification.

The Proclamation is expressly premised on legitimate purposes: preventing entry of nationals who cannot be adequately vetted and inducing other nations to improve their practices. The text says nothing about religion. Plaintiffs and the dissent nonetheless emphasize that five of the seven nations currently included in the Proclamation have Muslim-majority populations. Yet that fact alone does not support an inference of religious hostility, given that the policy covers just 8% of the world's Muslim population and is limited to countries that were previously designated by Congress or prior administrations as posing national security risks.

The Proclamation, moreover, reflects the results of a worldwide review process undertaken by multiple Cabinet officials and their agencies.

Finally, the dissent invokes *Korematsu v. United States* (1944). Whatever rhetorical advantage the dissent may see in doing so, *Korematsu* has nothing to do with this case. The forcible relocation of U.S. citizens to concentration camps, solely and explicitly on the basis of race, is objectively unlawful and outside the scope of Presidential authority. But it is wholly inapt to liken that morally repugnant order to a facially neutral policy denying certain foreign nationals the privilege of admission. The entry suspension is an act that is well within executive authority and could have been taken by any other President — the only question is evaluating the actions of this particular President in promulgating an otherwise valid Proclamation.

The dissent's reference to *Korematsu*, however, affords this Court the opportunity to make express what is already obvious: *Korematsu* was gravely wrong the day it was decided, has been overruled in the court of history, and — to be clear — "has no place in law under the Constitution."

Under these circumstances, the Government has set forth a sufficient national security justification to survive rational basis review. We express no view on the soundness of the policy. We simply hold today that plaintiffs have not demonstrated a likelihood of success on the merits of their constitutional claim. Because plaintiffs have not shown that they are likely to succeed on the merits of their claims, we reverse the grant of the preliminary injunction as an abuse of discretion.

Justice KENNEDY, concurring.

I join the Court's opinion in full. In all events, it is appropriate to make this further observation. There are numerous instances in which the statements and actions of Government officials are not subject to judicial scrutiny or intervention. That does not mean those officials are free to disregard the Constitution and the rights it proclaims and protects. The oath that all officials take to adhere to the Constitution is not confined to those spheres in which the Judiciary can correct or even comment upon what those officials say or do. Indeed, the very fact that an official may have broad discretion, discretion free from judicial scrutiny, makes it all the more imperative for him or her to adhere to the Constitution and to its meaning and its promise.

The First Amendment prohibits the establishment of religion and promises the free exercise of religion. From these safeguards, and from the guarantee of freedom of speech, it follows there is freedom of belief and expression. It is an urgent necessity that officials adhere to these constitutional guarantees and mandates in all their actions, even in the sphere of foreign affairs. An anxious world must know that our Government remains committed always to the liberties the Constitution seeks to preserve and protect, so that freedom extends outward, and lasts.

Justice BRYER, with whom Justice KAGAN joins, dissenting.

The question before us is whether Proclamation No. 9645 is lawful. If its promulgation or content was significantly affected by religious animus against Muslims, it would violate the relevant statute or the First Amendment itself. If, however, its sole *ratio decidendi* was one of national security, then it would be unlikely to violate either the statute or the Constitution. Which is it? Members of the Court principally disagree about the answer to this question, *i.e.*, about whether or the extent to which religious animus played a significant role in the Proclamation's promulgation or content.

In my view, the Proclamation's elaborate system of exemptions and waivers can and should help us answer this question. That system provides for case-by-case consideration of persons who may qualify for visas despite the Proclamation's general ban. Those persons include lawful permanent residents, asylum seekers, refugees, students, children, and numerous others. There are likely many such persons, perhaps in the thousands. And I believe it appropriate to take account of their Proclamation-granted status when considering the Proclamation's lawfulness.

Further, since the case-by-case exemptions and waivers apply without regard to the individual's religion, application of that system would help make clear that the Proclamation does not deny visas to numerous Muslim individuals (from those countries) who do not pose a security threat. And that fact would help to rebut the First Amendment claim that the Proclamation rests upon anti-Muslim bias rather than security need. Finally, of course, the very fact that Muslims from those countries would enter the United States (under Proclamation-provided exemptions and waivers) would help to show the same thing.

On the other hand, if the Government is *not* applying the system of exemptions and waivers that the Proclamation contains, then its argument for the Proclamation's lawfulness becomes significantly weaker. And, perhaps most importantly, if the Government is not applying the Proclamation's exemption and waiver system, the claim that the Proclamation is a "Muslim ban," rather than a "security-based" ban, becomes much stronger. How could the Government successfully claim that the Proclamation rests on security needs if it is excluding Muslims who satisfy the Proclamation's own terms? At the same time, denying visas to Muslims who meet the Proclamation's own security terms would support the view that the Government excludes them for reasons based upon their religion.

Unfortunately there is evidence that supports the second possibility, *i.e.*, that the Government is not applying the Proclamation as written. An examination of publicly available statistics also provides cause for concern. The State Department reported that during the Proclamation's first month, two waivers were approved out of 6,555 eligible applicants. In its reply brief, the Government claims that number increased from 2 to 430 during the first four months of implementation. That number, 430, however, when compared with the number of pre-Proclamation visitors, accounts for a miniscule percentage of those likely eligible for visas, in such categories as persons requiring medical treatment, academic visitors, students, family members, and others belonging to groups that, when considered as a group (rather than case by case), would not seem to pose security threats.

Amici have suggested that there are numerous applicants who could meet the waiver criteria. Other data suggest the same. The Proclamation does not apply to asylum seekers or refugees. Yet few refugees have been admitted since the Proclamation took effect. While more than 15,000 Syrian refugees arrived in the United States in 2016, only 13 have arrived since January 2018.

Declarations, anecdotal evidence, facts, and numbers taken from *amicus* briefs are not judicial factfindings. The Government has not had an opportunity to respond, and a court has not had an opportunity to decide. But, given the importance of the decision in this case, the need for assurance that the Proclamation does not rest upon a "Muslim ban," and the assistance in deciding the issue that answers to the "exemption and waiver" questions may provide, I would send this case back to the District Court for further proceedings. And, I would leave the injunction in effect while the matter is litigated. Regardless, the Court's decision today leaves the District Court free to explore these issues on remand.

Justice SOTOMAYOR, with whom Justice GINSBURG joins, dissenting.

The United States of America is a Nation built upon the promise of religious liberty. Our Founders honored that core promise by embedding the principle of religious neutrality in the First Amendment. The Court's decision today fails to safeguard that fundamental principle. It leaves undisturbed a policy first advertised openly and unequivocally as a "total and complete shutdown of Muslims entering the United States" because the policy now masquerades behind a facade of national-security concerns. But this repackaging does little to cleanse Presidential Proclamation No. 9645 of the appearance of discrimination that the President's words have created. Based on the evidence in the record, a reasonable observer would conclude that the Proclamation was motivated by anti-Muslim animus. That alone suffices to show that plaintiffs are likely to succeed on the merits of their Establishment Clause claim. The majority holds otherwise by ignoring the facts, misconstruing our legal precedent, and turning a blind eye to the pain and suffering the Proclamation inflicts upon countless families and individuals, many of whom are United States citizens. Because that troubling result runs contrary to the Constitution and our precedent, I dissent.

I

Whatever the merits of plaintiffs' complex statutory claims, the Proclamation must be enjoined for a more fundamental reason: It runs afoul of the Establishment Clause's guarantee of religious neutrality.

The Establishment Clause forbids government policies "respecting an establishment of religion." The "clearest command" of the Establishment Clause is that the Government cannot favor or disfavor one religion over another. "When the government acts with the ostensible and predominant purpose" of disfavoring a particular religion, "it violates that central Establishment Clause value of official religious neutrality, there being no neutrality when the government's ostensible object is to take sides." To determine whether plaintiffs have proved an Establishment Clause violation, the Court asks whether a reasonable observer would view the government action as enacted for the purpose of disfavoring a religion.

In answering that question, this Court has generally considered the text of the government policy, its operation, and any available evidence regarding "the historical background of the decision under challenge, the specific series of events leading to the enactment or official policy in question, and the legislative or administrative history, including contemporaneous statements made by" the decisionmaker.

Although the majority briefly recounts a few of the statements and background events that form the basis of plaintiffs' constitutional challenge, that highly abridged account does not tell even half of the story. The full record paints a far more harrowing picture, from which a reasonable observer would readily conclude that the Proclamation was motivated by hostility and animus toward the Muslim faith.

During his Presidential campaign, then-candidate Donald Trump pledged that, if elected, he would ban Muslims from entering the United States. Specifically, on December 7, 2015, he issued a formal statement "calling for a total and complete shutdown of Muslims entering the United States." That statement remained on his campaign website until May 2017 (several months into his Presidency).

On December 8, 2015, Trump justified his proposal during a television interview by noting that President Franklin D. Roosevelt "did the same thing" with respect to the internment of Japanese Americans during World War II. . In January 2016, during a Republican primary debate, Trump was asked whether he wanted to "rethink [his] position" on "banning Muslims from entering the country." He answered, "No." A month later, at a rally in South Carolina, Trump told an apocryphal story about United States General John J. Pershing killing a large group of Muslim insurgents in the Philippines with bullets dipped in pigs' blood in the early 1900's. . In March 2016, he expressed his belief that "Islam hates us. . . . [W]e can't allow people coming into this country who have this hatred of the United States . . . [a]nd of people that are not Muslim." That same month, Trump asserted that "[w]e're having problems with the Muslims, and we're having problems with Muslims coming into the country." He therefore called for surveillance of mosques in the United States, blaming terrorist attacks on Muslims' lack of "assimilation" and their commitment to "sharia law." A day later, he opined that Muslims "do not respect us at all" and "don't respect a lot of the things that are happening throughout not only our country, but they don't respect other things."

As Trump's presidential campaign progressed, he began to describe his policy proposal in slightly different terms. In June 2016, for instance, he characterized the policy proposal as a suspension of immigration from countries "where there's a proven history of terrorism." He also described the proposal as rooted in the need to stop "importing radical Islamic terrorism to the West through a failed immigration system." Asked in July 2016 whether he was "pull[ing] back from" his pledged Muslim ban, Trump responded, "I actually don't think it's a rollback. In fact, you could say it's an expansion." He then explained that he used different terminology because "[p]eople were so upset when [he] used the word Muslim."

A month before the 2016 election, Trump reiterated that his proposed "Muslim ban" had "morphed into a[n] extreme vetting from certain areas of the world." Then, on December 21, 2016, President-elect Trump was asked whether he would "rethink" his previous "plans to create a Muslim registry or ban Muslim immigration." He replied: "You know my plans. All along, I've proven to be right."

On January 27, 2017, one week after taking office, President Trump signed entitled "Protecting the Nation From Foreign Terrorist Entry Into the United States." As he signed it, President Trump read the title, looked up, and said "We all know what that means." That same day, President Trump explained to the media that, under EO-1, Christians would be given priority for entry as refugees into the United States. The following day, one of President Trump's key advisers candidly drew the connection between EO-1 and the "Muslim ban" that the President had pledged to implement if elected. According to that adviser, "[W]hen [Donald Trump] first announced it, he said, 'Muslim ban.' He called me up. He said, 'Put a commission together. Show me the right way to do it legally.'"

While litigation over EO-2 was ongoing, President Trump repeatedly made statements alluding to a desire to keep Muslims out of the country. For instance, he said at a rally of his supporters that EO-2 was just a "watered down version of the first one" and had been "tailor[ed]" at the behest of "the lawyers." He further added that he would prefer "to go back to the first [executive order] and go all the way" and reiterated his belief that it was "very hard" for Muslims to assimilate into Western culture. Then, on August 17, 2017, President Trump issued yet another tweet about Islam, once more referencing the story about General Pershing's massacre of Muslims in the Philippines: "Study what General Pershing . . . did to terrorists when caught. There was no more Radical Islamic Terror for 35 years!"

In September 2017, President Trump tweeted that "[t]he travel ban into the United States should be far larger, tougher and more specific — but stupidly, that would not be politically correct!" On November 29, 2017, President Trump "retweeted" three anti-Muslim videos, entitled "Muslim Destroys a Statue of Virgin Mary!", "Islamist mob pushes teenage boy off roof and beats him to death!", and "Muslim migrant beats up Dutch boy on crutches!"

As the majority correctly notes, "the issue before us is not whether to denounce" these offensive statements. Rather, the dispositive and narrow question here is whether a reasonable observer, presented with all "openly available data," the text and "historical context" of the Proclamation, and the "specific sequence of events" leading to it, would conclude that the primary purpose of the Proclamation is to disfavor Islam and its adherents by excluding them from the country. The answer is unquestionably yes.

Taking all the relevant evidence together, a reasonable observer would conclude that the Proclamation was driven primarily by anti-Muslim animus, rather than by the Government's asserted national-security justifications. Moreover, despite several opportunities to do so, President Trump has never disavowed any of his prior statements about Islam. Instead, he has continued to make remarks that a reasonable observer would view as an unrelenting attack on the Muslim religion and its followers. Given President Trump's failure to correct the reasonable perception of his apparent hostility toward the Islamic faith, it is unsurprising that the President's lawyers have, at every step in the lower courts, failed in their attempts to launder the Proclamation of its discriminatory taint.

Ultimately, what began as a policy explicitly "calling for a total and complete shutdown of Muslims entering the United States" has since morphed into a "Proclamation" putatively based on national-security concerns. But this new window dressing cannot conceal an unassailable fact: the words of the President and his advisers create the strong perception that the Proclamation is contaminated by impermissible discriminatory animus against Islam and its followers.

II

Rather than defend the President's problematic statements, the Government urges this Court to set them aside and defer to the President on issues related to immigration and national security. The majority accepts that invitation and incorrectly applies a watered-down legal standard in an effort to short circuit plaintiffs' Establishment Clause claim.

But even under rational-basis review, the Proclamation must fall. That is so because the Proclamation is "'divorced from any factual context from which we could discern a relationship to legitimate state interests,' and 'its sheer breadth [is] so discontinuous with the reasons offered for it'" that the policy is "'inexplicable by anything but animus.'"

In sum, none of the features of the Proclamation highlighted by the majority supports the Government's claim that the Proclamation is genuinely and primarily rooted in a legitimate national-security interest. What the unrebutted evidence actually shows is that a reasonable observer would conclude, quite easily, that the primary purpose and function of the Proclamation is to disfavor Islam by banning Muslims from entering our country.

[III]

The First Amendment stands as a bulwark against official religious prejudice and embodies our Nation's deep commitment to religious plurality and tolerance. That constitutional promise is why, "[f]or centuries now, people have come to this country from every corner of the world to share in the blessing of religious freedom." Instead of vindicating those principles, today's decision tosses them aside. In holding that the First Amendment gives way to an executive policy that a reasonable observer would view as motivated by animus against Muslims, the majority opinion upends this Court's precedent, repeats tragic mistakes of the past, and denies countless individuals the fundamental right of religious liberty.

Just weeks ago, the Court rendered its decision in which applied the bedrock principles of religious neutrality and tolerance in considering a First Amendment challenge to government action. Those principles should apply equally here. In both instances, the question is whether a government actor exhibited tolerance and neutrality in reaching a decision that affects individuals' fundamental religious freedom. But unlike in *Masterpiece*, where a state civil rights commission was found to have acted without "the neutrality that the Free Exercise Clause requires," the government actors in this case will not be held accountable for breaching the First Amendment's guarantee of religious neutrality and tolerance. Unlike in *Masterpiece*, where the majority considered the state commissioners' statements about religion to be persuasive evidence of unconstitutional government action, the majority here completely sets aside the President's charged statements about Muslims as irrelevant. That holding erodes the foundational principles of religious tolerance that the Court elsewhere has so emphatically protected, and it tells members of minority religions in our country "'that they are outsiders, not full members of the political community.'"

Today's holding is all the more troubling given the stark parallels between the reasoning of this case and that of *Korematsu v. United States* (1944). In *Korematsu*, the Court gave "a pass [to] an odious, gravely injurious racial classification" authorized by an executive order. As here, the Government invoked an ill-defined national-security threat to justify an exclusionary policy of sweeping proportion. As here, the exclusion order was rooted in dangerous stereotypes about, *inter alia*, a particular group's supposed inability to assimilate and desire to harm the United States. As here, the Government was unwilling to reveal its own intelligence agencies' views of the alleged security concerns to the very citizens it purported to protect. And as here, there was strong evidence that impermissible hostility and animus motivated the Government's policy.

Today, the Court takes the important step of finally overruling *Korematsu*, denouncing it as "gravely wrong the day it was decided." This formal repudiation of a shameful precedent is laudable and long overdue. But it does not make the majority's decision here acceptable or right. By blindly accepting the Government's misguided invitation to sanction a discriminatory policy motivated by animosity toward a disfavored group, all in the name of a superficial claim of national security, the Court redeploys the same dangerous logic underlying *Korematsu* and merely replaces one "gravely wrong" decision with another.

Our Constitution demands, and our country deserves, a Judiciary willing to hold the coordinate branches to account when they defy our most sacred legal commitments. Because the Court's decision today has failed in that respect, with profound regret, I dissent.

C. Constitutional Problems of the Administrative State

1. The Non-Delegation Doctrine and Its Demise (casebook p. 342)

As indicated in the casebook, the Court has not found a federal law unconstitutional as an impermissible delegation of powers since 1935. In *Gundy v. United States*, the Court again rejected a challenge to a federal law on this basis. But notice that the decision was 5-3 (Justice Kavanaugh had not been confirmed when the case was argued), and it is without a majority opinion. Although Justice Kagan's plurality opinion would give little effect to the non-delegation doctrine, Justice Alito's brief concurring opinion expresses a willingness to reconsider the law in this area. In light of the dissent and the confirmation of Justice Kavanaugh, there might be a majority willing to do so.

GUNDY v. UNITED STATES
139 S. Ct. 2116 (2019)

Justice KAGAN announced the judgment of the Court and delivered an opinion, in which Justice GINSBURG, Justice BREYER, and Justice SOTOMAYOR join.

The nondelegation doctrine bars Congress from transferring its legislative power to another branch of Government. This case requires us to decide whether 34 U.S.C. § 20913(d), enacted as part of the Sex Offender Registration and Notification Act (SORNA), violates that doctrine. We hold it does not. Under § 20913(d), the Attorney General must apply SORNA's registration requirements as soon as feasible to offenders convicted before the statute's enactment. That delegation easily passes constitutional muster.

I

Congress has sought, for the past quarter century, to combat sex crimes and crimes against children through sex-offender registration schemes. In 1994, Congress first conditioned certain federal funds on States' adoption of registration laws meeting prescribed minimum standards. Two years later, Congress strengthened those standards, most notably by insisting that States inform local communities of registrants' addresses. By that time, every State and the District of Columbia had enacted a sex-offender registration law. But the state statutes varied along many dimensions, and Congress came to realize that their "loopholes and deficiencies" had allowed over 100,000 sex offenders (about 20% of the total) to escape registration. In 2006, to address those failings, Congress enacted SORNA.

SORNA makes "more uniform and effective" the prior "patchwork" of sex-offender registration systems. The Act's express "purpose" is "to protect the public from sex offenders and offenders against children" by "establish[ing] a comprehensive national system for [their] registration." To that end, SORNA covers more sex offenders, and imposes more onerous registration requirements, than most States had before. The Act also backs up those requirements with new criminal penalties. Any person required to register under SORNA who knowingly fails to do so (and who travels in interstate commerce) may be imprisoned for up to ten years.

Section 20913—the disputed provision here—elaborates the "[i]nitial registration" requirements for sex offenders. Subsection (b) sets out the general rule: An offender must register "before completing a sentence of imprisonment with respect to the offense giving rise to the registration requirement" (or, if the offender is not sentenced to prison, "not later than [three] business days after being sentenced"). Two provisions down, subsection (d) addresses (in its title's words) the "[i]nitial registration of sex offenders unable to comply with subsection (b)." The provision states:

> "The Attorney General shall have the authority to specify the applicability of the requirements of this subchapter to sex offenders convicted before the enactment of

this chapter . . . and to prescribe rules for the registration of any such sex offenders and for other categories of sex offenders who are unable to comply with
subsection (b)."

Subsection (d), in other words, focuses on individuals convicted of a
sex offense before SORNA's enactment—a group we will call pre-Act
offenders. Many of these individuals were unregistered at the time of
SORNA's enactment, either because pre-existing law did not cover them
or because they had successfully evaded that law (so were "lost" to the
system). And of those potential new registrants, many or most could not
comply with subsection (b)'s registration rule because they had already
completed their prison sentences. For the entire group of pre-Act offenders, once again, the Attorney General "shall have the authority" to "specify
the applicability" of SORNA's registration requirements and "to prescribe
rules for [their] registration."

Under that delegated authority, the Attorney General issued an interim
rule in February 2007, specifying that SORNA's registration requirements
apply in full to "sex offenders convicted of the offense for which registration is required prior to the enactment of that Act." The final rule, issued
in December 2010, reiterated that SORNA applies to all pre- That rule has
remained the same to this day.

Petitioner Herman Gundy is a pre-Act offender. The year before
SORNA's enactment, he pleaded guilty under Maryland law for sexually
assaulting a minor. After his release from prison in 2012, Gundy came to
live in New York. But he never registered there as a sex offender. A few
years later, he was convicted for failing to register, in violation of § 2250.
He argued below (among other things) that Congress unconstitutionally
delegated legislative power when it authorized the Attorney General to
"specify the applicability" of SORNA's registration requirements to pre-
Act offenders. The District Court and Court of Appeals for the Second
Circuit rejected that claim, as had every other court (including eleven
Courts of Appeals) to consider the issue. Today, we join the consensus
and affirm.

II

Article I of the Constitution provides that "[a]ll legislative Powers herein
granted shall be vested in a Congress of the United States." Accompanying
that assignment of power to Congress is a bar on its further delegation.
Congress, this Court explained early on, may not transfer to another
branch "powers which are strictly and exclusively legislative." But the

Constitution does not "deny[ ] to the Congress the necessary resources of flexibility and practicality [that enable it] to perform its function[s]." Congress may "obtain[ ] the assistance of its coordinate Branches"—and in particular, may confer substantial discretion on executive agencies to implement and enforce the laws. "[I]n our increasingly complex society, replete with ever changing and more technical problems," this Court has understood that "Congress simply cannot do its job absent an ability to delegate power under broad general directives." So we have held, time and again, that a statutory delegation is constitutional as long as Congress "lay[s] down by legislative act an intelligible principle to which the person or body authorized to [exercise the delegated authority] is directed to conform."

Given that standard, a nondelegation inquiry always begins (and often almost ends) with statutory interpretation. The constitutional question is whether Congress has supplied an intelligible principle to guide the delegee's use of discretion. So the answer requires construing the challenged statute to figure out what task it delegates and what instructions it provides. Only after a court has determined a challenged statute's meaning can it decide whether the law sufficiently guides executive discretion to accord with Article I. And indeed, once a court interprets the statute, it may find that the constitutional question all but answers itself.

That is the case here, because § 20913(d) does not give the Attorney General anything like the "unguided" and "unchecked" authority that Gundy says. The provision, in Gundy's view, "grants the Attorney General plenary power to determine SORNA's applicability to pre-Act offenders—to require them to register, or not, as she sees fit, and to change her policy for any reason and at any time." If that were so, we would face a nondelegation question. But it is not. This Court has already interpreted § 20913(d) to say something different—to require the Attorney General to apply SORNA to all pre-Act offenders as soon as feasible. And revisiting that issue yet more fully today, we reach the same conclusion. The text, considered alongside its context, purpose, and history, makes clear that the Attorney General's discretion extends only to considering and addressing feasibility issues. Given that statutory meaning, Gundy's constitutional claim must fail. Section 20913(d)'s delegation falls well within permissible bounds.

Recall again the delegation provision at issue. Congress gave the Attorney General authority to "specify the applicability" of SORNA's requirements to pre-Act offenders. § 20913(d). And in the second half of the same sentence, Congress gave him authority to "prescribe rules for the registration of any such sex offenders . . . who are unable to comply with" subsection (b)'s initial registration requirement. What does the delegation in § 20913(d) allow the Attorney General to do?

The different answers on offer here reflect competing views of statutory interpretation. As noted above, Gundy urges us to read § 20913(d) to empower the Attorney General to do whatever he wants as to pre-Act offenders: He may make them all register immediately or he may exempt them from registration forever (or he may do anything in between). Gundy bases that argument on the first half of § 20913(d), isolated from everything else—from the second half of the same section, from surrounding provisions in SORNA, and from any conception of the statute's history and purpose. *Reynolds* [*v. United States* (2012)] took a different approach (as does the Government here), understanding statutory interpretation as a "holistic endeavor" which determines meaning by looking not to isolated words, but to text in context, along with purpose and history.

This Court has long refused to construe words "in a vacuum," as Gundy attempts. "It is a fundamental canon of statutory construction that the words of a statute must be read in their context and with a view to their place in the overall statutory scheme." And beyond context and structure, the Court often looks to "history [and] purpose" to divine the meaning of language. That non-blinkered brand of interpretation holds good for delegations, just as for other statutory provisions. To define the scope of delegated authority, we have looked to the text in "context" and in light of the statutory "purpose." In keeping with that method, we again do so today.

So begin at the beginning, with the "[d]eclaration of purpose" that is SORNA's first sentence. There, Congress announced that "to protect the public," it was "establish[ing] a comprehensive national system for the registration" of "sex offenders and offenders against children." The term "comprehensive" has a clear meaning—something that is all-encompassing or sweeping. That description could not fit the system SORNA created if the Attorney General could decline, for any reason or no reason at all, to apply SORNA to all pre-Act offenders. After all, for many years after SORNA's enactment, the great majority of sex offenders in the country would be pre-Act offenders. If Gundy were right, all of those offenders could be exempt from SORNA's registration requirements. So the mismatch between SORNA's statement of purpose and Gundy's view of § 20913(d) is as stark as stark comes.

The Act's definition of "sex offender" makes the same point. Under that definition, a "sex offender" is "an individual who was convicted of a sex offense." Note the tense: "was," not "is." This Court has often "looked to Congress' choice of verb tense to ascertain a statute's temporal reach," including when interpreting other SORNA provisions.

The Act's legislative history backs up everything said above by showing that the need to register pre-Act offenders was front and center in Congress's thinking. Recall that Congress designed SORNA to address "loopholes and deficiencies" in existing registration laws.

We thus end up, on close inspection of the statutory scheme, exactly where *Reynolds* left us. The Attorney General's authority goes to transition-period implementation issues, and no further.

Now that we have determined what § 20913(d) means, we can consider whether it violates the Constitution. The question becomes: Did Congress make an impermissible delegation when it instructed the Attorney General to apply SORNA's registration requirements to pre-Act offenders as soon as feasible? Under this Court's long-established law, that question is easy. Its answer is no.

As noted earlier, this Court has held that a delegation is constitutional so long as Congress has set out an "intelligible principle" to guide the delegee's exercise of authority. Or in a related formulation, the Court has stated that a delegation is permissible if Congress has made clear to the delegee "the general policy" he must pursue and the "boundaries of [his] authority." Those standards, the Court has made clear, are not demanding. "[W]e have 'almost never felt qualified to second-guess Congress regarding the permissible degree of policy judgment that can be left to those executing or applying the law.'" Only twice in this country's history (and that in a single year) have we found a delegation excessive — in each case because "Congress had failed to articulate *any* policy or standard" to confine discretion. see *A. L. A. Schechter Poultry Corp. v. United States* (1935); *Panama Refining Co. v. Ryan* (1935). By contrast, we have over and over upheld even very broad delegations. Here is a sample: We have approved delegations to various agencies to regulate in the "public interest." We have sustained authorizations for agencies to set "fair and equitable" prices and "just and reasonable" rates. We more recently affirmed a delegation to an agency to issue whatever air quality standards are "requisite to protect the public health."

In that context, the delegation in SORNA easily passes muster (as all eleven circuit courts to have considered the question found). The statute conveyed Congress's policy that the Attorney General require pre-Act offenders to register as soon as feasible. Under the law, the feasibility issues he could address were administrative — and, more specifically, transitional — in nature.

Indeed, if SORNA's delegation is unconstitutional, then most of Government is unconstitutional — dependent as Congress is on the need to give discretion to executive officials to implement its programs. Consider again this Court's long-time recognition: "Congress simply cannot do its job absent an ability to delegate power under broad general directives." Among the judgments often left to executive officials are ones involving feasibility.

It is wisdom and humility alike that this Court has always upheld such "necessities of government."

Justice KAVANAUGH took no part in the consideration or decision of this case.

Justice ALITO, concurring in the judgment.

The Constitution confers on Congress certain "legislative [p]owers," Art. I, § 1, and does not permit Congress to delegate them to another branch of the Government. Nevertheless, since 1935, the Court has uniformly rejected nondelegation arguments and has upheld provisions that authorized agencies to adopt important rules pursuant to extraordinarily capacious standards. If a majority of this Court were willing to reconsider the approach we have taken for the past 84 years, I would support that effort. But because a majority is not willing to do that, it would be freakish to single out the provision at issue here for special treatment.

Because I cannot say that the statute lacks a discernable standard that is adequate under the approach this Court has taken for many years, I vote to affirm.

Justice GORSUCH, with whom THE CHIEF JUSTICE and Justice THOMAS join, dissenting.

The Constitution promises that only the people's elected representatives may adopt new federal laws restricting liberty. Yet the statute before us scrambles that design. It purports to endow the nation's chief prosecutor with the power to write his own criminal code governing the lives of a half-million citizens. Yes, those affected are some of the least popular among us. But if a single executive branch official can write laws restricting the liberty of this group of persons, what does that mean for the next?

Today, a plurality of an eight-member Court endorses this extraconstitutional arrangement but resolves nothing. Working from an understanding of the Constitution at war with its text and history, the plurality reimagines the terms of the statute before us and insists there is nothing wrong with Congress handing off so much power to the Attorney General. But Justice

Alito supplies the fifth vote for today's judgment and he does not join either the plurality's constitutional or statutory analysis, indicating instead that he remains willing, in a future case with a full Court, to revisit these matters. Respectfully, I would not wait.

I

For individuals convicted of sex offenses *after* Congress adopted the Sex Offender Registration and Notification Act (SORNA) in 2006, the statute offers detailed instructions.

But what about those convicted of sex offenses *before* the Act's adoption? At the time of SORNA's enactment, the nation's population of sex offenders exceeded 500,000, and Congress concluded that something had to be done about these "pre-Act" offenders too. But it seems Congress couldn't agree what that should be. The treatment of pre-Act offenders proved a "controversial issue with major policy significance and practical ramifications for states." Among other things, applying SORNA immediately to this group threatened to impose unpopular and costly burdens on States and localities by forcing them to adopt or overhaul their own sex offender registration schemes. So Congress simply passed the problem to the Attorney General. For all half-million pre-Act offenders, the law says only this, in 34 U.S.C. § 20913(d):

> "The Attorney General shall have the authority to specify the applicability of the requirements of this subchapter to sex offenders convicted before the enactment of this chapter . . . and to prescribe rules for the registration of any such sex offender."

Yes, that's it. The breadth of the authority Congress granted to the Attorney General in these few words can only be described as vast. As the Department of Justice itself has acknowledged, SORNA "does not require the Attorney General" to impose registration requirements on pre-Act offenders "within a certain time frame or by a date certain; it does not require him to act at all." If the Attorney General does choose to act, he can require all pre-Act offenders to register, or he can "require some but not all to register." For those he requires to register, the Attorney General may impose "some but not all of [SORNA's] registration requirements," as he pleases. And he is free to change his mind on any of these matters "at any given time or over the course of different [political] administrations." Congress thus gave the Attorney General free rein to write the rules for virtually the entire existing sex offender population in this country — a situation that promised to persist for years or decades until pre-Act offenders passed away or fulfilled the terms of their registration obligations and post-Act offenders came to predominate.

Unsurprisingly, different Attorneys General have exercised their discretion in different ways. For six months after SORNA's enactment, Attorney General Gonzales left past offenders alone. Then the pendulum swung the other direction when the Department of Justice issued an interim rule requiring pre-Act offenders to follow all the same rules as post-Act offenders. A year later, Attorney General Mukasey issued more new guidelines, this time directing the States to register some but not all past offenders. Three years after that, Attorney General Holder required the States to register only those pre-Act offenders convicted of a new felony after SORNA's enactment. Various Attorneys General have also taken different positions on whether pre-Act offenders might be entitled to credit for time spent in the community before SORNA was enacted.

These unbounded policy choices have profound consequences for the people they affect. Take our case. Before SORNA's enactment, Herman Gundy pleaded guilty in 2005 to a sexual offense. After his release from prison five years later, he was arrested again, this time for failing to register as a sex offender according to the rules the Attorney General had then prescribed for pre-Act offenders. As a result, Mr. Gundy faced an additional 10-year prison term — 10 years more than if the Attorney General had, in his discretion, chosen to write the rules differently.

II

The framers understood, too, that it would frustrate "the system of government ordained by the Constitution" if Congress could merely announce vague aspirations and then assign others the responsibility of adopting legislation to realize its goals. Through the Constitution, after all, the people had vested the power to prescribe rules limiting their liberties in Congress alone. No one, not even Congress, had the right to alter that arrangement. As Chief Justice Marshall explained, Congress may not "delegate . . . powers which are strictly and exclusively legislative."

Why did the framers insist on this particular arrangement? They believed the new federal government's most dangerous power was the power to enact laws restricting the people's liberty. An "excess of law-making" was, in their words, one of "the diseases to which our governments are most liable." To address that tendency, the framers went to great lengths to make lawmaking difficult. Nor was the point only to limit the government's capacity to restrict the people's freedoms. Article I's detailed processes for new laws were also designed to promote deliberation.

Other purposes animated the framers' design as well. Because men are not angels and majorities can threaten minority rights, the framers insisted on a legislature composed of different bodies subject to different electorates as a means of ensuring that any new law would have to secure the approval of a supermajority of the people's representatives. This, in turn, assured minorities that their votes would often decide the fate of proposed legislation.

If Congress could pass off its legislative power to the executive branch, the "[v]esting [c]lauses, and indeed the entire structure of the Constitution," would "make no sense." Without the involvement of representatives from across the country or the demands of bicameralism and presentment, legislation would risk becoming nothing more than the will of the current President. And if laws could be simply declared by a single person, they would not be few in number, the product of widespread social consensus, likely to protect minority interests, or apt to provide stability and fair notice. Accountability would suffer too. Legislators might seek to take credit for addressing a pressing social problem by sending it to the executive for resolution, while at the same time blaming the executive for the problems that attend whatever measures he chooses to pursue. In turn, the executive might point to Congress as the source of the problem. These opportunities for finger-pointing might prove temptingly advantageous for the politicians involved, but they would also threaten to " 'disguise . . . responsibility for . . . the decisions.'"

Accepting, then, that we have an obligation to decide whether Congress has unconstitutionally divested itself of its legislative responsibilities, the question follows: What's the test?

First, we know that as long as Congress makes the policy decisions when regulating private conduct, it may authorize another branch to "fill up the details." Second, once Congress prescribes the rule governing private conduct, it may make the application of that rule depend on executive fact-finding. Third, Congress may assign the executive and judicial branches certain non-legislative responsibilities.

Before the 1930s, federal statutes granting authority to the executive were comparatively modest and usually easily upheld. But then the federal government began to grow explosively. And with the proliferation of new executive programs came new questions about the scope of congressional delegations. Twice the Court responded by striking down statutes for violating the separation of powers. (*A. L. A. Schechter Poultry Corp.* v. *United States*; *Panama Refining Co.* v. *Ryan*).

After *Schechter Poultry* and *Panama Refining*, Congress responded by writing a second wave of New Deal legislation more "[c]arefully crafted" to avoid the kind of problems that sank these early statutes. And since that

time the Court hasn't held another statute to violate the separation of powers in the same way. Of course, no one thinks that the Court's quiescence
can be attributed to an unwavering new tradition of more scrupulously
drawn statutes. Some lament that the real cause may have to do with a
mistaken "case of death by association" because *Schechter Poultry* and
Panama Refining happened to be handed down during the same era as certain of the Court's now-discredited substantive due process decisions. But
maybe the most likely explanation of all lies in the story of the evolving
"intelligible principle" doctrine.

This Court first used that phrase in 1928 in *J. W. Hampton, Jr., & Co.*
v. *United States*, where it remarked that a statute "lay[ing] down by legislative act an intelligible principle to which the [executive official] is
directed to conform" satisfies the separation of powers."

Still, it's undeniable that the "intelligible principle" remark eventually
began to take on a life of its own. This mutated version of the "intelligible
principle" remark has no basis in the original meaning of the Constitution,
in history, or even in the decision from which it was plucked.

To leave this aspect of the constitutional structure alone undefended
would serve only to accelerate the flight of power from the legislative
to the executive branch, turning the latter into a vortex of authority that
was constitutionally reserved for the people's representatives in order to
protect their liberties.

III

Returning to SORNA with this understanding of our charge in hand, problems quickly emerge. Start with this one: It's hard to see how SORNA
leaves the Attorney General with only details to fill up. As the government
itself admitted in *Reynolds*, SORNA leaves the Attorney General free to
impose on 500,000 pre-Act offenders all of the statute's requirements,
some of them, or none of them. The Attorney General may choose which
pre-Act offenders to subject to the Act. And he is free to change his mind
at any point or over the course of different political administrations. In the
end, there isn't a single policy decision concerning pre-Act offenders on
which Congress even tried to speak, and not a single other case where we
have upheld executive authority over matters like these on the ground they
constitute mere "details." This much appears to have been deliberate, too.
Because members of Congress could not reach consensus on the treatment
of pre-Act offenders, it seems this was one of those situations where they
found it expedient to hand off the job to the executive and direct there the
blame for any later problems that might emerge.

It would be easy enough to let this case go. After all, sex offenders are one of the most disfavored groups in our society. But the rule that prevents Congress from giving the executive *carte blanche* to write laws for sex offenders is the same rule that protects everyone else. Nor is it hard to imagine how the power at issue in this case—the power of a prosecutor to require a group to register with the government on pain of weighty criminal penalties—could be abused in other settings. To allow the nation's chief law enforcement officer to write the criminal laws he is charged with enforcing—to " 'unit[e]' " the " 'legislative and executive powers . . . in the same person' "—would be to mark the end of any meaningful enforcement of our separation of powers and invite the tyranny of the majority that follows when lawmaking and law enforcement responsibilities are united in the same hands.

Nor would enforcing the Constitution's demands spell doom for what some call the "administrative state." The separation of powers does not prohibit any particular policy outcome, let alone dictate any conclusion about the proper size and scope of government. Instead, it is a procedural guarantee that requires Congress to assemble a social consensus before choosing our nation's course on policy questions like those implicated by SORNA. What is more, Congress is hardly bereft of options to accomplish all it might wish to achieve. It may always authorize executive branch officials to fill in even a large number of details, to find facts that trigger the generally applicable rule of conduct specified in a statute, or to exercise non-legislative powers. Congress can also commission agencies or other experts to study and recommend legislative language. Respecting the separation of powers forecloses no substantive outcomes. It only requires us to respect along the way one of the most vital of the procedural protections of individual liberty found in our Constitution.

The only real surprise is that the Court fails to make good on the consequences the government invited, resolving nothing and deferring everything. In a future case with a full panel, I remain hopeful that the Court may yet recognize that, while Congress can enlist considerable assistance from the executive branch in filling up details and finding facts, it may never hand off to the nation's chief prosecutor the power to write his own criminal code. That "is delegation running riot."

3.   Checking Administrative Power (casebook p. 378)

In *Lucia v. Securities and Exchange Commission*, the Court considered when a person should be regarded as an "officer"—who must be appointed by the President, the heads of departments or the lower federal courts — as opposed to a government employee.

LUCIA v. SECURITIES AND EXCHANGE COMMISSION
138 S. Ct. 2044 (2018)

Justice KAGAN delivered the opinion of the Court.

The Appointments Clause of the Constitution lays out the permissible methods of appointing "Officers of the United States," a class of government officials distinct from mere employees. This case requires us to decide whether administrative law judges (ALJs) of the Securities and Exchange Commission (SEC or Commission) qualify as such "Officers." In keeping with *Freytag v. Commissioner* (1991), we hold that they do.

I

The SEC has statutory authority to enforce the nation's securities laws. One way it can do so is by instituting an administrative proceeding against an alleged wrongdoer. By law, the Commission may itself preside over such a proceeding. But the Commission also may, and typically does, delegate that task to an ALJ. The SEC currently has five ALJs. Other staff members, rather than the Commission proper, selected them all.

An ALJ assigned to hear an SEC enforcement action has extensive powers — the "authority to do all things necessary and appropriate to discharge his or her duties" and ensure a "fair and orderly" adversarial proceeding. Those powers "include, but are not limited to," supervising discovery; issuing, revoking, or modifying subpoenas; deciding motions; ruling on the admissibility of evidence; administering oaths; hearing and examining witnesses; generally "[r]egulating the course of" the proceeding and the "conduct of the parties and their counsel"; and imposing sanctions for "[c]ontemptuous conduct" or violations of procedural requirements. As that list suggests, an SEC ALJ exercises authority "comparable to" that of a federal district judge conducting a bench trial.

After a hearing ends, the ALJ issues an "initial decision." That decision must set out "findings and conclusions" about all "material issues of fact [and] law"; it also must include the "appropriate order, sanction, relief, or denial thereof." The Commission can then review the ALJ's decision, either upon request or *sua sponte*. But if it opts against review, the Commission "issue[s] an order that the [ALJ's] decision has become final." At that point, the initial decision is "deemed the action of the Commission."

This case began when the SEC instituted an administrative proceeding against petitioner Raymond Lucia and his investment company. Lucia marketed a retirement savings strategy called "Buckets of Money." In the SEC's view, Lucia used misleading slideshow presentations to deceive prospective clients. The SEC charged Lucia under the Investment Advisers Act, and assigned ALJ Cameron Elliot to adjudicate the case. After nine days of testimony and argument, Judge Elliot issued an initial decision concluding that Lucia had violated the Act and imposing sanctions, including civil penalties of $300,000 and a lifetime bar from the investment industry. In his decision, Judge Elliot made factual findings about only one of the four ways the SEC thought Lucia's slideshow misled investors. The Commission thus remanded for factfinding on the other three claims, explaining that an ALJ's "personal experience with the witnesses" places him "in the best position to make findings of fact" and "resolve any conflicts in the evidence." Judge Elliot then made additional findings of deception and issued a revised initial decision, with the same sanctions.

On appeal to the SEC, Lucia argued that the administrative proceeding was invalid because Judge Elliot had not been constitutionally appointed. According to Lucia, the Commission's ALJs are "Officers of the United States" and thus subject to the Appointments Clause. Under that Clause, Lucia noted, only the President, "Courts of Law," or "Heads of Departments" can appoint "Officers." And none of those actors had made Judge Elliot an ALJ. To be sure, the Commission itself counts as a "Head[ ] of Department[ ]." But the Commission had left the task of appointing ALJs, including Judge Elliot, to SEC staff members. As a result, Lucia contended, Judge Elliot lacked constitutional authority to do his job.

The Commission rejected Lucia's argument. It held that the SEC's ALJs are not "Officers of the United States." Instead, they are "mere employees" — officials with lesser responsibilities who fall outside the Appointments Clause's ambit. Lucia's claim fared no better in the Court of Appeals for the D.C. Circuit. A panel of that court seconded the Commission's view that SEC ALJs are employees rather than officers, and so are not subject to the Appointments Clause.

II

The sole question here is whether the Commission's ALJs are "Officers of the United States" or simply employees of the Federal Government. The Appointments Clause prescribes the exclusive means of appointing "Officers." Only the President, a court of law, or a head of department can do so. And as all parties agree, none of those actors appointed Judge Elliot before he heard Lucia's case; instead, SEC staff members gave him an ALJ slot. So if the Commission's ALJs are constitutional officers, Lucia raises a valid Appointments Clause claim. The only way to defeat his position is to show that those ALJs are not officers at all, but instead non-officer employees—part of the broad swath of "lesser functionaries" in the Government's workforce. For if that is true, the Appointments Clause cares not a whit about who named them.

[I]n *Freytag v. Commissioner* (1991), we applied the unadorned "significant authority" test to adjudicative officials who are near-carbon copies of the Commission's ALJs. As we now explain, our analysis there (sans any more detailed legal criteria) necessarily decides this case.

The officials at issue in *Freytag* were the "special trial judges" (STJs) of the United States Tax Court. The authority of those judges depended on the significance of the tax dispute before them. In "comparatively narrow and minor matters," they could both hear and definitively resolve a case for the Tax Court. In more major matters, they could preside over the hearing, but could not issue the final decision; instead, they were to "prepare proposed findings and an opinion" for a regular Tax Court judge to consider. This Court held that the Tax Court's STJs are officers, not mere employees.

Still more, the Commission's ALJs exercise the same "significant discretion" when carrying out the same "important functions" as STJs do. Both sets of officials have all the authority needed to ensure fair and orderly adversarial hearings—indeed, nearly all the tools of federal trial judges. Consider in order the four specific (if overlapping) powers *Freytag* mentioned. First, the Commission's ALJs (like the Tax Court's STJs) "take testimony." More precisely, they "[r]eceiv[e] evidence" and "[e]xamine witnesses" at hearings, and may also take pre-hearing depositions. Second, the ALJs (like STJs) "conduct trials." As detailed earlier, they administer oaths, rule on motions, and generally "regulat[e] the course of" a hearing, as well as the conduct of parties and counsel. Third, the ALJs (like STJs) "rule on the admissibility of evidence." They thus critically shape the administrative record (as they also do when issuing document subpoenas). And fourth, the ALJs (like STJs) "have the power to enforce compliance with discovery orders." In particular, they may punish all "[c]ontemptuous conduct," including violations of those orders, by means as severe as excluding the offender from the hearing. So point for point—straight from *Freytag*'s list—the Commission's ALJs have equivalent duties and powers as STJs in conducting adversarial inquiries.

And at the close of those proceedings, ALJs issue decisions much like that in *Freytag*—except with potentially more independent effect. As the *Freytag* Court recounted, STJs "prepare proposed findings and an opinion" adjudicating charges and assessing tax liabilities. Similarly, the Commission's ALJs issue decisions containing factual findings, legal conclusions, and appropriate remedies. And what happens next reveals that the ALJ can play the more autonomous role. In a major case like *Freytag*, a regular Tax Court judge must always review an STJ's opinion. And that opinion counts for nothing unless the regular judge adopts it as his own. By contrast, the SEC can decide against reviewing an ALJ decision at all. And when the SEC declines review (and issues an order saying so), the ALJ's decision itself "becomes final" and is "deemed the action of the Commission." That last-word capacity makes this an *a fortiori* case: If the Tax Court's STJs are officers, as *Freytag* held, then the Commission's ALJs must be too.

For all the reasons we have given, and all those *Freytag* gave before, the Commission's ALJs are "Officers of the United States," subject to the Appointments Clause. And as noted earlier, Judge Elliot heard and decided Lucia's case without the kind of appointment the Clause requires. This Court has held that "one who makes a timely challenge to the constitutional validity of the appointment of an officer who adjudicates his case" is entitled to relief. Lucia made just such a timely challenge: He contested the validity of Judge Elliot's appointment before the Commission, and continued pressing that claim in the Court of Appeals and this Court. So what relief follows? This Court has also held that the "appropriate" remedy for an adjudication tainted with an appointments violation is a new "hearing before a properly appointed" official. And we add today one thing more. That official cannot be Judge Elliot, even if he has by now received (or receives sometime in the future) a constitutional appointment. Judge Elliot has already both heard Lucia's case and issued an initial decision on the merits. He cannot be expected to consider the matter as though he had not adjudicated it before. To cure the constitutional error, another ALJ (or the Commission itself) must hold the new hearing to which Lucia is entitled.

Justice THOMAS, with whom Justice GORSUCH joins, concurring.

I agree with the Court that this case is indistinguishable from *Freytag v. Commissioner* (1991). If the special trial judges in *Freytag* were "Officers of the United States," Art. II, § 2, cl. 2, then so are the administrative law judges of the Securities and Exchange Commission. The Appointments Clause provides the exclusive process for appointing "Officers of the

United States." While principal officers must be nominated by the President and confirmed by the Senate, Congress can authorize the appointment of "inferior Officers" by "the President alone," "the Courts of Law," or "the Heads of Departments."

This alternative process for appointing inferior officers strikes a balance between efficiency and accountability. Given the sheer number of inferior officers, it would be too burdensome to require each of them to run the gauntlet of Senate confirmation. But, by specifying only a limited number of actors who can appoint inferior officers without Senate confirmation, the Appointments Clause maintains clear lines of accountability — encouraging good appointments and giving the public someone to blame for bad ones.

The Founders likely understood the term "Officers of the United States" to encompass all federal civil officials who perform an ongoing, statutory duty — no matter how important or significant the duty. "Officers of the United States" was probably not a term of art that the Constitution used to signify some special type of official. Based on how the Founders used it and similar terms, the phrase "of the United States" was merely a synonym for "federal," and the word "Office[r]" carried its ordinary meaning. The ordinary meaning of "officer" was anyone who performed a continuous public duty. The Founders considered individuals to be officers even if they performed only ministerial statutory duties — including recordkeepers, clerks, and tidewaiters (individuals who watched goods land at a customhouse). Early congressional practice reflected this understanding. With exceptions not relevant here, Congress required all federal officials with ongoing statutory duties to be appointed in compliance with the Appointments Clause.

Applying the original meaning here, the administrative law judges of the Securities and Exchange Commission easily qualify as "Officers of the United States." These judges exercise many of the agency's statutory duties, including issuing initial decisions in adversarial proceedings. As explained, the importance or significance of these statutory duties is irrelevant. All that matters is that the judges are continuously responsible for performing them.

Justice BREYER, with whom Justice GINSBURG and Justice SOTOMAYOR join as to Part III, concurring in the judgment in part and dissenting in part.

I agree with the Court that the Securities and Exchange Commission did not properly appoint the Administrative Law Judge who presided over petitioner Lucia's hearing. But I disagree with the majority in respect to two matters. First, I would rest our conclusion upon statutory, not constitutional, grounds. I believe it important to do so because I cannot answer the constitutional question that the majority answers without knowing the answer to a different, embedded constitutional question, which the Solicitor General urged us to answer in this case: the constitutionality of the statutory "for cause" removal protections that Congress provided for administrative law judges. Second, I disagree with the Court in respect to the proper remedy.

I

The relevant statute here is the Administrative Procedure Act. That Act governs the appointment of administrative law judges.

I do not believe that the Administrative Procedure Act permits the Commission to delegate its power to appoint its administrative law judges to its staff. We have held that, for purposes of the Constitution's Appointments Clause, the Commission itself is a "'Hea[d]'" of a "'Departmen[t].'" Thus, reading the statute as referring to the Commission itself, and not to its staff, avoids a difficult constitutional question, namely, the very question that the Court answers today: whether the Commission's administrative law judges are constitutional "inferior Officers" whose appointment Congress may vest only in the President, the "Courts of Law," or the "Heads of Departments."

I have found no other statutory provision that would permit the Commission to delegate the power to appoint its administrative law judges to its staff. Regardless, the same constitutional-avoidance reasons that should inform our construction of the Administrative Procedure Act should also lead us to interpret the Commission's general delegation authority as excluding the power to delegate to staff the authority to appoint its administrative law judges, so as to avoid the constitutional question the Court reaches in this case.

The upshot, in my view, is that for statutory, not constitutional, reasons, the Commission did not lawfully appoint the Administrative Law Judge here at issue. And this Court should decide no more than that.

II

The Administrative Procedure Act thus allows administrative law judges to be removed only "for good cause" found by the Merit Systems Protection Board. And the President may, in turn, remove members of the Merit Systems Protection Board only for "inefficiency, neglect of duty, or malfeasance in office." Thus, Congress seems to have provided administrative law judges with two levels of protection from removal without cause—just what *Free Enterprise Fund* interpreted the Constitution to forbid in the case of the Board members.

The substantial independence that the Administrative Procedure Act's removal protections provide to administrative law judges is a central part of the Act's overall scheme. Before the Administrative Procedure Act, hearing examiners "were in a dependent status" to their employing agency, with their classification, compensation, and promotion all dependent on how the agency they worked for rated them. As a result of that dependence, "[m]any complaints were voiced against the actions of the hearing examiners, it being charged that they were mere tools of the agency concerned and subservient to the agency heads in making their proposed findings of fact and recommendations." The Administrative Procedure Act responded to those complaints by giving administrative law judges "independence and tenure within the existing Civil Service system."

If the *Free Enterprise Fund* [*v. Bennett*]'s Court's holding applies equally to the administrative law judges—and I stress the "if"—then to hold that the administrative law judges are "Officers of the United States" is, *perhaps*, to hold that their removal protections are unconstitutional. This would risk transforming administrative law judges from independent adjudicators into *dependent* decisionmakers, serving at the pleasure of the Commission. Similarly, to apply *Free Enterprise Fund*'s holding to high-level civil servants threatens to change the nature of our merit-based civil service as it has existed from the time of President Chester Alan Arthur.

I have stressed the words "if" and "perhaps" in the previous paragraph because *Free Enterprise Fund*'s holding may not invalidate the removal protections applicable to the Commission's administrative law judges even if the judges are inferior "officers of the United States" for purposes of the Appointments Clause.

How is the Court to decide whether Congress intended that the holder of a particular Government position count as an "Office[r] of the United States"? Congress might, of course, write explicitly into the statute that the employee "is an officer of the United States under the Appointments Clause," but an explicit phrase of this kind is unlikely to appear. If it does not, then I would approach the question like any other difficult question of statutory interpretation. Several considerations, among others, are likely to be relevant. First, as the Court said in *Freytag v. Commissioner* (1991) and repeats today, where Congress grants an appointee "'significant authority pursuant to the laws to the United States,'" that supports the view that (but should not determinatively decide that) Congress made that appointee an "Office[r] of the United States." The means of appointment that

Congress chooses is also instructive. Where Congress provides a method of appointment that mimics a method the Appointments Clause allows for "Officers," that fact too supports the view that (but does not determinatively decide that) Congress viewed the position as one to be held by an "Officer," and vice versa. And the Court's decision in *Free Enterprise Fund* suggests a third indication of "Officer" status — did Congress provide the position with removal protections that would be unconstitutional if provided for an "That fact would support (but again not be determinative of) the opposite view — that Congress did not intend to confer "inferior Officer" status on the position.

As I said, these statutory features, while highly relevant, need not always prove determinative. The vast number of different civil service positions, with different tasks, different needs, and different requirements for independence, mean that this is not the place to lay down bright-line rules. Rather, as this Court has said, "[t]he versatility of circumstances often mocks a natural desire for definitiveness" in this area.

No case from this Court holds that Congress lacks this sort of constitutional leeway in determining whether a particular Government position will be filled by an "Office[r] of the United States."

The Court's decision to address the Appointments Clause question separately from the constitutional removal question is problematic. By considering each question in isolation, the Court risks (should the Court later extend *Free Enterprise Fund*) unraveling, step-by-step, the foundations of the Federal Government's administrative adjudication system as it has existed for decades, and perhaps of the merit-based civil-service system in general. And the Court risks doing so without considering that potential consequence. For these reasons, I concur in the judgment in part and, with respect, I dissent in part.

Justice SOTOMAYOR, with whom Justice GINSBURG joins, dissenting.

The Court today and scholars acknowledge that this Court's Appointments Clause jurisprudence offers little guidance on who qualifies as an "Officer of the United States." The lack of guidance is not without consequence. "[Q]uestions about the Clause continue to arise regularly both in the operation of the Executive Branch and in proposed legislation." This confusion can undermine the reliability and finality of proceedings and result in wasted resources.

As the majority notes, this Court's decisions currently set forth at least two prerequisites to officer status: (1) an individual must hold a "continuing" office established by law, and (2) an individual must wield "significant authority." The first requirement is relatively easy to grasp; the second, less so. To be sure, to exercise "significant authority," the person must wield considerable powers in comparison to the average person who works for the Federal Government. As this Court has noted, the vast majority of those who work for the Federal Government are not "Officers of the United States." But this Court's decisions have yet to articulate the types of powers that will be deemed significant enough to constitute "significant authority."

To provide guidance to Congress and the Executive Branch, I would hold that one requisite component of "significant authority" is the ability to make final, binding decisions on behalf of the Government. Accordingly, a person who merely advises and provides recommendations to an officer would not herself qualify as an officer.

There is some historical support for such a requirement. Confirming that final decisionmaking authority is a prerequisite to officer status would go a long way to aiding Congress and the Executive Branch in sorting out who is an officer and who is a mere employee. At the threshold, Congress and the Executive Branch could rule out as an officer any person who investigates, advises, or recommends, but who has no power to issue binding policies, execute the laws, or finally resolve adjudicatory questions.

Turning to the question presented here, it is true that the administrative law judges (ALJs) of the Securities and Exchange Commission wield "extensive powers." Nevertheless, I would hold that Commission ALJs are not officers because they lack final decisionmaking authority. As the Commission explained below, the Commission retains "'plenary authority over the course of [its] administrative proceedings and the rulings of [its] law judges.'" In other words, Commission ALJs do not exercise significant authority because they do not, and cannot, enter final, binding decisions against the Government or third parties.

Because I would conclude that Commission ALJs are not officers for purposes of the Appointments Clause, it is not necessary to reach the constitutionality of their removal protections.

4.   Review of Administrative Decisions: The Census Example

One of the most high-profile cases of the year involved the decision of the Commerce Department to include a question about citizenship on the 2020 census forms. The constitutional question was whether this violated the Constitution's requirement for an accurate enumeration of the population. The Court held that it did not violate the Constitution. The primary focus was on whether there was a violation of the Administrative

Procedures Act. The Court, 5-4, concluded that the Commerce Department had not offered an adequate rationale for doing so and remanded the case to provide an opportunity for this.

DEPARTMENT OF COMMERCE v. NEW YORK
139 S. Ct. 2551 (2019)

Chief Justice ROBERTS delivered the opinion of the Court.

The Secretary of Commerce decided to reinstate a question about citizenship on the 2020 census questionnaire. A group of plaintiffs challenged that decision on constitutional and statutory grounds. We now decide whether the Secretary violated the Enumeration Clause of the Constitution, the Census Act, or otherwise abused his discretion.

I

In order to apportion Members of the House of Representatives among the States, the Constitution requires an "Enumeration" of the population every 10 years, to be made "in such Manner" as Congress "shall by Law direct." In the Census Act, Congress delegated to the Secretary of Commerce the task of conducting the decennial census "in such form and content as he may determine." The Secretary is aided in that task by the Census Bureau, a statistical agency housed within the Department of Commerce.

The population count derived from the census is used not only to apportion representatives but also to allocate federal funds to the States and to draw electoral districts. The census additionally serves as a means of collecting demographic information, which "is used for such varied purposes as computing federal grant-in-aid benefits, drafting of legislation, urban and regional planning, business planning, and academic and social studies." Over the years, the census has asked questions about (for example) race, sex, age, health, education, occupation, housing, and military service. It has also asked about radio ownership, age at first marriage, and native tongue. The Census Act obliges everyone to answer census questions truthfully and requires the Secretary to keep individual answers confidential, including from other Government agencies.

There have been 23 decennial censuses from the first census in 1790 to the most recent in 2010. Every census between 1820 and 2000 (with the exception of 1840) asked at least some of the population about their citizenship or place of birth. Between 1820 and 1950, the question was asked of all households. Between 1960 and 2000, it was asked of about one-fourth to one-sixth of the population. That change was part of a larger effort to simplify the census by asking most people a few basic demographic questions (such as sex, age, race, and marital status) on a short-form questionnaire, while asking a sample of the population more detailed demographic questions on a long-form questionnaire. In explaining the decision to move the citizenship question to the long-form questionnaire, the Census Bureau opined that "general census information on citizenship had become of less importance compared with other possible questions to be included in the census, particularly in view of the recent statutory requirement for annual alien registration which could provide the Immigration and Naturalization Service, the principal user of such data, with the information it needed."

In 2010, the year of the latest census, the format changed again. All households received the same questionnaire, which asked about sex, age, race, Hispanic origin, and living arrangements. The more detailed demographic questions previously asked on the long-form questionnaire, including the question about citizenship, were instead asked in the American Community Survey (or ACS), which is sent each year to a rotating sample of about 2.6% of households.

The Census Bureau and former Bureau officials have resisted occasional proposals to resume asking a citizenship question of everyone, on the ground that doing so would discourage noncitizens from responding to the census and lead to a less accurate count of the total population.

In March 2018, Secretary of Commerce Wilbur Ross announced in a memo that he had decided to reinstate a question about citizenship on the 2020 decennial census questionnaire. The Secretary stated that he was acting at the request of the Department of Justice (DOJ), which sought improved data about citizen voting-age population for purposes of enforcing the Voting Rights Act (or VRA)—specifically the Act's ban on diluting the influence of minority voters by depriving them of single-member districts in which they can elect their preferred candidates. DOJ explained that federal courts determine whether a minority group could constitute a majority in a particular district by looking to the citizen voting-age population of the group.

He also noted the long history of the citizenship question on the census, as well as the facts that the United Nations recommends collecting census-based citizenship information, and other major democracies such as Australia, Canada, France, Indonesia, Ireland, Germany, Mexico, Spain, and the United Kingdom inquire about citizenship in their censuses. Altogether, the Secretary determined that "the need for accurate citizenship data and the limited burden that the reinstatement of the citizenship question would impose outweigh fears about a potentially lower response rate."

Shortly after the Secretary announced his decision, two groups of plaintiffs filed suit in Federal District Court in New York, challenging the decision on several grounds. The first group of plaintiffs included 18 States, the District of Columbia, various counties and cities, and the United States Conference of Mayors. They alleged that the Secretary's decision violated the Enumeration Clause of the Constitution and the requirements of the Administrative Procedure Act. The second group of plaintiffs consisted of several non-governmental organizations that work with immigrant and minority communities. They added an equal protection claim.

[II]

The Enumeration Clause of the Constitution does not provide a basis to set aside the Secretary's decision. The text of that clause "vests Congress with virtually unlimited discretion in conducting the decennial 'actual Enumeration,' " and Congress "has delegated its broad authority over the census to the Secretary." Given that expansive grant of authority, we have rejected challenges to the conduct of the census where the Secretary's decisions bore a "reasonable relationship to the accomplishment of an actual enumeration."

Respondents ask us to evaluate the Secretary's decision to reinstate a citizenship question under that "reasonable relationship" standard. We have never applied the standard to decisions about what kinds of demographic information to collect in the course of taking the census. Indeed, as the District Court recognized, applying the "reasonable relationship" standard to *every* census-related decision "would lead to the conclusion that it is unconstitutional to ask *any* demographic question on the census" because "asking such questions bears no relationship whatsoever to the goal of an accurate headcount." Yet demographic questions have been asked in *every* census since 1790, and questions about citizenship in particular have been asked for nearly as long. Like the District Court, we decline respondents' invitation to measure the constitutionality of the citizenship question by a standard that would seem to render every census since 1790 unconstitutional.

We look instead to Congress's broad authority over the census, as informed by long and consistent historical practice. All three branches of Government have understood the Constitution to allow Congress, and by extension the Secretary, to use the census for more than simply counting the population. Since 1790, Congress has sought, or permitted the Secretary to seek, information about matters as varied as age, sex, marital status, health, trade, profession, literacy, and value of real estate owned. Since 1820, it has sought, or permitted the Secretary to seek, information about citizenship in particular. Federal courts have approved the practice of collecting demographic data in the census. While we have never faced the question directly, we have assumed that Congress has the power to use the census for information-gathering purposes, and we have recognized the role of the census as a "linchpin of the federal statistical system by collecting data on the characteristics of individuals, households, and housing units throughout the country."

That history matters. Here, as in other areas, our interpretation of the Constitution is guided by a Government practice that "has been open, widespread, and unchallenged since the early days of the Republic." In light of the early understanding of and long practice under the Enumeration Clause, we conclude that it permits Congress, and by extension the Secretary, to inquire about citizenship on the census questionnaire. We need not, and do not, decide the constitutionality of any other question that Congress or the Secretary might decide to include in the census.

[III]

[Chief Justice Roberts then considered whether the question about citizenship violated the Administrative Procedures Act.] At the heart of this suit is respondents' claim that the Secretary abused his discretion in deciding to reinstate a citizenship question. We review the Secretary's exercise of discretion under the deferential "arbitrary and capricious" standard. Our scope of review is "narrow": we determine only whether the Secretary examined "the relevant data" and articulated "a satisfactory explanation" for his decision, "including a rational connection between the facts found and the choice made." We may not substitute our judgment for that of the Secretary, *ibid.*, but instead must confine ourselves to ensuring that he remained "within the bounds of reasoned decisionmaking,"

The District Court set aside the Secretary's decision for two independent reasons: His course of action was not supported by the evidence before him, and his stated rationale was pretextual. We focus on the first point here and take up the question of pretext later.

The Secretary examined the Bureau's analysis of various ways to collect improved citizenship data and explained why he thought the best course was to both reinstate a citizenship question and use citizenship data from administrative records to fill in the gaps.

The Secretary weighed the benefit of collecting more complete and accurate citizenship data against the risk that inquiring about citizenship would depress census response rates, particularly among noncitizen households. In the Secretary's view, that risk was difficult to assess. That decision was reasonable and reasonably explained, particularly in light of the long history of the citizenship question on the census.

Justice Breyer would conclude otherwise, but only by subordinating the Secretary's policymaking discretion to the Bureau's technocratic expertise. The Secretary was required to consider the evidence and give reasons for his chosen course of action. He did so. It is not for us to ask whether his decision was "the best one possible" or even whether it was "better than the alternatives." By second-guessing the Secretary's weighing of risks and benefits and penalizing him for departing from the Bureau's inferences and assumptions, Justice Breyer — like the District Court — substitutes his judgment for that of the agency.

We now consider the District Court's determination that the Secretary's decision must be set aside because it rested on a pretextual basis, which the Government conceded below would warrant a remand to the agency.

We start with settled propositions. First, in order to permit meaningful judicial review, an agency must "disclose the basis" of its action. Second, in reviewing agency action, a court is ordinarily limited to evaluating the agency's contemporaneous explanation in light of the existing administrative record. That principle reflects the recognition that further judicial inquiry into "executive motivation" represents "a substantial intrusion" into the workings of another branch of Government and should normally be avoided. Third, a court may not reject an agency's stated reasons for acting simply because the agency might also have had other unstated reasons. Relatedly, a court may not set aside an agency's policymaking decision solely because it might have been influenced by political considerations or prompted by an Administration's priorities. Finally, we have recognized a narrow exception to the general rule against inquiring into "the mental processes of administrative decisionmakers." On a "strong showing of bad faith or improper behavior," such an inquiry may be warranted and may justify extra-record discovery.

Several points, considered together, reveal a significant mismatch between the decision the Secretary made and the rationale he provided. The record shows that the Secretary began taking steps to reinstate a citizenship question about a week into his tenure, but it contains no hint that he was considering VRA enforcement in connection with that project. The Director initially attempted to elicit requests for citizenship data from the Department of Homeland Security and DOJ's Executive Office for Immigration Review, neither of which is responsible for enforcing the VRA. After those attempts failed, he asked Commerce staff to look into whether the Secretary could reinstate the question without receiving a request from another agency. The possibility that DOJ's Civil Rights Division might be willing to request citizenship data for VRA enforcement purposes was proposed by Commerce staff along the way and eventually pursued.

Even so, it was not until the Secretary contacted the Attorney General directly that DOJ's Civil Rights Division expressed interest in acquiring census-based citizenship data to better enforce the VRA. And even then, the record suggests that DOJ's interest was directed more to helping the Commerce Department than to securing the data.

Altogether, the evidence tells a story that does not match the explanation the Secretary gave for his decision. In the Secretary's telling, Commerce was simply acting on a routine data request from another agency. Yet the materials before us indicate that Commerce went to great lengths to elicit the request from DOJ (or any other willing agency). And unlike a typical case in which an agency may have both stated and unstated reasons for a decision, here the VRA enforcement rationale—the sole stated reason—seems to have been contrived.

We are presented, in other words, with an explanation for agency action that is incongruent with what the record reveals about the agency's priorities and decisionmaking process. It is rare to review a record as extensive as the one before us when evaluating informal agency action—and it should be. But having done so for the sufficient reasons we have explained, we cannot ignore the disconnect between the decision made and the explanation given. Our review is deferential, but we are "not required to exhibit a naiveté from which ordinary citizens are free." The reasoned explanation requirement of administrative law, after all, is meant to ensure that agencies offer genuine justifications for important decisions, reasons that can be scrutinized by courts and the interested public. Accepting contrived reasons would defeat the purpose of the enterprise. If judicial review is to be more than an empty ritual, it must demand something better than the explanation offered for the action taken in this case.

In these unusual circumstances, the District Court was warranted in remanding to the agency, and we affirm that disposition. We do not hold that the agency decision here was substantively invalid. But agencies must pursue their goals reasonably. Reasoned decisionmaking under the Administrative Procedure Act calls for an explanation for agency action. What was provided here was more of a distraction.

Justice THOMAS, with whom Justice GORSUCH and Justice KAVANAUGH join, concurring in part and dissenting in part.

In March 2018, the Secretary of Commerce exercised his broad discretion over the administration of the decennial census to resume a nearly unbroken practice of asking a question relating to citizenship. Our only role in this case is to decide whether the Secretary complied with the law and gave a reasoned explanation for his decision. The Court correctly answers these questions in the affirmative. That ought to end our inquiry.

The Court, however, goes further. For the first time ever, the Court invalidates an agency action solely because it questions the sincerity of the agency's otherwise adequate rationale. Echoing the din of suspicion and distrust that seems to typify modern discourse, the Court declares the Secretary's memorandum "pretextual" because, "viewing the evidence as a whole," his explanation that including a citizenship question on the census would help enforce the Voting Rights Act (VRA) "seems to have been contrived." The Court does not hold that the Secretary merely had *additional*, unstated reasons for reinstating the citizenship question. Rather, it holds that the Secretary's stated rationale did not factor *at all* into his decision.

The Court's holding reflects an unprecedented departure from our deferential review of discretionary agency decisions. And, if taken seriously as a rule of decision, this holding would transform administrative law. It is not difficult for political opponents of executive actions to generate controversy with accusations of pretext, deceit, and illicit motives. Significant policy decisions are regularly criticized as products of partisan influence, interest-group pressure, corruption, and animus. Crediting these accusations on evidence as thin as the evidence here could lead judicial review of administrative proceedings to devolve into an endless morass of discovery and policy disputes not contemplated by the Administrative Procedure Act (APA).

Unable to identify any legal problem with the Secretary's reasoning, the Court imputes one by concluding that he must not be telling the truth. The law requires a more impartial approach. Even assuming we are authorized to engage in the review undertaken by the Court—which is far from clear—we have often stated that courts reviewing agency action owe the Executive a "presumption of regularity." The Court pays only lipservice to this principle. But, the evidence falls far short of supporting its decision. The Court, I fear, will come to regret inventing the principles it uses to achieve today's result.

Justice BREYER, with whom Justice GINSBURG, Justice SOTOMAYOR, and Justice KAGAN join, concurring in part and dissenting in part.

I agree with the Court that the Secretary of Commerce provided a pretextual reason for placing a question about citizenship on the short-form census questionnaire and that a remand to the agency is appropriate on that ground. But I write separately because I also believe that the Secretary's decision to add the citizenship question was arbitrary and capricious and therefore violated the Administrative Procedure Act (APA).

There is no serious dispute that adding a citizenship question would diminish the accuracy of the enumeration of the population—the sole constitutional function of the census and a task of great practical importance. The record demonstrates that the question would likely cause a disproportionate number of noncitizens and Hispanics to go uncounted in the upcoming census. That, in turn, would create a risk that some States would wrongfully lose a congressional representative and funding for a host of federal programs. And, the Secretary was told, the adverse consequences would fall most heavily on minority communities. The Secretary decided to ask the question anyway, citing a need for more accurate citizenship data. But the evidence indicated that asking the question would produce citizenship data that is *less* accurate, not more. And the reason the Secretary gave for needing better citizenship data in the first place—to help enforce the Voting Rights Act of 1965—was not convincing.

In short, the Secretary's decision to add a citizenship question created a severe risk of harmful consequences, yet he did not adequately consider whether the question was necessary or whether it was an appropriate means of achieving his stated goal. The Secretary thus failed to "articulate a satisfactory explanation" for his decision, "failed to consider . . . important aspect[s] of the problem," and "offered an explanation for [his] decision that runs counter to the evidence." These failures, in my view, risked undermining public confidence in the integrity of our democratic system itself. I would therefore hold that the Secretary's decision—whether pretextual or not—was arbitrary, capricious, and an abuse of discretion.

Three sets of laws determine the legal outcome of this case. First, the Constitution requires an "actual Enumeration" of the "whole number of persons in each State" every 10 years. Art. I, § 2, cl. 3; Amdt. 14, § 2. It does so in order to "provide a basis for apportioning representatives among the states in the Congress." The inclusion of this provision in the Constitution itself underscores the importance of conducting an accurate census.

Second, the Census Act contains two directives that constrain the Secretary's ability to add questions to the census. Section 195 says that the Secretary "shall, if he considers it feasible," authorize the use of statistical "sampling" in collecting demographic information. That means the Secretary must, if feasible, obtain demographic information through a survey sent to a *sample* of households, rather than through the short-form census questionnaire to which *every* household must respond. The other relevant provision, § 6(c), says that "[t]*o the maximum extent possible* and consistent with the kind, timeliness, quality and scope of the statistics required, the Secretary shall acquire and use information available" from administrative sources "instead of conducting direct inquiries." These provisions, taken together, reflect a congressional preference for keeping the short form short, so that it does not burden recipients and thereby discourage them from responding.

Third, the APA prohibits administrative agencies from making choices that are "arbitrary, capricious, an abuse of discretion, or otherwise not in accordance with law." We have said that courts, in applying this provision, must decide "whether the decision was based on a consideration of the relevant factors and whether there has been a clear error of judgment." The agency must have "examine[d] the relevant data and articulate[d] a satisfactory explanation for its action[,] including a 'rational connection between the facts found and the choice made.'"

Now consider the Secretary's conclusion that, even if adding a citizenship question diminishes the accuracy of the enumeration, "the value of more complete and accurate data derived from surveying the entire population *outweighs* . . . concerns" about diminished accuracy. That conclusion was also arbitrary. The administrative record indicates that adding a citizenship question to the short form would produce less "complete and accurate data," not more.

The Census Bureau informed the Secretary that, for about 90% of the population, accurate citizenship data is available from administrative records maintained by the Social Security Administration and Internal Revenue Service. The Bureau further informed the Secretary that it had "high confidence" that it could develop a statistical model that would accurately impute citizenship status for the remaining 10% of the population. The Bureau stated that these methods alone — using existing administrative records for 90% of the population and statistical modeling for the remaining 10% — would yield more accurate citizenship data than also asking a citizenship question.

If my description of the record is correct, it raises a serious legal problem. How can an agency support the decision to add a question to the short form, thereby risking a significant undercount of the population, on the ground that it will *improve* the accuracy of citizenship data, when in fact the evidence indicates that adding the question will *harm* the accuracy of citizenship data? Of course it cannot. But, as I have just said, I have not been able to find evidence to suggest that adding the question would result in more accurate citizenship data. Neither could the District Court. After reviewing the record in detail, the District Court found that "all of the relevant evidence before Secretary Ross—*all* of it—demonstrated that using administrative records . . . would actually produce more accurate [citizenship] data than adding a citizenship question to the census."

The Secretary's failure to consider this evidence—that adding the question would harm the census count in the interest of obtaining less accurate citizenship data—provides a sufficient basis for setting the decision aside. But there is more. The reason that the Secretary provided for needing more accurate citizenship information in the first place—to help the DOJ enforce the Voting Rights Act—is unconvincing.

This rationale is difficult to accept. One obvious problem is that the DOJ provided no basis to believe that more precise data would in fact help with Voting Rights Act enforcement. Congress enacted the Voting Rights Act in 1965—15 years after the census last asked every household about citizenship. Actions to enforce the Act have therefore *always* used citizenship data derived from sampling. Yet I am aware of no one—not in the Department of Commerce proceeding, in the District Court, or in this Court—who has provided a single example in which enforcement of the Act has suffered due to lack of more precise citizenship data. Organizations with expertise in this area tell us that asking the citizenship question will not help enforce the Act. Rather, the question will, by depressing the count of minority groups, hurt those whom the Act seeks to help.

Another problem with the Secretary's rationale is that, even assuming the DOJ needed more detailed citizenship data, there were better ways of obtaining the needed data. The Census Bureau offered to provide the DOJ with data using administrative records, which, as I have pointed out, are likely just as accurate, if not more accurate, than responses to a citizenship question. The Census Bureau offered to provide this data at the census block level, which would resolve each of the DOJ's complaints about the existing ACS data. But the Secretary rejected this alternative without explaining why it would not fully respond to the DOJ's request. That failure was particularly problematic given that the Census Act requires the Secretary to use other methods of obtaining demographic information if at all possible.

Normally, the Secretary would be entitled to place considerable weight upon the DOJ's expertise in matters involving the Voting Rights Act, but there are strong reasons for discounting that expertise here. The administrative record shows that DOJ's request to add a citizenship question originated not with the DOJ, but with the Secretary himself. See Administrative

Record The Voting Rights Act rationale was in fact first proposed by Commerce Department officials. DOJ officials, for their part, were initially uninterested in obtaining more detailed citizenship data, and they agreed to request the data only after the Secretary personally spoke to the Attorney General about the matter. And when the acting director of the Census Bureau proposed alternative means of obtaining better citizenship data, DOJ officials declined to meet to discuss the proposal.

Taken as a whole, the evidence in the administrative record indicates that the Voting Rights Act rationale offered by the Secretary was not just unconvincing, but pretextual. And, as the Court concludes, further evidence outside the administrative record but present in the trial record supports the finding of pretext. Among other things, that evidence reveals that the DOJ official who wrote the letter agreed that adding the question "is not necessary for DOJ's VRA enforcement efforts."

I agree with the Court that the APA gives agencies broad leeway to carry out their legislatively delegated duties. And I recognize that Congress has specifically delegated to the Secretary of Commerce the authority to conduct a census of the population "in such form and content as he may determine." But although this delegation is broad, it is not without limits. The APA supplies one such limit. In an effort to ensure rational decisionmaking, the APA prohibits an agency from making decisions that are "arbitrary, capricious, [or] an abuse of discretion"

This provision, of course, does not insist that decisionmakers think through every minor aspect of every problem that they face. But here, the Secretary's decision was a major one, potentially affecting the proper workings of our democratic government and the proper allocation of hundreds of billions of dollars in federal funds. Yet the decision was ill considered in a number of critically important respects. The Secretary did not give adequate consideration to issues that should have been central to his judgment, such as the high likelihood of an undercount, the low likelihood that a question would yield more accurate citizenship data, and the apparent lack of any need for more accurate citizenship data to begin with. The Secretary's failures in considering those critical issues make his decision unreasonable. They are the kinds of failures for which, in my view, the APA's arbitrary and capricious provision was written.

As I have said, I agree with the Court's conclusion as to pretext and with the decision to send the matter back to the agency. I do not agree, however, with several of the Court's conclusions concerning application of the arbitrary and capricious standard. In my view, the Secretary's decision—whether pretextual or not—was arbitrary, capricious, and an abuse of his lawfully delegated discretion.

Justice ALITO, concurring in part and dissenting in part.

It is a sign of our time that the inclusion of a question about citizenship on the census has become a subject of bitter public controversy and has led to today's regrettable decision. While the decision to place such a question on the 2020 census questionnaire is attacked as racist, there is a broad international consensus that inquiring about citizenship on a census is not just appropriate but advisable. No one disputes that it is important to know how many inhabitants of this country are citizens. And the most direct way to gather this information is to ask for it in a census. The United Nations recommends that a census inquire about citizenship, and many countries do so.

Asking about citizenship on the census also has a rich history in our country. Every census, from the very first one in 1790 to the most recent in 2010, has sought not just a count of the number of inhabitants but also varying amounts of additional demographic information. In 1800, Thomas Jefferson, as president of the American Philosophical Society, signed a letter to Congress asking for the inclusion on the census of questions regarding "'the respective numbers of native citizens, citizens of foreign birth, and of aliens' " " 'for the purpose . . . of more exactly distinguishing the increase of population by birth and immigration.'" In 1820, John Quincy Adams, as Secretary of State, was responsible for conducting the census, and consistent with the 1820 Census Act, he instructed the marshals who were charged with gathering the information to ask about citizenship. In 1830, when Martin Van Buren was Secretary of State, a question about citizenship was again included. With the exception of the census of 1840, at least some portion of the population was asked a question about citizenship as part of the census through 2000, after which the question was moved to the American Community Survey, which is sent to only a small fraction of the population. All these census inquiries were made by the Executive pursuant to congressional authorization. None were reviewed by the courts.

Now, for the first time, this Court has seen fit to claim a role with respect to the inclusion of a citizenship question on the census, and in doing so, the Court has set a dangerous precedent, both with regard to the census itself and with regard to judicial review of all other executive agency actions. For the reasons ably stated by Justice Thomas today's decision is either an aberration or a license for widespread judicial inquiry into the motivations of Executive Branch officials. If this case is taken as a model, then any one of the approximately 1,000 district court judges in this country, upon receiving information that a controversial agency decision might have been motivated by some unstated consideration, may order the questioning of Cabinet officers and other high-ranking Executive Branch officials, and the judge may then pass judgment on whether the decision was pretextual. What Bismarck is reputed to have said about laws and sausages comes to mind. And that goes for decisionmaking by all three branches.

To put the point bluntly, the Federal Judiciary has no authority to stick its nose into the question whether it is good policy to include a citizenship question on the census or whether the reasons given by Secretary Ross for that decision were his only reasons or his real reasons. Of course, we may determine whether the decision is constitutional. But under the considerations that typically guide this Court in the exercise of its power of judicial review of agency action, we have no authority to decide whether the Secretary's decision was rendered in compliance with the Administrative Procedure Act (APA).

Throughout our Nation's history, the Executive Branch has decided without judicial supervision or interference whether and, if so, in what form the decennial census should inquire about the citizenship of the inhabitants of this country. Whether to put a citizenship question on the 2020 census questionnaire is a question that is committed by law to the discretion of the Secretary of Commerce and is therefore exempt from APA review.

Chapter 4

Limits on State Regulatory and Taxing Power

B.   The Dormant Commerce Clause (casebook p. 476)

c.   Analysis if a Law Is Deemed Discriminatory (casebook p. 503)

In *Tennessee Wine and Spirits Retailers Association v. Thomas*, the Court considered whether the power of states to regulate alcohol sales under the 21st Amendment allows laws that would otherwise violate the dormant commerce clause. The Court said no, with several of the opinions discussing the purposes and desirability of the dormant commerce clause.

TENNESSEE WINE AND SPIRITS RETAILERS ASSOCIATION v. THOMAS
139 S. Ct. 2449 (2019)

Justice ALITO delivered the opinion of the Court.

The State of Tennessee imposes demanding durational-residency requirements on all individuals and businesses seeking to obtain or renew a license to operate a liquor store. One provision precludes the renewal of a license unless the applicant has resided in the State for 10 consecutive years. Another provides that a corporation cannot obtain a license unless all of its stockholders are residents. The Court of Appeals for the Sixth Circuit struck down these provisions as blatant violations of the Commerce Clause, and neither petitioner—an association of Tennessee liquor retailers—nor the State itself defends them in this Court.

The Sixth Circuit also invalidated a provision requiring applicants for an initial license to have resided in the State for the prior two years, and petitioner does challenge that decision. But while this requirement is less extreme than the others that the Sixth Circuit found to be unconstitutional, we now hold that it also violates the Commerce Clause and is not shielded by § 2 of the Twenty-first Amendment. Section 2 was adopted as part of the scheme that ended prohibition on the national level. It gives each State

leeway in choosing the alcohol-related public health and safety measures
that its citizens find desirable. But § 2 is not a license to impose all manner
of protectionist restrictions on commerce in alcoholic beverages. Because
Tennessee's 2-year residency requirement for retail license applicants
blatantly favors the State's residents and has little relationship to public
health and safety, it is unconstitutional.

I

No person may lawfully participate in the sale of alcohol [in Tennessee]
without the appropriate license. Included in the Tennessee scheme are
onerous durational-residency requirements for all persons and companies
wishing to operate "retail package stores" that sell alcoholic beverages for
off-premises consumption (hereinafter liquor stores). To obtain an initial
retail license, an individual must demonstrate that he or she has "been a
bona fide resident" of the State for the previous two years.

II

A

The Court of Appeals held that Tennessee's 2-year residency requirement violates the Commerce Clause, which provides that "[t]he Congress
shall have Power . . . [t]o regulate Commerce with foreign Nations, and
among the several States, and with the Indian Tribes." "Although the
Clause is framed as a positive grant of power to Congress," we have long
held that this Clause also prohibits state laws that unduly restrict interstate
commerce. "This 'negative' aspect of the Commerce Clause" prevents the
States from adopting protectionist measures and thus preserves a national
market for goods and services.

In recent years, some Members of the Court have authored vigorous
and thoughtful critiques of this interpretation. But the proposition that the
Commerce Clause by its own force restricts state protectionism is deeply
rooted in our case law. And without the dormant Commerce Clause, we
would be left with a constitutional scheme that those who framed and ratified the Constitution would surely find surprising.

That is so because removing state trade barriers was a principal reason for the adoption of the Constitution. Under the Articles of
Confederation, States notoriously obstructed the interstate shipment of
goods. "Interference with the arteries of commerce was cutting off the
very life-blood of the nation." The Annapolis Convention of 1786 was

convened to address this critical problem, and it culminated in a call for the Philadelphia Convention that framed the Constitution in the summer of 1787. At that Convention, discussion of the power to regulate interstate commerce was almost uniformly linked to the removal of state trade barriers, and when the Constitution was sent to the state conventions, fostering free trade among the States was prominently cited as a reason for ratification.

In light of this background, it would be strange if the Constitution contained no provision curbing state protectionism, and at this point in the Court's history, no provision other than the Commerce Clause could easily do the job. So if we accept the Court's established interpretation of those provisions, that leaves the Commerce Clause as the primary safeguard against state protectionism. More recently, we observed that our dormant Commerce Clause cases reflect a "'central concern of the Framers that was an immediate reason for calling the Constitutional Convention: the conviction that in order to succeed, the new Union would have to avoid the tendencies toward economic Balkanization that had plagued relations among the Colonies and later among the States under the Articles of Confederation.'" In light of this history and our established case law, we reiterate that the Commerce Clause by its own force restricts state protectionism.

B

Under our dormant Commerce Clause cases, if a state law discriminates against out-of-state goods or nonresident economic actors, the law can be sustained only on a showing that it is narrowly tailored to "'advanc[e] a legitimate local purpose.'" Tennessee's 2-year durational-residency requirement plainly favors Tennesseans over nonresidents, and neither the Association nor the dissent below defends that requirement under the standard that would be triggered if the requirement applied to a person wishing to operate a retail store that sells a commodity other than alcohol. Instead, their arguments are based on § 2 of the Twenty-first Amendment, to which we will now turn.

III

Section 2 of the Twenty-first Amendment provides as follows:

> "The transportation or importation into any State, Territory, or possession of the United States for delivery or use therein of intoxicating liquors, in violation of the laws thereof, is hereby prohibited."

Although the interpretation of any provision of the Constitution must begin with a consideration of the literal meaning of that particular provision, reading § 2 to prohibit the transportation or importation of alcoholic beverages in violation of *any* state law would lead to absurd results that the provision cannot have been meant to produce. Under the established rule that a later adopted provision takes precedence over an earlier, conflicting provision of equal stature, such a reading of § 2 would mean that the provision would trump any irreconcilable provision of the original Constitution, the Bill of Rights, the Fourteenth Amendment, and every other constitutional provision predating ratification of the Twenty-first Amendment in 1933. This would mean, among other things, that a state law prohibiting the importation of alcohol for sale to persons of a particular race, religion, or sex would be immunized from challenge under the Equal Protection Clause. Similarly, if a state law prohibited the importation of alcohol for sale by proprietors who had expressed an unpopular point of view on an important public issue, the First Amendment would provide no protection. If a State imposed a duty on the importation of foreign wine or spirits, the Import-Export Clause would have to give way. If a state law retroactively made it a crime to have bought or sold imported alcohol under specified conditions, the *Ex Post Facto* Clause would provide no barrier to conviction. The list goes on.

Despite the ostensibly broad text of § 2, no one now contends that the provision must be interpreted in this way. Instead, we have held that § 2 must be viewed as one part of a unified constitutional scheme. In attempting to understand how § 2 and other constitutional provisions work together, we have looked to history for guidance, and history has taught us that the thrust of § 2 is to "constitutionaliz[e]" the basic structure of federal-state alcohol regulatory authority that prevailed prior to the adoption of the Eighteenth Amendment.

IV

By 1933, support for Prohibition had substantially diminished but not vanished completely. Thirty-eight state conventions eventually ratified the Twenty-first Amendment, but 10 States either rejected or took no action on the Amendment. Section 1 of the Twenty-first Amendment repealed the Eighteenth Amendment and thus ended nationwide Prohibition, but § 2, the provision at issue here, gave each State the option of banning alcohol if its citizens so chose. Accordingly, we have inferred that § 2 was meant to "constitutionaliz[e]" the basic understanding of the extent of the States' power to regulate alcohol that prevailed before Prohibition.

This understanding is supported by the debates on the Amendment in Congress[13] and the state ratifying conventions. The records of the state conventions provide no evidence that § 2 was understood to give States the power to enact protectionist laws, "a privilege [the States] had not enjoyed at any earlier time."

Although some Justices have argued that § 2 shields all state alcohol regulation—including discriminatory laws—from any application of dormant Commerce Clause doctrine, the Court's modern § 2 precedents have repeatedly rejected that view. We have examined whether state alcohol laws that burden interstate commerce serve a State's legitimate § 2 interests. And protectionism, we have stressed, is not such an interest.

Applying that principle, we have invalidated state alcohol laws aimed at giving a competitive advantage to in-state businesses. Most recently, in *Granholm* [*v. Heald*], we struck down a set of discriminatory direct-shipment laws that favored in-state wineries over out-of-state competitors. After surveying the history of § 2, we affirmed that "the Twenty-first Amendment does not immunize all laws from Commerce Clause challenge." We therefore examined whether the challenged laws were reasonably necessary to protect the States' asserted interests in policing underage drinking and facilitating tax collection. Concluding that the answer to that question was no, we invalidated the laws as inconsistent with the dormant Commerce Clause's nondiscrimination principle.

To summarize, the Court has acknowledged that § 2 grants States latitude with respect to the regulation of alcohol, but the Court has repeatedly declined to read § 2 as allowing the States to violate the "nondiscrimination principle" that was a central feature of the regulatory regime that the provision was meant to constitutionalize.

The Association resists this reading. Although it concedes (as it must under *Granholm*) that § 2 does not give the States the power to discriminate against out-of-state alcohol *products and producers*, the Association presses the argument, echoed by the dissent, that a different rule applies to state laws that regulate in-state alcohol distribution. There is no sound basis for this distinction.

The Association's argument encounters a problem at the outset. The argument concedes that § 2 does not shield state laws that discriminate against interstate commerce with respect to the very activity that the provision explicitly addresses—the importation of alcohol. But at the same time, the Association claims that § 2 protects something that § 2's text, if read literally, does not cover—laws restricting the licensing of domestic retail alcohol stores. That reading is implausible. Surely if § 2 granted States the power to discriminate in the field of alcohol regulation, that power would be at its apex when it comes to regulating the activity to which the provision expressly refers.

V

Having concluded that § 2 does not confer limitless authority to regulate the alcohol trade, we now apply the § 2 analysis dictated by the provision's history and our precedents.

If we viewed Tennessee's durational-residency requirements as a package, it would be hard to avoid the conclusion that their overall purpose and effect is protectionist. Indeed, two of those requirements — the 10-year residency requirement for license renewal and the provision that shuts out all publicly traded corporations — are so plainly based on unalloyed protectionism that neither the Association nor the State is willing to come to their defense. The provision that the Association and the State seek to preserve — the 2-year residency requirement for initial license applicants — forms part of that scheme. But we assume that it can be severed from its companion provisions, and we therefore analyze that provision on its own.

Since the 2-year residency requirement discriminates on its face against nonresidents, it could not be sustained if it applied across the board to all those seeking to operate any retail business in the State. But because of § 2, we engage in a different inquiry. Recognizing that § 2 was adopted to give each State the authority to address alcohol-related public health and safety issues in accordance with the preferences of its citizens, we ask whether the challenged requirement can be justified as a public health or safety measure or on some other legitimate nonprotectionist ground. Section 2 gives the States regulatory authority that they would not otherwise enjoy, but as we pointed out in *Granholm*, "mere speculation" or "unsupported assertions" are insufficient to sustain a law that would otherwise violate the Commerce Clause. Where the predominant effect of a law is protectionism, not the protection of public health or safety, it is not shielded by § 2.

The provision at issue here expressly discriminates against nonresidents and has at best a highly attenuated relationship to public health or safety. [T]he record is devoid of any "concrete evidence" showing that the 2-year residency requirement actually promotes public health or safety; nor is there evidence that nondiscriminatory alternatives would be insufficient to further those interests.

Given all this, the Association has fallen far short of showing that the 2-year durational-residency requirement for license applicants is valid.

Like the other discriminatory residency requirements that the Association is unwilling to defend, the predominant effect of the 2-year residency requirement is simply to protect the Association's members from out-of-state competition. We therefore hold that this provision violates the Commerce Clause and is not saved by the Twenty-first Amendment.

Justice GORSUCH with whom Justice THOMAS joins, dissenting.

Alcohol occupies a complicated place in this country's history. Some of the founders were enthusiasts; Benjamin Franklin thought wine was "proof that God loves us." Many in the Prohibition era were decidedly less enamored; they saw "liquor [a]s a lawlessness unto itself." Over time, the people have adopted two separate constitutional Amendments to adjust and then readjust alcohol's role in our society. But through it all, one thing has always held true: States may impose residency requirements on those who seek to sell alcohol within their borders to ensure that retailers comply with local laws and norms. In fact, States have enacted residency requirements for at least 150 years, and the Tennessee law at issue before us has stood since 1939. Today and for the first time, the Court claims to have discovered a duty and power to strike down laws like these as unconstitutional. Respectfully, I do not see it.

Start with the text of the Constitution. After the Nation's failed experiment with Prohibition, the people assembled in conventions in each State to adopt the Twenty-first Amendment. In § 1, they repealed the Eighteenth Amendment's nationwide prohibition on the sale of alcohol. But in § 2, they provided that "[t]he transportation or importation into any State . . . for delivery or use therein of intoxicating liquors, in violation of the laws thereof, is hereby prohibited." The Amendment thus embodied a classically federal compromise: Nationwide prohibition ended, but States gained broad discretion to calibrate alcohol regulations to local preferences. And under the terms of this compromise, Tennessee's law imposing a two-year residency requirement on those who seek to sell liquor within its jurisdiction would seem perfectly permissible.

Of course, § 2 does not immunize state laws from *all* constitutional claims. Everyone agrees that state laws must still comply with, say, the First Amendment or the Equal Protection Clause. But the challenge before us isn't based on any constitutional provision like that. Instead, we are asked to decide whether Tennessee's residency requirement impermissibly discriminates against out-of-state residents and recent arrivals in violation of the "dormant Commerce Clause" doctrine. And that doctrine is a peculiar one. Unlike most constitutional rights, the dormant Commerce Clause doctrine cannot be found in the text of any constitutional provision but is (at best) an implication from one. Under its banner, this Court has sometimes asserted the power to strike down state laws that discriminate against nonresidents on the ground that they usurp the authority to regulate interstate commerce that the Constitution assigns in Article I to Congress. But precisely because the Constitution assigns *Congress* the power to regulate interstate commerce, that body is free to rebut any implication of unconstitutionality that might otherwise arise under the dormant Commerce Clause doctrine by authorizing States to adopt laws favoring in-state residents.

And that's exactly what happened here. In the Webb-Kenyon Act of 1913, Congress gave the States wide latitude to restrict the sale of alcohol within their borders. Not only is that law still on the books today, § 2 of the Twenty-first Amendment closely "followed the wording of the 1913 Webb-Kenyon Act." Accordingly, the people who adopted the Amendment naturally would have understood it to constitutionalize an "exception to the normal operation of the [dormant] Commerce Clause." After all, what Congress can do by statute "surely the people may do . . . through the process of amending our Constitution." So in this area, at least, we should not be in the business of imposing our own judge-made "dormant Commerce Clause" limitations on state powers.

What the relevant constitutional and statutory texts suggest, history confirms. Licensing requirements for the sale of liquor are older than the Nation itself.

What are lower courts supposed to make of this? How much public health and safety benefit must there be to overcome this Court's worries about protectionism "predominat[ing]"? Does reducing competition in the liquor market, raising prices, and thus reducing demand still count as a public health benefit, as many States have long supposed? And if residency requirements are problematic, what about simple physical *presence* laws? After all, can't States "thoroughly investigate applicants" for liquor licenses without requiring them to have a brick-and-mortar store in the State? The Court offers lower courts no more guidance than to proclaim delphically that "each variation must be judged based on its own features."

As judges, we may be sorely tempted to "rationalize" the law and impose our own free-trade rules for all goods and services in interstate commerce. Certainly, that temptation seems to have proven nearly irresistible for this Court when it comes to alcohol. But real life is not always so tidy and satisfactory, and neither are the democratic compromises we are bound to respect as judges. Like it or not, those who adopted the Twenty-first Amendment took the view that reasonable people can disagree about the costs and benefits of free trade in alcohol. They left us with clear instructions that the free-trade rules this Court has devised for "cabbages and candlesticks" should not be applied to alcohol. Under the terms of the compromise they hammered out, the regulation of alcohol wasn't left to the imagination of a committee of nine sitting in Washington, D. C., but to the judgment of the people themselves and their local elected representatives. State governments were supposed to serve as "laborator[ies]" of democracy, with "broad power to regulate liquor under § 2." If the people wish to alter this arrangement, that is their sovereign right. But until then, I would enforce the Twenty-first Amendment as they wrote and originally understood it.

***

One application of the dormant commerce clause is as a limit on state taxation of interstate commerce. Previously the Supreme Court had ruled that a state could not require businesses to collect sales tax unless the business had a physical presence in the state. In *South Dakota v. Wayfair*, the Court overruled the earlier decisions and clarifies the ability of a state to impose taxes on interstate commerce.

SOUTH DAKOTA v. WAYFAIR, INC.
138 S. Ct. 2080 (2018)

Justice KENNEDY delivered the opinion of the Court.

When a consumer purchases goods or services, the consumer's State often imposes a sales tax. This case requires the Court to determine when an out-of-state seller can be required to collect and remit that tax. All concede that taxing the sales in question here is lawful. The question is whether the out-of-state seller can be held responsible for its payment, and this turns on a proper interpretation of the Commerce Clause.

In two earlier cases the Court held that an out-of-state seller's liability to collect and remit the tax to the consumer's State depended on whether the seller had a physical presence in that State, but that mere shipment of goods into the consumer's State, following an order from a catalog, did not satisfy the physical presence requirement. *National Bellas Hess, Inc. v. Department of Revenue of Ill.* (1967); *Quill Corp. v. North Dakota* (1992).

I

Like most States, South Dakota has a sales tax. It taxes the retail sales of goods and services in the State. Sellers are generally required to collect and remit this tax to the Department of Revenue. If for some reason the

sales tax is not remitted by the seller, then in-state consumers are separately responsible for paying a use tax at the same rate. Many States
employ this kind of complementary sales and use tax regime.

Under this Court's decisions in *Bellas Hess* and *Quill*, South Dakota
may not require a business to collect its sales tax if the business lacks
a physical presence in the State. Without that physical presence, South
Dakota instead must rely on its residents to pay the use tax owed on their
purchases from out-of-state sellers. "[T]he impracticability of [this] collection from the multitude of individual purchasers is obvious." And consumer compliance rates are notoriously low. It is estimated that *Bellas
Hess* and *Quill* cause the States to lose between $8 and $33 billion every
year. In South Dakota alone, the Department of Revenue estimates revenue loss at $48 to $58 million annually. Particularly because South Dakota
has no state income tax, it must put substantial reliance on its sales and
use taxes for the revenue necessary to fund essential services. Those taxes
account for over 60 percent of its general fund.

In 2016, South Dakota confronted the serious inequity *Quill* imposes
by enacting S. 106—"An Act to provide for the collection of sales taxes
from certain remote sellers, to establish certain Legislative findings, and
to declare an emergency." The legislature found that the inability to collect
sales tax from remote sellers was "seriously eroding the sales tax base"
and "causing revenue losses and imminent harm . . . through the loss of
critical funding for state and local services." The legislature also declared
an emergency: "Whereas, this Act is necessary for the support of the state
government and its existing public institutions, an emergency is hereby
declared to exist." Fearing further erosion of the tax base, the legislature
expressed its intention to "apply South Dakota's sales and use tax obligations to the limit of federal and state constitutional doctrines" and noted
the urgent need for this Court to reconsider its precedents.

To that end, the Act requires out-of-state sellers to collect and remit
sales tax "as if the seller had a physical presence in the state." The Act
applies only to sellers that, on an annual basis, deliver more than $100,000
of goods or services into the State or engage in 200 or more separate transactions for the delivery of goods or services into the State. The Act also
forecloses the retroactive application of this requirement and provides
means for the Act to be appropriately stayed until the constitutionality of
the law has been clearly established.

Respondents Wayfair, Inc., Overstock.com, Inc., and Newegg, Inc., are
merchants with no employees or real estate in South Dakota. Wayfair,
Inc., is a leading online retailer of home goods and furniture and had net
revenues of over $4.7 billion last year. Overstock.com, Inc., is one of the

top online retailers in the United States, selling a wide variety of products from home goods and furniture to clothing and jewelry; and it had net revenues of over $1.7 billion last year. Newegg, Inc., is a major online retailer of consumer electronics in the United States. Each of these three companies ships its goods directly to purchasers throughout the United States, including South Dakota. Each easily meets the minimum sales or transactions requirement of the Act, but none collects South Dakota sales tax.

II

From early in its history, a central function of this Court has been to adjudicate disputes that require interpretation of the Commerce Clause in order to determine its meaning, its reach, and the extent to which it limits state regulations of commerce. Modern precedents rest upon two primary principles that mark the boundaries of a State's authority to regulate interstate commerce. First, state regulations may not discriminate against interstate commerce; and second, States may not impose undue burdens on interstate commerce. State laws that discriminate against interstate commerce face "a virtually *per se* rule of invalidity." State laws that "regulat[e] even-handedly to effectuate a legitimate local public interest . . . will be upheld unless the burden imposed on such commerce is clearly excessive in relation to the putative local benefits." Although subject to exceptions and variations, these two principles guide the courts in adjudicating cases challenging state laws under the Commerce Clause.

These principles also animate the Court's Commerce Clause precedents addressing the validity of state taxes. The Court explained the now-accepted framework for state taxation in *Complete Auto Transit, Inc. v. Brady* (1977). The Court held that a State "may tax exclusively interstate commerce so long as the tax does not create any effect forbidden by the Commerce Clause." After all, "interstate commerce may be required to pay its fair share of state taxes." The Court will sustain a tax so long as it (1) applies to an activity with a substantial nexus with the taxing State, (2) is fairly apportioned, (3) does not discriminate against interstate commerce, and (4) is fairly related to the services the State provides.

Before *Complete Auto*, the Court had addressed a challenge to an Illinois tax that required out-of-state retailers to collect and remit taxes on sales made to consumers who purchased goods for use within Illinois. The Court held that a mail-order company "whose only connection with customers in the State is by common carrier or the United States mail" lacked the requisite minimum contacts with the State required by both the Due

Process Clause and the Commerce Clause. Unless the retailer maintained a physical presence such as "retail outlets, solicitors, or property within a State," the State lacked the power to require that retailer to collect a local use tax.

In 1992, the Court reexamined the physical presence rule in *Quill*. That case presented a challenge to North Dakota's "attempt to require an out-of-state mail-order house that has neither outlets nor sales representatives in the State to collect and pay a use tax on goods purchased for use within the State." Despite the fact that *Bellas Hess* linked due process and the Commerce Clause together, the Court in *Quill* overruled the due process holding, but not the Commerce Clause holding; and it thus reaffirmed the physical presence rule.

III

The physical presence rule has "been the target of criticism over many years from many quarters." *Quill*, it has been said, was "premised on assumptions that are unfounded" and "riddled with internal inconsistencies." *Quill* created an inefficient "online sales tax loophole" that gives out-of-state businesses an advantage. And "while nexus rules are clearly necessary," the Court "should focus on rules that are appropriate to the twenty-first century, not the nineteenth." Each year, the physical presence rule becomes further removed from economic reality and results in significant revenue losses to the States. These critiques underscore that the physical presence rule, both as first formulated and as applied today, is an incorrect interpretation of the Commerce Clause.

Quill is flawed on its own terms. First, the physical presence rule is not a necessary interpretation of the requirement that a state tax must be "applied to an activity with a substantial nexus with the taxing State." Second, *Quill* creates rather than resolves market distortions. And third, *Quill* imposes the sort of arbitrary, formalistic distinction that the Court's modern Commerce Clause precedents disavow.

All agree that South Dakota has the authority to tax these transactions. S.B. 106 applies to sales of "tangible personal property, products transferred electronically, or services *for delivery into South Dakota*." "It has long been settled" that the sale of goods or services "has a sufficient nexus to the State in which the sale is consummated to be treated as a local transaction taxable by that State."

The central dispute is whether South Dakota may require remote sellers to collect and remit the tax without some additional connection to the State. The Court has previously stated that "[t]he imposition on the seller of the duty to insure collection of the tax from the purchaser does not violate the [C]ommerce [C]lause." There just must be "a substantial nexus with the taxing State." This nexus requirement is "closely related" to the due process requirement that there be "some definite link, some minimum connection, between a state and the person, property or transaction it seeks to tax."

The Court has consistently explained that the Commerce Clause was designed to prevent States from engaging in economic discrimination so they would not divide into isolated, separable units. But it is "not the purpose of the [C]ommerce [C]lause to relieve those engaged in interstate commerce from their just share of state tax burden." And it is certainly not the purpose of the Commerce Clause to permit the Judiciary to create market distortions. "If the Commerce Clause was intended to put businesses on an even playing field, the [physical presence] rule is hardly a way to achieve that goal."

Quill puts both local businesses and many interstate businesses with physical presence at a competitive disadvantage relative to remote sellers. Remote sellers can avoid the regulatory burdens of tax collection and can offer *de facto* lower prices caused by the widespread failure of consumers to pay the tax on their own. This "guarantees a competitive benefit to certain firms simply because of the organizational form they choose" while the rest of the Court's jurisprudence "is all about preventing discrimination between firms." In effect, *Quill* has come to serve as a judicially created tax shelter for businesses that decide to limit their physical presence and still sell their goods and services to a State's consumers — something that has become easier and more prevalent as technology has advanced.

Worse still, the rule produces an incentive to avoid physical presence in multiple States. Distortions caused by the desire of businesses to avoid tax collection mean that the market may currently lack storefronts, distribution points, and employment centers that otherwise would be efficient or desirable. The Commerce Clause must not prefer interstate commerce only to the point where a merchant physically crosses state borders. Rejecting the physical presence rule is necessary to ensure that artificial competitive advantages are not created by this Court's precedents. This Court should not prevent States from collecting lawful taxes through a physical presence rule that can be satisfied only if there is an employee or a building in the State.

The Court's Commerce Clause jurisprudence has "eschewed formalism for a sensitive, case-by-case analysis of purposes and effects." *Quill*, in contrast, treats economically identical actors differently, and for arbitrary reasons.

The *Quill* Court itself acknowledged that the physical presence rule is "artificial at its edges." That was an understatement when *Quill* was decided; and when the day-to-day functions of marketing and distribution in the modern economy are considered, it is all the more evident that the physical presence rule is artificial in its entirety.

Modern e-commerce does not align analytically with a test that relies on the sort of physical presence defined in *Quill*. In a footnote, *Quill* rejected the argument that "title to 'a few floppy diskettes' present in a State" was sufficient to constitute a "substantial nexus." But it is not clear why a single employee or a single warehouse should create a substantial nexus while "physical" aspects of pervasive modern technology should not. For example, a company with a website accessible in South Dakota may be said to have a physical presence in the State via the customers' computers. A website may leave cookies saved to the customers' hard drives, or customers may download the company's app onto their phones. Or a company may lease data storage that is permanently, or even occasionally, located in South Dakota. What may have seemed like a "clear," "bright-line tes[t]" when *Quill* was written now threatens to compound the arbitrary consequences that should have been apparent from the outset.

The "dramatic technological and social changes" of our "increasingly interconnected economy" mean that buyers are "closer to most major retailers" than ever before — "regardless of how close or far the nearest storefront." Between targeted advertising and instant access to most consumers via any internet-enabled device, "a business may be present in a State in a meaningful way without" that presence "being physical in the traditional sense of the term." A virtual showroom can show far more inventory, in far more detail, and with greater opportunities for consumer and seller interaction than might be possible for local stores. Yet the continuous and pervasive virtual presence of retailers today is, under *Quill*, simply irrelevant. This Court should not maintain a rule that ignores these substantial virtual connections to the State.

The physical presence rule as defined and enforced in *Bellas Hess* and *Quill* is not just a technical legal problem — it is an extraordinary imposition by the Judiciary on States' authority to collect taxes and perform critical public functions. Forty-one States, two Territories, and the District of Columbia now ask this Court to reject the test formulated in *Quill*. *Quill*'s physical presence rule intrudes on States' reasonable choices in enacting their tax systems. And that it allows remote sellers to escape an obligation to remit a lawful state tax is unfair and unjust. It is unfair and unjust to those competitors, both local and out of State, who must remit the tax; to the consumers who pay the tax; and to the States that seek fair enforcement of the sales tax, a tax many States for many years have considered an indispensable source for raising revenue.

In essence, respondents ask this Court to retain a rule that allows their customers to escape payment of sales taxes — taxes that are essential to create and secure the active market they supply with goods and services.

It is essential to public confidence in the tax system that the Court avoid creating inequitable exceptions. This is also essential to the confidence placed in this Court's Commerce Clause decisions. Yet the physical presence rule undermines that necessary confidence by giving some online retailers an arbitrary advantage over their competitors who collect state sales taxes.

In the name of federalism and free markets, *Quill* does harm to both. The physical presence rule it defines has limited States' ability to seek long-term prosperity and has prevented market participants from competing on an even playing field.

"Although we approach the reconsideration of our decisions with the utmost caution, *stare decisis* is not an inexorable command." Here, *stare decisis* can no longer support the Court's prohibition of a valid exercise of the States' sovereign power.

If it becomes apparent that the Court's Commerce Clause decisions prohibit the States from exercising their lawful sovereign powers in our federal system, the Court should be vigilant in correcting the error. While it can be conceded that Congress has the authority to change the physical presence rule, Congress cannot change the constitutional default rule. It is inconsistent with the Court's proper role to ask Congress to address a false constitutional premise of this Court's own creation. Courts have acted as the front line of review in this limited sphere; and hence it is important that their principles be accurate and logical, whether or not Congress can or will act in response. It is currently the Court, and not Congress, that is limiting the lawful prerogatives of the States.

Further, the real world implementation of Commerce Clause doctrines now makes it manifest that the physical presence rule as defined by *Quill* must give way to the "far-reaching systemic and structural changes in the economy" and "many other societal dimensions" caused by the Cyber Age. Though *Quill* was wrong on its own terms when it was decided in 1992, since then the Internet revolution has made its earlier error all the more egregious and harmful.

This expansion has also increased the revenue shortfall faced by States seeking to collect their sales and use taxes. In 1992, it was estimated that the States were losing between $694 million and $3 billion per year in sales tax revenues as a result of the physical presence rule. Now estimates range from $8 to $33 billion. The South Dakota Legislature has declared an emergency, S.B. 106, § 9, which again demonstrates urgency of over-turning the physical presence rule.

The argument, moreover, that the physical presence rule is clear and easy to apply is unsound. Attempts to apply the physical presence rule to online retail sales are proving unworkable. States are already confronting the complexities of defining physical presence in the Cyber Age.

Respondents argue that "the physical presence rule has permitted start-ups and small businesses to use the Internet as a means to grow their companies and access a national market, without exposing them to the daunting complexity and business-development obstacles of nationwide sales tax collection." These burdens may pose legitimate concerns in some instances, particularly for small businesses that make a small volume of sales to customers in many States. State taxes differ, not only in the rate imposed but also in the categories of goods that are taxed and, some-times, the relevant date of purchase. Eventually, software that is available at a reasonable cost may make it easier for small businesses to cope with these problems. Indeed, as the physical presence rule no longer controls, those systems may well become available in a short period of time, either from private providers or from state taxing agencies themselves. And in all events, Congress may legislate to address these problems if it deems it necessary and fit to do so.

For these reasons, the Court concludes that the physical presence rule of *Quill* is unsound and incorrect. The Court's decisions in *Quill Corp. v. North Dakota*, (1992), and *National Bellas Hess, Inc. v. Department of Revenue of Ill.*, (1967), should be, and now are, overruled.

V

In the absence of *Quill* and *Bellas Hess*, the first prong of the *Complete Auto* test simply asks whether the tax applies to an activity with a substan-tial nexus with the taxing State. "[S]uch a nexus is established when the taxpayer [or collector] 'avails itself of the substantial privilege of carrying on business' in that jurisdiction."

Here, the nexus is clearly sufficient based on both the economic and vir-tual contacts respondents have with the State. The Act applies only to sell-ers that deliver more than $100,000 of goods or services into South Dakota or engage in 200 or more separate transactions for the delivery of goods and services into the State on an annual basis. This quantity of business could not have occurred unless the seller availed itself of the substantial privilege of carrying on business in South Dakota. And respondents are large, national companies that undoubtedly maintain an extensive virtual presence. Thus, the substantial nexus requirement of *Complete Auto* is satisfied in this case.

Chief Justice ROBERTS, with whom Justice BREYER, Justice SOTOMAYOR, and Justice KAGAN join, dissenting.

I agree that *Bellas Hess* was wrongly decided, for many of the reasons given by the Court. The Court argues in favor of overturning that decision because the "Internet's prevalence and power have changed the dynamics of the national economy." But that is the very reason I oppose discarding the physical-presence rule. E-commerce has grown into a significant and vibrant part of our national economy against the backdrop of established rules, including the physical-presence rule. Any alteration to those rules with the potential to disrupt the development of such a critical segment of the economy should be undertaken by Congress. The Court should not act on this important question of current economic policy, solely to expiate a mistake it made over 50 years ago.

I

This Court "does not overturn its precedents lightly." Departing from the doctrine of *stare decisis* is an "exceptional action" demanding "special justification." The bar is even higher in fields in which Congress "exercises primary authority" and can, if it wishes, override this Court's decisions with contrary legislation. In such cases, we have said that "the burden borne by the party advocating the abandonment of an established precedent" is "greater" than usual. That is so "even where the error is a matter of serious concern, provided correction can be had by legislation."

We have applied this heightened form of *stare decisis* in the dormant Commerce Clause context. Under our dormant Commerce Clause precedents, when Congress has not yet legislated on a matter of interstate commerce, it is the province of "the courts to formulate the rules." But because Congress "has plenary power to regulate commerce among the States," it may at any time replace such judicial rules with legislation of its own. The Court thus left it to Congress "to decide whether, when, and to what extent the States may burden interstate mail-order concerns with a duty to collect use taxes."

II

This is neither the first, nor the second, but the third time this Court has been asked whether a State may obligate sellers with no physical presence within its borders to collect tax on sales to residents. Whatever salience the adage "third time's a charm" has in daily life, it is a poor guide to Supreme Court decisionmaking. If *stare decisis* applied with special force in *Quill*, it should be an even greater impediment to overruling precedent now, particularly since this Court in *Quill* "tossed [the ball] into Congress's court, for acceptance or not as that branch elects."

Congress has in fact been considering whether to alter the rule established in *Bellas Hess* for some time. Nothing in today's decision precludes Congress from continuing to seek a legislative solution. But by suddenly changing the ground rules, the Court may have waylaid Congress's consideration of the issue. Armed with today's decision, state officials can be expected to redirect their attention from working with Congress on a national solution, to securing new tax revenue from remote retailers.

The Court, for example, breezily disregards the costs that its decision will impose on retailers. Correctly calculating and remitting sales taxes on all e-commerce sales will likely prove baffling for many retailers. Over 10,000 jurisdictions levy sales taxes, each with "different tax rates, different rules governing tax-exempt goods and services, different product category definitions, and different standards for determining whether an out-of-state seller has a substantial presence" in the jurisdiction.

The burden will fall disproportionately on small businesses. One vitalizing effect of the Internet has been connecting small, even "micro" businesses to potential buyers across the Nation. People starting a business selling their embroidered pillowcases or carved decoys can offer their wares throughout the country—but probably not if they have to figure out the tax due on every sale. And the software said to facilitate compliance is still in its infancy, and its capabilities and expense are subject to debate. The Court's decision today will surely have the effect of dampening opportunities for commerce in a broad range of new markets.

A good reason to leave these matters to Congress is that legislators may more directly consider the competing interests at stake. Unlike this Court, Congress has the flexibility to address these questions in a wide variety of ways. As we have said in other dormant Commerce Clause cases, Congress "has the capacity to investigate and analyze facts beyond anything the Judiciary could match."

Here, after investigation, Congress could reasonably decide that current trends might sufficiently expand tax revenues, obviating the need for an abrupt policy shift with potentially adverse consequences for e-commerce. Or Congress might decide that the benefits of allowing States to secure additional tax revenue outweigh any foreseeable harm to e-commerce. Or Congress might elect to accommodate these competing interests, by, for example, allowing States to tax Internet sales by remote retailers only if revenue from such sales exceeds some set amount per year. In any event, Congress can focus directly on current policy concerns rather than past legal mistakes. Congress can also provide a nuanced answer to the troubling question whether any change will have retroactive effect.

An erroneous decision from this Court may well have been an unintended factor contributing to the growth of e-commerce. The Court is of course correct that the Nation's economy has changed dramatically since the time that *Bellas Hess* and *Quill* roamed the earth. I fear the Court today is compounding its past error by trying to fix it in a totally different era. The Constitution gives Congress the power "[t]o regulate Commerce . . . among the several States." I would let Congress decide whether to depart from the physical-presence rule that has governed this area for half a century.

Chapter 5

The Structure of the Constitution's Protection of Civil Rights and Civil Liberties

B. The Application of the Bill of Rights to the States

3. The Incorporation of the Bill of Rights into the Due Process Clause of the Fourteenth Amendment (casebook p. 550)

The casebook, on p. 565, indicates that there were four provisions of the Bill of Rights that never had been deemed incorporated and to apply to state and local governments. In *Timbs v. Indiana*, the Court found one of these four—the excessive fines clause of the Eighth Amendment—to be incorporated and to apply to the states.

TIMBS v. INDIANA
139 S. Ct. 682 (2019)

Justice GINSBURG delivered the opinion of the Court.

Tyson Timbs pleaded guilty in Indiana state court to dealing in a controlled substance and conspiracy to commit theft. The trial court sentenced him to one year of home detention and five years of probation, which included a court-supervised addiction-treatment program. The sentence also required Timbs to pay fees and costs totaling $1,203. At the time of Timbs's arrest, the police seized his vehicle, a Land Rover SUV Timbs had purchased for about $ 42,000. Timbs paid for the vehicle with money he received from an insurance policy when his father died.

The State engaged a private law firm to bring a civil suit for forfeiture of Timbs's Land Rover, charging that the vehicle had been used to transport heroin. After Timbs's guilty plea in the criminal case, the trial court held a hearing on the forfeiture demand. Although finding that Timbs's vehicle had been used to facilitate violation of a criminal statute, the court denied the requested forfeiture, observing that Timbs had recently purchased the vehicle for $ 42,000, more than four times the maximum $ 10,000 monetary fine assessable against him for his drug conviction. Forfeiture of the Land Rover, the court determined, would be grossly disproportionate to the gravity of Timbs's offense, hence unconstitutional under the Eighth Amendment's Excessive Fines Clause. The Court of Appeals of Indiana affirmed that determination, but the Indiana Supreme Court reversed.

The question presented: Is the Eighth Amendment's Excessive Fines Clause an "incorporated" protection applicable to the States under the Fourteenth Amendment's Due Process Clause? Like the Eighth Amendment's proscriptions of "cruel and unusual punishment" and "[e]xcessive bail," the protection against excessive fines guards against abuses of government's punitive or criminal-law-enforcement authority. This safeguard, we hold, is "fundamental to our scheme of ordered liberty," with "dee[p] root[s] in *687 [our] history and tradition." The Excessive Fines Clause is therefore incorporated by the Due Process Clause of the Fourteenth Amendment.

I

When ratified in 1791, the Bill of Rights applied only to the Federal Government. *Barron ex rel. Tiernan* v. *Mayor of Baltimore* (1833). "The constitutional Amendments adopted in the aftermath of the Civil War," however, "fundamentally altered our country's federal system." With only "a handful" of exceptions, this Court has held that the Fourteenth Amendment's Due Process Clause incorporates the protections contained in the Bill of Rights, rendering them applicable to the States. A Bill of Rights protection is incorporated, we have explained, if it is "fundamental to our scheme of ordered liberty," or "deeply rooted in this Nation's history and tradition."

Incorporated Bill of Rights guarantees are "enforced against the States under the Fourteenth Amendment according to the same standards that protect those personal rights against federal encroachment." Thus, if a Bill of Rights protection is incorporated, there is no daylight between the federal and state conduct it prohibits or requires.[1]

Under the Eighth Amendment, "[e]xcessive bail shall not be required, nor excessive fines imposed, nor cruel and unusual punishments inflicted." Taken together, these Clauses place "parallel limitations" on "the power of those entrusted with the criminal-law function of government." Directly at issue here is the phrase "nor excessive fines imposed," which "limits the government's power to extract payments, whether in cash or in kind, 'as punishment for some offense.'" The Fourteenth Amendment, we hold, incorporates this protection.

The Excessive Fines Clause traces its venerable lineage back to at least 1215, when Magna Carta guaranteed that "[a] Free-man shall not be amerced for a small fault, but after the manner of the fault; and for a great fault after the greatness thereof, saving to him his contenement. . . ." As relevant here, Magna Carta required that economic sanctions "be proportioned to the wrong" and "not be so large as to deprive [an offender] of his livelihood."

Despite Magna Carta, imposition of excessive fines persisted. The 17th century Stuart kings, in particular, were criticized for using large fines to raise revenue, harass their political foes, and indefinitely detain those unable to pay. When James II was overthrown in the Glorious Revolution, the attendant English Bill of Rights reaffirmed Magna Carta's guarantee by providing that "excessive Bail ought not to be required, nor excessive Fines imposed; nor cruel and unusual Punishments inflicted."

Across the Atlantic, this familiar language was adopted almost verbatim, first in the Virginia Declaration of Rights, then in the Eighth Amendment, which states: "Excessive bail shall not be required, nor excessive fines imposed, nor cruel and unusual punishments inflicted."

Adoption of the Excessive Fines Clause was in tune not only with English law; the Clause resonated as well with similar colonial-era provisions.

An even broader consensus obtained in 1868 upon ratification of the Fourteenth Amendment. By then, the constitutions of 35 of the 37 States—accounting for over 90% of the U.S. population—expressly prohibited excessive fines. Today, acknowledgment of the right's fundamental nature remains widespread. As Indiana itself reports, all 50 States have a constitutional provision prohibiting the imposition of excessive fines either directly or by requiring proportionality.

For good reason, the protection against excessive fines has been a constant shield throughout Anglo-American history: Exorbitant tolls undermine other constitutional liberties. Excessive fines can be used, for example, to retaliate against or chill the speech of political enemies, as the Stuarts' critics learned several centuries ago. Even absent a political motive, fines may be employed "in a measure out of accord with the penal goals of retribution and deterrence," for "fines are a source of revenue," while other forms of punishment "cost a State money."

In short, the historical and logical case for concluding that the Fourteenth Amendment incorporates the Excessive Fines Clause is overwhelming. Protection against excessive punitive economic sanctions secured by the

Clause is, to repeat, both "fundamental to our scheme of ordered liberty" and "deeply rooted in this Nation's history and tradition."

II

The State of Indiana does not meaningfully challenge the case for incorporating the Excessive Fines Clause as a general matter. Instead, the State argues that the Clause does not apply to its use of civil *in rem* forfeitures because, the State says, the Clause's specific application to such forfeitures is neither fundamental nor deeply rooted.

In *Austin* v. *United States* (1993), however, this Court held that civil *in rem* forfeitures fall within the Clause's protection when they are at least partially punitive. *Austin* arose in the federal context. But when a Bill of Rights protection is incorporated, the protection applies "identically to both the Federal Government and the States."

Justice GORSUCH, concurring.

The majority faithfully applies our precedent and, based on a wealth of historical evidence, concludes that the Fourteenth Amendment incorporates the Eighth Amendment's Excessive Fines Clause against the States. I agree with that conclusion. As an original matter, I acknowledge, the appropriate vehicle for incorporation may well be the Fourteenth Amendment's Privileges or Immunities Clause, rather than, as this Court has long assumed, the Due Process Clause. But nothing in this case turns on that question, and, regardless of the precise vehicle, there can be no serious doubt that the Fourteenth Amendment requires the States to respect the freedom from excessive fines enshrined in the Eighth Amendment.

Justice THOMAS, concurring in the judgment.

I agree with the Court that the Fourteenth Amendment makes the Eighth Amendment's prohibition on excessive fines fully applicable to the States. But I cannot agree with the route the Court takes to reach this conclusion. Instead of reading the Fourteenth Amendment's Due Process Clause to encompass a substantive right that has nothing to do with "process," I would hold that the right to be free from excessive fines is one of the "privileges or immunities of citizens of the United States" protected by the Fourteenth Amendment.

The right against excessive fines traces its lineage back in English law nearly a millennium, and from the founding of our country, it has been consistently recognized as a core right worthy of constitutional protection. As a constitutionally enumerated right understood to be a privilege of

American citizenship, the Eighth Amendment's prohibition on excessive fines applies in full to the States.

C. The Application of the Bill of Rights and the Constitution to Private Conduct

2.   The Exceptions to the State Action Doctrine

a.   The Public Functions Exception (casebook p. 572)

In *Manhattan Community Access Corporation v. Halleck*, the Court reaffirmed the importance of the state action doctrine. The discussion primarily is about the public functions exception, but the majority and dissent discuss other exceptions as well.

MANHATTAN COMMUNITY ACCESS
CORPORATION v. HALLECK
139 S. Ct. 1921 (2019)

Justice KAVANAUGH delivered the opinion of the Court.

The Free Speech Clause of the First Amendment constrains governmental actors and protects private actors. To draw the line between governmental and private, this Court applies what is known as the state-action doctrine. Under that doctrine, as relevant here, a private entity may be considered a state actor when it exercises a function "traditionally exclusively reserved to the State." *Jackson v. Metropolitan Edison Co.* (1974).

This state-action case concerns the public access channels on Time Warner's cable system in Manhattan. Public access channels are available for private citizens to use. The public access channels on Time Warner's cable system in Manhattan are operated by a private nonprofit corporation known as MNN. The question here is whether MNN—even though it is a private entity—nonetheless is a state actor when it operates the public access channels. In other words, is operation of public access channels on a cable system a traditional, exclusive public function? If so, then the First Amendment would restrict MNN's exercise of editorial discretion over the speech and speakers on the public access channels.

Under the state-action doctrine as it has been articulated and applied by our precedents, we conclude that operation of public access channels on a cable system is not a traditional, exclusive public function. Moreover, a private entity such as MNN who opens its property for speech by others is not transformed by that fact alone into a state actor. In operating the public access channels, MNN is a private actor, not a state actor, and MNN therefore is not subject to First Amendment constraints on its editorial discretion.

I

Since the 1970s, public access channels have been a regular feature on cable television systems throughout the United States. In the 1970s, Federal Communications Commission regulations required certain cable operators to set aside channels on their cable systems for public access. In 1979, however, this Court ruled that the FCC lacked statutory authority to impose that mandate. A few years later, Congress passed and President Reagan signed the Cable Communications Policy Act of 1984. The Act authorized state and local governments to require cable operators to set aside channels on their cable systems for public access.

The New York State Public Service Commission regulates cable franchising in New York State and requires cable operators in the State to set aside channels on their cable systems for public access. State law requires that use of the public access channels be free of charge and first-come, first-served. Under state law, the cable operator operates the public access channels unless the local government in the area chooses to itself operate the channels or designates a private entity to operate the channels.

Time Warner (now known as Charter) operates a cable system in Manhattan. Under state law, Time Warner must set aside some channels on its cable system for public access. New York City (the City) has designated a private nonprofit corporation named Manhattan Neighborhood Network, commonly referred to as MNN, to operate Time Warner's public access channels in Manhattan. This case involves a complaint against MNN regarding its management of the public access channels.

Because this case comes to us on a motion to dismiss, we accept the allegations in the complaint as true. DeeDee Halleck and Jesus Papoleto Melendez produced public access programming in Manhattan. They made a film about MNN's alleged neglect of the East Harlem community. Halleck submitted the film to MNN for airing on MNN's public access channels, and MNN later televised the film. Afterwards, MNN fielded multiple complaints about the film's content. In response, MNN temporarily suspended Halleck from using the public access channels. Halleck and Melendez soon became embroiled in another dispute with MNN staff. In the wake of that dispute, MNN ultimately suspended Halleck and Melendez from all MNN services and facilities.

Halleck and Melendez then sued MNN, among other parties, in Federal District Court. The two producers claimed that MNN violated their First Amendment free-speech rights when MNN restricted their access to the public access channels because of the content of their film.

MNN moved to dismiss the producers' First Amendment claim on the ground that MNN is not a state actor and therefore is not subject to First Amendment restrictions on its editorial discretion.

II

The text and original meaning of [the First and Fourteenth] Amendments, as well as this Court's longstanding precedents, establish that the Free Speech Clause prohibits only *governmental* abridgment of speech. The Free Speech Clause does not prohibit *private* abridgment of speech. In accord with the text and structure of the Constitution, this Court's state-action doctrine distinguishes the government from individuals and private entities. By enforcing that constitutional boundary between the governmental and the private, the state-action doctrine protects a robust sphere of individual liberty.

Here, the producers claim that MNN, a private entity, restricted their access to MNN's public access channels because of the content of the producers' film. The producers have advanced a First Amendment claim against MNN. The threshold problem with that First Amendment claim is a fundamental one: MNN is a private entity.

Relying on this Court's state-action precedents, the producers assert that MNN is nonetheless a state actor subject to First Amendment constraints on its editorial discretion. Under this Court's cases, a private entity can qualify as a state actor in a few limited circumstances—including, for example, (i) when the private entity performs a traditional, exclusive public function, (ii) when the government compels the private entity to take a particular action; or (iii) when the government acts jointly with the private entity.

The producers' primary argument here falls into the first category: The producers contend that MNN exercises a traditional, exclusive public function when it operates the public access channels on Time Warner's cable system in Manhattan. We disagree.

Under the Court's cases, a private entity may qualify as a state actor when it exercises "powers traditionally exclusively reserved to the State." It is not enough that the federal, state, or local government exercised the function in the past, or still does. And it is not enough that the function serves the public good or the public interest in some way. Rather, to qualify as a traditional, exclusive public function within the meaning of our state-action precedents, the government must have traditionally *and* exclusively performed the function.

The Court has stressed that "very few" functions fall into that category. Under the Court's cases, those functions include, for example, running elections and operating a company town. The Court has ruled that a variety of functions do not fall into that category, including, for example: running sports associations and leagues, administering insurance payments, operating nursing homes, providing special education, representing indigent criminal defendants, resolving private disputes, and supplying electricity.

The relevant function in this case is operation of public access channels on a cable system. That function has not traditionally and exclusively been performed by government.

Since the 1970s, when public access channels became a regular feature on cable systems, a variety of private and public actors have operated public access channels, including: private cable operators; private nonprofit organizations; municipalities; and other public and private community organizations such as churches, schools, and libraries.

The history of public access channels in Manhattan further illustrates the point. In 1971, public access channels first started operating in Manhattan. Those early Manhattan public access channels were operated in large part by private cable operators, with some help from private nonprofit organizations. Those private cable operators continued to operate the public access channels until the early 1990s, when MNN (also a private entity) began to operate the public access channels.

In short, operating public access channels on a cable system is not a traditional, exclusive public function within the meaning of this Court's cases.

To avoid that conclusion, the producers widen the lens and contend that the relevant function here is not simply the operation of public access channels on a cable system, but rather is more generally the operation of a public forum for speech. And according to the producers, operation of a public forum for speech is a traditional, exclusive public function.

That analysis mistakenly ignores the threshold state-action question. When the government provides a forum for speech (known as a public forum), the government may be constrained by the First Amendment, meaning that the government ordinarily may not exclude speech or speakers from the forum on the basis of viewpoint, or sometimes even on the basis of content. By contrast, when a private entity provides a forum for speech, the private entity is not ordinarily constrained by the First Amendment because the private entity is not a state actor. The private entity may thus exercise editorial discretion over the speech and speakers in the forum. This Court so ruled in its 1976 decision in *Hudgens* v. *NLRB*. There, the Court held that a shopping center owner is not a state actor subject to First Amendment requirements such as the public forum doctrine.

In short, merely hosting speech by others is not a traditional, exclusive public function and does not alone transform private entities into state actors subject to First Amendment constraints.If the rule were otherwise, all private property owners and private lessees who open their property for speech would be subject to First Amendment constraints and would lose the ability to exercise what they deem to be appropriate editorial discretion within that open forum. Private property owners and private lessees would face the unappetizing choice of allowing all comers or closing the platform altogether. The producers here are seeking in effect to circumvent this Court's case law, including *Hudgens*. But *Hudgens* is sound, and we therefore reaffirm our holding in that case.

Next, the producers retort that this case differs from *Hudgens* because New York City has designated MNN to operate the public access channels on Time Warner's cable system, and because New York State heavily regulates MNN with respect to the public access channels. Under this Court's cases, however, those facts do not establish that MNN is a state actor.

New York City's designation of MNN to operate the public access channels is analogous to a government license, a government contract, or a government-granted monopoly. But as the Court has long held, the fact that the government licenses, contracts with, or grants a monopoly to a private entity does not convert the private entity into a state actor—unless the private entity is performing a traditional, exclusive public function.

Numerous private entities in America obtain government licenses, government contracts, or government-granted monopolies. If those facts sufficed to transform a private entity into a state actor, a large swath of private entities in America would suddenly be turned into state actors and be subject to a variety of constitutional constraints on their activities. As this Court's many state-action cases amply demonstrate, that is not the law. Here, therefore, the City's designation of MNN to operate the public access channels on Time Warner's cable system does not make MNN a state actor.So, too, New York State's extensive regulation of MNN's operation of the public access channels does not make MNN a state actor. In *Jackson* v. *Metropolitan Edison Co.*, the leading case on point, the Court stated that the "fact that a business is subject to state regulation does not by itself convert its action into that of the State."

In sum, we conclude that MNN is not subject to First Amendment constraints on how it exercises its editorial discretion with respect to the public access channels. To be sure, MNN is subject to state-law constraints on its editorial discretion (assuming those state laws do not violate a federal statute or the Constitution). If MNN violates those state laws, or violates any applicable contracts, MNN could perhaps face state-law sanctions or liability of some kind. We of course take no position on any potential state-law questions. We simply conclude that MNN, as a private actor, is not subject to First Amendment constraints on how it exercises editorial discretion over the speech and speakers on its public access channels.

III

Perhaps recognizing the problem with their argument that MNN is a state actor under ordinary state-action principles applicable to private entities and private property, the producers alternatively contend that the public access channels are actually the property of New York City, not the property of Time Warner or MNN. On this theory, the producers say (and the dissent agrees) that MNN is in essence simply managing government property on behalf of New York City.

The short answer to that argument is that the public access channels are not the property of New York City. Nothing in the record here suggests that a government (federal, state, or city) owns or leases either the cable system or the public access channels at issue here. Both Time Warner and MNN are private entities. Time Warner is the cable operator, and it owns its cable network, which contains the public access channels. MNN operates those public access channels with its own facilities and equipment. The City does not own or lease the public access channels, and the City does not possess a formal easement or other property interest in those channels. The franchise agreements between the City and Time Warner do not say that the City has any property interest in the public access channels.

It is true that the City has allowed the cable operator, Time Warner, to lay cable along public rights-of-way in the City. But Time Warner's access to public rights-of-way does not alter the state-action analysis. For Time Warner, as for other cable operators, access to public rights-of-way is essential to lay cable and construct a physical cable infrastructure. But the same is true for utility providers, such as the electric utility in *Jackson*. Put simply, a private entity's permission from government to use public rights-of-way does not render that private entity a state actor.

Having said all that, our point here should not be read too broadly. Under the laws in certain States, including New York, a local government may decide to itself operate the public access channels on a local cable system (as many local governments in New York State and around the country already do), or could take appropriate steps to obtain a property interest in the public access channels. Depending on the circumstances, the First Amendment might then constrain the local government's operation of the public access channels. We decide only the case before us in light of the record before us.

It is sometimes said that the bigger the government, the smaller the individual. Consistent with the text of the Constitution, the state-action doctrine enforces a critical boundary between the government and the individual, and thereby protects a robust sphere of individual liberty. Expanding the state-action doctrine beyond its traditional boundaries would expand governmental control while restricting individual liberty and private enterprise. We decline to do so in this case.

MNN is a private entity that operates public access channels on a cable system. Operating public access channels on a cable system is not a traditional, exclusive public function. A private entity such as MNN who opens its property for speech by others is not transformed by that fact alone into a state actor. Under the text of the Constitution and our precedents, MNN is not a state actor subject to the First Amendment.

Justice SOTOMAYOR, with whom Justice GINSBURG, Justice BREYER, and Justice KAGAN join, dissenting.

The Court tells a very reasonable story about a case that is not before us. I write to address the one that is. This is a case about an organization appointed by the government to administer a constitutional public forum. (It is not, as the Court suggests, about a private property owner that simply opened up its property to others.) New York City (the City) secured a property interest in public-access television channels when it granted a cable franchise to a cable company. State regulations require those public-access channels to be made open to the public on terms that render them a public forum. The City contracted out the administration of that forum to a private organization, petitioner Manhattan Community Access Corporation (MNN). By accepting that agency relationship, MNN stepped into the City's shoes and thus qualifies as a state actor, subject to the First Amendment like any other.

I

A cable-television franchise is, essentially, a license to create a system for distributing cable TV in a certain area. It is a valuable right, usually conferred on a private company by a local government. A private company cannot enter a local cable market without one.

Cable companies transmit content through wires that stretch "between a transmission facility and the television sets of individual subscribers." Creating this network of wires is a disruptive undertaking that "entails the use of public rights-of-way and easements."

New York State authorizes municipalities to grant cable franchises to cable companies of a certain size only if those companies agree to set aside at least one public access channel. New York then requires that those public-access channels be open to all comers on "a first-come, first-served, nondiscriminatory basis." Likewise, the State prohibits both cable franchisees and local governments from "exercis[ing] any editorial control" over the channels, aside from regulating obscenity and other unprotected content.

II

I would affirm the judgment below. The channels are clearly a public forum: The City has a property interest in them, and New York regulations require that access to those channels be kept open to all. And because the City (1) had a duty to provide that public forum once it granted a cable franchise and (2) had a duty to abide by the First Amendment once it provided that forum, those obligations did not evaporate when the City delegated the administration of that forum to a private entity. Just as the City would have been subject to the First Amendment had it chosen to run the forum itself, MNN assumed the same responsibility when it accepted the delegation.

Here, respondents alleged viewpoint discrimination. So a key question in this case concerns what the Manhattan public-access channels are: a public forum of some kind, in which a claim alleging viewpoint discrimination would be cognizable, or something else, such as government speech or purely private property, where picking favored viewpoints is appropriately commonplace. Neither MNN nor the majority suggests that this is an instance of government speech. This case thus turns first and foremost on whether the public-access channels are or are not purely private property.

This Court has not defined precisely what kind of governmental property interest (if any) is necessary for a public forum to exist. I assume for the sake of argument in this case that public-forum analysis is inappropriate where the government lacks a "significant property interest consistent with the communicative purpose of the forum."

Such an interest is present here. As described above, New York State required the City to obtain public-access channels from Time Warner in exchange for awarding a cable franchise. The exclusive right to use these channels (and, as necessary, Time Warner's infrastructure) qualifies as a property interest, akin at the very least to an easement.

As noted above, there is no disputing that Time Warner owns the wires themselves. If the wires were a road, it would be easy to define the public's right to walk on it as an easement. Similarly, if the wires were a theater, there would be no question that a government's long-term lease to use it would be sufficient for public-forum purposes. But some may find this case more complicated because the wires are not a road or a theater that one can physically occupy; they are a conduit for transmitting signals that appear as television channels. In other words, the question is how to understand the right to place content on those channels using those wires.

The right to convey expressive content using someone else's physical infrastructure is not new. To give another low-tech example, imagine that one company owns a billboard and another rents space on that billboard. The renter can have a property interest in placing content on the billboard for the lease term even though it does not own the billboard itself.

The same principle should operate in this higher tech realm. Just as if the channels were a billboard, the City obtained rights for exclusive use of the channels by the public for the foreseeable future; no one is free to take the channels away, short of a contract renegotiation. The City also obtained the right to administer, or delegate the administration of, the channels. The channels are more intangible than a billboard, but no one believes that a right must be tangible to qualify as a property interest. And it is hardly unprecedented for a government to receive a right to transmit something over a private entity's infrastructure in exchange for conferring something of value on that private entity; examples go back at least as far as the 1800s.

I do not suggest that the government always obtains a property interest in public-access channels created by franchise agreements. But the arrangement here is consistent with what the Court would treat as a governmental property interest in other contexts. New York City gave Time Warner the right to lay wires and sell cable TV. In exchange, the City received an exclusive right to send its own signal over Time Warner's infrastructure — no different than receiving a right to place ads on another's billboards. Those rights amount to a governmental property interest in the channels, and that property interest is clearly "consistent with the communicative purpose of the forum." Indeed, it is the right to transmit the very content to which New York law grants the public open and equal access.

With the question of a governmental property interest resolved, it should become clear that the public-access channels are a public forum. Outside of classic examples like sidewalks and parks, a public forum exists only where the government has deliberately opened up the setting for speech by at least a subset of the public. The requisite governmental intent is manifest here. As noted above, New York State regulations require that the channels be made available to the public "on a first-come, first-served, nondiscriminatory basis." The State, in other words, mandates that the doors be wide open for public expression. MNN's contract with Time Warner follows suit.

If New York's public-access channels are a public forum, it follows that New York cannot evade the First Amendment by contracting out administration of that forum to a private agent. When MNN took on the responsibility of administering the forum, it stood in the City's shoes and became a state actor for purposes of 42 U.S.C. § 1983.When a government (1) makes a choice that triggers constitutional obligations, and then (2) contracts out those constitutional responsibilities to a private entity, that entity—in agreeing to take on the job—becomes a state actor for purposes of § 1983.

III

The majority acknowledges that the First Amendment could apply when a local government either (1) has a property interest in public-access channels or (2) is more directly involved in administration of those channels than the City is here. And it emphasizes that it "decide[s] only the case before us in light of the record before us." These case-specific qualifiers sharply limit the immediate effect of the majority's decision, but that decision is still meaningfully wrong in two ways. First, the majority erroneously decides the property question against the plaintiffs as a matter of law. Second, and more fundamentally, the majority mistakes a case about the government choosing to hand off responsibility to an agent for a case about a private entity that simply enters a marketplace.

The majority's explanation for why there is no governmental property interest here, *ante*, at 1933 – 1934, does not hold up. The majority focuses on the fact that "[b]oth Time Warner and MNN are private entities"; that Time Warner "owns its cable network, which contains the public access channels"; and that "MNN operates those public access channels with its own facilities and equipment." Those considerations cannot resolve this case. The issue is not who owns the cable network or that MNN uses its own property to operate the channels. The key question, rather, is whether the channels themselves are purely private property. An advertiser may not own a billboard, but that does not mean that its long-term lease is not a property interest.

More fundamentally, the majority's opinion erroneously fixates on a type of case that is not before us: one in which a private entity simply enters the marketplace and is then subject to government regulation. The majority swings hard at the wrong pitch. The majority focuses on *Jackson v. Metropolitan Edison Co.* (1974), which is a paradigmatic example of a line of cases that reject § 1983 liability for private actors that simply operate against a regulatory backdrop.

The *Jackson* line of cases is inapposite here. MNN is not a private entity that simply ventured into the marketplace. It occupies its role because it was asked to do so by the City, which secured the public-access channels in exchange for giving up public rights of way, opened those channels up (as required by the State) as a public forum, and then deputized MNN to administer them. That distinguishes MNN from a private entity that simply sets up shop against a regulatory backdrop. To say that MNN is nothing more than a private organization regulated by the government is like saying that a waiter at a restaurant is an independent food seller who just happens to be highly regulated by the restaurant's owners.

IV

This is not a case about bigger governments and smaller individuals; it is a case about principals and agents. New York City opened up a public forum on public-access channels in which it has a property interest. It asked MNN to run that public forum, and MNN accepted the job. That makes MNN subject to the First Amendment, just as if the City had decided to run the public forum itself.

While the majority emphasizes that its decision is narrow and factbound, that does not make it any less misguided. It is crucial that the Court does not continue to ignore the reality, fully recognized by our precedents, that private actors who have been delegated constitutional responsibilities like this one should be accountable to the Constitution's demands.

Chapter 6

Economic Liberties

D. The Takings Clause

1. Introduction (casebook p. 670)

The usual rule is that there is no need to exhaust state administrative and judicial remedies before bringing a federal constitutional claim to court. In *Williamson County Regional Planning Commission v. Hamilton Bank*, 473 U.S. 172 (1985), the Court held that a takings claim is not ripe until there has been exhaustion of state remedies because it cannot be said until then that there has been a taking without just compensation. In *Knick v. Township of Scott*, the Court overruled *Williamson County*.

KNICK v. TOWNSHIP OF SCOTT, PENNSYLVANIA
139 S. Ct. 2162 (2019)

Chief Justice ROBERTS delivered the opinion of the Court.

The Takings Clause of the Fifth Amendment states that "private property [shall not] be taken for public use, without just compensation." In *Williamson County Regional Planning Comm'n v. Hamilton Bank of Johnson City* (1985), we held that a property owner whose property has been taken by a local government has not suffered a violation of his Fifth Amendment rights — and thus cannot bring a federal takings claim in federal court — until a state court has denied his claim for just compensation under state law.

The *Williamson County* Court anticipated that if the property owner failed to secure just compensation under state law in state court, he would be able to bring a "ripe" federal takings claim in federal court. But as we later held in *San Remo Hotel, L. P. v. City and County of San Francisco* (2005), a state court's resolution of a claim for just compensation under state law generally has preclusive effect in any subsequent federal suit.

The takings plaintiff thus finds himself in a Catch-22: He cannot go to federal court without going to state court first; but if he goes to state court and loses, his claim will be barred in federal court. The federal claim dies aborning.

The *San Remo* preclusion trap should tip us off that the state-litigation requirement rests on a mistaken view of the Fifth Amendment. The Civil Rights Act of 1871, after all, guarantees "a federal forum for claims of unconstitutional treatment at the hands of state officials," and the settled rule is that "exhaustion of state remedies 'is *not* a prerequisite to an action under [42 U.S.C.] § 1983.'" But the guarantee of a federal forum rings hollow for takings plaintiffs, who are forced to litigate their claims in state court.

We now conclude that the state-litigation requirement imposes an unjustifiable burden on takings plaintiffs, conflicts with the rest of our takings jurisprudence, and must be overruled. A property owner has an actionable Fifth Amendment takings claim when the government takes his property without paying for it. That does not mean that the government must provide compensation in advance of a taking or risk having its action invalidated: So long as the property owner has some way to obtain compensation after the fact, governments need not fear that courts will enjoin their activities. But it does mean that the property owner has suffered a violation of his Fifth Amendment rights when the government takes his property without just compensation, and therefore may bring his claim in federal court under § 1983 at that time.

I

Petitioner Rose Mary Knick owns 90 acres of land in Scott Township, Pennsylvania, a small community just north of Scranton. Knick lives in a single-family home on the property and uses the rest of the land as a grazing area for horses and other farm animals. The property includes a small graveyard where the ancestors of Knick's neighbors are allegedly buried. Such family cemeteries are fairly common in Pennsylvania, where "backyard burials" have long been permitted.

In December 2012, the Township passed an ordinance requiring that "[a]ll cemeteries . . . be kept open and accessible to the general public during daylight hours." The ordinance defined a "cemetery" as "[a] place or area of ground, whether contained on private or public property, which has been set apart for or otherwise utilized as a burial place for deceased human beings." The ordinance also authorized Township "code enforcement" officers to "enter upon any property" to determine the existence and location of a cemetery.

In 2013, a Township officer found several grave markers on Knick's property and notified her that she was violating the ordinance by failing to open the cemetery to the public during the day. Knick responded by seeking declaratory and injunctive relief in state court on the ground that the ordinance effected a taking of her property.

We granted certiorari to reconsider the holding of *Williamson County* that property owners must seek just compensation under state law in state court before bringing a federal takings claim under § 1983.

The state-litigation requirement relegates the Takings Clause "to the status of a poor relation" among the provisions of the Bill of Rights. Plaintiffs asserting any other constitutional claim are guaranteed a federal forum under § 1983, but the state-litigation requirement "hand[s] authority over federal takings claims to state courts." Fidelity to the Takings Clause and our cases construing it requires overruling *Williamson County* and restoring takings claims to the full-fledged constitutional status the Framers envisioned when they included the Clause among the other protections in the Bill of Rights.

[II]

Contrary to *Williamson County*, a property owner has a claim for a violation of the Takings Clause as soon as a government takes his property for public use without paying for it. The Clause provides: "[N]or shall private property be taken for public use, without just compensation." It does not say: "Nor shall private property be taken for public use, without an available procedure that will result in compensation." If a local government takes private property without paying for it, that government has violated the Fifth Amendment — just as the Takings Clause says — without regard to subsequent state court proceedings. And the property owner may sue the government at that time in federal court for the "deprivation" of a right "secured by the Constitution." 42 U.S.C. § 1983.

The Fifth Amendment right to full compensation arises at the time of the taking, regardless of post-taking remedies that may be available to the property owner. That principle was confirmed in *Jacobs v. United States* (1933), where we held that a property owner found to have a valid takings claim is entitled to compensation as if it had been "paid contemporaneously with the taking" — that is, the compensation must generally consist of the total value of the property when taken, plus interest from that time.

Jacobs made clear that, no matter what sort of procedures the government puts in place to remedy a taking, a property owner has a Fifth Amendment entitlement to compensation as soon as the government takes his property without paying for it.

Although *Jacobs* concerned a taking by the Federal Government, the same reasoning applies to takings by the States. The availability of any particular compensation remedy, such as an inverse condemnation claim under state law, cannot infringe or restrict the property owner's federal constitutional claim—just as the existence of a state action for battery does not bar a Fourth Amendment claim of excessive force. The fact that the State has provided a property owner with a procedure that may subsequently result in just compensation cannot deprive the owner of his Fifth Amendment right to compensation under the Constitution, leaving only the state law right. And that is key because it is the existence of the Fifth Amendment right that allows the owner to proceed directly to federal court under § 1983.

Williamson County had a different view of how the Takings Clause works. According to *Williamson County*, a taking does not give rise to a federal constitutional right to just compensation at that time, but instead gives a right to a state law procedure that will eventually result in just compensation. As the Court put it, "if a State provides an adequate procedure for seeking just compensation, the property owner cannot claim a violation of the [Takings] Clause until it has used the procedure and been denied just compensation." In the absence of a state remedy, the Fifth Amendment right to compensation would attach immediately. But, under *Williamson County*, the presence of a state remedy qualifies the right, preventing it from vesting until exhaustion of the state procedure. That is what *Jacobs* confirmed could not be done.

A later payment of compensation may remedy the constitutional violation that occurred at the time of the taking, but that does not mean the violation never took place. The violation is the only reason compensation was owed in the first place. A bank robber might give the loot back, but he still robbed the bank. The availability of a subsequent compensation remedy for a taking without compensation no more means there never was a constitutional violation in the first place than the availability of a damages action renders negligent conduct compliant with the duty of care.

In sum, because a taking without compensation violates the self-executing Fifth Amendment at the time of the taking, the property owner can bring a federal suit at that time. Just as someone whose property has been taken by the Federal Government has a claim "founded . . . upon the

Constitution" that he may bring under the Tucker Act, someone whose property has been taken by a local government has a claim under § 1983 for a "deprivation of [a] right[ ] . . . secured by the Constitution" that he may bring upon the taking in federal court. The "general rule" is that plaintiffs may bring constitutional claims under § 1983 "without first bringing any sort of state lawsuit, even when state court actions addressing the underlying behavior are available." This is as true for takings claims as for any other claim grounded in the Bill of Rights.

Williamson County effectively established an exhaustion requirement for § 1983 takings claims when it held that a property owner must pursue state procedures for obtaining compensation before bringing a federal suit. But the Court did not phrase its holding in those terms; if it had, its error would have been clear. Instead, *Williamson County* broke with the Court's longstanding position that a property owner has a constitutional claim to compensation at the time the government deprives him of his property, and held that there can be no uncompensated taking, and thus no Fifth Amendment claim actionable under § 1983, until the property owner has tried and failed to obtain compensation through the available state procedure. "[U]ntil it has used the procedure and been denied just compensation," the property owner " 'has no claim against the Government' for a taking."

Today, because the federal and nearly all state governments provide just compensation remedies to property owners who have suffered a taking, equitable relief is generally unavailable. As long as an adequate provision for obtaining just compensation exists, there is no basis to enjoin the government's action effecting a taking. But that is because such a procedure is a remedy for a taking that violated the Constitution, not because the availability of the procedure somehow prevented the violation from occurring in the first place.

We conclude that a government violates the Takings Clause when it takes property without compensation, and that a property owner may bring a Fifth Amendment claim under § 1983 at that time. That does not as a practical matter mean that government action or regulation may not proceed in the absence of contemporaneous compensation. Given the availability of post-taking compensation, barring the government from acting will ordinarily not be appropriate. But because the violation is complete at the time of the taking, pursuit of a remedy in federal court need not await any subsequent state action. Takings claims against local governments should be handled the same as other claims under the Bill of Rights. *Williamson County* erred in holding otherwise.

[III]

The next question is whether we should overrule *Williamson County*, or whether *stare decisis* counsels in favor of adhering to the decision, despite its error. The doctrine of *stare decisis* reflects a judgment "that 'in most matters it is more important that the applicable rule of law be settled than that it be settled right.'" The doctrine "is at its weakest when we interpret the Constitution," as we did in *Williamson County*, because only this Court or a constitutional amendment can alter our holdings.

We have identified several factors to consider in deciding whether to overrule a past decision, including "the quality of [its] reasoning, the workability of the rule it established, its consistency with other related decisions, . . . and reliance on the decision." All of these factors counsel in favor of overruling

Williamson County was not just wrong. Its reasoning was exceptionally ill founded and conflicted with much of our takings jurisprudence. The decision has come in for repeated criticism over the years from Justices of this Court and many respected commentators. Because of its shaky foundations, the state-litigation requirement has been a rule in search of a justification for over 30 years.

Governments need not fear that our holding will lead federal courts to invalidate their regulations as unconstitutional. As long as just compensation remedies are available—as they have been for nearly 150 years—injunctive relief will be foreclosed. For the same reason, the Federal Government need not worry that courts will set aside agency actions as unconstitutional under the Administrative Procedure Act. Federal courts will not invalidate an otherwise lawful uncompensated taking when the property owner can receive complete relief through a Fifth Amendment claim brought under the Tucker Act.

In light of all the foregoing, the dissent cannot, with respect, fairly maintain its extreme assertions regarding our application of the principle of *stare decisis*.

The state-litigation requirement of *Williamson County* is overruled. A property owner may bring a takings claim under § 1983 upon the taking of his property without just compensation by a local government.

Justice KAGAN, with whom Justice GINSBURG, Justice BREYER, and Justice SOTOMAYOR join, dissenting.

Today, the Court formally overrules *Williamson County Regional Planning Comm'n v. Hamilton Bank of Johnson City* (1985). But its decision rejects far more than that single case. *Williamson County* was rooted in an understanding of the Fifth Amendment's Takings Clause stretching back to the late 1800s. On that view, a government could take property so long as it provided a reliable mechanism to pay just compensation, even if the payment came after the fact. No longer. The majority today holds, in conflict with precedent after precedent, that a government violates the Constitution whenever it takes property without advance compensation—no matter how good its commitment to pay. That conclusion has no basis in the Takings Clause. Its consequence is to channel a mass of quintessentially local cases involving complex state-law issues into federal courts. And it transgresses all usual principles of *stare decisis*.

I

Begin with the basics—the meaning of the Takings Clause. The right that Clause confers is not to be free from government takings of property for public purposes. Instead, the right is to be free from those takings when the government fails to provide "just compensation." In other words, the government *can* take private property for public purposes, so long as it fairly pays the property owner. That precept, which the majority does not contest, comes straight out of the constitutional text: "[P]rivate property [shall not] be taken for public use, without just compensation." "As its language indicates, [the Takings Clause] does not prohibit the taking of private property, but instead places a condition on the exercise of that power." And that constitutional choice accords with ancient principles about what governments do. The eminent domain power—the capacity to "take private property for public uses"—is an integral "attribute of sovereignty." Small surprise, then, that the Constitution does not prohibit takings for public purposes, but only requires the government to pay fair value.

In that way, the Takings Clause is unique among the Bill of Rights' guarantees. It is, for example, unlike the Fourth Amendment's protection against excessive force—which the majority mistakenly proposes as an analogy. Suppose a law enforcement officer uses excessive force and the victim recovers damages for his injuries. Did a constitutional violation occur? Of course. The Constitution prohibits what the officer did; the payment of damages merely remedied the constitutional wrong. But the Takings Clause is different because it does not prohibit takings; to the contrary, it permits them provided the government gives just compensation. So when the government "takes and pays," it is not violating the Constitution at all.

Put another way, a Takings Clause violation has two necessary elements. First, the government must take the property. Second, it must
deny the property owner just compensation. If the government has not
done both, no constitutional violation has happened. All this is well-trod
ground. Even the majority (despite its faulty analogy) does not contest
it.

Similarly well-settled—until the majority's opinion today—was the
answer to a follow-on question: At what point has the government denied
a property owner just compensation, so as to complete a Fifth Amendment
violation? For over a hundred years, this Court held that advance or contemporaneous payment was not required, so long as the government had
established reliable procedures for an owner to later obtain just compensation (including interest for any time elapsed).

Today's decision thus overthrows the Court's long-settled view of the
Takings Clause. The majority declares, as against a mountain of precedent,
that a government taking private property for public purposes must pay
compensation at that moment or in advance. If the government fails to do
so, a constitutional violation has occurred, regardless of whether "reasonable, certain and adequate" compensatory mechanisms exist. And regardless of how many times this Court has said the opposite before. Under
cover of overruling "only" a single decision, today's opinion smashes a
hundred-plus years of legal rulings to smithereens.

II

So how does the majority defend taking down *Williamson County* and its
many precursors?

The first crack comes from the repeated assertion (already encountered in the majority's Fourth Amendment analogy, that *Williamson
County* treats takings claims worse than other claims founded in the Bill
of Rights. That is not so. The distinctive aspects of litigating a takings
claim merely reflect the distinctive aspects of the constitutional right.
Once again, a Fourth Amendment claim arises at the moment a police
officer uses excessive force, because the Constitution prohibits that thing
and that thing only. (Similarly, for the majority's other analogies, a bank
robber commits his offense when he robs a bank and a tortfeasor when
he acts negligently—because that conduct, and it alone, is what the law
forbids.)

Second, the majority contends that its rule follows from the constitutional text, because the Takings Clause does not say "[n]or shall private
property be taken for public use, without an available procedure that will

result in compensation." There is a reason the majority devotes only a few sentences to that argument. Because here's another thing the text does not say: "Nor shall private property be taken for public use, without advance or contemporaneous payment of just compensation, notwithstanding ordinary procedures." In other words, the text no more states the majority's rule than it does *Williamson County*'s (and its precursors'). As constitutional text often is, the Takings Clause is spare. It says that a government taking property must pay just compensation — but does not say through exactly what mechanism or at exactly what time. That was left to be worked out, consistent with the Clause's (minimal) text and purpose. And from 1890 until today, this Court worked it out *Williamson County*'s way, rather than the majority's. Under our caselaw, a government could use reliable post-taking compensatory mechanisms (with payment calculated from the taking) without violating the Takings Clause.

III

And not only wrong on prior law. The majority's overruling of *Williamson County* will have two damaging consequences. It will inevitably turn even well-meaning government officials into lawbreakers. And it will subvert important principles of judicial federalism.

To begin with, today's decision means that government regulators will often have no way to avoid violating the Constitution. There are a "nearly infinite variety of ways" for regulations to "affect property interests." And under modern takings law, there is "no magic formula" to determine "whether a given government interference with property is a taking." For that reason, a government actor usually cannot know in advance whether implementing a regulatory program will effect a taking, much less of whose property. Until today, such an official could do his work without fear of wrongdoing, in any jurisdiction that had set up a reliable means for property owners to obtain compensation. Even if some regulatory action turned out to take someone's property, the official would not have violated the Constitution. But no longer. Now, when a government undertakes land-use regulation (and what government doesn't?), the responsible employees will almost inescapably become constitutional malefactors. That is not a fair position in which to place persons carrying out their governmental duties.

Still more important, the majority's ruling channels to federal courts a (potentially massive) set of cases that more properly belongs, at least in the first instance, in state courts — where *Williamson County* put them. The regulation of land use, this Court has stated, is "perhaps the quintessential state activity." And a claim that a land-use regulation violates the Takings Clause usually turns on state-law issues. In that respect, takings claims have little in common with other constitutional challenges. The question in takings cases is not merely whether a given state action meets federal constitutional standards. Before those standards can come into play, a court must typically decide whether, under state law, the plaintiff has a property interest in the thing regulated. Often those questions—how does pre-existing state law define the property right?; what interests does that law grant?; and conversely what interests does it deny?—are nuanced and complicated. And not a one of them is familiar to federal courts.

This case highlights the difficulty. The ultimate constitutional question here is: Did Scott Township's cemetery ordinance "go[ ] too far" (in Justice Holmes's phrase), so as to effect a taking of Rose Mary Knick's property? But to answer that question, it is first necessary to address an issue about background state law. In the Township's view, the ordinance did little more than codify Pennsylvania common law, which (the Township says) has long required property owners to make land containing human remains open to the public. If the Township is right on that state-law question, Knick's constitutional claim will fail: The ordinance, on that account, didn't go far at all. But Knick contends that no common law rule of that kind exists in Pennsylvania. And if she is right, her takings claim may yet have legs. But is she? Or is the Township? I confess: I don't know. Nor, I would venture, do my colleagues on the federal bench. But under today's decision, it will be the Federal District Court for the Middle District of Pennsylvania that will have to resolve this question of local cemetery law. And if the majority thinks this case is an outlier, it's dead wrong; indeed, this case will be easier than many.

IV

Everything said above aside, *Williamson County* should stay on the books because of *stare decisis*. Adherence to precedent is "a foundation stone of the rule of law." "[I]t promotes the evenhanded, predictable, and consistent development of legal principles, fosters reliance on judicial decisions, and contributes to the actual and perceived integrity of the judicial process." *Stare decisis*, of course, is "not an inexorable command." But it is not enough that five Justices believe a precedent wrong. Reversing course demands a "special justification—over and above the belief that the precedent was wrongly decided." The majority offers no reason that qualifies.

In its only real stab at a special justification, the majority focuses on what it calls the "*San Remo* preclusion trap." As the majority notes, this Court held in a post-*Williamson County* decision interpreting the full faith and credit statute, 28 U.S.C. § 1738, that a state court's resolution of an inverse condemnation proceeding has preclusive effect in a later federal suit. The interaction between *San Remo* and *Williamson County* means that "many takings plaintiffs never have the opportunity to litigate in a federal forum." According to the majority, that unanticipated result makes *Williamson County* itself "unworkable."

But in highlighting the preclusion concern, the majority only adds to the case for respecting *stare decisis*—because that issue can always be addressed by Congress. When "correction can be had by legislation," Justice Brandeis once stated, the Court should let stand even "error[s on] matter[s] of serious concern." Here, Congress can reverse the *San Remo* preclusion rule any time it wants, and thus give property owners an opportunity—*after* a state-court proceeding—to litigate in federal court. The *San Remo* decision, as noted above, interpreted the federal full faith and credit statute; Congress need only add a provision to that law to flip the Court's result. In fact, Congress has already considered proposals responding to *San Remo*—though so far to no avail.

What is left is simply the majority's view that *Williamson County* was wrong. The majority repurposes all its merits arguments—all its claims that *Williamson County* was "ill founded"—to justify its overruling. But the entire idea of *stare decisis* is that judges do not get to reverse a decision just because they never liked it in the first instance. Once again, they need a reason *other than* the idea "that the precedent was wrongly decided." For it is hard to overstate the value, in a country like ours, of stability in the law.

Just last month, when the Court overturned another longstanding precedent, Justice Breyer penned a dissent. See *Franchise Tax Bd. of Cal.* v. *Hyatt* (2019). He wrote of the dangers of reversing legal course "only because five Members of a later Court" decide that an earlier ruling was incorrect. He concluded: "Today's decision can only cause one to wonder which cases the Court will overrule next." Well, that didn't take long. Now one may wonder yet again.

2. Is There a Taking? (casebook p. 671)

With regard to regulatory takings, the issue often arises as to how to determine what is the "property." That is the issue in *Murr v. Wisconsin*.

MURR v. WISCONSIN
137 S. Ct. 1933 (2017)

Justice KENNEDY delivered the opinion of the Court.

The classic example of a property taking by the government is when the property has been occupied or otherwise seized. In the case now before the Court, petitioners contend that governmental entities took their real property—an undeveloped residential lot—not by some physical occupation but instead by enacting burdensome regulations that forbid its improvement or separate sale because it is classified as substandard in size. The relevant governmental entities are the respondents.

Against the background justifications for the challenged restrictions, respondents contend there is no regulatory taking because petitioners own an adjacent lot. The regulations, in effecting a merger of the property, permit the continued residential use of the property including for a single improvement to extend over both lots. This retained right of the landowner, respondents urge, is of sufficient offsetting value that the regulation is not severe enough to be a regulatory taking. To resolve the issue whether the landowners can insist on confining the analysis just to the lot in question, without regard to their ownership of the adjacent lot, it is necessary to discuss the background principles that define regulatory takings.

I

The St. Croix River originates in northwest Wisconsin and flows approximately 170 miles until it joins the Mississippi River, forming the boundary between Minnesota and Wisconsin for much of its length. The lower portion of the river slows and widens to create a natural water area known as Lake St. Croix. Tourists and residents of the region have long extolled the picturesque grandeur of the river and surrounding area.

Under the Wild and Scenic Rivers Act, the river was designated, by 1972, for federal protection. The law required the States of Wisconsin and Minnesota to develop "a management and development program" for the river area. In compliance, Wisconsin authorized the State Department of Natural Resources to promulgate rules limiting development in order to "guarantee the protection of the wild, scenic and recreational qualities of the river for present and future generations."

Petitioners are two sisters and two brothers in the Murr family. Petitioners' parents arranged for them to receive ownership of two lots the family used for recreation along the Lower St. Croix River in the town of Troy, Wisconsin. The lots are adjacent, but the parents purchased them separately, put the title of one in the name of the family business, and later arranged for transfer of the two lots, on different dates, to petitioners. The lots, which are referred to in this litigation as Lots E and F, are described in more detail below.

For the area where petitioners' property is located, the Wisconsin rules prevent the use of lots as separate building sites unless they have at least one acre of land suitable for development. A grandfather clause relaxes this restriction for substandard lots which were "in separate ownership from abutting lands" on January 1, 1976, the effective date of the regulation. The clause permits the use of qualifying lots as separate building sites. The rules also include a merger provision, however, which provides that adjacent lots under common ownership may not be "sold or developed as separate lots" if they do not meet the size requirement. The Wisconsin rules require localities to adopt parallel provisions, so the St. Croix County zoning ordinance contains identical restrictions. The Wisconsin rules also authorize the local zoning authority to grant variances from the regulations where enforcement would create "unnecessary hardship."

B

Petitioners' parents purchased Lot F in 1960 and built a small recreational cabin on it. In 1961, they transferred title to Lot F to the family plumbing company. In 1963, they purchased neighboring Lot E, which they held in their own names.

The lots have the same topography. A steep bluff cuts through the middle of each, with level land suitable for development above the bluff and next to the water below it. The line dividing Lot E from Lot F runs from the riverfront to the far end of the property, crossing the blufftop along the way. Lot E has approximately 60 feet of river frontage, and Lot F has approximately 100 feet. Though each lot is approximately 1.25 acres in size, because of the waterline and the steep bank they each have less than one acre of land suitable for development. Even when combined, the lots' buildable land area is only 0.98 acres due to the steep terrain.

The lots remained under separate ownership, with Lot F owned by the plumbing company and Lot E owned by petitioners' parents, until transfers to petitioners. Lot F was conveyed to them in 1994, and Lot E was conveyed to them in 1995.

A decade later, petitioners became interested in moving the cabin on Lot F to a different portion of the lot and selling Lot E to fund the project. The unification of the lots under common ownership, however, had implicated the state and local rules barring their separate sale or development. Petitioners then sought variances from the St. Croix County Board of Adjustment to enable their building and improvement plan, including a variance to allow the separate sale or use of the lots. The Board denied the requests, and the state courts affirmed in relevant part. In particular, the Wisconsin Court of Appeals agreed with the Board's interpretation that the local ordinance "effectively merged" Lots E and F, so petitioners "could only sell or build on the single larger lot."

The Circuit Court of St. Croix County granted summary judgment to the State, explaining that petitioners retained "several available options for the use and enjoyment of their property." For example, they could preserve the existing cabin, relocate the cabin, or eliminate the cabin and build a new residence on Lot E, on Lot F, or across both lots. The court also found petitioners had not been deprived of all economic value of their property. Considering the valuation of the property as a single lot versus two separate lots, the court found the market value of the property was not significantly affected by the regulations because the decrease in value was less than 10 percent.

The Wisconsin Court of Appeals affirmed. . . . The Supreme Court of Wisconsin denied discretionary review. This Court granted certiorari . . . .

II

A central dynamic of the Court's regulatory takings jurisprudence is its flexibility. This has been and remains a means to reconcile two competing objectives central to regulatory takings doctrine. One is the individual's right to retain the interests and exercise the freedoms at the core of private property ownership. Property rights are necessary to preserve freedom, for property ownership empowers persons to shape and to plan their own destiny in a world where governments are always eager to do so for them. The other persisting interest is the government's well-established power to "adjus[t] rights for the public good." As Justice Holmes declared, "Government hardly could go on if to some extent values incident to property could not be diminished without paying for every such change in the general law." In adjudicating regulatory takings cases a proper balancing of these principles requires a careful inquiry informed by the specifics of the case. In all instances, the analysis must be driven "by the purpose of the Takings Clause, which is to prevent the government from'forcing some people alone to bear public burdens which, in all fairness and justice, should be borne by the public as a whole.'"

This case presents a question that is linked to the ultimate determination whether a regulatory taking has occurred: What is the proper unit of property against which to assess the effect of the challenged governmental action? Put another way, "[b]ecause our test for regulatory taking requires us to compare the value that has been taken from the property with the value that remains in the property, one of the critical questions is determining how to define the unit of property 'whose value is to furnish the denominator of the fraction.'" As commentators have noted, the answer to this question may be outcome determinative. This Court, too, has explained that the question is important to the regulatory takings inquiry. "To the extent that any portion of property is taken, that portion is always taken in its entirety; the relevant question, however, is whether the property taken is all, or only a portion of, the parcel in question."

Defining the property at the outset, however, should not necessarily preordain the outcome in every case. In some, though not all, cases the effect of the challenged regulation must be assessed and understood by the effect on the entire property held by the owner, rather than just some part of the property that, considered just on its own, has been diminished in value. This demonstrates the contrast between regulatory takings, where the goal is usually to determine how the challenged regulation affects the property's value to the owner, and physical takings, where the impact of physical appropriation or occupation of the property will be evident.

While the Court has not set forth specific guidance on how to identify the relevant parcel for the regulatory taking inquiry, there are two concepts which the Court has indicated can be unduly narrow.

First, the Court has declined to limit the parcel in an artificial manner to the portion of property targeted by the challenged regulation. The second concept about which the Court has expressed caution is the view that property rights under the Takings Clause should be coextensive with those under state law. By the same measure, defining the parcel by reference to state law could defeat a challenge even to a state enactment that alters permitted uses of property in ways inconsistent with reasonable investment-backed expectations. For example, a State might enact a law that consolidates nonadjacent property owned by a single person or entity in different parts of the State and then imposes development limits on the aggregate set. If a court defined the parcel according to the state law requiring consolidation, this improperly would fortify the state law against a takings claim, because the court would look to the retained value in the property as a whole rather than considering whether individual holdings had lost all value.

III

As the foregoing discussion makes clear, no single consideration can supply the exclusive test for determining the denominator. Instead, courts must consider a number of factors. These include the treatment of the land under state and local law; the physical characteristics of the land; and the prospective value of the regulated land. The endeavor should determine whether reasonable expectations about property ownership would lead a landowner to anticipate that his holdings would be treated as one parcel, or, instead, as separate tracts. The inquiry is objective, and the reasonable expectations at issue derive from background customs and the whole of our legal tradition.

First, courts should give substantial weight to the treatment of the land, in particular how it is bounded or divided, under state and local law. The reasonable expectations of an acquirer of land must acknowledge legitimate restrictions affecting his or her subsequent use and dispensation of the property.

Second, courts must look to the physical characteristics of the landowner's property. These include the physical relationship of any distinguishable tracts, the parcel's topography, and the surrounding human and ecological environment. In particular, it may be relevant that the property is located in an area that is subject to, or likely to become subject to, environmental or other regulation.

Third, courts should assess the value of the property under the challenged regulation, with special attention to the effect of burdened land on the value of other holdings. Though a use restriction may decrease the market value of the property, the effect may be tempered if the regulated land adds value to the remaining property, such as by increasing privacy, expanding recreational space, or preserving surrounding natural beauty. A law that limits use of a landowner's small lot in one part of the city by reason of the landowner's nonadjacent holdings elsewhere may decrease the market value of the small lot in an unmitigated fashion. The absence of a special relationship between the holdings may counsel against consideration of all the holdings as a single parcel, making the restrictive law susceptible to a takings challenge. On the other hand, if the landowner's other property is adjacent to the small lot, the market value of the properties may well increase if their combination enables the expansion of a structure, or if development restraints for one part of the parcel protect the unobstructed skyline views of another part. That, in turn, may counsel in favor of treatment as a single parcel and may reveal the weakness of a regulatory takings challenge to the law.

State and federal courts have considerable experience in adjudicating regulatory takings claims that depart from these examples in various ways. The Court anticipates that in applying the test above they will continue to exercise care in this complex area.

IV

Under the appropriate multifactor standard, it follows that for purposes of determining whether a regulatory taking has occurred here, petitioners' property should be evaluated as a single parcel consisting of Lots E and F together.

First, the treatment of the property under state and local law indicates petitioners' property should be treated as one when considering the effects of the restrictions. As the Wisconsin courts held, the state and local regulations merged Lots E and F. The decision to adopt the merger provision at issue here was for a specific and legitimate purpose, consistent with the widespread understanding that lot lines are not dominant or controlling in every case. Petitioners' land was subject to this regulatory burden, moreover, only because of voluntary conduct in bringing the lots under common ownership after the regulations were enacted. As a result, the valid merger of the lots under state law informs the reasonable expectation they will be treated as a single property.

Second, the physical characteristics of the property support its treatment as a unified parcel. The lots are contiguous along their longest edge. Their rough terrain and narrow shape make it reasonable to expect their range of potential uses might be limited. The land's location along the river is also significant. Petitioners could have anticipated public regulation might affect their enjoyment of their property, as the Lower St. Croix was a regulated area under federal, state, and local law long before petitioners possessed the land.

Third, the prospective value that Lot E brings to Lot F supports considering the two as one parcel for purposes of determining if there is a regulatory taking. Petitioners are prohibited from selling Lots E and F separately or from building separate residential structures on each. Yet this restriction is mitigated by the benefits of using the property as an integrated whole, allowing increased privacy and recreational space, plus the optimal location of any improvements.

The special relationship of the lots is further shown by their combined valuation. Were Lot E separately saleable but still subject to the development restriction, petitioners' appraiser would value the property at only $40,000. We express no opinion on the validity of this figure. We also note the number is not particularly helpful for understanding petitioners' retained value in the properties because Lot E, under the regulations, cannot be sold without Lot F. The point that is useful for these purposes is that the combined lots are valued at $698,300, which is far greater than the summed value of the separate regulated lots (Lot F with its cabin at $373,000, according to respondents' appraiser, and Lot E as an undevelopable plot at $40,000, according to petitioners' appraiser). The value added by the lots' combination shows their complementarity and supports their treatment as one parcel.

Considering petitioners' property as a whole, the state court was correct to conclude that petitioners cannot establish a compensable taking in these circumstances. Petitioners have not suffered a taking under *Lucas*, as they have not been deprived of all economically beneficial use of their property. They can use the property for residential purposes, including an enhanced, larger residential improvement. The property has not lost all economic value, as its value has decreased by less than 10 percent.

Petitioners furthermore have not suffered a taking under the more general test of *Penn Central*. The expert appraisal relied upon by the state courts refutes any claim that the economic impact of the regulation is severe. Petitioners cannot claim that they reasonably expected to sell or develop their lots separately given the regulations which predated their acquisition of both lots. Finally, the governmental action was a reasonable land-use regulation, enacted as part of a coordinated federal, state, and local effort to preserve the river and surrounding land.

Like the ultimate question whether a regulation has gone too far, the question of the proper parcel in regulatory takings cases cannot be solved by any simple test. Courts must instead define the parcel in a manner that reflects reasonable expectations about the property. Courts must strive for consistency with the central purpose of the Takings Clause: to "bar Government from forcing some people alone to bear public burdens which, in all fairness and justice, should be borne by the public as a whole." Treating the lot in question as a single parcel is legitimate for purposes of this takings inquiry, and this supports the conclusion that no regulatory taking occurred here.

Chief Justice ROBERTS, with whom Justice THOMAS and Justice ALITO join, dissenting.

Where the majority goes astray is in concluding that the definition of the "private property" at issue in a case such as this turns on an elaborate test looking not only to state and local law, but also to (1) "the physical characteristics of the land," (2) "the prospective value of the regulated land,"

(3) the "reasonable expectations" of the owner, and (4) "background customs and the whole of our legal tradition." Our decisions have, time and again, declared that the Takings Clause protects private property rights as state law creates and defines them. By securing such *established* property rights, the Takings Clause protects individuals from being forced to bear the full weight of actions that should be borne by the public at large. The majority's new, malleable definition of "private property"—adopted solely "for purposes of th[e] takings inquiry," undermines that protection.

I would stick with our traditional approach: State law defines the boundaries of distinct parcels of land, and those boundaries should determine the "private property" at issue in regulatory takings cases. Whether a regulation effects a taking of that property is a separate question, one in which common ownership of adjacent property may be taken into account. Because the majority departs from these settled principles, I respectfully dissent.

Because a regulation amounts to a taking if it completely destroys a property's productive use, there is an incentive for owners to define the relevant "private property" narrowly. This incentive threatens the careful balance between property rights and government authority that our regulatory takings doctrine strikes: Put in terms of the familiar "bundle" analogy, each "strand" in the bundle of rights that comes along with owning real property is a distinct property interest. If owners could define the relevant "private property" at issue as the specific "strand" that the challenged regulation affects, they could convert nearly all regulations into *per se* takings.

And so we do not allow it. In *Penn Central Transportation Co. v. New York City*, we held that property owners may not "establish a 'taking' simply by showing that they have been denied the ability to exploit a property interest." In that case, the owner of Grand Central Terminal in New York City argued that a restriction on the owner's ability to add an office building atop the station amounted to a taking of its air rights. We rejected that narrow definition of the "property" at issue, concluding that the correct unit of analysis was the owner's "rights in the parcel as a whole." "[W]here an owner possesses a full 'bundle' of property rights, the destruction of one strand of the bundle is not a taking, because the aggregate must be viewed in its entirety."

The question presented in today's case concerns the "parcel as a whole" language from *Penn Central*. This enigmatic phrase has created confusion about how to identify the relevant property in a regulatory takings case when the claimant owns more than one plot of land. Should the impact of the regulation be evaluated with respect to each individual plot, or with respect to adjacent plots grouped together as one unit? According to the majority, a court should answer this question by considering a number of facts about the land and the regulation at issue. The end result turns on whether those factors "would lead a landowner to anticipate that his holdings would be treated as one parcel, or, instead, as separate tracts."

I think the answer is far more straightforward: State laws define the boundaries of distinct units of land, and those boundaries should, in all but the most exceptional circumstances, determine the parcel at issue. Even in regulatory takings cases, the first step of the Takings Clause analysis is still to identify the relevant "private property." States create property rights with respect to particular "things." And in the context of real property, those "things" are horizontally bounded plots of land. States may define those plots differently—some using metes and bounds, others using government surveys, recorded plats, or subdivision maps. But the definition of property draws the basic line between, as P.G. Wodehouse would put it, *meum* and *tuum*. The question of who owns what is pretty important: The rules must provide a readily ascertainable definition of the land to which a particular bundle of rights attaches that does not vary depending upon the purpose at issue.

Following state property lines is also entirely consistent with *Penn Central*. Requiring consideration of the "parcel as a whole" is a response to the risk that owners will strategically pluck one strand from their bundle of property rights—such as the air rights at issue in *Penn Central*—and claim a complete taking based on that strand alone. That risk of strategic unbundling is not present when a legally distinct parcel is the basis of the regulatory takings claim. State law defines all of the interests that come along with owning a particular parcel, and both property owners and the government must take those rights as they find them.

The majority envisions that relying on state law will create other opportunities for "gamesmanship" by landowners and States: The former, it contends, "might seek to alter [lot] lines in anticipation of regulation," while the latter might pass a law that "consolidates . . . property" to avoid a successful takings claim. But such obvious attempts to alter the legal landscape in anticipation of a lawsuit are unlikely and not particularly difficult to detect and disarm. We rejected the strategic splitting of property rights in *Penn Central*, and courts could do the same if faced with an attempt to create a takings-specific definition of "private property."

Once the relevant property is identified, the real work begins. To decide whether the regulation at issue amounts to a "taking," courts should focus on the effect of the regulation on the "private property" at issue. Adjacent land under common ownership may be relevant to that inquiry. The owner's possession of such a nearby lot could, for instance, shed light on how the owner reasonably expected to use the parcel at issue before the regulation. If the court concludes that the government's action amounts to a taking, principles of "just compensation" may also allow the owner to recover damages "with regard to a separate parcel" that is contiguous and used in conjunction with the parcel at issue.

In sum, the "parcel as a whole" requirement prevents a property owner from identifying a single "strand" in his bundle of property rights and claiming that interest has been taken. Allowing that strategic approach to defining "private property" would undermine the balance struck by our regulatory takings cases. Instead, state law creates distinct parcels of land and defines the rights that come along with owning those parcels. Those established bundles of rights should define the "private property" in regulatory takings cases. While ownership of contiguous properties may bear on whether a person's plot has been "taken," *Penn Central* provides no basis for disregarding state property lines when identifying the "parcel as a whole."

II

The lesson that the majority draws from *Penn Central* is that defining "the proper parcel in regulatory takings cases cannot be solved by any simple test." Following through on that stand against simplicity, the majority lists a complex set of factors theoretically designed to reveal whether a hypothetical landowner might expect that his property "would be treated as one parcel, or, instead, as separate tracts." Those factors, says the majority, show that Lots E and F of the Murrs' property constitute a single parcel and that the local ordinance requiring the Murrs to develop and sell those lots as a pair does not constitute a taking.

In deciding that Lots E and F are a single parcel, the majority focuses on the importance of the ordinance at issue and the extent to which the Murrs may have been especially surprised, or unduly harmed, by the application of that ordinance to their property. But these issues should be considered when deciding if a regulation constitutes a "taking." Cramming them into the definition of "private property" undermines the effectiveness of the Takings Clause as a check on the government's power to shift the cost of public life onto private individuals.

In departing from state property principles, the majority authorizes governments to do precisely what we rejected in *Penn Central*: create a litigation-specific definition of "property" designed for a claim under

the Takings Clause. Whenever possible, governments in regulatory takings cases will ask courts to aggregate legally distinct properties into one
"parcel," solely for purposes of resisting a particular claim. And under the
majority's test, identifying the "parcel as a whole" in such cases will turn
on the reasonableness of the regulation as applied to the claimant. The
result is that the government's regulatory interests will come into play
not once, but twice—first when identifying the relevant parcel, and again
when determining whether the regulation has placed too great a public
burden on that property.

Regulatory takings, however—by their very nature—pit the common
good against the interests of a few. There is an inherent imbalance in
that clash of interests. The widespread benefits of a regulation will often
appear far weightier than the isolated losses suffered by individuals. And
looking at the bigger picture, the overall societal good of an economic system grounded on private property will appear abstract when cast against
a concrete regulatory problem. In the face of this imbalance, the Takings
Clause "prevents the public from loading upon one individual more than
his just share of the burdens of government," by considering the effect of
a regulation on specific property rights as they are established at state law.
But the majority's approach undermines that protection, defining property
only after engaging in an ad hoc, case-specific consideration of individual
and community interests. The result is that the government's goals shape
the playing field before the contest over whether the challenged regulation
goes "too far" even gets underway.

Put simply, today's decision knocks the definition of "private property"
loose from its foundation on stable state law rules and throws it into the
maelstrom of multiple factors that come into play at the second step of the
takings analysis. The result: The majority's new framework compromises
the Takings Clause as a barrier between individuals and the press of the
public interest.

III

As I see it, the Wisconsin Court of Appeals was wrong to apply a takings-specific definition of the property at issue. Instead, the court should
have asked whether, under general state law principles, Lots E and F are
legally distinct parcels of land. I would therefore vacate the judgment
below and remand for the court to identify the relevant property using
ordinary principles of Wisconsin property law.

Chapter 7

Equal Protection

C. Classifications Based on Race and National Origin

3. Proving the Existence of a Race or National Origin Classification

a. Race and National Origin Classifications on the Face of the Law (casebook p. 761)

In *Pena-Rodriguez v. Colorado*, the Court considered how a court should respond to information that a juror made racist statements during jury deliberations.

PENA-RODRIGUEZ v. COLORADO
137 S. Ct. 788 (2017)

Justice KENNEDY delivered the opinion of the Court.

The jury is a central foundation of our justice system and our democracy. Whatever its imperfections in a particular case, the jury is a necessary check on governmental power. The jury, over the centuries, has been an inspired, trusted, and effective instrument for resolving factual disputes and determining ultimate questions of guilt or innocence in criminal cases. Over the long course its judgments find acceptance in the community, an acceptance essential to respect for the rule of law. The jury is a tangible implementation of the principle that the law comes from the people.

In the era of our Nation's founding, the right to a jury trial already had existed and evolved for centuries, through and alongside the common law. The jury was considered a fundamental safeguard of individual liberty. The right to a jury trial in criminal cases was part of the Constitution as first drawn, and it was restated in the Sixth Amendment. By operation of the Fourteenth Amendment, it is applicable to the States.

Like all human institutions, the jury system has its flaws, yet experience shows that fair and impartial verdicts can be reached if the jury follows the court's instructions and undertakes deliberations that are honest, candid, robust, and based on common sense. A general rule has evolved to give substantial protection to verdict finality and to assure jurors that, once their verdict has been entered, it will not later be called into question based on the comments or conclusions they expressed during deliberations. This principle, itself centuries old, is often referred to as the no-impeachment rule. The instant case presents the question whether there is an exception to the no-impeachment rule when, after the jury is discharged, a juror comes forward with compelling evidence that another juror made clear and explicit statements indicating that racial animus was a significant motivating factor in his or her vote to convict.

I

State prosecutors in Colorado brought criminal charges against petitioner, Miguel Angel Peña-Rodriguez, based on the following allegations. In 2007, in the bathroom of a Colorado horse-racing facility, a man sexually assaulted two teenage sisters. The girls told their father and identified the man as an employee of the racetrack. The police located and arrested petitioner. Each girl separately identified petitioner as the man who had assaulted her.

The State charged petitioner with harassment, unlawful sexual contact, and attempted sexual assault on a child. Before the jury was empaneled, members of the venire were repeatedly asked whether they believed that they could be fair and impartial in the case. A written questionnaire asked if there was "anything about you that you feel would make it difficult for you to be a fair juror." The court repeated the question to the panel of prospective jurors and encouraged jurors to speak in private with the court if they had any concerns about their impartiality. Defense counsel likewise asked whether anyone felt that "this is simply not a good case" for them to be a fair juror. None of the empaneled jurors expressed any reservations based on racial or any other bias. And none asked to speak with the trial judge.

After a 3-day trial, the jury found petitioner guilty of unlawful sexual contact and harassment, but it failed to reach a verdict on the attempted sexual assault charge. Following the discharge of the jury, petitioner's counsel entered the jury room to discuss the trial with the jurors. As the room was emptying, two jurors remained to speak with counsel in private. They stated that, during deliberations, another juror had expressed anti-Hispanic bias toward petitioner and petitioner's alibi witness. Petitioner's counsel reported this to the court and, with the court's supervision, obtained sworn affidavits from the two jurors.

The affidavits by the two jurors described a number of biased statements made by another juror, identified as Juror H.C. According to the two jurors, H.C. told the other jurors that he "believed the defendant was guilty because, in [H.C.'s] experience as an ex-law enforcement officer, Mexican men had a bravado that caused them to believe they could do whatever they wanted with women." The jurors reported that H.C. stated his belief that Mexican men are physically controlling of women because of their sense of entitlement, and further stated, "'I think he did it because he's Mexican and Mexican men take whatever they want.'" According to the jurors, H.C. further explained that, in his experience, "nine times out of ten Mexican men were guilty of being aggressive toward women and young girls." Finally, the jurors recounted that Juror H.C. said that he did not find petitioner's alibi witness credible because, among other things, the witness was "'an illegal.'"

After reviewing the affidavits, the trial court acknowledged H.C.'s apparent bias. But the court denied petitioner's motion for a new trial, noting that "[t]he actual deliberations that occur among the jurors are protected from inquiry under [Colorado Rule of Evidence] 606(b)." Like its federal counterpart, Colorado's Rule 606(b) generally prohibits a juror from testifying as to any statement made during deliberations in a proceeding inquiring into the validity of the verdict. The Colorado Rule reads as follows:

> "(b) Inquiry into validity of verdict or indictment. Upon an inquiry into the validity of a verdict or indictment, a juror may not testify as to any matter or statement occurring during the course of the jury's deliberations or to the effect of anything upon his or any other juror's mind or emotions as influencing him to assent to or dissent from the verdict or indictment or concerning his mental processes in connection therewith. But a juror may testify about (1) whether extraneous prejudicial information was improperly brought to the jurors' attention, (2) whether any outside influence was improperly brought to bear upon any juror, or (3) whether there was a mistake in entering the verdict onto the verdict form. A juror's affidavit or evidence of any statement by the juror may not be received on a matter about which the juror would be precluded from testifying."

The verdict deemed final, petitioner was sentenced to two years' probation and was required to register as a sex offender.

Juror H.C.'s bias was based on petitioner's Hispanic identity, which the Court in prior cases has referred to as ethnicity, and that may be an instructive term here. Petitioner and respondent both refer to race, or to race and ethnicity, in this more expansive sense in their briefs to the Court. This opinion refers to the nature of the bias as racial in keeping with the primary terminology employed by the parties and used in our precedents.

II

At common law jurors were forbidden to impeach their verdict, either by affidavit or live testimony. This rule originated in *Vaise v. Delaval* (K.B. 1785). There, Lord Mansfield excluded juror testimony that the jury had decided the case through a game of chance. The Mansfield rule, as it came to be known, prohibited jurors, after the verdict was entered, from testifying either about their subjective mental processes or about objective events that occurred during deliberations.

American courts adopted the Mansfield rule as a matter of common law, though not in every detail. The common-law development of the no-impeachment rule reached a milestone in 1975, when Congress adopted the Federal Rules of Evidence, including Rule 606(b). Congress endorsed a broad no-impeachment rule, with only limited exceptions. The version of the rule that Congress adopted was "no accident." This version of the no-impeachment rule has substantial merit. It promotes full and vigorous discussion by providing jurors with considerable assurance that after being discharged they will not be summoned to recount their deliberations, and they will not otherwise be harassed or annoyed by litigants seeking to challenge the verdict. The rule gives stability and finality to verdicts.

Some version of the no-impeachment rule is followed in every State and the District of Columbia. Variations make classification imprecise, but, as a general matter, it appears that 42 jurisdictions follow the Federal Rule.

III

It must become the heritage of our Nation to rise above racial classifications that are so inconsistent with our commitment to the equal dignity of all persons. This imperative to purge racial prejudice from the administration of justice was given new force and direction by the ratification of the Civil War Amendments.

"[T]he central purpose of the Fourteenth Amendment was to eliminate racial discrimination emanating from official sources in the States." In the years before and after the ratification of the Fourteenth Amendment, it became clear that racial discrimination in the jury system posed a particular threat both to the promise of the Amendment and to the integrity of the jury trial. "Almost immediately after the Civil War, the South began a practice that would continue for many decades: All-white juries punished black defendants particularly harshly, while simultaneously refusing to punish violence by whites, including Ku Klux Klan members, against blacks and Republicans." To take one example, just in the years 1865 and 1866, all-white juries in Texas decided a total of 500 prosecutions of white defendants charged with killing African-Americans. All 500 were acquitted. The stark and unapologetic nature of race-motivated outcomes challenged the American belief that "the jury was a bulwark of liberty," and prompted Congress to pass legislation to integrate the jury system and to bar persons from eligibility for jury service if they had conspired to deny the civil rights of African-Americans. Members of Congress stressed that the legislation was necessary to preserve the right to a fair trial and to guarantee the equal protection of the laws.

The duty to confront racial animus in the justice system is not the legislature's alone. Time and again, this Court has been called upon to enforce the Constitution's guarantee against state-sponsored racial discrimination in the jury system. Beginning in 1880, the Court interpreted the Fourteenth Amendment to prohibit the exclusion of jurors on the basis of race. The Court has repeatedly struck down laws and practices that systematically exclude racial minorities from juries. To guard against discrimination in jury selection, the Court has ruled that no litigant may exclude a prospective juror on the basis of race. In an effort to ensure that individuals who sit on juries are free of racial bias, the Court has held that the Constitution at times demands that defendants be permitted to ask questions about racial bias during *voir dire*.

The unmistakable principle underlying these precedents is that discrimination on the basis of race, "odious in all aspects, is especially pernicious in the administration of justice." The jury is to be "a criminal defendant's fundamental 'protection of life and liberty against race or color prejudice.'" Permitting racial prejudice in the jury system damages "both the fact and the perception" of the jury's role as "a vital check against the wrongful exercise of power by the State."

IV

This case lies at the intersection of the Court's decisions endorsing the no-impeachment rule and its decisions seeking to eliminate racial bias in the jury system. The two lines of precedent, however, need not conflict.

[R]acial bias, a familiar and recurring evil that, if left unaddressed, would risk systemic injury to the administration of justice. This Court's decisions demonstrate that racial bias implicates unique historical, constitutional, and institutional concerns. An effort to address the most grave and serious statements of racial bias is not an effort to perfect the jury but to ensure that our legal system remains capable of coming ever closer to the promise of equal treatment under the law that is so central to a functioning democracy.

Racial bias is distinct in a pragmatic sense as well. In past cases this Court has relied on other safeguards to protect the right to an impartial jury. Some of those safeguards, to be sure, can disclose racial bias. *Voir dire* at the outset of trial, observation of juror demeanor and conduct during trial, juror reports before the verdict, and nonjuror evidence after trial are important mechanisms for discovering bias. Yet their operation may be compromised, or they may prove insufficient. For instance, this Court has noted the dilemma faced by trial court judges and counsel in deciding whether to explore potential racial bias at *voir dire*. Generic questions about juror impartiality may not expose specific attitudes or biases that can poison jury deliberations. Yet more pointed questions "could well exacerbate whatever prejudice might exist without substantially aiding in exposing it."

The stigma that attends racial bias may make it difficult for a juror to report inappropriate statements during the course of juror deliberations. It is one thing to accuse a fellow juror of having a personal experience that improperly influences her consideration of the case. It is quite another to call her a bigot.

For the reasons explained above, the Court now holds that where a juror makes a clear statement that indicates he or she relied on racial stereotypes or animus to convict a criminal defendant, the Sixth Amendment requires that the no-impeachment rule give way in order to permit the trial court to consider the evidence of the juror's statement and any resulting denial of the jury trial guarantee.

Not every offhand comment indicating racial bias or hostility will justify setting aside the no-impeachment bar to allow further judicial inquiry. For the inquiry to proceed, there must be a showing that one or more jurors made statements exhibiting overt racial bias that cast serious doubt on the fairness and impartiality of the jury's deliberations and resulting verdict. To qualify, the statement must tend to show that racial animus was a significant motivating factor in the juror's vote to convict. Whether that threshold showing has been satisfied is a matter committed to the substantial discretion of the trial court in light of all the circumstances, including the content and timing of the alleged statements and the reliability of the proffered evidence.

The practical mechanics of acquiring and presenting such evidence will no doubt be shaped and guided by state rules of professional ethics and local court rules, both of which often limit counsel's post-trial contact with jurors. These limits seek to provide jurors some protection when they return to their daily affairs after the verdict has been entered. But while a juror can always tell counsel they do not wish to discuss the case, jurors in some instances may come forward of their own accord.

That is what happened here. In this case the alleged statements by a juror were egregious and unmistakable in their reliance on racial bias. Not only did juror H.C. deploy a dangerous racial stereotype to conclude petitioner was guilty and his alibi witness should not be believed, but he also encouraged other jurors to join him in convicting on that basis.

Petitioner's counsel did not seek out the two jurors' allegations of racial bias. Pursuant to Colorado's mandatory jury instruction, the trial court had set limits on juror contact and encouraged jurors to inform the court if anyone harassed them about their role in the case. Similar limits on juror contact can be found in other jurisdictions that recognize a racial-bias exception.

While the trial court concluded that Colorado's Rule 606(b) did not permit it even to consider the resulting affidavits, the Court's holding today removes that bar. When jurors disclose an instance of racial bias as serious as the one involved in this case, the law must not wholly disregard its occurrence.

The Court relies on the experiences of the 17 jurisdictions that have recognized a racial-bias exception to the no-impeachment rule — some for over half a century — with no signs of an increase in juror harassment or a loss of juror willingness to engage in searching and candid deliberations. The experience of these jurisdictions, and the experience of the courts going forward, will inform the proper exercise of trial judge discretion in these and related matters. This case does not ask, and the Court need not address, what procedures a trial court must follow when confronted with a motion for a new trial based on juror testimony of racial bias. The Court also does not decide the appropriate standard for determining when evidence of racial bias is sufficient to require that the verdict be set aside and a new trial be granted.

The Nation must continue to make strides to overcome race-based discrimination. The progress that has already been made underlies the Court's insistence that blatant racial prejudice is antithetical to the functioning of the jury system and must be confronted in egregious cases like this one despite the general bar of the no-impeachment rule. It is the mark of a maturing legal system that it seeks to understand and to implement the lessons of history. The Court now seeks to strengthen the broader principle that society can and must move forward by achieving the thoughtful, rational dialogue at the foundation of both the jury system and the free society that sustains our Constitution.

Justice THOMAS, dissenting.

The Court today holds that the Sixth Amendment requires the States to provide a criminal defendant the opportunity to impeach a jury's guilty verdict with juror testimony about a juror's alleged racial bias, notwithstanding a state procedural rule forbidding such testimony. I agree with Justice Alito that the Court's decision is incompatible with the text of the Amendment it purports to interpret and with our precedents. I write separately to explain that the Court's holding also cannot be squared with the original understanding of the Sixth or Fourteenth Amendments.

The Sixth Amendment's protection of the right, "[i]n all criminal prosecutions," to a "trial, by an impartial jury," is limited to the protections that existed at common law when the Amendment was ratified. The Sixth Amendment's specific guarantee of impartiality incorporates the common-law understanding of that term. The common law required a juror to have "freedome of mind" and to be "indifferent as hee stands unsworne." 1 E. Coke, First Part of the Institutes of the Laws of England § 234, p. 155a (16th ed. 1809).

The common-law right to a jury trial did not, however, guarantee a defendant the right to impeach a jury verdict with juror testimony about juror misconduct, including "a principal species of [juror] misbehaviour" — "notorious partiality." 3 Blackstone 388. Although partiality was a ground for setting aside a jury verdict, the English common-law rule at the time the Sixth Amendment was ratified did not allow jurors to supply evidence of that misconduct.

Perhaps good reasons exist to curtail or abandon the no-impeachment rule. Some States have done so, and others have not. Ultimately, that question is not for us to decide. It should be left to the political process described by Justice Alito. In its attempt to stimulate a "thoughtful, rational dialogue" on race relations, the Court today ends the political process and imposes a uniform, national rule. The Constitution does not require such a rule. Neither should we.

Justice ALITO with whom THE CHIEF JUSTICE and Justice THOMAS join, dissenting.

Our legal system has many rules that restrict the admission of evidence of statements made under circumstances in which confidentiality is thought to be essential. Statements made to an attorney in obtaining legal advice, statements to a treating physician, and statements made to a spouse or member of the clergy are familiar examples. Even if a criminal defendant whose constitutional rights are at stake has a critical need to obtain and introduce evidence of such statements, long-established rules stand in the way. The goal of avoiding interference with confidential communications of great value has long been thought to justify the loss of important evidence and the effect on our justice system that this loss entails.

The present case concerns a rule like those just mentioned, namely, the age-old rule against attempting to overturn or "impeach" a jury's verdict by offering statements made by jurors during the course of deliberations. For centuries, it has been the judgment of experienced judges, trial attorneys, scholars, and lawmakers that allowing jurors to testify after a trial about what took place in the jury room would undermine the system of trial by jury that is integral to our legal system.

Juries occupy a unique place in our justice system. The other participants in a trial — the presiding judge, the attorneys, the witnesses — function in an arena governed by strict rules of law. Their every word is recorded and may be closely scrutinized for missteps.

When jurors retire to deliberate, however, they enter a space that is not regulated in the same way. Jurors are ordinary people. They are expected to speak, debate, argue, and make decisions the way ordinary people do in their daily lives. Our Constitution places great value on this way of thinking, speaking, and deciding. The jury trial right protects parties in court cases from being judged by a special class of trained professionals who do not speak the language of ordinary people and may not understand or appreciate the way ordinary people live their lives. To protect that right, the door to the jury room has been locked, and the confidentiality of jury deliberations has been closely guarded.

Today, with the admirable intention of providing justice for one criminal defendant, the Court not only pries open the door; it rules that respecting the privacy of the jury room, as our legal system has done for centuries, violates the Constitution. This is a startling development, and although the Court tries to limit the degree of intrusion, it is doubtful that there are principled grounds for preventing the expansion of today's holding.

The Court justifies its decision on the ground that the nature of the confidential communication at issue in this particular case — a clear expression of what the Court terms racial bias[1] — is uniquely harmful to our criminal justice system. And the Court is surely correct that even a tincture of racial bias can inflict great damage on that system, which is dependent on the public's trust. But until today, the argument that the Court now finds convincing has not been thought to be sufficient to overcome confidentiality rules like the one at issue here.

Suppose that a prosecution witness gives devastating but false testimony against a defendant, and suppose that the witness's motivation is racial bias. Suppose that the witness admits this to his attorney, his spouse, and a member of the clergy. Suppose that the defendant, threatened with conviction for a serious crime and a lengthy term of imprisonment, seeks to compel the attorney, the spouse, or the member of the clergy to testify about the witness's admissions. Even though the constitutional rights of the defendant hang in the balance, the defendant's efforts to obtain the testimony would fail. The Court provides no good reason why the result in this case should not be the same.

5.   Racial Classification Benefiting Minorities

Drawing Election Districts to Increase Minority Representation (casebook p. 878)

In *Cooper v. Harris*, the Supreme Court confronted whether and when the government can use race in drawing election districts. *Cooper v. Harris* seems particularly important because of the footnote in Justice Kagan's opinion that the use of race must meet strict scrutiny even if it is being considered as a proxy for political party affiliation. In light of this, *it* is unclear whether and to what extent *Easley v. Cromartie* (casebook p. 880) remains good law.

COOPER v. HARRIS
137 S. Ct. 1455 (2017)

Justice KAGAN delivered the opinion of the Court.

The Constitution entrusts States with the job of designing congressional districts. But it also imposes an important constraint: A State may not use race as the predominant factor in drawing district lines unless it has a compelling reason. In this case, a three-judge District Court ruled that North Carolina officials violated that bar when they created two districts whose voting-age populations were majority black. Applying a deferential standard of review to the factual findings underlying that decision, we affirm.

I

A

The Equal Protection Clause of the Fourteenth Amendment limits racial gerrymanders in legislative districting plans. It prevents a State, in the absence of "sufficient justification," from "separating its citizens into different voting districts on the basis of race." When a voter sues state officials for drawing such race-based lines, our decisions call for a two-step analysis.

First, the plaintiff must prove that "race was the predominant factor motivating the legislature's decision to place a significant number of voters within or without a particular district." That entails demonstrating that the legislature "subordinated" other factors — compactness, respect for political subdivisions, partisan advantage, what have you — to "racial considerations." The plaintiff may make the required showing through "direct evidence" of legislative intent, "circumstantial evidence of a district's shape and demographics," or a mix of both.

Second, if racial considerations predominated over others, the design of the district must withstand strict scrutiny. The burden thus shifts to the State to prove that its race-based sorting of voters serves a "compelling interest" and is "narrowly tailored" to that end. This Court has long assumed that one compelling interest is complying with operative provisions of the Voting Rights Act of 1965 (VRA or Act). When a State invokes the VRA to justify race-based districting, it must show (to meet the "narrow tailoring" requirement) that it had "a strong basis in evidence" for concluding that the statute required its action. Or said otherwise, the State must establish that it had "good reasons" to think that it would transgress the Act if it did *not* draw race-based district lines. That "strong basis" (or "good reasons") standard gives States "breathing room" to adopt reasonable compliance measures that may prove, in perfect hindsight, not to have been needed.

A district court's assessment of a districting plan, in accordance with the two-step inquiry just described, warrants significant deference on appeal to this Court. We of course retain full power to correct a court's errors of law, at either stage of the analysis. But the court's findings of fact — most notably, as to whether racial considerations predominated in drawing district lines — are subject to review only for clear error. Under that standard, we may not reverse just because we "would have decided the [matter] differently." A finding that is "plausible" in light of the full record — even if another is equally or more so — must govern.

B

This case concerns North Carolina's most recent redrawing of two congressional districts, both of which have long included substantial populations of black voters. In its current incarnation, District 1 is anchored in the northeastern part of the State, with appendages stretching both south and west (the latter into Durham). District 12 begins in the south-central part of the State (where it takes in a large part of Charlotte) and then travels northeast, zig-zagging much of the way to the State's northern border. Both have quite the history before this Court.

Registered voters in the two districts (David Harris and Christine Bowser, here called "the plaintiffs") brought this suit against North Carolina officials (collectively, "the State" or "North Carolina"), complaining of impermissible racial gerrymanders. After a bench trial, a three-judge District Court held both districts unconstitutional. All the judges agreed that racial considerations predominated in the design of District 1. And in then applying strict scrutiny, all rejected the State's argument that it had a "strong basis" for thinking that the VRA compelled such a race-based drawing of District 1's lines. As for District 12, a majority of the panel held that "race predominated" over all other factors, including partisanship.

[II]

[W]e turn to the merits of this case, beginning (appropriately enough) with District 1. As noted above, the court below found that race furnished the predominant rationale for that district's redesign. And it held that the State's interest in complying with the VRA could not justify that consideration of race. We uphold both conclusions.

Uncontested evidence in the record shows that the State's mapmakers, in considering District 1, purposefully established a racial target: African-Americans should make up no less than a majority of the voting-age population. The result is a district with stark racial borders: Within the same counties, the portions that fall inside District 1 have black populations two to three times larger than the portions placed in neighboring districts. Faced with this body of evidence — showing an announced racial target that subordinated other districting criteria and produced boundaries amplifying divisions between blacks and whites — the District Court did not clearly err in finding that race predominated in drawing District 1. Indeed, as all three judges recognized, the court could hardly have concluded anything but.

The more substantial question is whether District 1 can survive the strict scrutiny applied to racial gerrymanders. As noted earlier, we have long assumed that complying with the VRA is a compelling interest. And we have held that race-based districting is narrowly tailored to that objective if a State had "good reasons" for thinking that the Act demanded such steps.

This Court identified, in *Thornburg v. Gingles*, three threshold conditions for proving vote dilution under § 2 of the VRA. First, a "minority group" must be "sufficiently large and geographically compact to constitute a majority" in some reasonably configured legislative district. Second, the minority group must be "politically cohesive." And third, a district's white majority must "vote [ ] sufficiently as a bloc" to usually "defeat the minority's preferred candidate." *Ibid*. Those three showings, we have explained, are needed to establish that "the minority [group] has the potential to elect a representative of its own choice" in a possible district, but that racially polarized voting prevents it from doing so in the district as actually drawn because it is "submerg[ed] in a larger white voting population." If a State has good reason to think that all the "*Gingles* preconditions" are met, then so too it has good reason to believe that § 2 requires drawing a majority-minority district. But if not, then not.

Here, electoral history provided no evidence that a § 2 plaintiff could demonstrate the third *Gingles* prerequisite—effective white bloc-voting. For most of the twenty years prior to the new plan's adoption, African-Americans had made up less than a majority of District 1's voters . . . . So experience gave the State no reason to think that the VRA required it to ramp up District 1's BVAP.

Thus, North Carolina's belief that it was compelled to redraw District 1 (a successful crossover district) as a majority-minority district rested not on a "strong basis in evidence," but instead on a pure error of law. In sum: Although States enjoy leeway to take race-based actions reasonably judged necessary under a proper interpretation of the VRA, that latitude cannot rescue District 1. We by no means "insist that a state legislature, when redistricting, determine *precisely* what percent minority population [§ 2 of the VRA] demands." But neither will we approve a racial gerrymander whose necessity is supported by no evidence and whose *raison d'être* is a legal mistake. Accordingly, we uphold the District Court's conclusion that North Carolina's use of race as the predominant factor in designing District 1 does not withstand strict scrutiny.

[III]

We now look west to District 12, making its fifth(!) appearance before this Court. [T]he State altogether denied that racial considerations accounted for (or, indeed, played the slightest role in) District 12's redesign.

According to the State's version of events, Senator Rucho, Representative Lewis, and Dr. Hofeller moved voters in and out of the district as part of a "strictly" political gerrymander, without regard to race. The mapmakers drew their lines, in other words, to "pack" District 12 with Democrats, not African-Americans. After hearing evidence supporting both parties' accounts, the District Court accepted the plaintiffs'.

Getting to the bottom of a dispute like this one poses special challenges for a trial court. In the more usual case alleging a racial gerrymander—where no one has raised a partisanship defense—the court can make real headway by exploring the challenged district's conformity to traditional districting principles, such as compactness and respect for county lines. But such evidence loses much of its value when the State asserts partisanship as a defense, because a bizarre shape—as of the new District 12—can arise from a "political motivation" as well as a racial one. And crucially, political and racial reasons are capable of yielding similar oddities in a district's boundaries. That is because, of course, "racial identification is highly correlated with political affiliation." As a result of those redistricting realities, a trial court has a formidable task: It must make "a sensitive inquiry" into all "circumstantial and direct evidence of intent" to assess whether the plaintiffs have managed to disentangle race from politics and prove that the former drove a district's lines.[7]

Our job is different—and generally easier. As described earlier, we review a district court's finding as to racial predominance only for clear error, except when the court made a legal mistake. Under that standard of review, we affirm the court's finding so long as it is "plausible"; we reverse only when "left with the definite and firm conviction that a mistake has been committed." And in deciding which side of that line to come down on, we give singular deference to a trial court's judgments about the credibility of witnesses. That is proper, we have explained, because the various cues that "bear so heavily on the listener's understanding of and belief in what is said" are lost on an appellate court later sifting through a paper record.

---

7. As earlier noted, that inquiry is satisfied when legislators have "place[d] a significant number of voters within or without" a district predominantly because of their race, regardless of their ultimate objective in taking that step. So, for example, if legislators use race as their predominant districting criterion with the end goal of advancing their partisan interests—perhaps thinking that a proposed district is more "sellable" as a race-based VRA compliance measure than as a political gerrymander and will accomplish much the same thing—their action still triggers strict scrutiny. In other words, the sorting of voters on the grounds of their race remains suspect even if race is meant to function as a proxy for other (including political) characteristics. [Footnote by Justice Kagan.]

In light of those principles, we uphold the District Court's finding of racial predominance respecting District 12. The evidence offered at trial, including live witness testimony subject to credibility determinations, adequately supports the conclusion that race, not politics, accounted for the district's reconfiguration. And no error of law infected that judgment: Contrary to North Carolina's view, the District Court had no call to dismiss this challenge just because the plaintiffs did not proffer an alternative design for District 12 as circumstantial evidence of the legislature's intent.

The State mounts a final, legal rather than factual, attack on the District Court's finding of racial predominance. When race and politics are competing explanations of a district's lines, argues North Carolina, the party challenging the district must introduce a particular kind of circumstantial evidence: "an alternative [map] that achieves the legislature's political objectives while improving racial balance." That is true, the State says, irrespective of what other evidence is in the case—so even if the plaintiff offers powerful direct proof that the legislature adopted the map it did for racial reasons. Because the plaintiffs here (as all agree) did not present such a counter-map, North Carolina concludes that they cannot prevail. The dissent echoes that argument.

We have no doubt that an alternative districting plan, of the kind North Carolina describes, can serve as key evidence in a race-versus-politics dispute. One, often highly persuasive way to disprove a State's contention that politics drove a district's lines is to show that the legislature had the capacity to accomplish all its partisan goals without moving so many members of a minority group into the district. If you were *really* sorting by political behavior instead of skin color (so the argument goes) you would have done—or, at least, could just as well have done—*this*. Such would-have, could-have, and (to round out the set) should-have arguments are a familiar means of undermining a claim that an action was based on a permissible, rather than a prohibited, ground.

But they are hardly the *only* means. Suppose that the plaintiff in a dispute like this one introduced scores of leaked emails from state officials instructing their mapmaker to pack as many black voters as possible into a district, or telling him to make sure its BVAP hit 75%. Based on such evidence, a court could find that racial rather than political factors predominated in a district's design, with or without an alternative map. And so too in cases lacking that kind of smoking gun, as long as the evidence offered satisfies the plaintiff's burden of proof. Similarly, it does not matter in this case, where the plaintiffs' introduction of mostly direct and some circumstantial evidence—documents issued in the redistricting process, testimony of government officials, expert analysis of demographic patterns—gave the District Court a sufficient basis, sans any map, to resolve the race-or-politics question.

Plaintiff's task, in other words, is simply to persuade the trial court—without any special evidentiary prerequisite—that race (not politics) was the "predominant consideration in deciding to place a significant number of voters within or without a particular district." That burden of proof, we have often held, is "demanding." And because that is so, a plaintiff will sometimes need an alternative map, as a practical matter, to make his case. But in no area of our equal protection law have we forced plaintiffs to submit one particular form of proof to prevail. Nor would it make sense to do so here. The Equal Protection Clause prohibits the unjustified drawing of district lines based on race. An alternative map is merely an evidentiary tool to show that such a substantive violation has occurred; neither its presence nor its absence can itself resolve a racial gerrymandering claim.

V

Applying a clear error standard, we uphold the District Court's conclusions that racial considerations predominated in designing both District 1 and District 12. For District 12, that is all we must do, because North Carolina has made no attempt to justify race-based districting there. For District 1, we further uphold the District Court's decision that § 2 of the VRA gave North Carolina no good reason to reshuffle voters because of their race.

Justice THOMAS, concurring.

I join the opinion of the Court because it correctly applies our precedents under the Constitution and the Voting Rights Act of 1965 (VRA). I write briefly to explain the additional grounds on which I would affirm the three-judge District Court and to note my agreement, in particular, with the Court's clear-error analysis.

As to District 1, I think North Carolina's concession that it created the district as a majority-black district is by itself sufficient to trigger strict scrutiny. I also think that North Carolina cannot satisfy strict scrutiny based on its efforts to comply with § 2 of the VRA. In my view, § 2 does not apply to redistricting and therefore cannot justify a racial gerrymander.

As to District 12, I agree with the Court that the District Court did not clearly err when it determined that race was North Carolina's predominant motive in drawing the district. This is the same conclusion I reached when we last reviewed District 12. *Easley v. Cromartie* (2001) (*Cromartie II*) (dissenting opinion).

Justice ALITO, with whom THE CHIEF JUSTICE and Justice KENNEDY join, concurring in the judgment in part and dissenting in part.

A precedent of this Court should not be treated like a disposable household item — say, a paper plate or napkin — to be used once and then tossed in the trash. But that is what the Court does today in its decision regarding North Carolina's 12th Congressional District: The Court junks a rule adopted in a prior, remarkably similar challenge to this very same congressional district.

In *Easley v. Cromartie* (2001) (*Cromartie II*), the Court considered the constitutionality of the version of District 12 that was adopted in 1997. That district had the same basic shape as the district now before us, and the challengers argued that the legislature's predominant reason for adopting this configuration was race. The State responded that its motive was not race but politics. Its objective, the State insisted, was to create a district in which the Democratic candidate would win. Rejecting that explanation, a three-judge court found that the legislature's predominant motive was racial, specifically to pack African-Americans into District 12. But this Court held that this finding of fact was clearly erroneous.

A critical factor in our analysis was the failure of those challenging the district to come forward with an alternative redistricting map that served the legislature's political objective as well as the challenged version without producing the same racial effects. Noting that race and party affiliation in North Carolina were "highly correlated," we laid down this rule:

"In a case such as this one . . . the party attacking the legislatively drawn boundaries must show at the least that the legislature could have achieved its legitimate political objectives in alternative ways that are comparably consistent with traditional districting principles. That party must also show that those districting alternatives would have brought about significantly greater racial balance. Appellees failed to make any such showing here."

Now, District 12 is back before us. After the 2010 census, the North Carolina Legislature, with the Republicans in the majority, drew the present version of District 12. The challengers contend that this version violates equal protection because the predominant motive of the legislature was racial: to pack the district with African-American voters. The legislature responds that its objective was political: to pack the district with Democrats and thus to increase the chances of Republican candidates in neighboring districts.

You might think that the *Cromartie II* rule would be equally applicable in this case, which does not differ in any relevant particular, but the majority executes a stunning about-face. Now, the challengers' failure to produce an alternative map that meets the *Cromartie II* test is inconsequential. It simply "does not matter."

This is not the treatment of precedent that state legislatures have the right to expect from this Court. The failure to produce an alternative map doomed the challengers in *Cromartie II*, and the same should be true now. Partisan gerrymandering is always unsavory, but that is not the issue here. The issue is whether District 12 was drawn predominantly because of race. The record shows that it was not.

The alternative-map requirement deserves better. It is a logical response to the difficult problem of distinguishing between racial and political motivations when race and political party preference closely correlate. This is a problem with serious institutional and federalism implications. When a federal court says that race was a legislature's predominant purpose in drawing a district, it accuses the legislature of "offensive and demeaning" conduct. Indeed, we have said that racial gerrymanders "bea[r] an uncomfortable resemblance to political apartheid." That is a grave accusation to level against a state legislature.

In addition, "[f]ederal-court review of districting legislation represents a serious intrusion on the most vital of local functions" because "[i]t is well settled that reapportionment is primarily the duty and responsibility of the State." When a federal court finds that race predominated in the redistricting process, it inserts itself into that process. That is appropriate — indeed, constitutionally required — if the legislature truly did draw district boundaries on the basis of race. But if a court mistakes a political gerrymander for a racial gerrymander, it illegitimately invades a traditional domain of state authority, usurping the role of a State's elected representatives. This does violence to both the proper role of the Judiciary and the powers reserved to the States under the Constitution.

There is a final, often-unstated danger where race and politics correlate: that the federal courts will be transformed into weapons of political warfare. Unless courts "exercise extraordinary caution" in distinguishing race-based redistricting from politics-based redistricting, they will invite the losers in the redistricting process to seek to obtain in court what they could not achieve in the political arena. If the majority party draws districts to favor itself, the minority party can deny the majority its political victory by prevailing on a racial gerrymandering claim. Even if the minority party loses in court, it can exact a heavy price by using the judicial process to engage in political trench warfare for years on end.

The majority nevertheless absolves the challengers of their failure to submit an alternative map. It argues that an alternative map cannot be "the *only* means" of proving racial predominance, and it concludes from this that an alternative map "does not matter in this case." But even if there are cases in which a plaintiff could prove a racial gerrymandering claim without an alternative map, they would be exceptional ones in which the evidence of racial predominance is overwhelming. This most definitely is not one of those cases, and the plaintiffs' failure to produce an alternative map mandates reversal. Moreover, even in an exceptional case, the absence of such a map would still be strong evidence that a district's boundaries were determined by politics rather than race.

Even if we set aside the challengers' failure to submit an alternative map, the District Court's finding that race predominated in the drawing of District 12 is clearly erroneous. The State offered strong and coherent evidence that politics, not race, was the legislature's predominant aim, and the evidence supporting the District Court's contrary finding is weak and manifestly inadequate in light of the high evidentiary standard that our cases require challengers to meet in order to prove racial predominance.

Chapter 8

Fundamental Rights Under Due Process and Equal Protection

C. Constitutional Protection for Family Autonomy

1. The Right to Marry (casebook p. 955)

In *Obergefell v. Hodges* (casebook p. 967), the Court held that gay and lesbian couples have the same right to marry as opposite sex couples. In *Pavan v. Smith*, the Court reversed — without briefs or oral arguments — an Arkansas Supreme Court decision preventing lesbian couples from listing both parents on the birth certificate. But three justices dissented.

PAVAN v. SMITH
137 S. Ct. 2075 (2017)

PER CURIAM.

As this Court explained in *Obergefell v. Hodges* (2015), the Constitution entitles same-sex couples to civil marriage "on the same terms and conditions as opposite-sex couples." In the decision below, the Arkansas Supreme Court considered the effect of that holding on the State's rules governing the issuance of birth certificates. When a married woman gives birth in Arkansas, state law generally requires the name of the mother's male spouse to appear on the child's birth certificate — regardless of his biological relationship to the child. According to the court below, however, Arkansas need not extend that rule to similarly situated same-sex couples: The State need not, in other words, issue birth certificates including the female spouses of women who give birth in the State. Because that differential treatment infringes *Obergefell*'s commitment to provide same-sex couples "the constellation of benefits that the States have linked to marriage," we reverse the state court's judgment.

The petitioners here are two married same-sex couples who conceived children through anonymous sperm donation. Leigh and Jana Jacobs were married in Iowa in 2010, and Terrah and Marisa Pavan were married in New Hampshire in 2011. Leigh and Terrah each gave birth to a child in Arkansas in 2015. When it came time to secure birth certificates for the newborns, each couple filled out paperwork listing both spouses as parents — Leigh and Jana in one case, Terrah and Marisa in the other. Both times, however, the Arkansas Department of Health issued certificates bearing only the birth mother's name.

The department's decision rested on a provision of Arkansas law, Ark. Code § 20-18-401(2014), that specifies which individuals will appear as parents on a child's state-issued birth certificate. "For the purposes of birth registration," that statute says, "the mother is deemed to be the woman who gives birth to the child." And "[i]f the mother was married at the time of either conception or birth," the statute instructs that "the name of [her] husband shall be entered on the certificate as the father of the child." There are some limited exceptions to the latter rule — for example, another man may appear on the birth certificate if the "mother" and "husband" and "putative father" all file affidavits vouching for the putative father's paternity. But as all parties agree, the requirement that a married woman's husband appear on her child's birth certificate applies in cases where the couple conceived by means of artificial insemination with the help of an anonymous sperm donor.

The Jacobses and Pavans brought this suit in Arkansas state court against the director of the Arkansas Department of Health — seeking, among other things, a declaration that the State's birth-certificate law violates the Constitution. The trial court agreed, holding that the relevant portions of § 20-18-401 are inconsistent with *Obergefell* because they "categorically prohibi[t] every same-sex married couple . . . from enjoying the same spousal benefits which are available to every opposite-sex married couple." But a divided Arkansas Supreme Court reversed that judgment, concluding that the statute "pass[es] constitutional muster." In that court's view, "the statute centers on the relationship of the biological mother and the biological father to the child, not on the marital relationship of husband and wife," and so it "does not run afoul of *Obergefell*."

The Arkansas Supreme Court's decision, we conclude, denied married same-sex couples access to the "constellation of benefits that the Stat [e] ha[s] linked to marriage." As already explained, when a married woman in Arkansas conceives a child by means of artificial insemination, the State will — indeed, *must* — list the name of her male spouse on the child's birth certificate. And yet state law, as interpreted by the court below, allows

Arkansas officials in those very same circumstances to omit a married woman's female spouse from her child's birth certificate. As a result, same-sex parents in Arkansas lack the same right as opposite-sex parents to be listed on a child's birth certificate, a document often used for important transactions like making medical decisions for a child or enrolling a child in school.

Obergefell proscribes such disparate treatment. As we explained there, a State may not "exclude same-sex couples from civil marriage on the same terms and conditions as opposite-sex couples." Indeed, in listing those terms and conditions—the "rights, benefits, and responsibilities" to which same-sex couples, no less than opposite-sex couples, must have access—we expressly identified "birth and death certificates." That was no accident: Several of the plaintiffs in *Obergefell* challenged a State's refusal to recognize their same-sex spouses on their children's birth certificates. In considering those challenges, we held the relevant state laws unconstitutional to the extent they treated same-sex couples differently from opposite-sex couples. That holding applies with equal force to § 20-18-401.

Arkansas has thus chosen to make its birth certificates more than a mere marker of biological relationships: The State uses those certificates to give married parents a form of legal recognition that is not available to unmarried parents. Having made that choice, Arkansas may not, consistent with *Obergefell*, deny married same-sex couples that recognition.

Justice GORSUCH, with whom Justice THOMAS and Justice ALITO join, dissenting.

Summary reversal is usually reserved for cases where "the law is settled and stable, the facts are not in dispute, and the decision below is clearly in error." Respectfully, I don't believe this case meets that standard.

To be sure, *Obergefell* addressed the question whether a State must recognize same-sex marriages. But nothing in *Obergefell* spoke (let alone clearly) to the question whether § 20-18-401 of the Arkansas Code, or a state supreme court decision upholding it, must go. The statute in question establishes a set of rules designed to ensure that the biological parents of a child are listed on the child's birth certificate. Before the state supreme court, the State argued that rational reasons exist for a biology based birth registration regime, reasons that in no way offend *Obergefell*—like ensuring government officials can identify public health trends and helping individuals determine their biological lineage, citizenship, or susceptibility to genetic disorders. In an opinion that did not in any way seek to defy but rather earnestly engage *Obergefell*, the state supreme court agreed. And it is very hard to see what is wrong with this conclusion for, just as the state court recognized, nothing in *Obergefell* indicates that a birth registration regime based on biology, one no doubt with many analogues across the country and throughout history, offends the Constitution. To the contrary, to the extent they speak to the question at all, this Court's precedents suggest just the opposite conclusion. Neither does anything in today's opinion purport to identify any constitutional problem with a biology based birth registration regime. So whatever else we might do with this case, summary reversal would not exactly seem the obvious course.

Given all this, it seems far from clear what here warrants the strong medicine of summary reversal. Indeed, it is not even clear what the Court expects to happen on remand that hasn't happened already. The Court does not offer any remedial suggestion, and none leaps to mind. Perhaps the state supreme court could memorialize the State's concession on § 9-10-201, even though that law wasn't fairly challenged and such a chore is hardly the usual reward for seeking faithfully to apply, not evade, this Court's mandates.

D.   *Constitutional Protection for Reproductive Autonomy*

3.   The Right to Abortion (casebook p. 1014)

In *Box v. Planned Parenthood of Indiana and Kentucky*, 139 S. Ct. 1780 (2019), the federal district enjoined Indiana laws regulating abortion providers' disposition of fetal remains and prohibiting abortion providers from knowingly providing selective abortions based on sex, race, or disability. The Seventh Circuit affirmed. The Supreme Court said: "We reverse the judgment of the Seventh Circuit with respect to the first question presented, and we deny the petition with respect to the second question presented."

As for the law regulating disposal of fetal remains, the law "altered the manner in which abortion providers may dispose of fetal remains. Among other changes, it excluded fetal remains from the definition of infectious and pathological waste, thereby preventing incineration of fetal remains along with surgical byproducts. It also authorized simultaneous cremation of fetal remains, which Indiana does not generally allow for human remains. The law did not affect a woman's right under existing law "to determine the final disposition of the aborted fetus."

The Supreme Court, in a *per curium* opinion without briefing or oral argument, reversed the Seventh Circuit. The Court explained: "Respondents have never argued that Indiana's law creates an undue burden on a woman's right to obtain an abortion. Respondents have instead litigated this case on the assumption that the law does not implicate a fundamental right and is therefore subject only to ordinary rational basis review.

"This Court has already acknowledged that a State has a 'legitimate interest in proper disposal of fetal remains.' The Seventh Circuit clearly erred in failing to recognize that interest as a permissible basis for Indiana's disposition law. The only remaining question, then, is whether Indiana's law is rationally related to the State's interest in proper disposal of fetal remains. We conclude that it is, even if it is not perfectly tailored to that end. We therefore uphold Indiana's law under rational basis review."

Justice Thomas wrote a concurring opinion to say that he would uphold the part of the Indiana law that prohibits abortions based on race, sex, or disability. He stressed the relationship of abortion to the eugenics movement. He concluded: "Enshrining a constitutional right to an abortion based solely on the race, sex, or disability of an unborn child, as Planned Parenthood advocates, would constitutionalize the views of the 20th-century eugenics movement. In other contexts, the Court has been zealous in vindicating the rights of people even potentially subjected to race, sex, and disability discrimination."

Justice Ginsburg concurred in part and dissented in part. She would have denied the entire petition for certiorari (which also was Justice Sotomayor's position). She said that "'rational basis' is not the proper review standard. This case implicates 'the right of [a] woman to choose to have an abortion before viability and to obtain it without undue interference from the State."

Chapter 9

First Amendment: Freedom of Expression

B. Free Speech Methodology

1. The Distinction Between Content-Based and Content-Neutral Laws (casebook p. 1244)

In *Matal v. Tam*, the Court considered whether it violated the First Amendment to deny a band the ability to register its name as a trademark because it was racially offensive. Notice all of the justices agree that this is unconstitutional because it is viewpoint discrimination.

MATAL v. TAM
138 S. Ct. 1744 (2017)

Justice ALITO announced the judgment of the Court and delivered the opinion of the Court with respect to Parts I, II, and III-A, and an opinion with respect to Parts III-B, III-C, and IV, in which THE CHIEF JUSTICE, Justice THOMAS, and Justice BREYER join.

This case concerns a dance-rock band's application for federal trademark registration of the band's name, "The Slants." "Slants" is a derogatory term for persons of Asian descent, and members of the band are Asian-Americans. But the band members believe that by taking that slur as the name of their group, they will help to "reclaim" the term and drain its denigrating force.

The Patent and Trademark Office (PTO) denied the application based on a provision of federal law prohibiting the registration of trademarks that may "disparage . . . or bring . . . into contemp[t] or disrepute" any "persons, living or dead." We now hold that this provision violates the Free Speech Clause of the First Amendment. It offends a bedrock First Amendment principle: Speech may not be banned on the ground that it expresses ideas that offend.

I

"The principle underlying trademark protection is that distinctive marks—words, names, symbols, and the like—can help distinguish a particular artisan's goods from those of others." A trademark "designate [s] the goods as the product of a particular trader" and "protect[s] his good will against the sale of another's product as his." It helps consumers identify goods and services that they wish to purchase, as well as those they want to avoid.

"[F]ederal law does not create trademarks." Trademarks and their precursors have ancient origins, and trademarks were protected at common law and in equity at the time of the founding of our country. The foundation of current federal trademark law is the Lanham Act, enacted in 1946. Under the Lanham Act, trademarks that are "used in commerce" may be placed on the "principal register," that is, they may be federally registered. There are now more than two million marks that have active federal certificates of registration. This system of federal registration helps to ensure that trademarks are fully protected and supports the free flow of commerce. "[N]ational protection of trademarks is desirable," we have explained, "because trademarks foster competition and the maintenance of quality by securing to the producer the benefits of good reputation."

Without federal registration, a valid trademark may still be used in commerce. And an unregistered trademark can be enforced against would-be infringers in several ways. Most important, even if a trademark is not federally registered, it may still be enforceable under § 43(a) of the Lanham Act, which creates a federal cause of action for trademark infringement. And an unregistered trademark can be enforced under state common law, or if it has been registered in a State, under that State's registration system.

Federal registration, however, "confers important legal rights and benefits on trademark owners who register their marks." Registration on the principal register (1) "serves as 'constructive notice of the registrant's claim of ownership' of the mark," (2) "is 'prima facie evidence of the validity of the registered mark and of the registration of the mark, of the owner's ownership of the mark, and of the owner's exclusive right to use the registered mark in commerce on or in connection with the goods or services specified in the certificate,'" and (3) can make a mark "'incontestable'" once a mark has been registered for five years. Registration also enables the trademark holder "to stop the importation into the United States of articles bearing an infringing mark."

The Lanham Act contains provisions that bar certain trademarks from the principal register. For example, a trademark cannot be registered if it is "merely descriptive or deceptively misdescriptive" of goods, or if it is so similar to an already registered trademark or trade name that it is "likely . . . to cause confusion, or to cause mistake, or to deceive." At issue in this case is one such provision, which we will call "the disparagement clause." This provision prohibits the registration of a trademark "which may disparage . . . persons, living or dead, institutions, beliefs, or national symbols, or bring them into contempt, or disrepute." § 1052(a). This clause appeared in the original Lanham Act and has remained the same to this day.

Simon Tam is the lead singer of "The Slants." He chose this moniker in order to "reclaim" and "take ownership" of stereotypes about people of Asian ethnicity. The group "draws inspiration for its lyrics from childhood slurs and mocking nursery rhymes" and has given its albums names such as "The Yellow Album" and "Slanted Eyes, Slanted Hearts."

Tam sought federal registration of "THE SLANTS," on the principal register, but an examining attorney at the PTO rejected the request, finding that "there is . . . a substantial composite of persons who find the term in the applied-for mark offensive." The examining attorney relied in part on the fact that "numerous dictionaries define 'slants' or 'slant-eyes' as a derogatory or offensive term." The examining attorney also relied on a finding that "the band's name has been found offensive numerous times" — citing a performance that was canceled because of the band's moniker and the fact that "several bloggers and commenters to articles on the band have indicated that they find the term and the applied-for mark offensive." *Id.*, at 29-30.

Tam contested the denial of registration before the examining attorney and before the PTO's Trademark Trial and Appeal Board (TTAB) but to no avail.

II

[In Part II of the opinion the Court held that the statutory provision does prohibit trademarks that are disparaging to racial groups.]

III

Because the disparagement clause applies to marks that disparage the members of a racial or ethnic group, we must decide whether the clause violates the Free Speech Clause of the First Amendment. And at the outset, we must consider three arguments that would either eliminate any First Amendment protection or result in highly permissive rational-basis review. Specifically, the Government contends (1) that trademarks are government speech, not private speech, (2) that trademarks are a form of government subsidy, and (3) that the constitutionality of the disparagement clause should be tested under a new "government-program" doctrine. We address each of these arguments below.

A

The First Amendment prohibits Congress and other government entities and actors from "abridging the freedom of speech"; the First Amendment does not say that Congress and other government entities must abridge their own ability to speak freely. And our cases recognize that "[t]he Free Speech Clause . . . does not regulate government speech." When a government entity embarks on a course of action, it necessarily takes a particular viewpoint and rejects others. The Free Speech Clause does not require government to maintain viewpoint neutrality when its officers and employees speak about that venture.

But while the government-speech doctrine is important — indeed, essential — it is a doctrine that is susceptible to dangerous misuse. If private speech could be passed off as government speech by simply affixing a government seal of approval, government could silence or muffle the expression of disfavored viewpoints. For this reason, we must exercise great caution before extending our government-speech precedents.

At issue here is the content of trademarks that are registered by the PTO, an arm of the Federal Government. The Federal Government does not dream up these marks, and it does not edit marks submitted for registration. Except as required by the statute involved here, an examiner may not reject a mark based on the viewpoint that it appears to express. Thus, unless that section is thought to apply, an examiner does not inquire whether any viewpoint conveyed by a mark is consistent with Government policy or whether any such viewpoint is consistent with that expressed by other marks already on the principal register. Instead, if the mark meets the Lanham Act's viewpoint-neutral requirements, registration is mandatory. And if an examiner finds that a mark is eligible for placement on the principal register, that decision is not reviewed by any higher official unless the registration is challenged.

In light of all this, it is far-fetched to suggest that the content of a registered mark is government speech. If the federal registration of a trademark makes the mark government speech, the Federal Government is babbling prodigiously and incoherently. It is saying many unseemly things. It is expressing contradictory views. It is unashamedly endorsing a vast array of commercial products and services.

None of our government speech cases even remotely supports the idea that registered trademarks are government speech.

[T]rademarks often have an expressive content. Companies spend huge amounts to create and publicize trademarks that convey a message. It is true that the necessary brevity of trademarks limits what they can say. But powerful messages can sometimes be conveyed in just a few words. Trademarks are private, not government, speech.

B

We next address the Government's argument that this case is governed by cases in which this Court has upheld the constitutionality of government programs that subsidized speech expressing a particular viewpoint. These cases implicate a notoriously tricky question of constitutional law. "[W]e have held that the Government 'may not deny a benefit to a person on a basis that infringes his constitutionally protected . . . freedom of speech even if he has no entitlement to that benefit.'" But at the same time, government is not required to subsidize activities that it does not wish to promote. Determining which of these principles applies in a particular case "is not always self-evident," but no difficult question is presented here.

Unlike the present case, the decisions on which the Government relies all involved cash subsidies or their equivalent. The federal registration of a trademark is nothing like the programs at issue in these cases. The PTO does not pay money to parties seeking registration of a mark. Quite the contrary is true: An applicant for registration must pay the PTO a filing fee of $225-$600. And to maintain federal registration, the holder of a mark must pay a fee of $300-$500 every 10 years.

The Government responds that registration provides valuable non-monetary benefits that "are directly traceable to the resources devoted by the federal government to examining, publishing, and issuing certificates of registration for those marks." But just about every government service requires the expenditure of government funds. This is true of services that benefit everyone, like police and fire protection, as well as services that are utilized by only some, *e.g.*, the adjudication of private lawsuits and the use of public parks and highways.

Trademark registration is not the only government registration scheme. For example, the Federal Government registers copyrights and patents. State governments and their subdivisions register the title to real property and security interests; they issue driver's licenses, motor vehicle registrations, and hunting, fishing, and boating licenses or permits.

C

Finally, the Government urges us to sustain the disparagement clause under a new doctrine that would apply to "government-program" cases. For the most part, this argument simply merges our government-speech cases and the previously discussed subsidy cases in an attempt to construct a broader doctrine that can be applied to the registration of trademarks. The only new element in this construct consists of two cases involving a public employer's collection of union dues from its employees. But those cases occupy a special area of First Amendment case law, and they are far removed from the registration of trademarks.

Potentially more analogous are cases in which a unit of government creates a limited public forum for private speech. When government creates such a forum, in either a literal or "metaphysical" sense, some content- and speaker-based restrictions may be allowed. However, even in such cases, what we have termed "viewpoint discrimination" is forbidden.

Our cases use the term "viewpoint" discrimination in a broad sense, and in that sense, the disparagement clause discriminates on the bases of "viewpoint." To be sure, the clause evenhandedly prohibits disparagement of all groups. It applies equally to marks that damn Democrats and Republicans, capitalists and socialists, and those arrayed on both sides of every possible issue. It denies registration to any mark that is offensive to a substantial percentage of the members of any group. But in the sense relevant here, that is viewpoint discrimination: Giving offense is a viewpoint.

We have said time and again that "the public expression of ideas may not be prohibited merely because the ideas are themselves offensive to some of their hearers." For this reason, the disparagement clause cannot be saved by analyzing it as a type of government program in which some content- and speaker-based restrictions are permitted.

IV

Having concluded that the disparagement clause cannot be sustained under our government-speech or subsidy cases or under the Government's proposed "government-program" doctrine, we must confront a dispute between the parties on the question whether trademarks are commercial speech and are thus subject to the relaxed scrutiny outlined in *Central Hudson Gas & Elec. Corp. v. Public Serv. Comm'n of N.Y.* (1980). The Government and *amici* supporting its position argue that all trademarks are commercial speech. They note that the central purposes of trademarks are commercial and that federal law regulates trademarks to promote fair and orderly interstate commerce. Tam and his *amici*, on the other hand, contend that many, if not all, trademarks have an expressive component. In other words, these trademarks do not simply identify the source of a product or service but go on to say something more, either about the product or service or some broader issue. The trademark in this case illustrates this point. The name "The Slants" not only identifies the band but expresses a view about social issues.

We need not resolve this debate between the parties because the disparagement clause cannot withstand even *Central Hudson* review. Under *Central Hudson*, a restriction of speech must serve "a substantial interest," and it must be "narrowly drawn." This means, among other things, that "[t]he regulatory technique may extend only as far as the interest it serves." The disparagement clause fails this requirement.

It is claimed that the disparagement clause serves two interests. The first is phrased in a variety of ways in the briefs. Echoing language in one of the opinions below, the Government asserts an interest in preventing "underrepresented groups" from being "bombarded with demeaning messages in commercial advertising.'" But no matter how the point is phrased, its unmistakable thrust is this: The Government has an interest in preventing speech expressing ideas that offend. And, as we have explained, that idea strikes at the heart of the First Amendment. Speech that demeans on the basis of race, ethnicity, gender, religion, age, disability, or any other similar ground is hateful; but the proudest boast of our free speech jurisprudence is that we protect the freedom to express "the thought that we hate." *United States v. Schwimmer* (1929) (Holmes, J., dissenting).

The second interest asserted is protecting the orderly flow of commerce. Commerce, we are told, is disrupted by trademarks that "involv[e] disparagement of race, gender, ethnicity, national origin, religion, sexual orientation, and similar demographic classification." A simple answer to this argument is that the disparagement clause is not "narrowly drawn" to drive out trademarks that support invidious discrimination. The clause reaches any trademark that disparages *any person, group, or institution.* It applies to trademarks like the following: "Down with racists," "Down with sexists," "Down with homophobes." It is not an anti-discrimination clause; it is a happy-talk clause. In this way, it goes much further than is necessary to serve the interest asserted.

The clause is far too broad in other ways as well. The clause protects every person living or dead as well as every institution. Is it conceivable that commerce would be disrupted by a trademark saying: "James Buchanan was a disastrous president" or "Slavery is an evil institution"?

There is also a deeper problem with the argument that commercial speech may be cleansed of any expression likely to cause offense. The commercial market is well stocked with merchandise that disparages prominent figures and groups, and the line between commercial and non-commercial speech is not always clear, as this case illustrates. If affixing the commercial label permits the suppression of any speech that may lead to political or social "volatility," free speech would be endangered.

For these reasons, we hold that the disparagement clause violates the Free Speech Clause of the First Amendment.

Justice KENNEDY, with whom Justice GINSBURG, Justice SOTOMAYOR, and Justice KAGAN join, concurring in part and concurring in the judgment.

As the Court is correct to hold, § 1052(a) constitutes viewpoint discrimination—a form of speech suppression so potent that it must be subject to rigorous constitutional scrutiny. The Government's action and the statute on which it is based cannot survive this scrutiny.

The Court is correct in its judgment, and I join Parts I, II, and III-A of its opinion. This separate writing explains in greater detail why the First Amendment's protections against viewpoint discrimination apply to the trademark here. It submits further that the viewpoint discrimination rationale renders unnecessary any extended treatment of other questions raised by the parties.

I

Those few categories of speech that the government can regulate or punish—for instance, fraud, defamation, or incitement—are well established within our constitutional tradition. Aside from these and a few other narrow exceptions, it is a fundamental principle of the First Amendment that the government may not punish or suppress speech based on disapproval of the ideas or perspectives the speech conveys.

The First Amendment guards against laws "targeted at specific subject matter," a form of speech suppression known as content based discrimination. This category includes a subtype of laws that go further, aimed at the suppression of "particular views . . . on a subject." A law found to discriminate based on viewpoint is an "egregious form of content discrimination," which is "presumptively unconstitutional."

At its most basic, the test for viewpoint discrimination is whether—within the relevant subject category—the government has singled out a subset of messages for disfavor based on the views expressed. In the instant case, the disparagement clause the Government now seeks to implement and enforce identifies the relevant subject as "persons, living or dead, institutions, beliefs, or national symbols." Within that category, an applicant may register a positive or benign mark but not a derogatory one. The law thus reflects the Government's disapproval of a subset of messages it finds offensive. This is the essence of viewpoint discrimination.

The Government disputes this conclusion. It argues, to begin with, that the law is viewpoint neutral because it applies in equal measure to any trademark that demeans or offends. This misses the point. A subject that is first defined by content and then regulated or censored by mandating only one sort of comment is not viewpoint neutral. To prohibit all sides from criticizing their opponents makes a law more viewpoint based, not less so. The logic of the Government's rule is that a law would be viewpoint neutral even if it provided that public officials could be praised but not condemned. The First Amendment's viewpoint neutrality principle protects more than the right to identify with a particular side. It protects the right to create and present arguments for particular positions in particular ways, as the speaker chooses. By mandating positivity, the law here might silence dissent and distort the marketplace of ideas.

The Government next suggests that the statute is viewpoint neutral because the disparagement clause applies to trademarks regardless of the applicant's personal views or reasons for using the mark. Instead, registration is denied based on the expected reaction of the applicant's audience. The Government may not insulate a law from charges of viewpoint discrimination by tying censorship to the reaction of the speaker's audience. The Court has suggested that viewpoint discrimination occurs when the government intends to suppress a speaker's beliefs, but viewpoint discrimination need not take that form in every instance. The danger of viewpoint discrimination is that the government is attempting to remove certain ideas or perspectives from a broader debate. That danger is all the greater if the ideas or perspectives are ones a particular audience might think offensive, at least at first hearing. An initial reaction may prompt further reflection, leading to a more reasoned, more tolerant position.

Indeed, a speech burden based on audience reactions is simply government hostility and intervention in a different guise. The speech is targeted, after all, based on the government's disapproval of the speaker's choice of message. And it is the government itself that is attempting in this case to decide whether the relevant audience would find the speech offensive. For reasons like these, the Court's cases have long prohibited the government from justifying a First Amendment burden by pointing to the offensiveness of the speech to be suppressed.

II

The parties dispute whether trademarks are commercial speech and whether trademark registration should be considered a federal subsidy. The former issue may turn on whether certain commercial concerns for the protection of trademarks might, as a general matter, be the basis for regulation. However that issue is resolved, the viewpoint based discrimination at issue here necessarily invokes heightened scrutiny. "Commercial speech is no exception," the Court has explained, to the principle that the First Amendment "requires heightened scrutiny whenever the government creates a regulation of speech because of disagreement with the message it conveys." Unlike content based discrimination, discrimination based on viewpoint, including a regulation that targets speech for its offensiveness, remains of serious concern in the commercial context.

A law that can be directed against speech found offensive to some portion of the public can be turned against minority and dissenting views to the detriment of all. The First Amendment does not entrust that power to the government's benevolence. Instead, our reliance must be on the substantial safeguards of free and open discussion in a democratic society. For these reasons, I join the Court's opinion in part and concur in the judgment.

***

Two years after *Matal v. Tam*, the Court considered the constitutionality of another provision of the Lanham Act, one that prohibited registration of a trademark that is "scandalous" or "immoral." Once more, the Court found it to be impermissible viewpoint discrimination.

IANCU v. BRUNETTI
139 S. Ct. 2294 (2019)

Justice KAGAN delivered the opinion of the Court.

Two Terms ago, in *Matal v. Tam* (2017), this Court invalidated the Lanham Act's bar on the registration of "disparag[ing]" trademarks. Although split between two non-majority opinions, all Members of the Court agreed that the provision violated the First Amendment because it discriminated on the basis of viewpoint. Today we consider a First Amendment challenge to a neighboring provision of the Act, prohibiting the registration of "immoral[ ] or scandalous" trademarks. We hold that this provision infringes the First Amendment for the same reason: It too disfavors certain ideas.

I

Respondent Erik Brunetti is an artist and entrepreneur who founded a clothing line that uses the trademark FUCT. According to Brunetti, the mark (which functions as the clothing's brand name) is pronounced as four letters, one after the other: F-U-C-T. But you might read it differently and, if so, you would hardly be alone. That common perception caused difficulties for Brunetti when he tried to register his mark with the U.S. Patent and Trademark Office (PTO).

Under the Lanham Act, the PTO administers a federal registration system for trademarks. Registration of a mark is not mandatory. The owner of an unregistered mark may still use it in commerce and enforce it against infringers. But registration gives trademark owners valuable benefits. For example, registration constitutes "prima facie evidence" of the mark's validity. § 1115(a). And registration serves as "constructive notice of the registrant's claim of ownership," which forecloses some defenses in infringement actions. Generally, a trademark is eligible for registration, and receipt of such benefits, if it is "used in commerce." But the Act directs the PTO to "refuse[ ] registration" of certain marks. For instance, the PTO cannot register a mark that "so resembles" another mark as to create a likelihood of confusion. It cannot register a mark that is "merely descriptive" of the goods on which it is used. It cannot register a mark containing the flag or insignia of any nation or State. There are five or ten more (depending on how you count). And until we invalidated the criterion two years ago, the PTO could not register a mark that "disparage[d]" a "person[ ], living or dead."

This case involves another of the Lanham Act's prohibitions on registration — one applying to marks that "[c]onsist[ ] of or comprise[ ] immoral[ ] or scandalous matter." The PTO applies that bar as a "unitary provision," rather than treating the two adjectives in it separately. To determine whether a mark fits in the category, the PTO asks whether a "substantial composite of the general public" would find the mark "shocking to the sense of truth, decency, or propriety"; "giving offense to the conscience or moral feelings"; "calling out for condemnation"; "disgraceful"; "offensive"; "disreputable"; or "vulgar."

Both a PTO examining attorney and the PTO's Trademark Trial and Appeal Board decided that Brunetti's mark flunked that test. The attorney determined that FUCT was "a total vulgar" and "therefore[ ] unregistrable." On review, the Board stated that the mark was "highly offensive" and "vulgar," and that it had "decidedly negative sexual connotations." As part of its review, the Board also considered evidence of how Brunetti used the mark. It found that Brunetti's website and products contained imagery, near the mark, of "extreme nihilism" and "anti-social" behavior. In that context, the Board thought, the mark communicated "misogyny, depravity, [and] violence." The Board concluded: "Whether one considers [the mark] as a sexual term, or finds that [Brunetti] has used [the mark] in the context of extreme misogyny, nihilism or violence, we have no question but that [the term is] extremely offensive."

II

This Court first considered a First Amendment challenge to a trademark registration restriction in *Tam*, just two Terms ago. There, the Court declared unconstitutional the Lanham Act's ban on registering marks that "disparage" any "person[ ], living or dead." The Justices found common ground in a core postulate of free speech law: The government may not discriminate against speech based on the ideas or opinions it conveys. The bar violated the "bedrock First Amendment principle" that the government cannot discriminate against "ideas that offend." Viewpoint discrimination doomed the disparagement bar.

If the "immoral or scandalous" bar similarly discriminates on the basis of viewpoint, it must also collide with our First Amendment doctrine. So the key question becomes: Is the "immoral or scandalous" criterion in the Lanham Act viewpoint-neutral or viewpoint-based?

It is viewpoint-based. The meanings of "immoral" and "scandalous" are not mysterious, but resort to some dictionaries still helps to lay bare the problem. When is expressive material "immoral"? According to a standard definition, when it is "inconsistent with rectitude, purity, or good morals"; "wicked"; or "vicious." Webster's New International Dictionary 1246 (2d ed. 1949). Or again, when it is "opposed to or violating morality"; or "morally evil." Shorter Oxford English Dictionary 961 (3d ed. 1947). So the Lanham Act permits registration of marks that champion society's sense of rectitude and morality, but not marks that denigrate those concepts. And when is such material "scandalous"? Says a typical definition, when it "give[es] offense to the conscience or moral feelings"; "excite[s] reprobation"; or "call[s] out condemnation." Webster's New International Dictionary, at 2229. Or again, when it is "shocking to the sense of truth, decency, or propriety"; "disgraceful"; "offensive"; or "disreputable." Funk & Wagnalls New Standard Dictionary 2186 (1944). So the Lanham Act allows registration of marks when their messages accord with, but not when their messages defy, society's sense of decency or propriety.

Put the pair of overlapping terms together and the statute, on its face, distinguishes between two opposed sets of ideas: those aligned with conventional moral standards and those hostile to them; those inducing societal nods of approval and those provoking offense and condemnation. The statute favors the former, and disfavors the latter. "Love rules"? "Always be good"? Registration follows. "Hate rules"? "Always be cruel"? Not according to the Lanham Act's "immoral or scandalous" bar.

The facial viewpoint bias in the law results in viewpoint-discriminatory application. Recall that the PTO itself describes the "immoral or scandalous" criterion using much the same language as in the dictionary definitions recited above. The PTO, for example, asks whether the public would view the mark as "shocking to the sense of truth, decency, or propriety"; "calling out for condemnation"; "offensive"; or "disreputable." Using those guideposts, the PTO has refused to register marks communicating "immoral" or "scandalous" views about (among other things) drug use, religion, and terrorism. But all the while, it has approved registration of marks expressing more accepted views on the same topics.

Here are some samples. The PTO rejected marks conveying approval of drug use (YOU CAN'T SPELL HEALTHCARE WITHOUT THC for pain-relief medication, MARIJUANA COLA and KO KANE for beverages) because it is scandalous to "inappropriately glamoriz[e] drug abuse." But at the same time, the PTO registered marks with such sayings as D.A.R.E. TO RESIST DRUGS AND VIOLENCE and SAY NO TO DRUGS—REALITY IS THE BEST TRIP IN LIFE. Similarly, the PTO disapproved registration for the mark BONG HITS 4 JESUS because it "suggests that people should engage in an illegal activity [in connection with] worship" and because "Christians would be morally outraged by a statement that connects Jesus Christ with illegal drug use." And the PTO refused to register trademarks associating religious references with products (AGNUS DEI for safes and MADONNA for wine) because they would be "offensive to most individuals of the Christian faith" and "shocking to the sense of propriety." But once again, the PTO approved marks—PRAISE THE LORD for a game and JESUS DIED FOR YOU on clothing—whose message suggested religious faith rather than blasphemy or irreverence. Finally, the PTO rejected marks reflecting support for al-Qaeda (BABY AL QAEDA and AL-QAEDA on t-shirts) "because the bombing of civilians and other terrorist acts are shocking to the sense of decency and call out for condemnation." Yet it approved registration of a mark with the words WAR ON TERROR MEMORIAL. Of course, all these decisions are understandable. The rejected marks express opinions that are, at the least, offensive to many Americans. But as the Court made clear in *Tam*, a law disfavoring "ideas that offend" discriminates based on viewpoint, in violation of the First Amendment.

How, then, can the Government claim that the "immoral or scandalous" bar is viewpoint-neutral? The Government basically asks us to treat decisions like those described above as PTO examiners' mistakes. Still more, the Government tells us to ignore how the Lanham Act's language, on its face, disfavors some ideas. In urging that course, the Government does not dispute that the statutory language—and words used to define it—have just that effect. The Government's idea, abstractly phrased, is to narrow the statutory bar to "marks that are offensive [or] shocking to a substantial segment of the public because of their *mode* of expression, independent of any views that they may express." More concretely, the Government explains that this reinterpretation would mostly restrict the PTO to refusing marks that are "vulgar"—meaning "lewd," "sexually explicit or profane." Such a reconfigured bar, the Government says, would not turn on viewpoint, and so we could uphold it.

But we cannot accept the Government's proposal, because the statute says something markedly different. This Court, of course, may interpret "ambiguous statutory language" to "avoid serious constitutional doubts." But that canon of construction applies only when ambiguity exists. "We will not rewrite a law to conform it to constitutional requirements." So even assuming the Government's reading would eliminate First Amendment problems, we may adopt it only if we can see it in the statutory language. And we cannot. The "immoral or scandalous" bar stretches far beyond the Government's proposed construction. The statute as written does not draw the line at lewd, sexually explicit, or profane marks. Nor does it refer only to marks whose "mode of expression," independent of viewpoint, is particularly offensive. It covers the universe of immoral or scandalous—or (to use some PTO synonyms) offensive or disreputable—material. Whether or not lewd or profane. Whether the scandal and immorality comes from mode or instead from viewpoint. To cut the statute off where the Government urges is not to interpret the statute Congress enacted, but to fashion a new one.

And once the "immoral or scandalous" bar is interpreted fairly, it must be invalidated. T. But in any event, the "immoral or scandalous" bar is substantially overbroad. There are a great many immoral and scandalous ideas in the world (even more than there are swearwords), and the Lanham Act covers them all. It therefore violates the First Amendment.

Justice ALITO, concurring.

For the reasons explained in the opinion of the Court, the provision of the Lanham Act at issue in this case violates the Free Speech Clause of the

First Amendment because it discriminates on the basis of viewpoint and cannot be fixed without rewriting the statute. Viewpoint discrimination is poison to a free society. But in many countries with constitutions or legal traditions that claim to protect freedom of speech, serious viewpoint discrimination is now tolerated, and such discrimination has become increasingly prevalent in this country. At a time when free speech is under attack, it is especially important for this Court to remain firm on the principle that the First Amendment does not tolerate viewpoint discrimination. We reaffirm that principle today.

Our decision is not based on moral relativism but on the recognition that a law banning speech deemed by government officials to be "immoral" or "scandalous" can easily be exploited for illegitimate ends. Our decision does not prevent Congress from adopting a more carefully focused statute that precludes the registration of marks containing vulgar terms that play no real part in the expression of ideas. The particular mark in question in this case could be denied registration under such a statute. The term suggested by that mark is not needed to express any idea and, in fact, as commonly used today, generally signifies nothing except emotion and a severely limited vocabulary. The registration of such marks serves only to further coarsen our popular culture. But we are not legislators and cannot substitute a new statute for the one now in force.

Chief Justice ROBERTS, concurring in part and dissenting in part.

The Court rejects that proposal on the ground that it would in effect rewrite the statute. I agree with the majority that the "immoral" portion of the provision is not susceptible of a narrowing construction that would eliminate its viewpoint bias. As Justice Sotomayor explains, however, the "scandalous" portion of the provision is susceptible of such a narrowing construction. Standing alone, the term "scandalous" need not be understood to reach marks that offend because of the ideas they convey; it can be read more narrowly to bar only marks that offend because of their mode of expression—marks that are obscene, vulgar, or profane. That is how the PTO now understands the term. In light of our decision in *Matal v. Tam*, I agree with Justice Sotomayor that such a narrowing construction is appropriate in this context.

I also agree that, regardless of how exactly the trademark registration system is best conceived under our precedents—a question we left open in *Tam*—refusing registration to obscene, vulgar, or profane marks does not offend the First Amendment. Whether such marks can be registered does not affect the extent to which their owners may use them in commerce to identify goods. No speech is being restricted; no one is being punished. The owners of such marks are merely denied certain additional benefits associated with federal trademark registration. The Government, meanwhile, has an interest in not associating itself with trademarks whose content is obscene, vulgar, or profane. The First Amendment protects the freedom of speech; it does not require the Government to give aid and comfort to those using obscene, vulgar, and profane modes of expression.

Justice BREYER, concurring in part and dissenting in part.

Our precedents warn us against interpreting statutes in ways that would likely render them unconstitutional. Following these precedents, I agree with Justice Sotomayor that, for the reasons she gives, we should interpret the word "scandalous" in the present statute to refer only to certain highly "vulgar" or "obscene" modes of expression.

The question, then, is whether the First Amendment permits the Government to rely on this statute, as narrowly construed, to deny the benefits of federal trademark registration to marks like the one at issue here, which involves the use of the term "FUCT" in connection with a clothing line that includes apparel for children and infants. Like Justice Sotomayor, I believe the answer is "yes," though my reasons differ slightly.

In my view, a category-based approach to the First Amendment cannot adequately resolve the problem before us. I would place less emphasis on trying to decide whether the statute at issue should be categorized as an example of "viewpoint discrimination," "content discrimination," "commercial speech," "government speech," or the like. Rather, as I have written before, I believe we would do better to treat this Court's speech-related categories not as outcome-determinative rules, but instead as rules of thumb.

After all, these rules are not absolute. The First Amendment is not the Tax Code. Indeed, even when we consider a regulation that is ostensibly "viewpoint discriminatory" or that is subject to "strict scrutiny," we sometimes find the regulation to be constitutional after weighing the competing interests involved.

Unfortunately, the Court has sometimes applied these rules — especially the category of "content discrimination" — too rigidly. In a number of cases, the Court has struck down what I believe are ordinary, valid regulations that pose little or no threat to the speech interests that the First Amendment protects.

Rather than deducing the answers to First Amendment questions strictly from categories, as the Court often does, I would appeal more often and more directly to the values the First Amendment seeks to protect. As I have previously written, I would ask whether the regulation at issue "works speech-related harm that is out of proportion to its justifications."

Justice SOTOMAYOR, with whom Justice BREYER joins, concurring in part and dissenting in part.

The Court's decision today will beget unfortunate results. With the Lanham Act's scandalous-marks provision struck down as unconstitutional viewpoint discrimination, the Government will have no statutory basis to refuse (and thus no choice but to begin) registering marks containing the most vulgar, profane, or obscene words and images imaginable.

The coming rush to register such trademarks—and the Government's immediate powerlessness to say no—is eminently avoidable. Rather than read the relevant text as the majority does, it is equally possible to read that provision's bar on the registration of "scandalous" marks to address only obscenity, vulgarity, and profanity. Such a narrowing construction would save that duly enacted legislative text by rendering it a reasonable, viewpoint-neutral restriction on speech that is permissible in the context of a beneficial governmental initiative like the trademark-registration system. I would apply that narrowing construction to the term "scandalous" and accordingly reject petitioner Erik Brunetti's facial challenge.

Prohibiting the registration of obscene, profane, or vulgar marks qualifies as reasonable, viewpoint-neutral, content-based regulation. Apart from any interest in regulating commerce itself, the Government has an interest in not promoting certain kinds of speech, whether because such speech could be perceived as suggesting governmental favoritism or simply because the Government does not wish to involve itself with that kind of speech. While "there is no evidence that the public associates the contents of trademarks with the Federal Government," registration nevertheless entails Government involvement in promoting a particular mark. Registration requires the Government to publish the mark, as well as to take steps to combat international infringement. The Government has a reasonable interest in refraining from lending its ancillary support to marks that are obscene, vulgar, or profane.

2. Vagueness and Overbreadth

b. *Overbreadth* (casebook p. 1285)

Although the Court did not explicitly use overbreadth analysis, in *Packingham v. North Carolina*, the Court concluded that a law preventing those convicted of sex crimes from being on social media was too broad and violated the First Amendment. Justice Kennedy's opinion may be particularly important for its discussion of the importance of protecting speech on the internet.

PACKINGHAM v. NORTH CAROLINA
137 S. Ct. 1730 (2018)

Justice KENNEDY delivered the opinion of the Court.

In 2008, North Carolina enacted a statute making it a felony for a registered sex offender to gain access to a number of websites, including commonplace social media websites like Facebook and Twitter. The question presented is whether that law is permissible under the First Amendment's Free Speech Clause, applicable to the States under the Due Process Clause of the Fourteenth Amendment.

I

North Carolina law makes it a felony for a registered sex offender "to access a commercial social networking Web site where the sex offender knows that the site permits minor children to become members or to create or maintain personal Web pages." A "commercial social networking Web site" is defined as a website that meets four criteria. First, it "[i]s operated by a person who derives revenue from membership fees, advertising, or other sources related to the operation of the Website." Second, it "[f]acilitates the social introduction between two or more persons for the purposes of friendship, meeting other persons, or information exchanges." Third, it "[a]llows users to create Web pages or personal profiles that contain information such as the name or nickname of the user, photographs placed on the personal Web page by the user, other personal information about the user, and links to other personal Web pages on the commercial social networking Web site of friends or associates of the user that may be accessed by other users or visitors to the Web site." And fourth, it "[p]rovides users or visitors . . . mechanisms to communicate with other users, such as a message board, chat room, electronic mail, or instant messenger."

The statute includes two express exemptions. The statutory bar does not extend to websites that "[p]rovid[e] only one of the following discrete services: photo-sharing, electronic mail, instant messenger, or chat room or message board platform." The law also does not encompass websites that have as their "primary purpose the facilitation of commercial transactions involving goods or services between [their] members or visitors."

According to sources cited to the Court, § 14-202.5 applies to about 20,000 people in North Carolina and the State has prosecuted over 1,000 people for violating it.

B

In 2002, petitioner Lester Gerard Packingham—then a 21-year-old college student—had sex with a 13-year-old girl. He pleaded guilty to taking indecent liberties with a child. Because this crime qualifies as "an offense against a minor," petitioner was required to register as a sex offender—a status that can endure for 30 years or more. As a registered sex offender, petitioner was barred under § 14-202.5 from gaining access to commercial social networking sites.

In 2010, a state court dismissed a traffic ticket against petitioner. In response, he logged on to Facebook.com and posted the following statement on his personal profile:

"Man God is Good! How about I got so much favor they dismissed the ticket before court even started? No fine, no court cost, no nothing spent . . . Praise be to GOD, WOW! Thanks JESUS!"

At the time, a member of the Durham Police Department was investigating registered sex offenders who were thought to be violating § 14-202.5. The officer noticed that a "'J.R. Gerrard'" had posted the statement quoted above. By checking court records, the officer discovered that a traffic citation for petitioner had been dismissed around the time of the post. Evidence obtained by search warrant confirmed the officer's suspicions that petitioner was J.R. Gerrard.

Petitioner was indicted by a grand jury for violating § 14-202.5. The trial court denied his motion to dismiss the indictment on the grounds that the charge against him violated the First Amendment. Petitioner was ultimately convicted and given a suspended prison sentence. At no point during trial or sentencing did the State allege that petitioner contacted a minor—or committed any other illicit act—on the Internet.

II

A fundamental principle of the First Amendment is that all persons have access to places where they can speak and listen, and then, after reflection, speak and listen once more. The Court has sought to protect the right to speak in this spatial context. A basic rule, for example, is that a street or a park is a quintessential forum for the exercise of First Amendment rights. Even in the modern era, these places are still essential venues for public gatherings to celebrate some views, to protest others, or simply to learn and inquire.

While in the past there may have been difficulty in identifying the most important places (in a spatial sense) for the exchange of views, today the answer is clear. It is cyberspace—the "vast democratic forums of the Internet" in general and social media in particular. Seven in ten American adults use at least one Internet social networking service. One of the most popular of these sites is Facebook, the site used by petitioner leading to his conviction in this case. According to sources cited to the Court in this case, Facebook has 1.79 billion active users. This is about three times the population of North America.

Social media offers "relatively unlimited, low-cost capacity for communication of all kinds." On Facebook, for example, users can debate religion and politics with their friends and neighbors or share vacation photos. On LinkedIn, users can look for work, advertise for employees, or review tips on entrepreneurship. And on Twitter, users can petition their elected representatives and otherwise engage with them in a direct manner. Indeed, Governors in all 50 States and almost every Member of Congress have set up accounts for this purpose. In short, social media users employ these websites to engage in a wide array of protected First Amendment activity on topics "as diverse as human thought."

The nature of a revolution in thought can be that, in its early stages, even its participants may be unaware of it. And when awareness comes, they still may be unable to know or foresee where its changes lead. So too here. While we now may be coming to the realization that the Cyber Age is a revolution of historic proportions, we cannot appreciate yet its full dimensions and vast potential to alter how we think, express ourselves, and define who we want to be. The forces and directions of the Internet are so new, so protean, and so far reaching that courts must be conscious that what they say today might be obsolete tomorrow.

This case is one of the first this Court has taken to address the relationship between the First Amendment and the modern Internet. As a result, the Court must exercise extreme caution before suggesting that the First Amendment provides scant protection for access to vast networks in that medium.

III

This background informs the analysis of the North Carolina statute at issue. Even making the assumption that the statute is content neutral and thus subject to intermediate scrutiny, the provision cannot stand. In order to survive intermediate scrutiny, a law must be "narrowly tailored to serve a significant governmental interest."

For centuries now, inventions heralded as advances in human progress have been exploited by the criminal mind. New technologies, all too soon, can become instruments used to commit serious crimes. The railroad is one example, and the telephone another, So it will be with the Internet and social media.

There is also no doubt that, as this Court has recognized, "[t]he sexual abuse of a child is a most serious crime and an act repugnant to the moral instincts of a decent people." And it is clear that a legislature "may pass valid laws to protect children" and other victims of sexual assault "from abuse." The government, of course, need not simply stand by and allow these evils to occur. But the assertion of a valid governmental interest "cannot, in every context, be insulated from all constitutional protections."

It is necessary to make two assumptions to resolve this case. First, given the broad wording of the North Carolina statute at issue, it might well bar access not only to commonplace social media websites but also to websites as varied as Amazon.com, Washingtonpost.com, and Webmd. com. The Court need not decide the precise scope of the statute. It is enough to assume that the law applies (as the State concedes it does) to social networking sites "as commonly understood"—that is, websites like Facebook, LinkedIn, and Twitter.

Second, this opinion should not be interpreted as barring a State from enacting more specific laws than the one at issue. Specific criminal acts are not protected speech even if speech is the means for their commission. Though the issue is not before the Court, it can be assumed that the First Amendment permits a State to enact specific, narrowly tailored laws that prohibit a sex offender from engaging in conduct that often presages a sexual crime, like contacting a minor or using a website to gather information about a minor. Specific laws of that type must be the State's first resort to ward off the serious harm that sexual crimes inflict. (Of importance, the troubling fact that the law imposes severe restrictions on persons who already have served their sentence and are no longer subject to the supervision of the criminal justice system is also not an issue before the Court.)

Even with these assumptions about the scope of the law and the State's interest, the statute here enacts a prohibition unprecedented in the scope of First Amendment speech it burdens. Social media allows users to gain access to information and communicate with one another about it on any subject that might come to mind. By prohibiting sex offenders from using those websites, North Carolina with one broad stroke bars access to what for many are the principal sources for knowing current events, checking ads for employment, speaking and listening in the modern public square, and otherwise exploring the vast realms of human thought and knowledge. These websites can provide perhaps the most powerful mechanisms available to a private citizen to make his or her voice heard. They allow a person with an Internet connection to "become a town crier with a voice that resonates farther than it could from any soapbox."

In sum, to foreclose access to social media altogether is to prevent the user from engaging in the legitimate exercise of First Amendment rights. It is unsettling to suggest that only a limited set of websites can be used even by persons who have completed their sentences. Even convicted criminals — and in some instances especially convicted criminals — might receive legitimate benefits from these means for access to the world of ideas, in particular if they seek to reform and to pursue lawful and rewarding lives.

IV

The primary response from the State is that the law must be this broad to serve its preventative purpose of keeping convicted sex offenders away from vulnerable victims. The State has not, however, met its burden to show that this sweeping law is necessary or legitimate to serve that purpose. It is instructive that no case or holding of this Court has approved of a statute as broad in its reach.

It is well established that, as a general rule, the Government "may not suppress lawful speech as the means to suppress unlawful speech." That is what North Carolina has done here. Its law must be held invalid.

Justice ALITO, with whom THE CHIEF JUSTICE and Justice THOMAS join, concurring in the judgment.

The North Carolina statute at issue in this case was enacted to serve an interest of "surpassing importance" — but it has a staggering reach. It makes it a felony for a registered sex offender simply to visit a vast array of websites, including many that appear to provide no realistic opportunity for communications that could facilitate the abuse of children. Because of the law's extraordinary breadth, I agree with the Court that it violates the Free Speech Clause of the First Amendment.

I cannot join the opinion of the Court, however, because of its undisciplined dicta. The Court is unable to resist musings that seem to equate the entirety of the internet with public streets and parks. And this language is bound to be interpreted by some to mean that the States are largely powerless to restrict even the most dangerous sexual predators from visiting any internet sites, including, for example, teenage dating sites and sites designed to permit minors to discuss personal problems with their peers. I am troubled by the implications of the Court's unnecessary rhetoric.

I

As we have frequently noted, "[t]he prevention of sexual exploitation and abuse of children constitutes a government objective of surpassing importance." "Sex offenders are a serious threat," and "the victims of sexual assault are most often juveniles." "[T]he . . . interest [of] safeguarding the physical and psychological well-being of a minor . . . is a compelling one," and "we have sustained legislation aimed at protecting the physical and emotional well-being of youth even when the laws have operated in the sensitive area of constitutionally protected rights." Repeat sex offenders pose an especially grave risk to children. "When convicted sex offenders reenter society, they are much more likely than any other type of offender to be rearrested for a new rape or sexual assault."

The State's interest in protecting children from recidivist sex offenders plainly applies to internet use. Several factors make the internet a powerful tool for the would-be child abuser. First, children often use the internet in a way that gives offenders easy access to their personal information — by, for example, communicating with strangers and allowing sites to disclose their location. Second, the internet provides previously unavailable ways of communicating with, stalking, and ultimately abusing children. An abuser can create a false profile that misrepresents the abuser's age and gender. The abuser can lure the minor into engaging in sexual conversations, sending explicit photos, or even meeting in person. And an abuser can use a child's location posts on the internet to determine the pattern of the child's day-to-day activities — and even the child's location at a given moment. Such uses of the internet are already well documented, both in research and in reported decisions.

Because protecting children from abuse is a compelling state interest and sex offenders can (and do) use the internet to engage in such abuse, it is legitimate and entirely reasonable for States to try to stop abuse from occurring before it happens.

It is not enough, however, that the law before us is designed to serve a compelling state interest; it also must not "burden substantially more speech than is necessary to further the government's legitimate interests." The North Carolina law fails this requirement.

A straightforward reading of the text of N.C. Gen. Stat. Ann. § 14-202.5 compels the conclusion that it prohibits sex offenders from accessing an enormous number of websites.

The fatal problem for § 14-202.5 is that its wide sweep precludes access to a large number of websites that are most unlikely to facilitate the commission of a sex crime against a child. A handful of examples illustrates this point. Take, for example, the popular retail website Amazon.com, which allows minors to use its services and meets all four requirements of § 14-202.5's definition of a commercial social networking website. Many news websites are also covered by this definition. For example, the Washington Post's website gives minors access and satisfies the four elements that define a commercial social networking website. Or consider WebMD — a website that contains health-related resources, from tools that help users find a doctor to information on preventative care and the symptoms associated with particular medical problems. WebMD, too, allows children on the site. And it exhibits the four hallmarks of a "commercial social networking" website.

As these examples illustrate, the North Carolina law has a very broad reach and covers websites that are ill suited for use in stalking or abusing children. The focus of the discussion on these sites — shopping, news, health — does not provide a convenient jumping off point for conversations that may lead to abuse. In addition, the social exchanges facilitated by these websites occur in the open, and this reduces the possibility of a child being secretly lured into an abusive situation. These websites also give sex offenders little opportunity to gather personal details about a child; the information that can be listed in a profile is limited, and the profiles are brief. What is more, none of these websites make it easy to determine a child's precise location at a given moment. For example, they do not permit photo streams (at most, a child could upload a single profile photograph), and they do not include up-to-the minute location services. Such websites would provide essentially no aid to a would-be child abuser.

Placing this set of websites categorically off limits from registered sex offenders prohibits them from receiving or engaging in speech that the First Amendment protects and does not appreciably advance the State's goal of protecting children from recidivist sex offenders. I am therefore compelled to conclude that, while the law before us addresses a critical problem, it sweeps far too broadly to satisfy the demands of the Free Speech Clause.

II

While I thus agree with the Court that the particular law at issue in this case violates the First Amendment, I am troubled by the Court's loose rhetoric. After noting that "a street or a park is a quintessential forum for the exercise of First Amendment rights," the Court states that "cyberspace" and "social media in particular" are now "the most important places (in a spatial sense) for the exchange of views." But if the entirety of the internet or even just "social media" sites[16] are the 21st century equivalent of public streets and parks, then States may have little ability to restrict the sites that may be visited by even the most dangerous sex offenders. May a State preclude an adult previously convicted of molesting children from visiting a dating site for teenagers? Or a site where minors communicate with each other about personal problems? The Court should be more attentive to the implications of its rhetoric for, contrary to the Court's suggestion, there are important differences between cyberspace and the physical world.

I will mention a few that are relevant to internet use by sex offenders. First, it is easier for parents to monitor the physical locations that their children visit and the individuals with whom they speak in person than it is to monitor their internet use. Second, if a sex offender is seen approaching children or loitering in a place frequented by children, this conduct may be observed by parents, teachers, or others. Third, the internet offers an unprecedented degree of anonymity and easily permits a would-be molester to assume a false identity.

The Court is correct that we should be cautious in applying our free speech precedents to the internet. Cyberspace is different from the physical world, and if it is true, as the Court believes, that "we cannot appreciate yet" the "full dimensions and vast potential" of "the Cyber Age," we should proceed circumspectly, taking one step at a time. It is regrettable that the Court has not heeded its own admonition of caution.

4.   What Is an Infringement of Freedom of Speech?

Compelled Speech (casebook p. 1324)

In October Term 2017, the Court decided two cases concerning compelled speech. Both found laws unconstitutional as impermissibly compelling speech. One, *National Institute of Family and Life Advocates v. Becerra*, declared unconstitutional a state law requiring disclosures by reproductive health care facilities. The other, *Janus v. American Federation*, is presented below in the discussion on compelled association. It, too, found the law unconstitutional as impermissible compelled speech.

NATIONAL FEDERATION OF FAMILY AND LIFE ADVOCATES v. BECERRA
138 S. Ct. 2361 (2018)

Justice THOMAS delivered the opinion of the Court.

The California Reproductive Freedom, Accountability, Comprehensive Care, and Transparency Act (FACT Act) requires clinics that primarily serve pregnant women to provide certain notices. Licensed clinics must notify women that California provides free or low-cost services, including abortions, and give them a phone number to call. Unlicensed clinics must notify women that California has not licensed the clinics to provide medical services. The question in this case is whether these notice requirements violate the First Amendment.

I

The California State Legislature enacted the FACT Act to regulate crisis pregnancy centers. Crisis pregnancy centers—according to a report commissioned by the California State Assembly,—are "pro-life (largely Christian belief-based) organizations that offer a limited range of free pregnancy options, counseling, and other services to individuals that visit a center." "[U]nfortunately," the author of the FACT Act stated, "there are nearly 200 licensed and unlicensed" crisis pregnancy centers in California. These centers "aim to discourage and prevent women from seeking abortions." The author of the FACT Act observed that crisis pregnancy centers "are commonly affiliated with, or run by organizations whose stated goal" is to oppose abortion—including "the National Institute of Family and Life Advocates," one of the petitioners here. To address this perceived problem, the FACT Act imposes two notice requirements on facilities that provide pregnancy-related services—one for licensed facilities and one for unlicensed facilities.

The first notice requirement applies to "licensed covered facilit[ies]." To fall under the definition of "licensed covered facility," a clinic must be a licensed primary care or specialty clinic or qualify as an intermittent clinic under California law. A licensed covered facility also must have the "primary purpose" of "providing family planning or pregnancy-related services." And it must satisfy at least two of the following six requirements:

(1) The facility offers obstetric ultrasounds, obstetric sonograms, or prenatal care to pregnant women.
(2) The facility provides, or offers counseling about, contraception or contraceptive methods.
(3) The facility offers pregnancy testing or pregnancy diagnosis.
(4) The facility advertises or solicits patrons with offers to provide prenatal sonography, pregnancy tests, or pregnancy options counseling.
(5) The facility offers abortion services.
(6) The facility has staff or volunteers who collect health information from clients.

The FACT Act exempts several categories of clinics that would otherwise qualify as licensed covered facilities. Clinics operated by the United States or a federal agency are excluded, as are clinics that are "enrolled as a Medi-Cal provider" and participate in "the Family Planning, Access, Care, and Treatment Program" (Family PACT program). To participate in the Family PACT program, a clinic must provide "the full scope of family planning . . . services specified for the program," including sterilization and emergency contraceptive pills.

If a clinic is a licensed covered facility, the FACT Act requires it to disseminate a government-drafted notice on site. The notice states that "California has public programs that provide immediate free or low-cost access to comprehensive family planning services (including all FDA-approved methods of contraception), prenatal care, and abortion for eligible women. To determine whether you qualify, contact the county social services office at [insert the telephone number]." This notice must be posted in the waiting room, printed and distributed to all clients, or provided digitally at check-in. The notice must be in English and any additional languages identified by state law. In some counties, that means the notice must be spelled out in 13 different languages.

The stated purpose of the FACT Act, including its licensed notice requirement, is to "ensure that California residents make their personal reproductive health care decisions knowing their rights and the health care services available to them." The Legislature posited that "thousands of women remain unaware of the public programs available to provide them with contraception, health education and counseling, family planning, prenatal care, abortion, or delivery." Citing the "time sensitive" nature of pregnancy-related decisions, the Legislature concluded that requiring licensed facilities to inform patients themselves would be "[t]he most effective" way to convey this information.

The second notice requirement in the FACT Act applies to "unlicensed covered facilit[ies]." To fall under the definition of "unlicensed covered facility," a facility must not be licensed by the State, not have a licensed medical provider on staff or under contract, and have the "primary purpose" of "providing pregnancy-related services." An unlicensed covered facility also must satisfy at least two of the following four requirements:

(1) The facility offers obstetric ultrasounds, obstetric sonograms, or prenatal care to pregnant women.
(2) The facility offers pregnancy testing or pregnancy diagnosis.
(3) The facility advertises or solicits patrons with offers to provide prenatal sonography, pregnancy tests, or pregnancy options counseling.
(4) The facility has staff or volunteers who collect health information from clients.

Clinics operated by the United States and licensed primary care clinics enrolled in Medi-Cal and Family PACT are excluded.

Unlicensed covered facilities must provide a government-drafted notice stating that "[t]his facility is not licensed as a medical facility by the State of California and has no licensed medical provider who provides or directly supervises the provision of services." Cal. Health & Safety Code Ann. This notice must be provided on site and in all advertising materials. Onsite, the notice must be posted "conspicuously" at the entrance of the facility and in at least one waiting area. It must be "at least 8.5 inches by 11 inches and written in no less than 48-point type." *Ibid.* In advertisements, the notice must be in the same size or larger font than the surrounding text, or otherwise set off in a way that draws attention to it. Like the licensed notice, the unlicensed notice must be in English and any additional languages specified by state law. Its stated purpose is to ensure "that pregnant women in California know when they are getting medical care from licensed professionals."

After the Governor of California signed the FACT Act, petitioners — a licensed pregnancy center, an unlicensed pregnancy center, and an organization composed of crisis pregnancy centers — filed this suit. Petitioners alleged that the licensed and unlicensed notices abridge the freedom of speech protected by the First Amendment. The District Court denied their motion for a preliminary injunction. The Court of Appeals for the Ninth Circuit affirmed. We reverse with respect to both notice requirements.

II

We first address the licensed notice. The First Amendment, applicable to the States through the Fourteenth Amendment, prohibits laws that abridge the freedom of speech. When enforcing this prohibition, our precedents distinguish between content-based and content-neutral regulations of speech. Content-based regulations "target speech based on its communicative content." As a general matter, such laws "are presumptively unconstitutional and may be justified only if the government proves that they are narrowly tailored to serve compelling state interests." This stringent standard reflects the fundamental principle that governments have "'no power to restrict expression because of its message, its ideas, its subject matter, or its content.'"

The licensed notice is a content-based regulation of speech. By compelling individuals to speak a particular message, such notices "alte[r] the content of [their] speech." Here, for example, licensed clinics must provide a government-drafted script about the availability of state-sponsored services, as well as contact information for how to obtain them. One of those services is abortion—the very practice that petitioners are devoted to opposing. By requiring petitioners to inform women how they can obtain state-subsidized abortions—at the same time petitioners try to dissuade women from choosing that option—the licensed notice plainly "alters the content" of petitioners' speech.

Although the licensed notice is content based, the Ninth Circuit did not apply strict scrutiny because it concluded that the notice regulates "professional speech." Some Courts of Appeals have recognized "professional speech" as a separate category of speech that is subject to different rules. These courts define "professionals" as individuals who provide personalized services to clients and who are subject to "a generally applicable licensing and regulatory regime." "Professional speech" is then defined as any speech by these individuals that is based on "[their] expert knowledge and judgment," or that is "within the confines of [the] professional relationship." So defined, these courts except professional speech from the rule that content-based regulations of speech are subject to strict scrutiny.

But this Court has not recognized "professional speech" as a separate category of speech. Speech is not unprotected merely because it is uttered by "professionals." This Court has "been reluctant to mark off new categories of speech for diminished constitutional protection." And it has been especially reluctant to "exemp[t] a category of speech from the normal prohibition on content-based restrictions." This Court's precedents do not permit governments to impose content-based restrictions on speech without "'persuasive evidence . . . of a long (if heretofore unrecognized) tradition'" to that effect.

This Court's precedents do not recognize such a tradition for a category called "professional speech." This Court has afforded less protection for professional speech in two circumstances — neither of which turned on the fact that professionals were speaking. First, our precedents have applied more deferential review to some laws that require professionals to disclose factual, noncontroversial information in their "commercial speech." Second, under our precedents, States may regulate professional conduct, even though that conduct incidentally involves speech. But neither line of precedents is implicated here.

This Court's precedents have applied a lower level of scrutiny to laws that compel disclosures in certain contexts. Most obviously, the licensed notice is not limited to "purely factual and uncontroversial information about the terms under which . . . services will be available."

In addition, this Court has upheld regulations of professional conduct that incidentally burden speech. In *Planned Parenthood of Southeastern Pa. v. Casey*, for example, this Court upheld a law requiring physicians to obtain informed consent before they could perform an abortion. Pennsylvania law required physicians to inform their patients of "the nature of the procedure, the health risks of the abortion and childbirth, and the 'probable gestational age of the unborn child.'" The joint opinion in *Casey* rejected a free-speech challenge to this informed-consent requirement. It described the Pennsylvania law as "a requirement that a doctor give a woman certain information as part of obtaining her consent to an abortion," which "for constitutional purposes, [was] no different from a requirement that a doctor give certain specific information about any medical procedure." The joint opinion explained that the law regulated speech only "as part of the *practice* of medicine, subject to reasonable licensing and regulation by the State." Indeed, the requirement that a doctor obtain informed consent to perform an operation is "firmly entrenched in American tort law."

The licensed notice at issue here is not an informed-consent requirement or any other regulation of professional conduct. The notice does not facilitate informed consent to a medical procedure. In fact, it is not tied to a procedure at all. It applies to all interactions between a covered facility and its clients, regardless of whether a medical procedure is ever sought, offered, or performed. If a covered facility does provide medical procedures, the notice provides no information about the risks or benefits of those procedures. Tellingly, many facilities that provide the exact same services as covered facilities — such as general practice clinics, — are not required to provide the licensed notice. The licensed notice regulates speech as speech.

The dangers associated with content-based regulations of speech are also present in the context of professional speech. As with other kinds of speech, regulating the content of professionals' speech "pose[s] the inherent risk that the Government seeks not to advance a legitimate regulatory goal, but to suppress unpopular ideas or information." Take medicine, for example. "Doctors help patients make deeply personal decisions, and their candor is crucial." Throughout history, governments have "manipulat[ed] the content of doctor-patient discourse" to increase state power and suppress minorities. Further, when the government polices the content of professional speech, it can fail to "'preserve an uninhibited marketplace of ideas in which truth will ultimately prevail.'"

"Professional speech" is also a difficult category to define with precision. As defined by the courts of appeals, the professional-speech doctrine would cover a wide array of individuals — doctors, lawyers, nurses, physical therapists, truck drivers, bartenders, barbers, and many others. One court of appeals has even applied it to fortune tellers. All that is required to make something a "profession," according to these courts, is that it involves personalized services and requires a professional license from the State. But that gives the States unfettered power to reduce a group's First Amendment rights by simply imposing a licensing requirement. States cannot choose the protection that speech receives under the First Amendment, as that would give them a powerful tool to impose "invidious discrimination of disfavored subjects."

In sum, neither California nor the Ninth Circuit has identified a persuasive reason for treating professional speech as a unique category that is exempt from ordinary First Amendment principles. We do not foreclose the possibility that some such reason exists. We need not do so because the licensed notice cannot survive even intermediate scrutiny. California asserts a single interest to justify the licensed notice: providing low-income women with information about state-sponsored services. Assuming that this is a substantial state interest, the licensed notice is not sufficiently drawn to achieve it.

If California's goal is to educate low-income women about the services it provides, then the licensed notice is "wildly underinclusive." The notice applies only to clinics that have a "primary purpose" of "providing family planning or pregnancy-related services" and that provide two of six categories of specific services. Other clinics that have another primary purpose, or that provide only one category of those services, also serve low-income women and could educate them about the State's services. According to

the legislative record, California has "nearly 1,000 community clinics"—
including "federally designated community health centers, migrant health
centers, rural health centers, and frontier health centers"—that "serv[e]
more than 5.6 million patients . . . annually through over 17 million patient
encounters." But most of those clinics are excluded from the licensed notice
requirement without explanation. Such "[u]nderinclusiveness raises serious doubts about whether the government is in fact pursuing the interest
it invokes, rather than disfavoring a particular speaker or viewpoint." The
FACT Act also excludes, without explanation, federal clinics and Family
PACT providers from the licensed-notice requirement.

The FACT Act's exemption for these clinics, which serve many women
who are pregnant or could become pregnant in the future, demonstrates
the disconnect between its stated purpose and its actual scope. Yet
"[p]recision . . . must be the touchstone" when it comes to regulations of
speech, which "so closely touc[h] our most precious freedoms."

Further, California could inform low-income women about its services
"without burdening a speaker with unwanted speech." Most obviously,
it could inform the women itself with a public-information campaign.
California could even post the information on public property near crisis
pregnancy centers. California argues that it has already tried an advertising campaign, and that many women who are eligible for publicly-funded
healthcare have not enrolled. But California has identified no evidence
to that effect. And regardless, a "tepid response" does not prove that an
advertising campaign is not a sufficient alternative. California cannot
co-opt the licensed facilities to deliver its message for it. "[T]he First
Amendment does not permit the State to sacrifice speech for efficiency."

In short, petitioners are likely to succeed on the merits of their challenge
to the licensed notice. Contrary to the suggestion in the dissent, we do
not question the legality of health and safety warnings long considered
permissible, or purely factual and uncontroversial disclosures about commercial products.

III

We need not decide what type of state interest is sufficient to sustain a disclosure requirement like the unlicensed notice. California has not demonstrated any justification for the unlicensed notice that is more than "purely
hypothetical." The only justification that the California Legislature put
forward was ensuring that "pregnant women in California know when
they are getting medical care from licensed professionals." At oral argument, however, California denied that the justification for the FACT Act

was that women "go into [crisis pregnancy centers] and they don't realize what they are." Indeed, California points to nothing suggesting that pregnant women do not already know that the covered facilities are staffed by unlicensed medical professionals. The services that trigger the unlicensed notice—such as having "volunteers who collect health information from clients," "advertis[ing] . . . pregnancy options counseling," and offering over-the-counter "pregnancy testing,"—do not require a medical license. And California already makes it a crime for individuals without a medical license to practice medicine. At this preliminary stage of the litigation, we agree that petitioners are likely to prevail on the question whether California has proved a justification for the unlicensed notice.[4]

Even if California had presented a nonhypothetical justification for the unlicensed notice, the FACT Act unduly burdens protected speech. The unlicensed notice imposes a government-scripted, speaker-based disclosure requirement that is wholly disconnected from California's informational interest. It requires covered facilities to post California's precise notice, no matter what the facilities say on site or in their advertisements. And it covers a curiously narrow subset of speakers. While the licensed notice applies to facilities that provide "family planning" services and "contraception or contraceptive methods," the California Legislature dropped these triggering conditions for the unlicensed notice. The unlicensed notice applies only to facilities that primarily provide "pregnancy-related" services. Thus, a facility that advertises and provides pregnancy tests is covered by the unlicensed notice, but a facility across the street that advertises and provides nonprescription contraceptives is excluded—even though the latter is no less likely to make women think it is licensed. This Court's precedents are deeply skeptical of laws that "distinguis [h] among different speakers, allowing speech by some but not others." Speaker-based laws run the risk that "the State has left unburdened those speakers whose messages are in accord with its own views."

The application of the unlicensed notice to advertisements demonstrates just how burdensome it is. The notice applies to all "print and digital advertising materials" by an unlicensed covered facility. These materials must include a government-drafted statement that "[t]his facility is not licensed as a medical facility by the State of California and has no licensed medical provider who provides or directly supervises the provision of services." An unlicensed facility must call attention to the notice, instead of its own message, by some method such as larger text or contrasting type or color. This scripted language must be posted in English and as many other languages as California chooses to require. As California conceded at oral argument, a billboard for an unlicensed facility that says "Choose

Life" would have to surround that two-word statement with a 29-word statement from the government, in as many as 13 different languages. In this way, the unlicensed notice drowns out the facility's own message. More likely, the "detail required" by the unlicensed notice "effectively rules out" the possibility of having such a billboard in the first place. We express no view on the legality of a similar disclosure requirement that is better supported or less burdensome.

We hold that petitioners are likely to succeed on the merits of their claim that the FACT Act violates the First Amendment.

Justice KENNEDY, with whom THE CHIEF JUSTICE, Justice ALITO, and Justice GORSUCH join, concurring.

I join the Court's opinion in all respects. This separate writing seeks to underscore that the apparent viewpoint discrimination here is a matter of serious constitutional concern. The Court, in my view, is correct not to reach this question. It was not sufficiently developed, and the rationale for the Court's decision today suffices to resolve the case. And had the Court's analysis been confined to viewpoint discrimination, some legislators might have inferred that if the law were reenacted with a broader base and broader coverage it then would be upheld.

It does appear that viewpoint discrimination is inherent in the design and structure of this Act. This law is a paradigmatic example of the serious threat presented when government seeks to impose its own message in the place of individual speech, thought, and expression. For here the State requires primarily pro-life pregnancy centers to promote the State's own preferred message advertising abortions. This compels individuals to contradict their most deeply held beliefs, beliefs grounded in basic philosophical, ethical, or religious precepts, or all of these. And the history of the Act's passage and its underinclusive application suggest a real possibility that these individuals were targeted because of their beliefs.

The California Legislature included in its official history the congratulatory statement that the Act was part of California's legacy of "forward thinking." But it is not forward thinking to force individuals to "be an instrument for fostering public adherence to an ideological point of view [they] fin[d] unacceptable." It is forward thinking to begin by reading the First Amendment as ratified in 1791; to understand the history of authoritarian government as the Founders then knew it; to confirm that history since then shows how relentless authoritarian regimes are in their attempts to stifle free speech; and to carry those lessons onward as we seek to preserve and teach the necessity of freedom of speech for the generations to come. Governments must not be allowed to force persons to express a message contrary to their deepest convictions. Freedom of speech secures freedom of thought and belief. This law imperils those liberties.

Justice BREYER, with whom Justice GINSBURG, Justice SOTOMAYOR, and Justice KAGAN joins dissenting.

The petitioners ask us to consider whether two sections of a California statute violate the First Amendment. The first section requires licensed medical facilities (that provide women with assistance involving pregnancy or family planning) to tell those women where they might obtain help, including financial help, with comprehensive family planning services, prenatal care, and abortion. The second requires *un*licensed facilities offering somewhat similar services to make clear that they are unlicensed. In my view both statutory sections are likely constitutional, and I dissent from the Court's contrary conclusions.

I

Before turning to the specific law before us, I focus upon the general interpretation of the First Amendment that the majority says it applies. It applies heightened scrutiny to the Act because the Act, in its view, is "content based." "As a general matter," the majority concludes, such laws are "presumptively unconstitutional" and are subject to "stringent" review.

This constitutional approach threatens to create serious problems. Because much, perhaps most, human behavior takes place through speech and because much, perhaps most, law regulates that speech in terms of its content, the majority's approach at the least threatens considerable litigation over the constitutional validity of much, perhaps most, government regulation. Virtually every disclosure law could be considered "content based," for virtually every disclosure law requires individuals "to speak a particular message." Thus, the majority's view, if taken literally, could radically change prior law, perhaps placing much securities law or consumer protection law at constitutional risk, depending on how broadly its exceptions are interpreted.

The majority, at the end of Part II of its opinion, perhaps recognizing this problem, adds a general disclaimer. It says that it does not "question the legality of health and safety warnings long considered permissible, or purely factual and uncontroversial disclosures about commercial products." But this generally phrased disclaimer would seem more likely to invite litigation than to provide needed limitation and clarification. The majority, for example, does not explain why the Act here, which is justified in part by health and safety considerations, does not fall within its "health" category. Nor does the majority opinion offer any reasoned basis that might help apply its disclaimer for distinguishing lawful from unlawful disclosures. In the absence of a reasoned explanation of the disclaimer's meaning and rationale, the disclaimer is unlikely to withdraw the invitation to litigation that the majority's general broad "content-based" test issues. That test invites courts around the Nation to apply an unpredictable First Amendment to ordinary social and economic regulation, striking down disclosure laws that judges may disfavor, while upholding others, all without grounding their decisions in reasoned principle.

Precedent does not require a test such as the majority's. Rather, in saying the Act is not a longstanding health and safety law, the Court substitutes its own approach — without a defining standard — for an approach that was reasonably clear. Historically, the Court has been wary of claims that regulation of business activity, particularly health-related activity, violates the Constitution. Ever since this Court departed from the approach it set forth in *Lochner v. New York* (1905), ordinary economic and social legislation has been thought to raise little constitutional concern.

Even during the *Lochner* era, when this Court struck down numerous economic regulations concerning industry, this Court was careful to defer to state legislative judgments concerning the medical profession. The Court took the view that a State may condition the practice of medicine on any number of requirements, and physicians, in exchange for following those reasonable requirements, could receive a license to practice medicine from the State. Medical professionals do not, generally speaking, have a right to use the Constitution as a weapon allowing them rigorously to control the content of those reasonable conditions.

I, too, value this role that the First Amendment plays — in an appropriate case. But here, the majority enunciates a general test that reaches far beyond the area where this Court has examined laws closely in the service of those goals. And, in suggesting that heightened scrutiny applies to much economic and social legislation, the majority pays those First Amendment goals a serious disservice through dilution. Using the First Amendment to strike down economic and social laws that legislatures long would have thought themselves free to enact will, for the American public, obscure, not clarify, the true value of protecting freedom of speech.

Still, what about this specific case? The disclosure at issue here concerns speech related to abortion. It involves health, differing moral values, and differing points of view. Thus, rather than set forth broad, new, First Amendment principles, I believe that we should focus more directly upon precedent more closely related to the case at hand. This Court has more than once considered disclosure laws relating to reproductive health. Though those rules or holdings have changed over time, they should govern our disposition of this case.

In *Planned Parenthood of Southeastern Pa. v. Casey* (1992), the Court again considered a state law that required doctors to provide information to a woman deciding whether to proceed with an abortion. That law required the doctor to tell the woman about the nature of the abortion procedure, the health risks of abortion and of childbirth, the "'probable gestational age of the unborn child,'" and the availability of printed materials describing the fetus, medical assistance for childbirth, potential child support, and the agencies that would provide adoption services (or other alternatives to abortion). This time a joint opinion of the Court, in judging whether the State could impose these informational requirements, asked whether doing so imposed an "undue burden" upon women seeking an abortion. It held that it did not. Hence the statute was constitutional. The joint opinion stated that the statutory requirements amounted to "reasonable measure[s] to ensure an informed choice, one which might cause the woman to choose childbirth over abortion."

The joint opinion specifically discussed the First Amendment, the constitutional provision now directly before us. It concluded that the statute did not violate the First Amendment. It wrote: "All that is left of petitioners' argument is an asserted First Amendment right of a physician not to provide information about the risks of abortion, and childbirth, in a manner mandated by the State. To be sure, the physician's First Amendment rights not to speak are implicated, but only as part of the practice of medicine, subject to reasonable licensing and regulation by the State. We see no constitutional infirmity in the requirement that the physician provide the information mandated by the State here."

Thus, the Court considered the State's statutory requirements, including the requirement that the doctor must inform his patient about where she could learn how to have the newborn child adopted (if carried to term) and how she could find related financial assistance. To repeat the point, the Court then held that the State's requirements did *not* violate either the Constitution's protection of free speech or its protection of a woman's right to choose to have an abortion.

If a State can lawfully require a doctor to tell a woman seeking an abortion about adoption services, why should it not be able, as here, to require a medical counselor to tell a woman seeking prenatal care or other reproductive healthcare about childbirth and abortion services? As the question suggests, there is no convincing reason to distinguish between information about adoption and information about abortion in this context. After all, the rule of law embodies evenhandedness, and "what is sauce for the goose is normally sauce for the gander."

The majority also finds it "[t]ellin[g]" that general practice clinics — *i.e.*, paid clinics — are not required to provide the licensed notice. But the lack-of-information problem that the statute seeks to ameliorate is a problem that the State explains is commonly found among low-income women. That those with low income might lack the time to become fully informed and that this circumstance might prove disproportionately correlated with income is not intuitively surprising. Nor is it surprising that those with low income, whatever they choose in respect to pregnancy, might find information about financial assistance particularly useful. There is "nothing inherently suspect" about this distinction, which is not "based on the content of [the advocacy] each group offers," but upon the patients the group generally serves and the needs of that population.

Accordingly, the majority's reliance on cases that prohibit rather than require speech is misplaced. I agree that "'in the fields of medicine and public heath, . . . information can save lives,'" but the licensed disclosure *serves* that informational interest by requiring clinics to notify patients of the availability of state resources for family planning services, prenatal care, and abortion, which — unlike the majority's examples of normative statements, — is truthful and nonmisleading information. Abortion is a controversial topic and a source of normative debate, but the availability of state resources is not a normative statement or a fact of debatable truth. The disclosure includes information about resources available should a woman seek to continue her pregnancy or terminate it, and it expresses no official preference for one choice over the other. Similarly, the majority highlights an interest that often underlies our decisions in respect to speech prohibitions — the marketplace of ideas. But that marketplace is fostered, not hindered, by providing information to patients to enable them to make fully informed medical decisions in respect to their pregnancies.

Of course, one might take the majority's decision to mean that speech about abortion is special, that it involves in this case not only professional medical matters, but also views based on deeply held religious and moral beliefs about the nature of the practice. But assuming that is so, the law's insistence upon treating like cases alike should lead us to reject the petitioners' arguments that I have discussed. This insistence, the need for evenhandedness, should prove particularly weighty in a case involving abortion rights. That is because Americans hold strong, and differing, views about the matter. Some Americans believe that abortion involves the death of a live and innocent human being. Others believe that the ability to choose an abortion is "central to personal dignity and autonomy," and note that the failure to allow women to choose an abortion involves the deaths of innocent women. We have previously noted that we cannot try to adjudicate who is right and who is wrong in this moral debate. But we can do our best to interpret American constitutional law so that it applies fairly within a Nation whose citizens strongly hold these different points of view. That is one reason why it is particularly important to interpret the First Amendment so that it applies evenhandedly as between those who disagree so strongly. For this reason too a Constitution that allows States to insist that medical providers tell women about the possibility of adoption should also allow States similarly to insist that medical providers tell women about the possibility of abortion.

II

The second statutory provision covers pregnancy-related facilities that provide women with certain medical-type services (such as obstetric ultrasounds or sonograms, pregnancy diagnosis, counseling about pregnancy options, or prenatal care), are not licensed as medical facilities by the State, and do not have a licensed medical provider on site. The statute says that such a facility must disclose that it is not "licensed as a medical facility." And it must make this disclosure in a posted notice and in advertising.

The majority does not question that the State's interest (ensuring that "pregnant women in California know when they are getting medical care from licensed professionals") is the type of informational interest that [prior decisions encompass]. There is no basis for finding the State's interest "hypothetical." The legislature heard that information-related delays in qualified healthcare negatively affect women seeking to terminate their pregnancies as well as women carrying their pregnancies to term, with delays in qualified prenatal care causing life-long health problems for infants. Even without such testimony, it is "self-evident" that patients might think they are receiving qualified medical care when they enter facilities that collect health information, perform obstetric ultrasounds or sonograms, diagnose pregnancy, and provide counseling about pregnancy options or other prenatal care. The State's conclusion to that effect is certainly reasonable.

Relatedly, the majority suggests that the Act is suspect because it covers some speakers but not others. There is no cause for such concern here. The Act does not, on its face, distinguish between facilities that favor pro-life and those that favor pro-choice points of view. Nor is there any convincing evidence before us or in the courts below that discrimination was the purpose or the effect of the statute. Notably, California does not single out pregnancy-related facilities for this type of disclosure requirement. And it is unremarkable that the State excluded the provision of family planning and contraceptive services as triggering conditions. After all, the State was seeking to ensure that "pregnant women in California know when they are getting medical care from licensed professionals," and pregnant women generally do not need contraceptive services.

Finally, the majority concludes that the Act is overly burdensome. But these and similar claims are claims that the statute could be applied unconstitutionally, not that it is unconstitutional on its face. As I understand the Act, it would require disclosure in no more than two languages—English and Spanish—in the vast majority of California's 58 counties. The exception is Los Angeles County, where, given the large number of different-language speaking groups, expression in many languages may prove necessary to communicate the message to those whom that message will help. Whether the requirement of 13 different languages goes too far and is unnecessarily burdensome in light of the need to secure the statutory objectives is a matter that concerns Los Angeles County alone, and it is a proper subject for a Los Angeles-based as applied challenge in light of whatever facts a plaintiff finds relevant. At most, such facts might show a need for fewer languages, not invalidation of the statute.

C. Types of Unprotected and Less Protected Speech

5. Commercial Speech

b. What Is Commercial Speech? (p. 1478)

As *Sorrell v. IMS Health Care* (p. 1480) shows, the issue often arises as to when regulation of commercial transactions should be regarded as a regulation of commercial speech. That is the issue in *Expressions Hair Design v. Schneiderman*.

EXPRESSIONS HAIR DESIGN v. SCHNEIDERMAN
137 S. Ct. 1144 (2017)

Chief Justice ROBERTS delivered the opinion of the Court.

Each time a customer pays for an item with a credit card, the merchant selling that item must pay a transaction fee to the credit card issuer.

Some merchants balk at paying the fees and want to discourage the use of credit cards, or at least pass on the fees to customers who use them. One method of achieving those ends is through differential pricing—charging credit card users more than customers using cash. Merchants who wish to employ differential pricing may do so in two ways relevant here: impose a surcharge for the use of a credit card, or offer a discount for the use of cash. In N.Y. Gen. Bus. Law § 518, New York has banned the former practice. The question presented is whether § 518 regulates merchants' speech and—if so—whether the statute violates the First Amendment. We conclude that § 518 does regulate speech and remand for the Court of Appeals to determine in the first instance whether that regulation is unconstitutional.

I

When credit cards were first introduced, contracts between card issuers and merchants barred merchants from charging credit card users higher prices than cash customers. Congress put a partial stop to this practice in the 1974 amendments to the Truth in Lending Act (TILA). The amendments prohibited card issuers from contractually preventing merchants from giving discounts to customers who paid in cash. The law, however, said nothing about surcharges for the use of credit.

Two years later, Congress refined its dissimilar treatment of discounts and surcharges. First, the 1976 version of TILA barred merchants from imposing surcharges on customers who use credit cards. Second, Congress added definitions of the two terms. A discount was "a reduction made from the regular price," while a surcharge was "any means of increasing the regular price to a cardholder which is not imposed upon customers paying by cash, check, or similar means."

In 1981, Congress further delineated the distinction between discounts and surcharges by defining "regular price." Where a merchant "tagged or posted" a single price, the regular price was that single price. If no price was tagged or posted, or if a merchant employed a two-tag approach—posting one price for credit and another for cash—the regular price was whatever was charged to credit card users. Because a surcharge was defined as an increase from the regular price, there could be no credit card surcharge where the regular price was the same as the amount charged to customers using credit cards. The effect of all this was that a merchant could violate the surcharge ban only by posting a single price and charging credit card users more than that posted price.

The federal surcharge ban was short lived. Congress allowed it to expire in 1984 and has not renewed the ban since. The provision preventing credit card issuers from contractually barring discounts for cash, however, remained in place. With the lapse of the federal surcharge ban, several States, New York among them, immediately enacted their own surcharge bans. Passed in 1984, N.Y. Gen. Bus. Law § 518 adopted the operative language of the federal ban verbatim, providing that "[n]o seller in any sales transaction may impose a surcharge on a holder who elects to use a credit card in lieu of payment by cash, check, or similar means." Unlike the federal ban, the New York legislation included no definition of "surcharge."

In addition to these state legislative bans, credit card companies — though barred from prohibiting discounts for cash — included provisions in their contracts prohibiting merchants from imposing surcharges for credit card use. For most of its history, the New York law was essentially coextensive with these contractual prohibitions. In recent years, however, merchants have brought antitrust challenges to contractual no-surcharge provisions. Those suits have created uncertainty about the legal validity of such contractual surcharge bans. The result is that otherwise redundant legislative surcharge bans like § 518 have increasingly gained importance, and increasingly come under scrutiny.

Petitioners, five New York businesses and their owners, wish to impose surcharges on customers who use credit cards. Each time one of their customers pays with a credit card, these merchants must pay some transaction fee to the company that issued the credit card. The fee is generally two to three percent of the purchase price. Those fees add up, and the merchants allege that they pay tens of thousands of dollars every year to credit card companies. Rather than increase prices across the board to absorb those costs, the merchants want to pass the fees along only to their customers who choose to use credit cards. They also want to make clear that they are not the bad guys — that the credit card companies, not the merchants, are responsible for the higher prices. The merchants believe that surcharges for credit are more effective than discounts for cash in accomplishing these goals.

In 2013, after several major credit card issuers agreed to drop their contractual surcharge prohibitions, the merchants filed suit against the New York Attorney General and three New York District Attorneys to challenge § 518 — the only remaining obstacle to their charging surcharges for credit card use. As relevant here, they argued that the law violated the First Amendment by regulating how they communicated their prices, and that it was unconstitutionally vague because liability under the law "turn[ed] on the blurry difference" between surcharges and discounts.

The District Court ruled in favor of the merchants. It read the statute as "draw[ing a] line between prohibited 'surcharges' and permissible 'discounts' based on words and labels, rather than economic realities." The court concluded that the law therefore regulated speech, and violated the First Amendment under this Court's commercial speech doctrine. In addition, because the law turned on the "virtually incomprehensible distinction between what a vendor can and cannot tell its customers," the District Court found that the law was unconstitutionally vague.

The Court of Appeals for the Second Circuit vacated the judgment of the District Court with instructions to dismiss the merchants' claims. It began by considering single-sticker pricing, where merchants post one price and would like to charge more to customers who pay by credit card. All the law did in this context, the Court of Appeals explained, was regulate a relationship between two prices — the sticker price and the price charged to a credit card user — by requiring that the two prices be equal. Relying on our precedent holding that price regulation alone regulates conduct, not speech, the Court of Appeals concluded that § 518 did not violate the First Amendment.

II

As a preliminary matter, we note that petitioners present us with a limited challenge. Observing that the merchants were not always particularly clear about the scope of their suit, the Court of Appeals deemed them to be bringing a facial attack on § 518 as well as a challenge to the application of the statute to two particular pricing regimes: single-sticker pricing and two-sticker pricing. Before us, however, the merchants have disclaimed a facial challenge, assuring us that theirs is an as-applied challenge only.

There remains the question of what precise application of the law they seek to challenge. Although the merchants have presented a wide array of hypothetical pricing regimes, they have expressly identified only one pricing scheme that they seek to employ: posting a cash price and an additional credit card surcharge, expressed either as a percentage surcharge or a "dollars-and-cents" additional amount. Under this pricing approach, petitioner Expressions Hair Design might, for example, post a sign outside its salon reading "Haircuts $10 (we add a 3% surcharge if you pay by credit card)." Or, petitioner Brooklyn Farmacy & Soda Fountain might list one of the sundaes on its menu as costing "$10 (with a $0.30 surcharge for credit card users)." We take petitioners at their word and limit our review to the question whether § 518 is unconstitutional as applied to this particular pricing practice.

III

The next question is whether § 518 prohibits the pricing regime petitioners wish to employ. The Court of Appeals concluded that it does. The court read "surcharge" in § 518 to mean "an additional amount above the seller's regular price," and found it "basically self-evident" how § 518 applies to sellers who post a single sticker price: "the sticker price is the 'regular' price, so sellers may not charge credit-card customers an additional amount above the sticker price that is not also charged to cash customers." Under this interpretation, signs of the kind that the merchants wish to post — "$10, with a $0.30 surcharge for credit card users" — violate § 518 because they identify one sticker price — $10 — and indicate that credit card users are charged more than that amount.

"We generally accord great deference to the interpretation and application of state law by the courts of appeals." This deference is warranted to "render unnecessary review of their decisions in this respect" and because lower federal courts "are better schooled in and more able to interpret the laws of their respective States." "[W]e surely have the authority to differ with the lower federal courts as to the meaning of a state statute," and have done so in instances where the lower court's construction was "clearly wrong" or "plain error." But that is not the case here. Section 518 does not define "surcharge," but the Court of Appeals looked to the ordinary meaning of the term: "a charge in excess of the usual or normal amount." Where a seller posts a single sticker price, it is reasonable to treat that sticker price as the "usual or normal amount" and conclude, as the court below did, that a merchant imposes a surcharge when he charges a credit card user more than that sticker price. In short, we cannot dismiss the Court of Appeals' interpretation of § 518 as "clearly wrong." Accordingly, consistent with our customary practice, we follow that interpretation.

IV

Having concluded that § 518 bars the pricing regime petitioners wish to employ, we turn to their constitutional arguments: that the law unconstitutionally regulates speech and is impermissibly vague.

The Court of Appeals concluded that § 518 posed no First Amendment problem because the law regulated conduct, not speech. In reaching this conclusion, the Court of Appeals began with the premise that price controls regulate conduct alone. Section 518 regulates the relationship between "(1) the seller's sticker price and (2) the price the seller charges to credit card customers," requiring that these two amounts be equal. 808

F.3d, at 131. A law regulating the relationship between two prices regulates speech no more than a law regulating a single price. The Court of Appeals concluded that § 518 was therefore simply a conduct regulation.

But § 518 is not like a typical price regulation. Such a regulation—for example, a law requiring all New York delis to charge $10 for their sandwiches—would simply regulate the amount that a store could collect. In other words, it would regulate the sandwich seller's conduct. To be sure, in order to actually collect that money, a store would likely have to put "$10" on its menus or have its employees tell customers that price. Those written or oral communications would be speech, and the law—by determining the amount charged—would indirectly dictate the content of that speech. But the law's effect on speech would be only incidental to its primary effect on conduct, and "it has never been deemed an abridgment of freedom of speech or press to make a course of conduct illegal merely because the conduct was in part initiated, evidenced, or carried out by means of language, either spoken, written, or printed."

Section 518 is different. The law tells merchants nothing about the amount they are allowed to collect from a cash or credit card payer. Sellers are free to charge $10 for cash and $9.70, $10, $10.30, or any other amount for credit. What the law does regulate is how sellers may communicate their prices. A merchant who wants to charge $10 for cash and $10.30 for credit may not convey that price any way he pleases. He is not free to say "$10, with a 3% credit card surcharge" or "$10, plus $0.30 for credit" because both of those displays identify a single sticker price—$10—that is less than the amount credit card users will be charged. Instead, if the merchant wishes to post a single sticker price, he must display $10.30 as his sticker price. Accordingly, while we agree with the Court of Appeals that § 518 regulates a relationship between a sticker price and the price charged to credit card users, we cannot accept its conclusion that § 518 is nothing more than a mine-run price regulation. In regulating the communication of prices rather than prices themselves, § 518 regulates speech.

Because it concluded otherwise, the Court of Appeals had no occasion to conduct a further inquiry into whether § 518, as a speech regulation, survived First Amendment scrutiny. On that question, the parties dispute whether § 518 is a valid commercial speech regulation under *Central Hudson Gas & Elec. Corp. v. Public Serv. Comm'n of N.Y.* (1980), and whether the law can be upheld as a valid disclosure requirement. "[W]e are a court of review, not of first view." Accordingly, we decline to consider those questions in the first instance. Instead, we remand for the Court of Appeals to analyze § 518 as a speech regulation.

Justice BREYER, concurring in the judgment.

I agree with the Court that New York's statute regulates speech. But that is because virtually all government regulation affects speech. Human relations take place through speech. And human relations include community activities of all kinds—commercial and otherwise.

When the government seeks to regulate those activities, it is often wiser not to try to distinguish between "speech" and "conduct." Instead, we can, and normally do, simply ask whether, or how, a challenged statute, rule, or regulation affects an interest that the First Amendment protects. If, for example, a challenged government regulation negatively affects the processes through which political discourse or public opinion is formed or expressed (interests close to the First Amendment's protective core), courts normally scrutinize that regulation with great care.

If the challenged regulation restricts the "informational function" provided by truthful commercial speech, courts will apply a "lesser" (but still elevated) form of scrutiny. If, however, a challenged regulation simply requires a commercial speaker to disclose "purely factual and uncontroversial information," courts will apply a more permissive standard of review. Because that kind of regulation normally has only a "minimal" effect on First Amendment interests, it normally need only be "reasonably related to the State's interest in preventing deception of consumers." Courts apply a similarly permissive standard of review to "regulatory legislation affecting ordinary commercial transactions." *United States v. Carolene Products Co.* (1938). Since that legislation normally does not significantly affect the interests that the First Amendment protects, we normally look only for assurance that the legislation "rests upon some rational basis."

I repeat these well-known general standards or judicial approaches both because I believe that determining the proper approach is typically more important than trying to distinguish "speech" from "conduct," and because the parties here differ as to which approach applies. That difference reflects the fact that it is not clear just what New York's law does. On its face, the law seems simply to tell merchants that they cannot charge higher prices to credit-card users. If so, then it is an ordinary piece of commercial legislation subject to "rational basis" review. It may, however, make more sense to interpret the statute as working like the expired federal law that it replaced. If so, it would require a merchant, who posts prices and who wants to charge a higher credit-card price, simply to disclose that credit-card price. In that case, though affecting the merchant's "speech," it would not hinder the transmission of information to the public; the merchant would remain free to say whatever it wanted so long as it also revealed its credit-card price to customers. Accordingly, the law would still receive a deferential form of review.

Nonetheless, petitioners suggest that the statute does more. Because the statute's operation is unclear and because its interpretation is a matter of state law, I agree with the majority that we should remand the case to the Second Circuit. I also agree with Justice Sotomayor that on remand, it may well be helpful for the Second Circuit to ask the New York Court of Appeals to clarify the nature of the obligations the statute imposes.

Justice SOTOMAYOR, with whom Justice ALITO joins, concurring in the judgment.

The Court addresses only one part of one half of petitioners' First Amendment challenge to the New York statute at issue here. This quarter-loaf outcome is worse than none. I would vacate the judgment below and remand with directions to certify the case to the New York Court of Appeals for a definitive interpretation of the statute that would permit the full resolution of petitioners' claims.

D.   What Places Are Available for Speech?

1.   Government Properties and Speech

f.   Nonpublic Forums (casebook p. 1628)

In *Burson v. Freeman* (1992) (casebook p. 1597), the Supreme Court upheld a Tennessee law that prohibited distribution of campaign literature within 100 feet of a polling place. But in *Minnesota Voters Alliance v. Mansky*, 138 S. Ct. 1876 (2018), the Court declared unconstitutional a Minnesota law that prohibits individuals, including voters, from wearing a "political badge, political button, or other political insignia" inside a polling place on Election Day. The Court explicitly said that the inside of polling places "qualifies as a nonpublic forum. It is, at least on Election Day, government-controlled property set aside for the sole purpose of voting." The Court said that the restriction on speech had to be reasonable and viewpoint neutral. The Court said that the Minnesota law was unconstitutional because the meaning of "political" is too ambiguous and uncertain. Chief Justice Roberts writing for the Court explained: "the statute prohibits wearing a 'political badge, political button, or other political insignia.' It does not define the term 'political.' And the word can be expansive. It can encompass anything 'of or relating to government, a government, or the conduct of governmental affairs,' Webster's Third New International Dictionary 1755 (2002), or anything '[o]f, relating to, or dealing with the structure or affairs of government, politics, or the state,' American Heritage Dictionary 1401 (3d ed. 1996). Under a literal reading of those definitions, a button or T-shirt merely imploring others to "Vote!" could qualify." The Court concluded: "But we do hold that if a State wishes to set its polling places apart as areas free of partisan discord, it must employ a more discernible approach than the one Minnesota has offered here."

E. Freedom of Association

3. Compelled Association (casebook p. 1674)

In *Abood v. Detroit Board of Education* (casebook p. 1674), the Court held that no one can be forced to join a public employees' union, but that non-union members can be required to pay the share of the dues that go to support the collective bargaining activities of the union. In *Janus v. American Federation* (2018), the Court expressly overruled *Abood*.

JANUS v. AMERICAN FEDERATION OF STATE, COUNTY, AND MUNICIPAL EMPLOYEES, COUNCIL 31
138 S. Ct. 2448 (2018)

Justice ALITO delivered the opinion of the Court.

Under Illinois law, public employees are forced to subsidize a union, even if they choose not to join and strongly object to the positions the union takes in collective bargaining and related activities. We conclude that this arrangement violates the free speech rights of nonmembers by compelling them to subsidize private speech on matters of substantial public concern.

We upheld a similar law in *Abood v. Detroit Bd. of Ed.* (1977), and we recognize the importance of following precedent unless there are strong reasons for not doing so. But there are very strong reasons in this case. Fundamental free speech rights are at stake. *Abood* was poorly reasoned. It has led to practical problems and abuse. It is inconsistent with other First Amendment cases and has been undermined by more recent decisions.

Developments since *Abood* was handed down have shed new light on the issue of agency fees, and no reliance interests on the part of public-sector unions are sufficient to justify the perpetuation of the free speech violations that *Abood* has countenanced for the past 41 years. *Abood* is therefore overruled.

I

Under the Illinois Public Labor Relations Act (IPLRA), employees of the State and its political subdivisions are permitted to unionize. If a majority of the employees in a bargaining unit vote to be represented by a union, that union is designated as the exclusive representative of all the employees. Employees in the unit are not obligated to join the union selected by their co-workers, but whether they join or not, that union is deemed to be their sole permitted representative.

Once a union is so designated, it is vested with broad authority. Only the union may negotiate with the employer on matters relating to "pay, wages, hours [,] and other conditions of employment." And this authority extends to the negotiation of what the IPLRA calls "policy matters," such as merit pay, the size of the work force, layoffs, privatization, promotion methods, and non-discrimination policies.

Designating a union as the employees' exclusive representative substantially restricts the rights of individual employees. Among other things, this designation means that individual employees may not be represented by any agent other than the designated union; nor may individual employees negotiate directly with their employer. Protection of the employees' interests is placed in the hands of the union, and therefore the union is required by law to provide fair representation for all employees in the unit, members and nonmembers alike.

Employees who decline to join the union are not assessed full union dues but must instead pay what is generally called an "agency fee," which amounts to a percentage of the union dues. Under *Abood*, nonmembers may be charged for the portion of union dues attributable to activities that are "germane to [the union's] duties as collective-bargaining representative," but nonmembers may not be required to fund the union's political and ideological projects. bor-law parlance, the outlays in the first category are known as "chargeable" expenditures, while those in the latter are labeled "nonchargeable."

Illinois law does not specify in detail which expenditures are chargeable and which are not. The IPLRA provides that an agency fee may compensate a union for the costs incurred in "the collective bargaining process, contract administration[,] and pursuing matters affecting wages, hours [,] and conditions of employment." Excluded from the agency-fee calculation are union expenditures "related to the election or support of any candidate for political office."

As illustrated by the record in this case, unions charge nonmembers, not just for the cost of collective bargaining *per se*, but also for many other supposedly connected activities. Here, the nonmembers were told that they had to pay for "[l]obbying," "[s]ocial and recreational activities," "advertising," "[m]embership meetings and conventions," and "litigation," as well as other unspecified "[s]ervices" that "may ultimately inure to the benefit of the members of the local bargaining unit." The total chargeable amount for nonmembers was 78.06% of full union dues.

Petitioner Mark Janus is employed by the Illinois Department of Healthcare and Family Services as a child support specialist. The employees in his unit are among the 35,000 public employees in Illinois who are represented by respondent American Federation of State, County, and Municipal Employees, Council 31 (Union). Janus refused to join the Union because he opposes "many of the public policy positions that [it] advocates," including the positions it takes in collective bargaining. Janus believes that the Union's "behavior in bargaining does not appreciate the current fiscal crises in Illinois and does not reflect his best interests or the interests of Illinois citizens." Therefore, if he had the choice, he "would not pay any fees or otherwise subsidize [the Union]." Under his unit's collective-bargaining agreement, however, he was required to pay an agency fee of $44.58 per month, —which would amount to about $535 per year.

[II]

We first consider whether *Abood*'s holding is consistent with standard First Amendment principles. We have held time and again that freedom of speech "includes both the right to speak freely and the right to refrain from speaking at all." The right to eschew association for expressive purposes is likewise protected. As Justice Jackson memorably put it: "If there is any fixed star in our constitutional constellation, it is that no official, high or petty, can prescribe what shall be orthodox in politics, nationalism, religion, or other matters of opinion or *force citizens to confess by word or act their faith therein.*"

Compelling individuals to mouth support for views they find objectionable violates that cardinal constitutional command, and in most contexts, any such effort would be universally condemned. Suppose, for example, that the State of Illinois required all residents to sign a document expressing support for a particular set of positions on controversial public issues — say, the platform of one of the major political parties. No one, we trust, would seriously argue that the First Amendment permits this.

Perhaps because such compulsion so plainly violates the Constitution, most of our free speech cases have involved restrictions on what can be said, rather than laws compelling speech. But measures compelling speech are at least as threatening.

Whenever the Federal Government or a State prevents individuals from saying what they think on important matters or compels them to voice ideas with which they disagree, it undermines these ends. When speech is compelled, however, additional damage is done. In that situation, individuals are coerced into betraying their convictions. Forcing free and independent individuals to endorse ideas they find objectionable is always demeaning, and for this reason, one of our landmark free speech cases said that a law commanding "involuntary affirmation" of objected-to beliefs would require "even more immediate and urgent grounds" than a law demanding silence.

Compelling a person to *subsidize* the speech of other private speakers raises similar First Amendment concerns. As Jefferson famously put it, "to compel a man to furnish contributions of money for the propagation of opinions which he disbelieves and abhor[s] is sinful and tyrannical." We have therefore recognized that a "'significant impingement on First Amendment rights'" occurs when public employees are required to provide financial support for a union that "takes many positions during collective bargaining that have powerful political and civic consequences."

Because the compelled subsidization of private speech seriously impinges on First Amendment rights, it cannot be casually allowed.

[P]etitioner in the present case contends that the Illinois law at issue should be subjected to "strict scrutiny." The dissent, on the other hand, proposes that we apply what amounts to rational-basis review, that is, that we ask only whether a government employer could reasonably believe that the exaction of agency fees serves its interests. This form of minimal scrutiny is foreign to our free-speech jurisprudence, and we reject it here. At the same time, we again find it unnecessary to decide the issue of strict scrutiny because the Illinois scheme cannot survive under even the more permissive standard.

In *Abood*, the main defense of the agency-fee arrangement was that it served the State's interest in "labor peace." By "labor peace," the *Abood* Court meant avoidance of the conflict and disruption that it envisioned would occur if the employees in a unit were represented by more than one union. In such a situation, the Court predicted, "inter-union rivalries" would foster "dissension within the work force," and the employer could face "conflicting demands from different unions." Confusion would ensue if the employer entered into and attempted to "enforce two or more agreements specifying different terms and conditions of employment." And a settlement with one union would be "subject to attack from [a] rival labor organizatio[n."

We assume that "labor peace," in this sense of the term, is a compelling state interest, but *Abood* cited no evidence that the pandemonium it imagined would result if agency fees were not allowed, and it is now clear that *Abood*'s fears were unfounded. The *Abood* Court assumed that designation of a union as the exclusive representative of all the employees in a unit and the exaction of agency fees are inextricably linked, but that is simply not true.

Whatever may have been the case 41 years ago when *Abood* was handed down, it is now undeniable that "labor peace" can readily be achieved "through means significantly less restrictive of associational freedoms" than the assessment of agency fees.

In addition to the promotion of "labor peace," *Abood* cited "the risk of 'free riders'" as justification for agency fees. Respondents and some of their *amici* endorse this reasoning, contending that agency fees are needed to prevent nonmembers from enjoying the benefits of union representation without shouldering the costs.

Petitioner strenuously objects to this free-rider label. He argues that he is not a free rider on a bus headed for a destination that he wishes to reach but is more like a person shanghaied for an unwanted voyage.

Whichever description fits the majority of public employees who would not subsidize a union if given the option, avoiding free riders is not a compelling interest. As we have noted, "free-rider arguments . . . are generally insufficient to overcome First Amendment objections." To hold otherwise across the board would have startling consequences. Many private groups speak out with the objective of obtaining government action that will have the effect of benefiting nonmembers. May all those who are thought to benefit from such efforts be compelled to subsidize this speech?

Suppose that a particular group lobbies or speaks out on behalf of what it thinks are the needs of senior citizens or veterans or physicians, to take just a few examples. Could the government require that all seniors, veterans, or doctors pay for that service even if they object? It has never been thought that this is permissible. "[P]rivate speech often furthers the interests of nonspeakers," but "that does not alone empower the state to compel the speech to be paid for.". In simple terms, the First Amendment does not permit the government to compel a person to pay for another party's speech just because the government thinks that the speech furthers the interests of the person who does not want to pay.

In any event, whatever unwanted burden is imposed by the representation of nonmembers in disciplinary matters can be eliminated "through means significantly less restrictive of associational freedoms" than the imposition of agency fees. Individual nonmembers could be required to pay for that service or could be denied union representation altogether. Thus, agency fees cannot be sustained on the ground that unions would otherwise be unwilling to represent nonmembers.

In sum, we do not see any reason to treat the free-rider interest any differently in the agency-fee context than in any other First Amendment context. We therefore hold that agency fees cannot be upheld on free-rider grounds.

[III]

Implicitly acknowledging the weakness of *Abood*'s own reasoning, proponents of agency fees have come forward with alternative justifications for the decision, and we now address these arguments.

The most surprising of these new arguments is the Union respondent's originalist defense of *Abood*. According to this argument, *Abood* was correctly decided because the First Amendment was not originally understood to provide *any* protection for the free speech rights of public employees.

As an initial matter, we doubt that the Union — or its members — actually want us to hold that public employees have *"no* [free speech] rights." It is particularly discordant to find this argument in a brief that trumpets the importance of *stare decisis*. See Brief for Union Taking away free speech protection for public employees would mean overturning decades of landmark precedent. In short, the Union has offered no basis for concluding that *Abood* is supported by the original understanding of the First Amendment.

The principal defense of *Abood* advanced by respondents and the dissent is based on our decision in *Pickering* [v. *Board of Education* (1968)], which held that a school district violated the First Amendment by firing a teacher for writing a letter critical of the school administration. Under *Pickering* and later cases in the same line, employee speech is largely unprotected if it is part of what the employee is paid to do, see *Garcetti v. Ceballos* (2006), or if it involved a matter of only private concern. On the other hand, when a public employee speaks as a citizen on a matter of public concern, the employee's speech is protected unless "'the interest of the state, as an employer, in promoting the efficiency of the public services it performs through its employees' outweighs 'the interests of the [employee], as a citizen, in commenting upon matters of public concern.'" *Abood* was not based on *Pickering*. The *Abood* majority cited the case exactly once—in a footnote—and then merely to acknowledge that "there may be limits on the extent to which an employee in a sensitive or policymaking position may freely criticize his superiors and the policies they espouse." We see no good reason, at this late date, to try to shoehorn *Abood* into the *Pickering* framework.

Even if we were to apply some form of *Pickering*, Illinois' agency-fee arrangement would not survive. Respondents begin by suggesting that union speech in collective-bargaining and grievance proceedings should be treated like the employee speech in *Garcetti*, *i.e.*, as speech "pursuant to [an employee's] official duties." Many employees, in both the public and private sectors, are paid to write or speak for the purpose of furthering the interests of their employers. There are laws that protect public employees from being compelled to say things that they reasonably believe to be untrue or improper, but in general when public employees are performing their job duties, their speech may be controlled by their employer. Trying to fit union speech into this framework, respondents now suggest that the union speech funded by agency fees forms part of the official duties of the union officers who engage in the speech.

This argument distorts collective bargaining and grievance adjustment beyond recognition. When an employee engages in speech that is part of the employee's job duties, the employee's words are really the words of the employer. The employee is effectively the employer's spokesperson. But when a union negotiates with the employer or represents employees in disciplinary proceedings, the union speaks for the *employees*, not the employer. Otherwise, the employer would be negotiating with itself and disputing its own actions. That is not what anybody understands to be happening.

What is more, if the union's speech is really the employer's speech, then the employer could dictate what the union says. Unions, we trust, would be appalled by such a suggestion. For these reasons, *Garcetti* is totally inapposite here.

Although the dissent would accept without any serious independent evaluation the State's assertion that the absence of agency fees would cripple public-sector unions and thus impair the efficiency of government operations, ample experience, as we have noted, shows that this is questionable. It is also not disputed that the State may require that a union serve as exclusive bargaining agent for its employees—itself a significant impingement on associational freedoms that would not be tolerated in other contexts. We simply draw the line at allowing the government to go further still and require all employees to support the union irrespective of whether they share its views. Nothing in the *Pickering* line of cases requires us to uphold every speech restriction the government imposes as an employer.

[V]

For the reasons given above, we conclude that public-sector agency-shop arrangements violate the First Amendment, and *Abood* erred in concluding otherwise. There remains the question whether *stare decisis* nonetheless counsels against overruling *Abood*. It does not.

The doctrine "is at its weakest when we interpret the Constitution because our interpretation can be altered only by constitutional amendment or by overruling our prior decisions." And *stare decisis* applies with perhaps least force of all to decisions that wrongly denied First Amendment rights: "This Court has not hesitated to overrule decisions offensive to the First Amendment (a fixed star in our constitutional constellation, if there is one)."

Our cases identify factors that should be taken into account in deciding whether to overrule a past decision. Five of these are most important here: the quality of *Abood*'s reasoning, the workability of the rule it established, its consistency with other related decisions, developments since the decision was handed down, and reliance on the decision.

An important factor in determining whether a precedent should be overruled is the quality of its reasoning. "*Abood* failed to appreciate the conceptual difficulty of distinguishing in public-sector cases between union expenditures that are made for collective-bargaining purposes and those that are made to achieve political ends." Likewise, "*Abood* does not seem to have anticipated the magnitude of the practical administrative problems that would result in attempting to classify public-sector union expenditures as either 'chargeable' . . . or nonchargeable." Nor did *Abood* "foresee the practical problems that would face objecting nonmembers."

In sum, *Abood* was not well reasoned.

Another relevant consideration in the *stare decisis* calculus is the workability of the precedent in question, and that factor also weighs against *Abood*. *Abood*'s line between chargeable and nonchargeable union expenditures has proved to be impossible to draw with precision.

Respondents agree that *Abood*'s chargeable-nonchargeable line suffers from "a vagueness problem," that it sometimes "allows what it shouldn't allow," and that "a firm[er] line c[ould] be drawn." This concession only underscores the reality that *Abood* has proved unworkable: Not even the parties defending agency fees support the line that it has taken this Court over 40 years to draw.

Developments since *Abood*, both factual and legal, have also "eroded" the decision's "underpinnings" and left it an outlier among our First Amendment cases. *Abood* is also an "anomaly" in our First Amendment jurisprudence., as we recognized in *Harris* and *Knox*.

Abood particularly sticks out when viewed against our cases holding that public employees generally may not be required to support a political party. It is an odd feature of our First Amendment cases that political patronage has been deemed largely unconstitutional, while forced subsidization of union speech (which has no such pedigree) has been largely permitted.

In some cases, reliance provides a strong reason for adhering to established law, and this is the factor that is stressed most strongly by respondents, their *amici*, and the dissent. They contend that collective-bargaining agreements now in effect were negotiated with agency fees in mind and that unions may have given up other benefits in exchange for provisions granting them such fees. In this case, however, reliance does not carry decisive weight.

For one thing, it would be unconscionable to permit free speech rights to be abridged in perpetuity in order to preserve contract provisions that will expire on their own in a few years' time. "The fact that [public-sector unions] may view [agency fees] as an entitlement does not establish the sort of reliance interest that could outweigh the countervailing interest that [nonmembers] share in having their constitutional rights fully protected." For another, *Abood* does not provide "a clear or easily applicable standard, so arguments for reliance based on its clarity are misplaced." This is especially so because public-sector unions have been on notice for years regarding this Court's misgivings about *Abood*.

In short, the uncertain status of *Abood*, the lack of clarity it provides, the short-term nature of collective-bargaining agreements, and the ability of unions to protect themselves if an agency-fee provision was crucial to its bargain all work to undermine the force of reliance as a factor supporting *Abood*.

We recognize that the loss of payments from nonmembers may cause unions to experience unpleasant transition costs in the short term, and may require unions to make adjustments in order to attract and retain members. But we must weigh these disadvantages against the considerable windfall that unions have received under *Abood* for the past 41 years.

It is hard to estimate how many billions of dollars have been taken from nonmembers and transferred to public-sector unions in violation of the First Amendment. Those unconstitutional exactions cannot be allowed to continue indefinitely.

[VI]

For these reasons, States and public-sector unions may no longer extract agency fees from nonconsenting employees. Under Illinois law, if a public-sector collective-bargaining agreement includes an agency-fee provision and the union certifies to the employer the amount of the fee, that amount is automatically deducted from the nonmember's wages. No form of employee consent is required.

This procedure violates the First Amendment and cannot continue. Neither an agency fee nor any other payment to the union may be deducted from a nonmember's wages, nor may any other attempt be made to collect such a payment, unless the employee affirmatively consents to pay. By agreeing to pay, nonmembers are waiving their First Amendment rights, and such a waiver cannot be presumed. Rather, to be effective, the waiver must be freely given and shown by "clear and compelling" evidence. Unless employees clearly and affirmatively consent before any money is taken from them, this standard cannot be met.

Abood was wrongly decided and is now overruled.

Justice KAGAN, with whom Justice GINSBURG, Justice BREYER, and Justice SOTOMAYOR join, dissenting.

For over 40 years, *Abood v. Detroit Bd. of Ed.* (1977), struck a stable balance between public employees' First Amendment rights and government entities' interests in running their workforces as they thought proper. Under that decision, a government entity could require public employees to pay a fair share of the cost that a union incurs when negotiating on their behalf over terms of employment. But no part of that fair-share payment could go to any of the union's political or ideological activities.

That holding fit comfortably with this Court's general framework for evaluating claims that a condition of public employment violates the First Amendment. The Court's decisions have long made plain that government entities have substantial latitude to regulate their employees' speech — especially about terms of employment — in the interest of operating their workplaces effectively. *Abood* allowed governments to do just that. While protecting public employees' expression about non-workplace matters, the decision enabled a government to advance important managerial interests—by ensuring the presence of an exclusive employee representative to bargain with. Far from an "anomaly," the *Abood* regime was a paradigmatic example of how the government can regulate speech in its capacity as an employer.

Not any longer. Its decision will have large-scale consequences. Public employee unions will lose a secure source of financial support. State and local governments that thought fair-share provisions furthered their interests will need to find new ways of managing their workforces. Across the country, the relationships of public employees and employers will alter in both predictable and wholly unexpected ways.

Rarely if ever has the Court overruled a decision—let alone one of this import—with so little regard for the usual principles of *stare decisis*. There are no special justifications for reversing *Abood*. It has proved workable. No recent developments have eroded its underpinnings. And it is deeply entrenched, in both the law and the real world. More than 20 States have statutory schemes built on the decision. Those laws underpin thousands of ongoing contracts involving millions of employees. Reliance interests do not come any stronger than those surrounding *Abood*. And likewise, judicial disruption does not get any greater than what the Court does today. I respectfully dissent.

[I]

Unlike the majority, I see nothing "questionable" about *Abood*'s analysis. The decision's account of why some government entities have a strong interest in agency fees (now often called fair-share fees) is fundamentally sound. And the balance *Abood* struck between public employers' interests and public employees' expression is right at home in First Amendment doctrine.

In many cases over many decades, this Court has addressed how the First Amendment applies when the government, acting not as sovereign but as employer, limits its workers' speech. Those decisions have granted substantial latitude to the government, in recognition of its significant interests in managing its workforce so as to best serve the public. *Abood* fit neatly with that caselaw, in both reasoning and result. Indeed, its reversal today creates a significant anomaly—an exception, applying to union fees alone, from the usual rules governing public employees' speech.

In striking the proper balance between employee speech rights and managerial interests, the Court has long applied a test originating in *Pickering v. Board of Ed. of Township High School Dist. 205, Will Cty.* (1968). *Abood* coheres with that framework. *Abood* and *Pickering* raised variants of the same basic issue: the extent of the government's authority to make employ-ment decisions affecting expression. And in both, the Court struck the same basic balance, enabling the government to curb speech when—but only when—the regulation was designed to protect its managerial interests.

The key point about *Abood* is that it fit naturally with this Court's con-sistent teaching about the permissibility of regulating public employees' speech. The Court allows a government entity to regulate that expression in aid of managing its workforce to effectively provide public services. That is just what a government aims to do when it enforces a fair-share agreement. And so, the key point about today's decision is that it creates an unjustified hole in the law, applicable to union fees alone. This case is *sui generis* among those addressing public employee speech—and will almost surely remain so.

[II]

But the worse part of today's opinion is where the majority subverts all known principles of *stare decisis*. The majority makes plain, in the first 33 pages of its decision, that it believes *Abood* was wrong.[4] But even if that were true (which it is not), it is not enough. "Respecting *stare decisis* means sticking to some wrong decisions." Any departure from settled precedent (so the Court has often stated) demands a "special jus-tification—over and above the belief that the precedent was wrongly decided." And the majority does not have anything close. To the con-trary: all that is "special" in this case—especially the massive reliance interests at stake—demands retaining *Abood*, beyond even the normal precedent.

And *Abood* is not just any precedent: It is embedded in the law (not to mention, as I'll later address, in the world) in a way not many decisions are. Over four decades, this Court has cited *Abood* favorably many times, and has affirmed and applied its central distinction between the costs of collective bargaining (which the government can charge to all employees) and those of political activities (which it cannot).

The majority is likewise wrong to invoke "workability" as a reason for overruling *Abood*. Does *Abood* require drawing a line? Yes, between a union's collective-bargaining activities and its political activities. Is that line perfectly and pristinely "precis[e]," as the majority demands? Well, not quite that—but as exercises of constitutional linedrawing go, *Abood* stands well above average. In the 40 years since *Abood*, this Court has had to resolve only a handful of cases raising questions about the distinction. To my knowledge, the circuit courts are not divided on any classification issue; neither are they issuing distress signals of the kind that sometimes prompt the Court to reverse a decision. And that tranquility is unsurprising: There may be some gray areas (there always are), but in the mine run of cases, everyone knows the difference between politicking and collective bargaining.

And in any event, one *stare decisis* factor—reliance—dominates all others here and demands keeping *Abood*. *Stare decisis*, this Court has held, "has added force when the legislature, in the public sphere, and citizens, in the private realm, have acted in reliance on a previous decision." That is because overruling a decision would then "require an extensive legislative response" or "dislodge settled rights and expectations." Both will happen here: The Court today wreaks havoc on entrenched legislative and contractual arrangements.

Over 20 States have by now enacted statutes authorizing fair-share provisions. To be precise, 22 States, the District of Columbia, and Puerto Rico—plus another two States for police and firefighter unions. Many of those States have multiple statutory provisions, with variations for different categories of public employees. Every one of them will now need to come up with new ways—elaborated in new statutes—to structure relations between government employers and their workers. Still more, thousands of current contracts covering millions of workers provide for agency fees. Usually, this Court recognizes that "[c]onsiderations in favor of *stare decisis* are at their acme in cases involving property and contract rights." Not today. The majority undoes bargains reached all over the country. It prevents the parties from fulfilling other commitments they have made based on those agreements. It forces the parties—immediately—to renegotiate once-settled terms and create new tradeoffs. It does so knowing that many of the parties will have to revise (or redo) multiple contracts simultaneously. It does so knowing that those renegotiations will occur in an environment of legal uncertainty, as state governments scramble to enact new labor legislation. It does so with no real clue of what will happen next—of how its action will alter public-sector labor relations. It does so even though the government services affected—policing, firefighting, teaching, transportation, sanitation (and more)—affect the quality of life of tens of millions of Americans.

[III]

There is no sugarcoating today's opinion. The majority overthrows a decision entrenched in this Nation's law—and in its economic life—for over 40 years. As a result, it prevents the American people, acting through their state and local officials, from making important choices about workplace governance. And it does so by weaponizing the First Amendment, in a way that unleashes judges, now and in the future, to intervene in economic and regulatory policy.

The majority has overruled *Abood* for no exceptional or special reason, but because it never liked the decision. It has overruled *Abood* because it wanted to.

Because, that is, it wanted to pick the winning side in what should be — and until now, has been — an energetic policy debate. Some state and local governments (and the constituents they serve) think that stable unions promote healthy labor relations and thereby improve the provision of services to the public. Other state and local governments (and their constituents) think, to the contrary, that strong unions impose excessive costs and impair those services. Americans have debated the pros and cons for many decades — in large part, by deciding whether to use fair-share arrangements. Yesterday, 22 States were on one side, 28 on the other (ignoring a couple of in-betweeners). Today, that healthy — that democratic — debate ends. The majority has adjudged who should prevail.

And maybe most alarming, the majority has chosen the winners by turning the First Amendment into a sword, and using it against workaday economic and regulatory policy. And it threatens not to be the last. Speech is everywhere — a part of every human activity (employment, health care, securities trading, you name it). For that reason, almost all economic and regulatory policy affects or touches speech. So the majority's road runs long. And at every stop are black-robed rulers overriding citizens' choices. The First Amendment was meant for better things. It was meant not to undermine but to protect democratic governance — including over the role of public-sector unions.

Chapter 10

The First Amendment: Religion

B. The Free Exercise Clause

2. The Current Test (p. 1732)

The Supreme Court has held that the government violates free exercise of religion when it acts with hostility to religion. In *Masterpiece Cakeshop v. Colorado Civil Rights Commission*, the Court found hostility to religion when the Colorado Civil Rights Commission ruled against a baker who refused to design and bake a case to celebrate the wedding of a same-sex couple. The Court left unresolved whether it violates free exercise of religion or freedom of speech to hold a baker—or other business—liable for refusal to serve a same-sex couple.

MASTERPIECE CAKE SHOP, LTD. v.
COLORADO CIVIL RIGHTS COMMISSION
138 S. Ct. 1719 (2018)

Justice KENNEDY delivered the opinion of the Court.

In 2012 a same-sex couple visited Masterpiece Cakeshop, a bakery in Colorado, to make inquiries about ordering a cake for their wedding reception. The shop's owner told the couple that he would not create a cake for their wedding because of his religious opposition to same-sex marriages—marriages the State of Colorado itself did not recognize at that time. The couple filed a charge with the Colorado Civil Rights Commission alleging discrimination on the basis of sexual orientation in violation of the Colorado Anti-Discrimination Act.

The Commission determined that the shop's actions violated the Act and ruled in the couple's favor. The Colorado state courts affirmed the ruling and its enforcement order, and this Court now must decide whether the Commission's order violated the Constitution.

The case presents difficult questions as to the proper reconciliation of at least two principles. The first is the authority of a State and its governmental entities to protect the rights and dignity of gay persons who are, or wish to be, married but who face discrimination when they seek goods or services. The second is the right of all persons to exercise fundamental freedoms under the First Amendment, as applied to the States through the Fourteenth Amendment.

The freedoms asserted here are both the freedom of speech and the free exercise of religion. The free speech aspect of this case is difficult, for few persons who have seen a beautiful wedding cake might have thought of its creation as an exercise of protected speech. This is an instructive example, however, of the proposition that the application of constitutional freedoms in new contexts can deepen our understanding of their meaning.

One of the difficulties in this case is that the parties disagree as to the extent of the baker's refusal to provide service. If a baker refused to design a special cake with words or images celebrating the marriage — for instance, a cake showing words with religious meaning — that might be different from a refusal to sell any cake at all. In defining whether a baker's creation can be protected, these details might make a difference.

The same difficulties arise in determining whether a baker has a valid free exercise claim. A baker's refusal to attend the wedding to ensure that the cake is cut the right way, or a refusal to put certain religious words or decorations on the cake, or even a refusal to sell a cake that has been baked for the public generally but includes certain religious words or symbols on it are just three examples of possibilities that seem all but endless.

Whatever the confluence of speech and free exercise principles might be in some cases, the Colorado Civil Rights Commission's consideration of this case was inconsistent with the State's obligation of religious neutrality. The reason and motive for the baker's refusal were based on his sincere religious beliefs and convictions. The Court's precedents make clear that the baker, in his capacity as the owner of a business serving the public, might have his right to the free exercise of religion limited by generally applicable laws. Still, the delicate question of when the free exercise of his religion must yield to an otherwise valid exercise of state power needed to be determined in an adjudication in which religious hostility on the part of the State itself would not be a factor in the balance the State sought to reach. That requirement, however, was not met here. When the Colorado Civil Rights Commission considered this case, it did not do so with the religious neutrality that the Constitution requires.

Given all these considerations, it is proper to hold that whatever the outcome of some future controversy involving facts similar to these, the

Commission's actions here violated the Free Exercise Clause; and its order must be set aside.

I

Masterpiece Cakeshop, Ltd., is a bakery in Lakewood, Colorado, a suburb of Denver. The shop offers a variety of baked goods, ranging from everyday cookies and brownies to elaborate custom-designed cakes for birthday parties, weddings, and other events.

Jack Phillips is an expert baker who has owned and operated the shop for 24 years. Phillips is a devout Christian. He has explained that his "main goal in life is to be obedient to" Jesus Christ and Christ's "teachings in all aspects of his life." And he seeks to "honor God through his work at Masterpiece Cakeshop." One of Phillips' religious beliefs is that "God's intention for marriage from the beginning of history is that it is and should be the union of one man and one woman." To Phillips, creating a wedding cake for a same-sex wedding would be equivalent to participating in a celebration that is contrary to his own most deeply held beliefs.

Phillips met Charlie Craig and Dave Mullins when they entered his shop in the summer of 2012. Craig and Mullins were planning to marry. At that time, Colorado did not recognize same-sex marriages, so the couple planned to wed legally in Massachusetts and afterwards to host a reception for their family and friends in Denver. To prepare for their celebration, Craig and Mullins visited the shop and told Phillips that they were interested in ordering a cake for "our wedding." They did not mention the design of the cake they envisioned.

Phillips informed the couple that he does not "create" wedding cakes for same-sex weddings. He explained, "I'll make your birthday cakes, shower cakes, sell you cookies and brownies, I just don't make cakes for same sex weddings." The couple left the shop without further discussion.

The following day, Craig's mother, who had accompanied the couple to the cakeshop and been present for their interaction with Phillips, telephoned to ask Phillips why he had declined to serve her son. Phillips explained that he does not create wedding cakes for same-sex weddings because of his religious opposition to same-sex marriage, and also because Colorado (at that time) did not recognize same-sex marriages. He later explained his belief that "to create a wedding cake for an event that celebrates something that directly goes against the teachings of the Bible, would have been a personal endorsement and participation in the ceremony and relationship that they were entering into."

Today, the Colorado Anti-Discrimination Act (CADA) carries forward the state's tradition of prohibiting discrimination in places of public accommodation. Amended in 2007 and 2008 to prohibit discrimination on the basis of sexual orientation as well as other protected characteristics, CADA in relevant part provides as follows:

> It is a discriminatory practice and unlawful for a person, directly or indirectly, to refuse, withhold from, or deny to an individual or a group, because of disability, race, creed, color, sex, sexual orientation, marital status, national origin, or ancestry, the full and equal enjoyment of the goods, services, facilities, privileges, advantages, or accommodations of a place of public accommodation.

The Act defines "public accommodation" broadly to include any "place of business engaged in any sales to the public and any place offering services . . . to the public," but excludes "a church, synagogue, mosque, or other place that is principally used for religious purposes."

Craig and Mullins filed a discrimination complaint against Masterpiece Cakeshop and Phillips in September 2012, shortly after the couple's visit to the shop. App. 31. The complaint alleged that Craig and Mullins had been denied "full and equal service" at the bakery because of their sexual orientation, and that it was Phillips' "standard business practice" not to provide cakes for same-sex weddings.

The Civil Rights Division opened an investigation. The investigator found that "on multiple occasions," Phillips "turned away potential customers on the basis of their sexual orientation, stating that he could not create a cake for a same-sex wedding ceremony or reception" because his religious beliefs prohibited it and because the potential customers "were doing something illegal" at that time. The investigation found that Phillips had declined to sell custom wedding cakes to about six other same-sex couples on this basis. The investigator also recounted that, according to affidavits submitted by Craig and Mullins, Phillips' shop had refused to sell cupcakes to a lesbian couple for their commitment celebration because the shop "had a policy of not selling baked goods to same-sex couples for this type of event." Based on these findings, the Division found probable cause that Phillips violated CADA and referred the case to the Civil Rights Commission.

The Commission found it proper to conduct a formal hearing, and it sent the case to a State ALJ. Finding no dispute as to material facts, the ALJ entertained cross-motions for summary judgment and ruled in the couple's favor. The ALJ first rejected Phillips' argument that declining to make or create a wedding cake for Craig and Mullins did not violate Colorado law. It was undisputed that the shop is subject to state public accommodations laws. And the ALJ determined that Phillips' actions constituted prohibited discrimination on the basis of sexual orientation, not simply opposition to same-sex marriage as Phillips contended.

The Commission affirmed the ALJ's decision in full. The Commission ordered Phillips to "cease and desist from discriminating against . . . same-sex couples by refusing to sell them wedding cakes or any product [they] would sell to heterosexual couples." It also ordered additional remedial measures, including "comprehensive staff training on the Public Accommodations section" of CADA "and changes to any and all company policies to comply with . . . this Order." The Commission additionally required Phillips to prepare "quarterly compliance reports" for a period of two years documenting "the number of patrons denied service" and why, along with "a statement describing the remedial actions taken."

Phillips appealed to the Colorado Court of Appeals, which affirmed the Commission's legal determinations and remedial order.

II

Our society has come to the recognition that gay persons and gay couples cannot be treated as social outcasts or as inferior in dignity and worth. For that reason the laws and the Constitution can, and in some instances must, protect them in the exercise of their civil rights. The exercise of their freedom on terms equal to others must be given great weight and respect by the courts. At the same time, the religious and philosophical objections to gay marriage are protected views and in some instances protected forms of expression. As this Court observed in *Obergefell v. Hodges* (2015), "[t]he First Amendment ensures that religious organizations and persons are given proper protection as they seek to teach the principles that are so fulfilling and so central to their lives and faiths." Nevertheless, while those religious and philosophical objections are protected, it is a general rule that such objections do not allow business owners and other actors in the economy and in society to deny protected persons equal access to goods and services under a neutral and generally applicable public accommodations law.

When it comes to weddings, it can be assumed that a member of the clergy who objects to gay marriage on moral and religious grounds could not be compelled to perform the ceremony without denial of his or her right to the free exercise of religion. This refusal would be well understood in our constitutional order as an exercise of religion, an exercise that gay persons could recognize and accept without serious diminishment to their own dignity and worth. Yet if that exception were not confined, then a long list of persons who provide goods and services for marriages and weddings might refuse to do so for gay persons, thus resulting in a community-wide stigma inconsistent with the history and dynamics of civil rights laws that ensure equal access to goods, services, and public accommodations.

It is unexceptional that Colorado law can protect gay persons, just as it can protect other classes of individuals, in acquiring whatever products and services they choose on the same terms and conditions as are offered to other members of the public. And there are no doubt innumerable goods and services that no one could argue implicate the First Amendment. Petitioners conceded, moreover, that if a baker refused to sell any goods or any cakes for gay weddings, that would be a different matter and the State would have a strong case under this Court's precedents that this would be a denial of goods and services that went beyond any protected rights of a baker who offers goods and services to the general public and is subject to a neutrally applied and generally applicable public accommodations law.

Phillips claims, however, that a narrower issue is presented. He argues that he had to use his artistic skills to make an expressive statement, a wedding endorsement in his own voice and of his own creation. As Phillips would see the case, this contention has a significant First Amendment speech component and implicates his deep and sincere religious beliefs. In this context the baker likely found it difficult to find a line where the customers' rights to goods and services became a demand for him to exercise the right of his own personal expression for their message, a message he could not express in a way consistent with his religious beliefs.

Phillips' dilemma was particularly understandable given the background of legal principles and administration of the law in Colorado at that time. His decision and his actions leading to the refusal of service all occurred in the year 2012. At that point, Colorado did not recognize the validity of gay marriages performed in its own State. Since the State itself did not allow those marriages to be performed in Colorado, there is some force to the argument that the baker was not unreasonable in deeming it lawful to decline to take an action that he understood to be an expression of support for their validity when that expression was contrary to his sincerely held religious beliefs, at least insofar as his refusal was limited to refusing to create and express a message in support of gay marriage, even one planned to take place in another State.

At the time, state law also afforded storekeepers some latitude to decline to create specific messages the storekeeper considered offensive. Indeed, while enforcement proceedings against Phillips were ongoing, the Colorado Civil Rights Division itself endorsed this proposition in cases involving other bakers' creation of cakes, concluding on at least three occasions that a baker acted lawfully in declining to create cakes with decorations that demeaned gay persons or gay marriages.

[A]ny decision in favor of the baker would have to be sufficiently constrained, lest all purveyors of goods and services who object to gay marriages for moral and religious reasons in effect be allowed to put up signs saying "no goods or services will be sold if they will be used for gay marriages," something that would impose a serious stigma on gay persons. But, nonetheless, Phillips was entitled to the neutral and respectful consideration of his claims in all the circumstances of the case.

The neutral and respectful consideration to which Phillips was entitled was compromised here, however. The Civil Rights Commission's treatment of his case has some elements of a clear and impermissible hostility toward the sincere religious beliefs that motivated his objection.

That hostility surfaced at the Commission's formal, public hearings, as shown by the record. On May 30, 2014, the seven-member Commission convened publicly to consider Phillips' case. At several points during its meeting, commissioners endorsed the view that religious beliefs cannot legitimately be carried into the public sphere or commercial domain, implying that religious beliefs and persons are less than fully welcome in Colorado's business community. One commissioner suggested that Phillips can believe "what he wants to believe," but cannot act on his religious beliefs "if he decides to do business in the state." A few moments later, the commissioner restated the same position: "[I]f a businessman wants to do business in the state and he's got an issue with the — the law's impacting his personal belief system, he needs to look at being able to compromise." Standing alone, these statements are susceptible of different interpretations. On the one hand, they might mean simply that a business cannot refuse to provide services based on sexual orientation, regardless of the proprietor's personal views. On the other hand, they might be seen as inappropriate and dismissive comments showing lack of due consideration for Phillips' free exercise rights and the dilemma he faced. In view of the comments that followed, the latter seems the more likely.

On July 25, 2014, the Commission met again. This meeting, too, was conducted in public and on the record. On this occasion another commissioner made specific reference to the previous meeting's discussion but said far more to disparage Phillips' beliefs. The commissioner stated:

"I would also like to reiterate what we said in the hearing or the last meeting. Freedom of religion and religion has been used to justify all kinds of discrimination throughout history, whether it be slavery, whether it be the holocaust, whether it be — I mean, we — we can list hundreds of situations where freedom of religion has been used to justify discrimination. And to me it is one of the most despicable pieces of rhetoric that people can use to — to use their religion to hurt others."

To describe a man's faith as "one of the most despicable pieces of rhetoric that people can use" is to disparage his religion in at least two distinct ways: by describing it as despicable, and also by characterizing it as merely rhetorical — something insubstantial and even insincere. The commissioner even went so far as to compare Phillips' invocation of his sincerely held religious beliefs to defenses of slavery and the Holocaust. This sentiment is inappropriate for a Commission charged with the solemn responsibility of fair and neutral enforcement of Colorado's antidiscrimination law — a law that protects against discrimination on the basis of religion as well as sexual orientation.

The record shows no objection to these comments from other commissioners. And the later state-court ruling reviewing the Commission's decision did not mention those comments, much less express concern with their content. Nor were the comments by the commissioners disavowed in the briefs filed in this Court. For these reasons, the Court cannot avoid the conclusion that these statements cast doubt on the fairness and impartiality of the Commission's adjudication of Phillips' case. Members of the Court have disagreed on the question whether statements made by lawmakers may properly be taken into account in determining whether a law intentionally discriminates on the basis of religion. In this case, however, the remarks were made in a very different context — by an adjudicatory body deciding a particular case.

Another indication of hostility is the difference in treatment between Phillips' case and the cases of other bakers who objected to a requested cake on the basis of conscience and prevailed before the Commission. As noted above, on at least three other occasions the Civil Rights Division considered the refusal of bakers to create cakes with images that conveyed disapproval of same-sex marriage, along with religious text. Each time, the Division found that the baker acted lawfully in refusing service. It made these determinations because, in the words of the Division, the requested cake included "wording and images [the baker] deemed derogatory," featured "language and images [the baker] deemed hateful," or displayed a message the baker "deemed as discriminatory."

The treatment of the conscience-based objections at issue in these three cases contrasts with the Commission's treatment of Phillips' objection. The Commission ruled against Phillips in part on the theory that any message the requested wedding cake would carry would be attributed to the customer, not to the baker. Yet the Division did not address this point in any of the other cases with respect to the cakes depicting anti-gay marriage symbolism. Additionally, the Division found no violation of CADA in the other cases in part because each bakery was willing to sell other products, including those depicting Christian themes, to the prospective customers. But the Commission dismissed Phillips' willingness to sell "birthday cakes, shower cakes, [and] cookies and brownies," to gay and lesbian customers as irrelevant. The treatment of the other cases and Phillips' case could reasonably be interpreted as being inconsistent as to the question of whether speech is involved, quite apart from whether the cases should ultimately be distinguished. In short, the Commission's consideration of Phillips' religious objection did not accord with its treatment of these other objections.

For the reasons just described, the Commission's treatment of Phillips' case violated the State's duty under the First Amendment not to base laws or regulations on hostility to a religion or religious viewpoint. In view of these factors the record here demonstrates that the Commission's consideration of Phillips' case was neither tolerant nor respectful of Phillips' religious beliefs. The Commission gave "every appearance," of adjudicating Phillips' religious objection based on a negative normative "evaluation of the particular justification" for his objection and the religious grounds for it. It hardly requires restating that government has no role in deciding or even suggesting whether the religious ground for Phillips' conscience-based objection is legitimate or illegitimate. On these facts, the Court must draw the inference that Phillips' religious objection was not considered with the neutrality that the Free Exercise Clause requires.

While the issues here are difficult to resolve, it must be concluded that the State's interest could have been weighed against Phillips' sincere religious objections in a way consistent with the requisite religious neutrality that must be strictly observed. The official expressions of hostility to religion in some of the commissioners' comments—comments that were not disavowed at the Commission or by the State at any point in the proceedings that led to affirmance of the order—were inconsistent with what the Free Exercise Clause requires. The Commission's disparate consideration of Phillips' case compared to the cases of the other bakers suggests the same. For these reasons, the order must be set aside.

III

The Commission's hostility was inconsistent with the First Amendment's guarantee that our laws be applied in a manner that is neutral toward religion. Phillips was entitled to a neutral decisionmaker who would give full and fair consideration to his religious objection as he sought to assert it in all of the circumstances in which this case was presented, considered, and decided. However later cases raising these or similar concerns are resolved in the future, for these reasons the rulings of the Commission and of the state court that enforced the Commission's order must be invalidated.

The outcome of cases like this in other circumstances must await further elaboration in the courts, all in the context of recognizing that these disputes must be resolved with tolerance, without undue disrespect to sincere religious beliefs, and without subjecting gay persons to indignities when they seek goods and services in an open market.

Justice KAGAN, with whom Justice BREYER joins, concurring.

"[I]t is a general rule that [religious and philosophical] objections do not allow business owners and other actors in the economy and in society to deny protected persons equal access to goods and services under a neutral and generally applicable public accommodations law." But in upholding that principle, state actors cannot show hostility to religious views; rather, they must give those views "neutral and respectful consideration." I join the Court's opinion in full because I believe the Colorado Civil Rights Commission did not satisfy that obligation. I write separately to elaborate on one of the bases for the Court's holding.

The Court partly relies on the "disparate consideration of Phillips' case compared to the cases of [three] other bakers" who "objected to a requested cake on the basis of conscience." What makes the state agencies' consideration yet more disquieting is that a proper basis for distinguishing the cases was available—in fact, was obvious. The Colorado Anti-Discrimination Act (CADA) makes it unlawful for a place of public accommodation to deny "the full and equal enjoyment" of goods and services to individuals based on certain characteristics, including sexual orientation and creed. The three bakers in the Jack cases did not violate that law. Jack requested them to make a cake (one denigrating gay people and same-sex marriage) that they would not have made for any customer. In refusing that request, the bakers did not single out Jack because of his religion, but instead treated him in the same way they would have treated anyone else—just as CADA requires. By contrast, the same-sex couple in this case requested a wedding cake that Phillips would have made for an opposite-sex couple. In refusing that request, Phillips contravened CADA's demand that customers receive "the full and equal enjoyment" of public accommodations irrespective of their sexual orientation.

The different outcomes in the Jack cases and the Phillips case could thus have been justified by a plain reading and neutral application of Colorado law—untainted by any bias against a religious belief.*

Justice GORSUCH, with whom Justice ALITO joins, concurring.

In *Employment Div., Dept. of Human Resources of Ore. v. Smith*, this Court held that a neutral and generally applicable law will usually survive a constitutional free exercise challenge. *Smith* remains controversial in many quarters. But we know this with certainty: when the government fails to act neutrally toward the free exercise of religion, it tends to run into trouble. Then the government can prevail only if it satisfies strict scrutiny, showing that its restrictions on religion both serve a compelling interest and are narrowly tailored.

Today's decision respects these principles. As the Court explains, the Colorado Civil Rights Commission failed to act neutrally toward Jack Phillips's religious faith. Maybe most notably, the Commission allowed three other bakers to refuse a customer's request that would have required them to violate their secular commitments. Yet it denied the same accommodation to Mr. Phillips when he refused a customer's request that would have required him to violate his religious beliefs. As the Court also explains, the only reason the Commission seemed to supply for its discrimination was that it found Mr. Phillips's religious beliefs "offensive." That kind of judgmental dismissal of a sincerely held religious belief is, of course, antithetical to the First Amendment and cannot begin to satisfy strict scrutiny. The Constitution protects not just popular religious exercises from the condemnation of civil authorities. It protects them all.

The only wrinkle is this. In the face of so much evidence suggesting hostility toward Mr. Phillips's sincerely held religious beliefs, two of our colleagues have written separately to suggest that the Commission acted neutrally toward his faith when it treated him differently from the other bakers—or that it could have easily done so consistent with the First Amendment.

Justice THOMAS, with whom Justice GORSUCH joins, concurring in part and concurring in the judgment.

I agree that the Colorado Civil Rights Commission (Commission) violated Jack Phillips' right to freely exercise his religion. While Phillips rightly prevails on his free-exercise claim, I write separately to address his free-speech claim. The Court does not address this claim because it has some uncertainties about the record.

The conduct that the Colorado Court of Appeals ascribed to Phillips—creating and designing custom wedding cakes—is expressive. Phillips considers himself an artist. The logo for Masterpiece Cakeshop is an artist's paint palette with a paintbrush and baker's whisk. Behind the counter Phillips has a picture that depicts him as an artist painting on a canvas. Phillips takes exceptional care with each cake that he creates—sketching the design out on paper, choosing the color scheme, creating the frosting and decorations, baking and sculpting the cake, decorating it, and delivering it to the wedding. Examples of his creations can be seen on Masterpiece's website.

Phillips is an active participant in the wedding celebration. He sits down with each couple for a consultation before he creates their custom wedding cake. He discusses their preferences, their personalities, and the details of their wedding to ensure that each cake reflects the couple who ordered it. In addition to creating and delivering the cake—a focal point of the wedding celebration—Phillips sometimes stays and interacts with the guests at the wedding. And the guests often recognize his creations and seek his bakery out afterward. Phillips also sees the inherent symbolism in wedding cakes. To him, a wedding cake inherently communicates that "a wedding has occurred, a marriage has begun, and the couple should be celebrated."

Wedding cakes do, in fact, communicate this message. A tradition from Victorian England that made its way to America after the Civil War, "[w]edding cakes are so packed with symbolism that it is hard to know where to begin." If an average person walked into a room and saw a white, multi-tiered cake, he would immediately know that he had stumbled upon a wedding. The cake is "so standardised and inevitable a part of getting married that few ever think to question it." Almost no wedding, no matter how spartan, is missing the cake.

Accordingly, Phillips' creation of custom wedding cakes is expressive. The use of his artistic talents to create a well-recognized symbol that celebrates the beginning of a marriage clearly communicates a message—certainly more so than nude dancing, or flying a plain red flag. By forcing Phillips to create custom wedding cakes for same-sex weddings, Colorado's public-accommodations law "alter[s] the expressive content" of his message. Forcing Phillips to make custom wedding cakes for same-sex marriages requires him to, at the very least, acknowledge that same-sex weddings are "weddings" and suggest that they should be celebrated—the precise message he believes his faith forbids. The First Amendment prohibits Colorado from requiring Phillips to "bear witness to [these] fact[s]," or to "affir[m] . . . a belief with which [he] disagrees."

In *Obergefell*, I warned that the Court's decision would "inevitabl[y] . . . come into conflict" with religious liberty, "as individuals . . . are confronted with demands to participate in and endorse civil marriages between same-sex couples." This case proves that the conflict has already emerged. Because the Court's decision vindicates Phillips' right to free exercise, it seems that religious liberty has lived to fight another day. But, in future cases, the freedom of speech could be essential to preventing *Obergefell* from being used to "stamp out every vestige of dissent" and "vilify Americans who are unwilling to assent to the new orthodoxy."

Justice GINSBURG, with whom Justice SOTOMAYOR joins, dissenting.

There is much in the Court's opinion with which I agree. "[I]t is a general rule that [religious and philosophical] objections do not allow business owners and other actors in the economy and in society to deny protected persons equal access to goods and services under a neutral and generally applicable public accommodations law." "Colorado law can protect gay persons, just as it can protect other classes of individuals, in acquiring whatever products and services they choose on the same terms and conditions as are offered to other members of the public." "[P]urveyors of goods and services who object to gay marriages for moral and religious reasons [may not] put up signs saying 'no goods or services will be sold if they will be used for gay marriages.'" Gay persons may be spared from "indignities when they seek goods and services in an open market." I strongly disagree, however, with the Court's conclusion that Craig and Mullins should lose this case. All of the above-quoted statements point in the opposite direction.

The Court concludes that "Phillips' religious objection was not considered with the neutrality that the Free Exercise Clause requires." This conclusion rests on evidence said to show the Colorado Civil Rights Commission's (Commission) hostility to religion. Hostility is discernible, the Court maintains, from the asserted "disparate consideration of Phillips' case compared to the cases of" three other bakers who refused to make cakes requested by William Jack. The Court also finds hostility in statements made at two public hearings on Phillips' appeal to the Commission. The different outcomes the Court features do not evidence hostility to religion of the kind we have previously held to signal a free-exercise violation, nor do the comments by one or two members of one of the four decisionmaking entities considering this case justify reversing the judgment below.

The Court concludes that "the Commission's consideration of Phillips' religious objection did not accord with its treatment of [the other bakers'] objections." But the cases the Court aligns are hardly comparable. The bakers would have refused to make a cake with Jack's requested message for any customer, regardless of his or her religion. And the bakers visited by Jack would have sold him any baked goods they would have sold anyone else. The bakeries' refusal to make Jack cakes of a kind they would not make for any customer scarcely resembles Phillips' refusal to serve Craig and Mullins: Phillips would *not* sell to Craig and Mullins, for no reason other than their sexual orientation, a cake of the kind he regularly sold to others. When a couple contacts a bakery for a wedding cake, the product they are seeking is a cake celebrating *their* wedding—not a cake celebrating heterosexual weddings or same-sex weddings—and that is the service Craig and Mullins were denied. Colorado, the Court does not gainsay, prohibits precisely the discrimination Craig and Mullins encountered. Jack, on the other hand, suffered no service refusal on the basis of his religion or any other protected characteristic. He was treated as any other customer would have been treated—no better, no worse.

The fact that Phillips might sell other cakes and cookies to gay and lesbian customers[4] was irrelevant to the issue Craig and Mullins' case presented. What matters is that Phillips would not provide a good or service to a same-sex couple that he would provide to a heterosexual couple. In contrast, the other bakeries' sale of other goods to Christian customers was relevant: It shows that there were no goods the bakeries would sell to a non-Christian customer that they would refuse to sell to a Christian customer.

Statements made at the Commission's public hearings on Phillips' case provide no firmer support for the Court's holding today. Whatever one may think of the statements in historical context, I see no reason why the comments of one or two Commissioners should be taken to overcome Phillips' refusal to sell a wedding cake to Craig and Mullins. The proceedings involved several layers of independent decisionmaking, of which the Commission was but one. First, the Division had to find probable cause that Phillips violated CADA. Second, the ALJ entertained the parties' cross-motions for summary judgment. Third, the Commission heard Phillips' appeal. Fourth, after the Commission's ruling, the Colorado Court of Appeals considered the case *de novo*. What prejudice infected the determinations of the adjudicators in the case before and after the Commission? The Court does not say. Phillips' case is thus far removed from the only precedent upon which the Court relies, *Church of Lukumi Babalu Aye, Inc. v. Hialeah* (1993), where the government action that violated a principle of religious neutrality implicated a sole decisionmaking body, the city council.

3. Is Denial of Funding for Religious Education a Violation of Free Exercise of Religion? (casebook p. 1756)

TRINITY LUTHERAN CHURCH OF COLUMBIA, MISSOURI v. PAULEY
137 S. Ct. 2012 (2017)

Chief Justice ROBERTS delivered the opinion of the Court, except as to footnote 3.

The Missouri Department of Natural Resources offers state grants to help public and private schools, nonprofit daycare centers, and other non-profit entities purchase rubber playground surfaces made from recycled tires. Trinity Lutheran Church applied for such a grant for its preschool and daycare center and would have received one, but for the fact that Trinity Lutheran is a church. The Department had a policy of categorically disqualifying churches and other religious organizations from receiving grants under its playground resurfacing program. The question presented is whether the Department's policy violated the rights of Trinity Lutheran under the Free Exercise Clause of the First Amendment.

I

A

The Trinity Lutheran Church Child Learning Center is a preschool and daycare center open throughout the year to serve working families in Boone County, Missouri, and the surrounding area. Established as a nonprofit organization in 1980, the Center merged with Trinity Lutheran Church in 1985 and operates under its auspices on church property. The Center admits students of any religion, and enrollment stands at about 90 children ranging from age two to five.

The Center includes a playground that is equipped with the basic playground essentials: slides, swings, jungle gyms, monkey bars, and sandboxes. Almost the entire surface beneath and surrounding the play equipment is coarse pea gravel. Youngsters, of course, often fall on the playground or tumble from the equipment. And when they do, the gravel can be unforgiving.

In 2012, the Center sought to replace a large portion of the pea gravel with a pour-in-place rubber surface by participating in Missouri's Scrap Tire Program. Run by the State's Department of Natural Resources to reduce the number of used tires destined for landfills and dump sites, the program offers reimbursement grants to qualifying nonprofit organizations that purchase playground surfaces made from recycled tires. It is funded through a fee imposed on the sale of new tires in the State.

Due to limited resources, the Department cannot offer grants to all applicants and so awards them on a competitive basis to those scoring highest based on several criteria, such as the poverty level of the population in the surrounding area and the applicant's plan to promote recycling. When the Center applied, the Department had a strict and express policy of denying grants to any applicant owned or controlled by a church, sect, or other religious entity. That policy, in the Department's view, was compelled by Article I, Section 7 of the Missouri Constitution, which provides: "That no money shall ever be taken from the public treasury, directly or indirectly, in aid of any church, sect or denomination of religion, or in aid of any priest, preacher, minister or teacher thereof, as such; and that no preference shall be given to nor any discrimination made against any church, sect or creed of religion, or any form of religious faith or worship."

The Center ranked fifth among the 44 applicants in the 2012 Scrap Tire Program. But despite its high score, the Center was deemed categorically ineligible to receive a grant. In a letter rejecting the Center's application, the program director explained that, under Article I, Section 7 of the Missouri Constitution, the Department could not provide financial assistance directly to a church.

The Department ultimately awarded 14 grants as part of the 2012 program. Because the Center was operated by Trinity Lutheran Church, it did not receive a grant.

B

Trinity Lutheran sued the Director of the Department in Federal District Court. The Church alleged that the Department's failure to approve the Center's application, pursuant to its policy of denying grants to religiously affiliated applicants, violates the Free Exercise Clause of the First Amendment. Trinity Lutheran sought declaratory and injunctive relief prohibiting the Department from discriminating against the Church on that basis in future grant applications.

The District Court granted the Department's motion to dismiss. The Free Exercise Clause, the District Court stated, prohibits the government from outlawing or restricting the exercise of a religious practice; it generally does not prohibit withholding an affirmative benefit on account of religion. The District Court likened the Department's denial of the scrap tire grant to the situation this Court encountered in *Locke v. Davey* (2004). In that case, we upheld against a free exercise challenge the State of Washington's decision not to fund degrees in devotional theology as part of a state scholarship program. Finding the present case "nearly indistinguishable from *Locke*," the District Court held that the Free Exercise Clause did not require the State to make funds available under the Scrap Tire Program to religious institutions like Trinity Lutheran. The Court of Appeals for the Eighth Circuit affirmed.

II

The First Amendment provides, in part, that "Congress shall make no law respecting an establishment of religion, or prohibiting the free exercise thereof." The parties agree that the Establishment Clause of that Amendment does not prevent Missouri from including Trinity Lutheran in the Scrap Tire Program. That does not, however, answer the question under the Free Exercise Clause, because we have recognized that there is "play in the joints" between what the Establishment Clause permits and the Free Exercise Clause compels.

The Free Exercise Clause "protect[s] religious observers against unequal treatment" and subjects to the strictest scrutiny laws that target the religious for "special disabilities" based on their "religious status." Applying that basic principle, this Court has repeatedly confirmed that denying a generally available benefit solely on account of religious identity imposes a penalty on the free exercise of religion that can be justified only by a state interest "of the highest order."

In *Everson v. Board of Education of Ewing* (1947), for example, we upheld against an Establishment Clause challenge a New Jersey law enabling a local school district to reimburse parents for the public transportation costs of sending their children to public and private schools, including parochial schools. In the course of ruling that the Establishment Clause allowed New Jersey to extend that public benefit to all its citizens regardless of their religious belief, we explained that a State "cannot hamper its citizens in the free exercise of their own religion. Consequently, it cannot exclude individual Catholics, Lutherans, Mohammedans, Baptists, Jews, Methodists, Non-believers, Presbyterians, or the members of any other faith, *because of their faith, or lack of it*, from receiving the benefits of public welfare legislation."

III

A

The Department's policy expressly discriminates against otherwise eligible recipients by disqualifying them from a public benefit solely because of their religious character. If the cases just described make one thing clear, it is that such a policy imposes a penalty on the free exercise of religion that triggers the most exacting scrutiny. This conclusion is unremarkable in light of our prior decisions.

The Department contends that merely declining to extend funds to Trinity Lutheran does not *prohibit* the Church from engaging in any religious conduct or otherwise exercising its religious rights. Here the Department has simply declined to allocate to Trinity Lutheran a subsidy the State had no obligation to provide in the first place. That decision does not meaningfully burden the Church's free exercise rights. And absent any such burden, the argument continues, the Department is free to heed the State's antiestablishment objection to providing funds directly to a church.

It is true the Department has not criminalized the way Trinity Lutheran worships or told the Church that it cannot subscribe to a certain view of the Gospel. But, as the Department itself acknowledges, the Free Exercise Clause protects against "indirect coercion or penalties on the free exercise of religion, not just outright prohibitions." As the Court put it more than 50 years ago, "[i]t is too late in the day to doubt that the liberties of religion and expression may be infringed by the denial of or placing of conditions upon a benefit or privilege."

Trinity Lutheran is not claiming any entitlement to a subsidy. It instead asserts a right to participate in a government benefit program without having to disavow its religious character. The "imposition of such a condition upon even a gratuitous benefit inevitably deter[s] or discourage[s] the exercise of First Amendment rights." The express discrimination against religious exercise here is not the denial of a grant, but rather the refusal to allow the Church—solely because it is a church—to compete with secular organizations for a grant. Trinity Lutheran is a member of the community too, and the State's decision to exclude it for purposes of this public program must withstand the strictest scrutiny.

B

The Department attempts to get out from under the weight of our precedents by arguing that the free exercise question in this case is instead controlled by our decision in *Locke v. Davey*. It is not. In *Locke*, the State of Washington created a scholarship program to assist high-achieving students with the costs of postsecondary education. The scholarships were paid out of the State's general fund, and eligibility was based on criteria such as an applicant's score on college admission tests and family income. While scholarship recipients were free to use the money at accredited religious and non-religious schools alike, they were not permitted to use the funds to pursue a devotional theology degree—one "devotional in nature or designed to induce religious faith." Davey was selected for a scholarship but was denied the funds when he refused to certify that he would not use them toward a devotional degree. He sued, arguing that the State's refusal to allow its scholarship money to go toward such degrees violated his free exercise rights.

At the outset the Court made clear that *Locke* was not like the case now before us.

Washington's restriction on the use of its scholarship funds was different. According to the Court, the State had "merely chosen not to fund a distinct category of instruction." Davey was not denied a scholarship because of who he *was*; he was denied a scholarship because of what he proposed *to do*—use the funds to prepare for the ministry. Here there is no question that Trinity Lutheran was denied a grant simply because of what it is—a church.

The Court in *Locke* also stated that Washington's choice was in keeping with the State's antiestablishment interest in not using taxpayer funds to pay for the training of clergy; in fact, the Court could "think of few areas in which a State's antiestablishment interests come more into play." The claimant in *Locke* sought funding for an "essentially religious endeavor . . . akin to a religious calling as well as an academic pursuit," and opposition to such funding "to support church leaders" lay at the historic core of the Religion Clauses. Here nothing of the sort can be said about a program to use recycled tires to resurface playgrounds.

Relying on *Locke*, the Department nonetheless emphasizes Missouri's similar constitutional tradition of not furnishing taxpayer money directly to churches. But *Locke* took account of Washington's antiestablishment interest only after determining, as noted, that the scholarship program did not "require students to choose between their religious beliefs and receiving a government benefit." As the Court put it, Washington's scholarship program went "a long way toward including religion in its benefits." Students in the program were free to use their scholarships at "pervasively religious schools." Davey could use his scholarship to pursue a secular degree at one institution while studying devotional theology at another. He could also use his scholarship money to attend a religious college and take devotional theology courses there. The only thing he could not do was use the scholarship to pursue a degree in that subject.

In this case, there is no dispute that Trinity Lutheran *is* put to the choice between being a church and receiving a government benefit. The rule is simple: No churches need apply.[3]

C

The State in this case expressly requires Trinity Lutheran to renounce its religious character in order to participate in an otherwise generally available public benefit program, for which it is fully qualified. Our cases make clear that such a condition imposes a penalty on the free exercise of religion that must be subjected to the "most rigorous" scrutiny.

Under that stringent standard, only a state interest "of the highest order" can justify the Department's discriminatory policy. Yet the Department offers nothing more than Missouri's policy preference for skating as far as possible from religious establishment concerns. In the face of the clear infringement on free exercise before us, that interest cannot qualify as compelling. As we said when considering Missouri's same policy preference on a prior occasion, "the state interest asserted here—in achieving greater separation of church and State than is already ensured under the Establishment Clause of the Federal Constitution—is limited by the Free Exercise Clause."

The State has pursued its preferred policy to the point of expressly denying a qualified religious entity a public benefit solely because of its religious character. Under our precedents, that goes too far. The Department's policy violates the Free Exercise Clause.

Nearly 200 years ago, a legislator urged the Maryland Assembly to adopt a bill that would end the State's disqualification of Jews from public office: "If, on account of my religious faith, I am subjected to disqualifications, from which others are free, . . . I cannot but consider myself a persecuted man. . . . An odious exclusion from any of the benefits common to the rest of my fellow-citizens, is a persecution, differing only in degree, but of a nature equally unjustifiable with that, whose instruments are chains and torture."

The Missouri Department of Natural Resources has not subjected anyone to chains or torture on account of religion. And the result of the State's policy is nothing so dramatic as the denial of political office. The

---

3. This case involves express discrimination based on religious identity with respect to playground resurfacing. We do not address religious uses of funding or other forms of discrimination. [Footnote by the Court.]

consequence is, in all likelihood, a few extra scraped knees. But the exclusion of Trinity Lutheran from a public benefit for which it is otherwise qualified, solely because it is a church, is odious to our Constitution all the same, and cannot stand.

Justice THOMAS, with whom Justice GORSUCH joins, concurring in part.

This Court's endorsement in *Locke* of even a "mil[d] kind" of discrimination against religion remains troubling. But because the Court today appropriately construes *Locke* narrowly, and because no party has asked us to reconsider it, I join nearly all of the Court's opinion. I do not, however, join footnote 3, for the reasons expressed by Justice Gorsuch.

Justice GORSUCH, with whom Justice THOMAS joins, concurring in part.

Missouri's law bars Trinity Lutheran from participating in a public benefits program only because it is a church. I agree this violates the First Amendment and I am pleased to join nearly all of the Court's opinion. I offer only two modest qualifications.

First, the Court leaves open the possibility a useful distinction might be drawn between laws that discriminate on the basis of religious *status* and religious *use*. Respectfully, I harbor doubts about the stability of such a line. Does a religious man say grace before dinner? Or does a man begin his meal in a religious manner? Is it a religious group that built the playground? Or did a group build the playground so it might be used to advance a religious mission? The distinction blurs in much the same way the line between acts and omissions can blur when stared at too long, leaving us to ask (for example) whether the man who drowns by awaiting the incoming tide does so by act (coming upon the sea) or omission (allowing the sea to come upon him). Often enough the same facts can be described both ways.

Neither do I see why the First Amendment's Free Exercise Clause should care. After all, that Clause guarantees the free *exercise* of religion, not just the right to inward belief (or status). And this Court has long explained that government may not "devise mechanisms, overt or disguised, designed to persecute or oppress a religion or its practices." Generally the government may not force people to choose between participation in a public program and their right to free exercise of religion. I don't see why it should matter whether we describe that benefit, say, as closed to Lutherans (status) or closed to people who do Lutheran things (use). It is free exercise either way. For these reasons, reliance on the status-use distinction does not suffice for me to distinguish.

Second and for similar reasons, I am unable to join the footnoted observation that "[t]his case involves express discrimination based on religious identity with respect to playground resurfacing." Of course the footnote is entirely correct, but I worry that some might mistakenly read it to suggest that only "playground resurfacing" cases, or only those with some association with children's safety or health, or perhaps some other social good we find sufficiently worthy, are governed by the legal rules recounted in and faithfully applied by the Court's opinion. Such a reading would be unreasonable for our cases are "governed by general principles, rather than ad hoc improvisations." And the general principles here do not permit discrimination against religious exercise — whether on the playground or anywhere else.

Justice BREYER concurring in the judgment.

I agree with much of what the Court says and with its result. But I find relevant, and would emphasize, the particular nature of the "public benefit" here at issue. The Court stated in *Everson* that "cutting off church schools from" such "general government services as ordinary police and fire protection . . . is obviously not the purpose of the Here, the State would cut Trinity Lutheran off from participation in a general program designed to secure or to improve the health and safety of children. I see no significant difference. The fact that the program at issue ultimately funds only a limited number of projects cannot itself justify a religious distinction. Nor is there any administrative or other reason to treat church schools differently. The sole reason advanced that explains the difference is faith. And it is that last-mentioned fact that calls the Free Exercise Clause into play. We need not go further. Public benefits come in many shapes and sizes. I would leave the application of the Free Exercise Clause to other kinds of public benefits for another day.

Justice SOTOMAYOR, with whom Justice GINSBURG joins, dissenting.

To hear the Court tell it, this is a simple case about recycling tires to resurface a playground. The stakes are higher. This case is about nothing less than the relationship between religious institutions and the civil government — that is, between church and state. The Court today profoundly changes that relationship by holding, for the first time, that the Constitution requires the government to provide public funds directly to a church. Its decision slights both our precedents and our history, and its reasoning weakens this country's longstanding commitment to a separation of church and state beneficial to both.

I

Founded in 1922, Trinity Lutheran Church (Church) "operates . . . for the express purpose of carrying out the commission of . . . Jesus Christ as directed to His church on earth." The Church uses "preaching, teaching, worship, witness, service, and fellowship according to the Word of God" to carry out its mission "to 'make disciples.'" The Church's religious beliefs include its desire to "associat[e] with the [Trinity Church Child] Learning Center." The Learning Center serves as "a ministry of the Church and incorporates daily religion and developmentally appropriate activities into . . . [its] program." In this way, "[t]hrough the Learning Center, the Church teaches a Christian world view to children of members of the Church, as well as children of non-member residents" of the area. These activities represent the Church's "sincere religious belief . . . to use [the Learning Center] to teach the Gospel to children of its members, as well to bring the Gospel message to non-members."

II

Properly understood then, this is a case about whether Missouri can decline to fund improvements to the facilities the Church uses to practice and spread its religious views. This Court has repeatedly warned that funding of exactly this kind — payments from the government to a house of worship — would cross the line drawn by the Establishment Clause. So it is surprising that the Court mentions the Establishment Clause only to note the parties' agreement that it "does not prevent Missouri from including Trinity Lutheran in the Scrap Tire Program." Constitutional questions are decided by this Court, not the parties' concessions. The Establishment Clause does not allow Missouri to grant the Church's funding request because the Church uses the Learning Center, including its playground, in conjunction with its religious mission. The Court's silence on this front signals either its misunderstanding of the facts of this case or a startling departure from our precedents.

The government may not directly fund religious exercise. Nowhere is this rule more clearly implicated than when funds flow directly from the public treasury to a house of worship. A house of worship exists to foster and further religious exercise. When a government funds a house of worship, it underwrites this religious exercise.

This case is no different. The Church seeks state funds to improve the Learning Center's facilities, which, by the Church's own avowed description, are used to assist the spiritual growth of the children of its members and to spread the Church's faith to the children of nonmembers. The Church's playground surface — like a Sunday School room's walls or the sanctuary's pews — are integrated with and integral to its religious mission. The conclusion that the funding the Church seeks would impermissibly advance religion is inescapable.

True, this Court has found some direct government funding of religious institutions to be consistent with the Establishment Clause. But the funding in those cases came with assurances that public funds would not be used for religious activity, despite the religious nature of the institution. The Church has not and cannot provide such assurances here. The Church has a religious mission, one that it pursues through the Learning Center. The playground surface cannot be confined to secular use any more than lumber used to frame the Church's walls, glass stained and used to form its windows, or nails used to build its altar.

The Court may simply disagree with this account of the facts and think that the Church does not put its playground to religious use. If so, its mistake is limited to this case. But if it agrees that the State's funding would further religious activity and sees no Establishment Clause problem, then it must be implicitly applying a rule other than the one agreed to in our precedents.

When the Court last addressed direct funding of religious institutions, in *Mitchell*, it adhered to the rule that the Establishment Clause prohibits the direct funding of religious activities.

Today's opinion suggests the Court has made the leap the *Mitchell* plurality could not. For if it agrees that the funding here will finance religious activities, then only a rule that considers that fact irrelevant could support a conclusion of constitutionality. It has no basis in the history to which the Court has repeatedly turned to inform its understanding of the Establishment Clause. It permits direct subsidies for religious indoctrination, with all the attendant concerns that led to the Establishment Clause. And it favors certain religious groups, those with a belief system that allows them to compete for public dollars and those well-organized and well-funded enough to do so successfully.

Such a break with precedent would mark a radical mistake. The Establishment Clause protects both religion and government from the dangers that result when the two become entwined, "*not* by providing every religion with an *equal opportunity* (say, to secure state funding or to pray in the public schools), but by drawing fairly clear lines of *separation* between church and state — at least where the heartland of religious belief, such as primary religious [worship], is at issue."

III

Even assuming the absence of an Establishment Clause violation and proceeding on the Court's preferred front—the Free Exercise Clause—the
Court errs. It claims that the government may not draw lines based on an
entity's religious "status." But we have repeatedly said that it can. When
confronted with government action that draws such a line, we have carefully considered whether the interests embodied in the Religion Clauses
justify that line. The question here is thus whether those interests support
the line drawn in Missouri's Article I, § 7, separating the State's treasury
from those of houses of worship. They unquestionably do.

The Establishment Clause prohibits laws "respecting an establishment of
religion" and the Free Exercise Clause prohibits laws "prohibiting the free
exercise thereof." "[I]f expanded to a logical extreme," these prohibitions
"would tend to clash with the other." Even in the absence of a violation of
one of the Religion Clauses, the interaction of government and religion can
raise concerns that sound in both Clauses. For that reason, the government
may sometimes act to accommodate those concerns, even when not required
to do so by the Free Exercise Clause, without violating the Establishment
Clause. And the government may sometimes act to accommodate those
concerns, even when not required to do so by the Establishment Clause,
without violating the Free Exercise Clause. "[T]here is room for play in
the joints productive of a benevolent neutrality which will permit religious
exercise to exist without sponsorship and without interference." This space
between the two Clauses gives government some room to recognize the
unique status of religious entities and to single them out on that basis for
exclusion from otherwise generally applicable laws.

Invoking this principle, this Court has held that the government may
sometimes relieve religious entities from the requirements of government programs. A State need not, for example, require nonprofit houses
of worship to pay property taxes. Nor must a State require nonprofit religious entities to abstain from making employment decisions on the basis
of religion. But the government may not invoke the space between the
Religion Clauses in a manner that "devolve[s] into an unlawful fostering
of religion."

Missouri has decided that the unique status of houses of worship requires
a special rule when it comes to public funds. Its Constitution reflects that
choice and provides:

"That no money shall ever be taken from the public treasury, directly
or indirectly, in aid of any church, sect, or denomination of religion, or in
aid of any priest, preacher, minister or teacher thereof, as such; and that

no preference shall be given to nor any discrimination made against any church, sect or creed of religion, or any form of religious faith or worship." Art. I, § 7.

Missouri's decision, which has deep roots in our Nation's history, reflects a reasonable and constitutional judgment.

This Court has consistently looked to history for guidance when applying the Constitution's Religion Clauses. Those Clauses guard against a return to the past, and so that past properly informs their meaning. This case is no different.

Those who fought to end the public funding of religion based their opposition on a powerful set of arguments, all stemming from the basic premise that the practice harmed both civil government and religion. The civil government, they maintained, could claim no authority over religious belief. For them, support for religion compelled by the State marked an overstep of authority that would only lead to more. Equally troubling, it risked divisiveness by giving religions reason to compete for the State's beneficence. Faith, they believed, was a personal matter, entirely between an individual and his god. Religion was best served when sects reached out on the basis of their tenets alone, unsullied by outside forces, allowing adherents to come to their faith voluntarily. Over and over, these arguments gained acceptance and led to the end of state laws exacting payment for the support of religion.

In *Locke*, this Court expressed an understanding of, and respect for, this history.

The same is true of this case, about directing taxpayer funds to houses of worship. Like the use of public dollars for ministers at issue in *Locke*, turning over public funds to houses of worship implicates serious anti-establishment and free exercise interests. The history just discussed fully supports this conclusion. As states disestablished, they repealed laws allowing taxation to support religion because the practice threatened other forms of government support for, involved some government control over, and weakened supporters' control of religion. Common sense also supports this conclusion. Recall that a state may not fund religious activities without violating the Establishment Clause. A state can reasonably use status as a "house of worship" as a stand-in for "religious activities." Inside a house of worship, dividing the religious from the secular would require intrusive line-drawing by government, and monitoring those lines would entangle government with the house of worship's activities. And so while not every activity a house of worship undertakes will be inseparably linked to religious activity, "the likelihood that many are makes a categorical rule a suitable means to avoid chilling the exercise of religion."

Finally, and of course, such funding implicates the free exercise rights of taxpayers by denying them the chance to decide for themselves whether and how to fund religion. If there is any "'room for play in the joints' between" the Religion Clauses, it is here.

As was true in *Locke*, a prophylactic rule against the use of public funds for houses of worship is a permissible accommodation of these weighty interests. The rule has a historical pedigree identical to that of the provision in Today, thirty-eight States have a counterpart to Missouri's Article I, § 7. The provisions, as a general matter, date back to or before these States' original Constitutions. That so many States have for so long drawn a line that prohibits public funding for houses of worship, based on principles rooted in this Nation's understanding of how best to foster religious liberty, supports the conclusion that public funding of houses of worship "is of a different ilk."

Missouri has recognized the simple truth that, even absent an Establishment Clause violation, the transfer of public funds to houses of worship raises concerns that sit exactly between the Religion Clauses. To avoid those concerns, and only those concerns, it has prohibited such funding. In doing so, it made the same choice made by the earliest States centuries ago and many other States in the years since. The Constitution permits this choice.

In the Court's view, none of this matters. It focuses on one aspect of Missouri's Article I, § 7, to the exclusion of all else: that it denies funding to a house of worship, here the Church, "simply because of what it [i]s — a church."

Start where the Court stays silent. Its opinion does not acknowledge that our precedents have expressly approved of a government's choice to draw lines based on an entity's religious status. Those cases did not deploy strict scrutiny to create a presumption of unconstitutionality, as the Court does today. Instead, they asked whether the government had offered a strong enough reason to justify drawing a line based on that status.

The Court takes two steps to avoid these precedents. First, it recasts *Locke* as a case about a restriction that prohibited the would-be minister from "us[ing] the funds to prepare for the ministry." A faithful reading of *Locke* gives it a broader reach. *Locke* stands for the reasonable proposition that the government may, but need not, choose not to fund certain religious entities (there, ministers) where doing so raises "historic and substantial" establishment and free exercise concerns.

Second, it suggests that this case is different because it involves "discrimination" in the form of the denial of access to a possible benefit. But in this area of law, a decision to treat entities differently based on distinctions that the Religion Clauses make relevant does not amount to discrimination. To understand why, keep in mind that "the Court has unambiguously concluded that the individual freedom of conscience protected by the First Amendment embraces the right to select any religious faith or none at all." If the denial of a benefit others may receive is discrimination that violates the Free Exercise Clause, then the accommodations of religious entities we have approved would violate the free exercise rights of nonreligious entities. We have, with good reason, rejected that idea and instead focused on whether the government has provided a good enough reason, based in the values the Religion Clauses protect, for its decision.

The Court offers no real reason for rejecting the balancing approach in our precedents in favor of strict scrutiny, beyond its references to discrimination. The Court's desire to avoid what it views as discrimination is understandable. But in this context, the description is particularly inappropriate. A State's decision not to fund houses of worship does not disfavor religion; rather, it represents a valid choice to remain secular in the face of serious establishment and free exercise concerns. That does not make the State "atheistic or antireligious." The Court's conclusion "that the only alternative to governmental support of religion is governmental hostility to it represents a giant step backward in our Religion Clause jurisprudence."

At bottom, the Court creates the following rule today: The government may draw lines on the basis of religious status to grant a benefit to religious persons or entities but it may not draw lines on that basis when doing so would further the interests the Religion Clauses protect in other ways. Nothing supports this lopsided outcome. Not the Religion Clauses, as they protect establishment and free exercise interests in the same constitutional breath, neither privileged over the other. Not precedent, since we have repeatedly explained that the Clauses protect not religion but "the individual's freedom of conscience,"—that which allows him to choose religion, reject it, or remain undecided. And not reason, because as this case shows, the same interests served by lifting government-imposed burdens on certain religious entities may sometimes be equally served by denying government-provided benefits to certain religious entities.[14] Today's decision discounts centuries of history and jeopardizes the government's ability to remain secular.

14. In the end, the soundness of today's decision may matter less than what it might enable tomorrow. The principle it establishes can be manipulated to call for a similar fate for lines drawn on the basis of religious use. It is enough for today to explain why the Court's decision is wrong. The error of the concurrences' hoped-for decisions can be left for tomorrow. [Footnote by Justice Sotomayor.]

IV

The Court today dismantles a core protection for religious freedom provided in these Clauses. It holds not just that a government may support houses of worship with taxpayer funds, but that—at least in this case and perhaps in others, it must do so whenever it decides to create a funding program. History shows that the Religion Clauses separate the public treasury from religious coffers as one measure to secure the kind of freedom of conscience that benefits both religion and government. If this separation means anything, it means that the government cannot, or at the very least need not, tax its citizens and turn that money over to houses of worship. The Court today blinds itself to the outcome this history requires and leads us instead to a place where separation of church and state is a constitutional slogan, not a constitutional commitment.

C.   The Establishment Clause

4.   Religious Speech and the First Amendment

d.   Religious Symbols on Government Property (casebook p. 1782)

In *American Legion v. American Humanist Association*, the Court returned to the issue of a prominent religious symbol on government property. In a 7-2 decision, the Court held that it did not violate the Establishment Clause. In reading the various opinions, it is worth considering whether the *Lemon v. Kurtzman* test survives and if so, when it is to be used.

AMERICAN LEGION v. AMERICAN HUMANIST ASSOCIATION
139 S. Ct. 2067 (2019)

Justice ALITO announced the judgment of the Court and delivered the opinion of the Court with respect to Parts I, II–B, II–C, III, and IV, and an opinion with respect to Parts II–A and II–D, in which the CHIEF JUSTICE, Justice BREYER, and Justice KAVANAUGH join.

Since 1925, the Bladensburg Peace Cross (Cross) has stood as a tribute to 49 area soldiers who gave their lives in the First World War. Eighty-nine years after the dedication of the Cross, respondents filed this lawsuit, claiming that they are offended by the sight of the memorial on public land

and that its presence there and the expenditure of public funds to maintain it violate the Establishment Clause of the First Amendment. To remedy this violation, they asked a federal court to order the relocation or demolition of the Cross or at least the removal of its arms. The Court of Appeals for the Fourth Circuit agreed that the memorial is unconstitutional and remanded for a determination of the proper remedy. We now reverse.

Although the cross has long been a preeminent Christian symbol, its use in the Bladensburg memorial has a special significance. After the First World War, the picture of row after row of plain white crosses marking the overseas graves of soldiers who had lost their lives in that horrible conflict was emblazoned on the minds of Americans at home, and the adoption of the cross as the Bladensburg memorial must be viewed in that historical context. For nearly a century, the Bladensburg Cross has expressed the community's grief at the loss of the young men who perished, its thanks for their sacrifice, and its dedication to the ideals for which they fought. It has become a prominent community landmark, and its removal or radical alteration at this date would be seen by many not as a neutral act but as the manifestation of "a hostility toward religion that has no place in our Establishment Clause traditions." And contrary to respondents' intimations, there is no evidence of discriminatory intent in the selection of the design of the memorial or the decision of a Maryland commission to maintain it. The Religion Clauses of the Constitution aim to foster a society in which people of all beliefs can live together harmoniously, and the presence of the Bladensburg Cross on the land where it has stood for so many years is fully consistent with that aim.

I

The cross came into widespread use as a symbol of Christianity by the fourth century, and it retains that meaning today. But there are many contexts in which the symbol has also taken on a secular meaning. Indeed, there are instances in which its message is now almost entirely secular.

A cross appears as part of many registered trademarks held by businesses and secular organizations, including Blue Cross Blue Shield, the Bayer Group, and some Johnson & Johnson products. Many of these marks relate to health care, and it is likely that the association of the cross with healing had a religious origin. But the current use of these marks is indisputably secular.

The familiar symbol of the Red Cross—a red cross on a white background—shows how the meaning of a symbol that was originally religious can be transformed. The International Committee of the Red Cross

(ICRC) selected that symbol in 1863 because it was thought to call to mind the flag of Switzerland, a country widely known for its neutrality. The Swiss flag consists of a white cross on a red background. In an effort to invoke the message associated with that flag, the ICRC copied its design with the colors inverted. Thus, the ICRC selected this symbol for an essentially secular reason, and the current secular message of the symbol is shown by its use today in nations with only tiny Christian populations. But the cross was originally chosen for the Swiss flag for religious reasons. So an image that began as an expression of faith was transformed.

The image used in the Bladensburg memorial — a plain Latin cross — also took on new meaning after World War I. "During and immediately after the war, the army marked soldiers' graves with temporary wooden crosses or Stars of David" — a departure from the prior practice of marking graves in American military cemeteries with uniform rectangular slabs. The vast majority of these grave markers consisted of crosses, and thus when Americans saw photographs of these cemeteries, what struck them were rows and rows of plain white crosses. As a result, the image of a simple white cross "developed into a 'central symbol' " of the conflict. Contemporary literature, poetry, and art reflected this powerful imagery. Perhaps most famously, John McCrae's poem, In Flanders Fields, began with these memorable lines:

> "In Flanders fields the poppies blow
> Between the crosses, row on row."

Recognition of the cross's symbolism extended to local communities across the country. In late 1918, residents of Prince George's County, Maryland, formed a committee for the purpose of erecting a memorial for the county's fallen soldiers. Among the committee's members were the mothers of 10 deceased soldiers. The committee decided that the memorial should be a cross and hired sculptor and architect John Joseph Earley to design it.

The Cross was to stand at the terminus of another World War I memorial — the National Defense Highway, which connects Washington to Annapolis. The community gathered for a joint groundbreaking ceremony for both memorials on September 28, 1919; the mother of the first Prince George's County resident killed in France broke ground for the Cross.

The completed monument is a 32-foot tall Latin cross that sits on a large pedestal. The American Legion's emblem is displayed at its center, and the words "Valor," "Endurance," "Courage," and "Devotion" are inscribed at its base, one on each of the four faces. The pedestal also features a 9- by 2.5-foot bronze plaque explaining that the monument is "Dedicated to the heroes of Prince George's County, Maryland who lost their lives in the Great War for the liberty of the world."

In 2012, nearly 90 years after the Cross was dedicated and more than 50 years after the Commission acquired it, the American Humanist Association (AHA) lodged a complaint with the Commission. The complaint alleged that the Cross's presence on public land and the Commission's maintenance of the memorial violate the Establishment Clause of the First Amendment.

II

The Establishment Clause of the First Amendment provides that "Congress shall make no law respecting an establishment of religion." While the concept of a formally established church is straightforward, pinning down the meaning of a "law respecting an establishment of religion" has proved to be a vexing problem. After grappling with such cases for more than 20 years, *Lemon* ambitiously attempted to distill from the Court's existing case law a test that would bring order and predictability to Establishment Clause decisionmaking. That test, as noted, called on courts to examine the purposes and effects of a challenged government action, as well as any entanglement with religion that it might entail. The Court later elaborated that the "effect[s]" of a challenged action should be assessed by asking whether a "reasonable observer" would conclude that the action constituted an "endorsement" of religion.

For at least four reasons, the *Lemon* test presents particularly daunting problems in cases, including the one now before us, that involve the use, for ceremonial, celebratory, or commemorative purposes, of words or symbols with religious associations. Together, these considerations counsel against efforts to evaluate such cases under *Lemon* and toward application of a presumption of constitutionality for longstanding monuments, symbols, and practices.

First, these cases often concern monuments, symbols, or practices that were first established long ago, and in such cases, identifying their original purpose or purposes may be especially difficult.

Second, as time goes by, the purposes associated with an established monument, symbol, or practice often multiply.

Third, just as the purpose for maintaining a monument, symbol, or practice may evolve, "[t]he 'message' conveyed . . . may change over time." Consider, for example, the message of the Statue of Liberty, which began as a monument to the solidarity and friendship between France and the United States and only decades later came to be seen "as a beacon welcoming immigrants to a land of freedom." With sufficient time, religiously expressive monuments, symbols, and practices can become embedded features of a community's landscape and identity.

In the same way, consider the many cities and towns across the United States that bear religious names. Religion undoubtedly motivated those who named Bethlehem, Pennsylvania; Las Cruces, New Mexico; Providence, Rhode Island; Corpus Christi, Texas; Nephi, Utah, and the countless other places in our country with names that are rooted in religion. Yet few would argue that this history requires that these names be erased from the map.

Fourth, when time's passage imbues a religiously expressive monument, symbol, or practice with this kind of familiarity and historical significance, removing it may no longer appear neutral, especially to the local community for which it has taken on particular meaning. A government that roams the land, tearing down monuments with religious symbolism and scrubbing away any reference to the divine will strike many as aggressively hostile to religion. Militantly secular regimes have carried out such projects in the past, and for those with a knowledge of history, the image of monuments being taken down will be evocative, disturbing, and divisive.

These four considerations show that retaining established, religiously expressive monuments, symbols, and practices is quite different from erecting or adopting new ones. The passag of time gives rise to a strong presumption of constitutionality.

The role of the cross in World War I memorials is illustrative of each of the four preceding considerations. Immediately following the war, "[c]ommunities across America built memorials to commemorate those who had served the nation in the struggle to make the world safe for democracy." "[T]he First World War witnessed a dramatic change in . . . the symbols used to commemorate th[e] service" of the fallen soldiers. In the wake of the war, the United States adopted the cross as part of its military honors, establishing the Distinguished Service Cross and the Navy Cross in 1918 and 1919, respectively. And as already noted, the fallen soldiers' final resting places abroad were marked by white crosses or Stars of David. The solemn image of endless rows of white crosses became inextricably linked with and symbolic of the ultimate price paid by 116,000 soldiers. And this relationship between the cross and the war undoubtedly influenced the design of the many war memorials that sprang up across the Nation.

This is not to say that the cross's association with the war was the sole or dominant motivation for the inclusion of the symbol in every World

War I memorial that features it. But today, it is all but impossible to tell whether that was so. The passage of time means that testimony from those actually involved in the decisionmaking process is generally unavailable, and attempting to uncover their motivations invites rampant speculation. And no matter what the original purposes for the erection of a monument, a community may wish to preserve it for very different reasons, such as the historic preservation and traffic-safety concerns the Commission has pressed here.

In addition, the passage of time may have altered the area surrounding a monument in ways that change its meaning and provide new reasons for its preservation. Such changes are relevant here, since the Bladensburg Cross now sits at a busy traffic intersection, and numerous additional monuments are located nearby.

Finally, as World War I monuments have endured through the years and become a familiar part of the physical and cultural landscape, requiring their removal would not be viewed by many as a neutral act. A monument may express many purposes and convey many different messages, both secular and religious. Thus, a campaign to obliterate items with religious associations may evidence hostility to religion even if those religious associations are no longer in the forefront.

While the *Lemon* Court ambitiously attempted to find a grand unified theory of the Establishment Clause, in later cases, we have taken a more modest approach that focuses on the particular issue at hand and looks to history for guidance. Our cases involving prayer before a legislative session are an example.

The prevalence of this philosophy at the time of the founding is reflected in other prominent actions taken by the First Congress. It requested — and President Washington proclaimed — a national day of prayer and it reenacted the Northwest Territory Ordinance, which provided that "[r]eligion, morality, and knowledge, being necessary to good government and the happiness of mankind, schools and the means of education shall forever be encouraged." President Washington echoed this sentiment in his Farewell Address, calling religion and morality "indispensable supports" to "political prosperity."

III

Applying these principles, we conclude that the Bladensburg Cross does not violate the Establishment Clause. As we have explained, the Bladensburg Cross carries special significance in commemorating World War I. Due in large part to the image of the simple wooden crosses that originally marked the graves of American soldiers killed in the war, the cross became a symbol of their sacrifice, and the design of the Bladensburg Cross must be understood in light of that background. That the cross originated as a Christian symbol and retains that meaning in many contexts does not change the fact that the symbol took on an added secular meaning when used in World War I memorials.

Not only did the Bladensburg Cross begin with this meaning, but with the passage of time, it has acquired historical importance. It reminds the people of Bladensburg and surrounding areas of the deeds of their predecessors and of the sacrifices they made in a war fought in the name of democracy. As long as it is retained in its original place and form, it speaks as well of the community that erected the monument nearly a century ago and has maintained it ever since. The memorial represents what the relatives, friends, and neighbors of the fallen soldiers felt at the time and how they chose to express their sentiments. And the monument has acquired additional layers of historical meaning in subsequent years. The Cross now stands among memorials to veterans of later wars. It has become part of the community.

The monument would not serve that role if its design had deliberately disrespected area soldiers who perished in World War I. More than 3,500 Jewish soldiers gave their lives for the United States in that conflict, and some have wondered whether the names of any Jewish soldiers from the area were deliberately left off the list on the memorial or whether the names of any Jewish soldiers were included on the Cross against the wishes of their families.

Finally, it is surely relevant that the monument commemorates the death of particular individuals. It is natural and appropriate for those seeking to honor the deceased to invoke the symbols that signify what death meant for those who are memorialized And this is why the memorial for soldiers from the Bladensburg community features the cross—the same symbol that marks the graves of so many of their comrades near the battlefields where they fell.

IV

The cross is undoubtedly a Christian symbol, but that fact should not blind us to everything else that the Bladensburg Cross has come to represent. For some, that monument is a symbolic resting place for ancestors who never returned home. For others, it is a place for the community to gather and honor all veterans and their sacrifices for our Nation. For others still, it is a historical landmark. For many of these people, destroying or defacing the Cross that has stood undisturbed for nearly a century would not be neutral and would not further the ideals of respect and tolerance embodied in the First Amendment.

Justice BREYER, with whom Justice KAGAN joins, concurring.

I have long maintained that there is no single formula for resolving Establishment Clause challenges. The Court must instead consider each case in light of the basic purposes that the Religion Clauses were meant to serve: assuring religious liberty and tolerance for all, avoiding religiously based social conflict, and maintaining that separation of church and state that allows each to flourish in its "separate spher[e]."

I agree with the Court that allowing the State of Maryland to display and maintain the Peace Cross poses no threat to those ends. The Court's opinion eloquently explains why that is so: The Latin cross is uniquely associated with the fallen soldiers of World War I; the organizers of the Peace Cross acted with the undeniably secular motive of commemorating local soldiers; no evidence suggests that they sought to disparage or exclude any religious group; the secular values inscribed on the Cross and its place among other memorials strengthen its message of patriotism and commemoration; and, finally, the Cross has stood on the same land for 94 years, generating no controversy in the community until this lawsuit was filed. Nothing in the record suggests that the lack of public outcry "was due to a climate of intimidation." In light of all these circumstances, the Peace Cross cannot reasonably be understood as "a government effort to favor a particular religious sect" or to "promote religion over nonreligion." And, as the Court explains, ordering its removal or alteration at this late date would signal "a hostility toward religion that has no place in our Establishment Clause traditions."

The case would be different, in my view, if there were evidence that the organizers had "deliberately disrespected" members of minority faiths or if the Cross had been erected only recently, rather than in the aftermath of World War I. But those are not the circumstances presented to us here, and I see no reason to order *this* cross torn down simply because *other* crosses would raise constitutional concerns.

Nor do I understand the Court's opinion today to adopt a "history and tradition test" that would permit any newly constructed religious memorial on public land. The Court appropriately "looks to history for guidance," but it upholds the constitutionality of the Peace Cross only after considering its particular historical context and its long-held place in the community. A newer memorial, erected under different circumstances, would not necessarily be permissible under this approach.

Justice Kavanaugh, concurring.

I join the Court's eloquent and persuasive opinion in full. I write separately to emphasize two points.

Consistent with the Court's case law, the Court today applies a history and tradition test in examining and upholding the constitutionality of the Bladensburg Cross. As this case again demonstrates, this Court no longer applies the old test articulated in *Lemon* v. *Kurtzman* (1971).

The opinion identifies five relevant categories of Establishment Clause cases: (1) religious symbols on government property and religious speech at government events; (2) religious accommodations and exemptions from generally applicable laws; (3) government benefits and tax exemptions for religious organizations; (4) religious expression in public schools; and (5) regulation of private religious speech in public forums. The *Lemon* test does not explain the Court's decisions in any of those five categories.

The practice of displaying religious memorials, particularly religious war memorials, on public land is not coercive and is rooted in history and tradition. The Bladensburg Cross does not violate the Establishment Clause.

II

The Bladensburg Cross commemorates soldiers who gave their lives for America in World War I. I agree with the Court that the Bladensburg Cross is constitutional. At the same time, I have deep respect for the plaintiffs' sincere objections to seeing the cross on public land. I have great respect for the Jewish war veterans who in an *amicus* brief say that the cross on public land sends a message of exclusion. I recognize their sense of distress and alienation. Moreover, I fully understand the deeply religious nature of the cross. It would demean both believers and nonbelievers to say that the cross is not religious, or not all that religious. A case like this is difficult because it represents a clash of genuine and important interests. Applying our precedents, we uphold the constitutionality of the cross. In doing so, it is appropriate to also restate this bedrock constitutional principle: All citizens are equally American, no matter what religion they are, or if they have no religion at all.

The conclusion that the cross does not violate the Establishment Clause does not necessarily mean that those who object to it have no other recourse. The Court's ruling *allows* the State to maintain the cross on public land. The Court's ruling does not *require* the State to maintain the cross on public land. The Maryland Legislature could enact new laws requiring removal of the cross or transfer of the land. The Maryland Governor or other state or local executive officers may have authority to do so under current Maryland law. And if not, the legislature could enact new laws to authorize such executive action. The Maryland Constitution, as interpreted by the Maryland Court of Appeals, may speak to this question. And if not, the people of Maryland can amend the State Constitution.

Those alternative avenues of relief illustrate a fundamental feature of our constitutional structure: This Court is not the *only* guardian of individual rights in America. This Court fiercely protects the individual rights secured by the U.S. Constitution. But the Constitution sets a floor for the protection of individual rights. The constitutional floor is sturdy and often high, but it is a floor. Other federal, state, and local government entities generally possess authority to safeguard individual rights above and beyond the rights secured by the U.S. Constitution.

Justice KAGAN, concurring in part.

I fully agree with the Court's reasons for allowing the Bladensburg Peace Cross to remain as it is. Although I agree that rigid application of the *Lemon* test does not solve every Establishment Clause problem, I think that test's focus on purposes and effects is crucial in evaluating government action in this sphere—as this very suit shows. Although I too "look[ ] to history for guidance." I prefer at least for now to do so case-by-case, rather than to sign on to any broader statements about history's role in Establishment Clause analysis.

Justice THOMAS, concurring in the judgment.

The Establishment Clause states that "Congress shall make no law respecting an establishment of religion." The text and history of this Clause suggest that it should not be incorporated against the States. Even if the Clause expresses an individual right enforceable against the States, it is limited by its text to "law[s]" enacted by a legislature, so it is unclear whether the Bladensburg Cross would implicate any incorporated right. And even if it did, this religious display does not involve the type of actual legal coercion that was a hallmark of historical establishments of religion. Therefore, the Cross is clearly constitutional.

Justice GORSUCH, with whom Justice THOMAS joins, concurring in the judgment.

The American Humanist Association wants a federal court to order the destruction of a 94 year-old war memorial because its members are offended. Today, the Court explains that the plaintiffs are not entitled to demand the destruction of longstanding monuments, and I find much of its opinion compelling. In my judgment, however, it follows from the Court's analysis that suits like this one should be dismissed for lack of standing. Accordingly, while I concur in the judgment to reverse and remand the court of appeals' decision, I would do so with additional instructions to dismiss the case.

The Association claims that its members "regularly" come into "unwelcome direct contact" with a World War I memorial cross in Bladensburg, Maryland "while driving in the area." And this, the Association suggests, is enough to allow it to insist on a federal judicial decree ordering the memorial's removal. Maybe, the Association concedes, others who are less offended lack standing to sue. Maybe others still who are equally affected but who come into contact with the memorial too infrequently lack standing as well. But, the Association assures us, its members are offended enough — and with sufficient frequency — that they may sue.

This "offended observer" theory of standing has no basis in law. Federal courts may decide only those cases and controversies that the Constitution and Congress have authorized them to hear. Unsurprisingly, this Court has already rejected the notion that offense alone qualifies as a "concrete and particularized" injury sufficient to confer standing. Offended observer standing cannot be squared with this Court's longstanding teachings about the limits of Article III.

In a large and diverse country, offense can be easily found. Really, most every governmental action probably offends *somebody*. No doubt, too, that offense can be sincere, sometimes well taken, even wise. But recourse for disagreement and offense does not lie in federal litigation. Instead, in a society that holds among its most cherished ambitions mutual respect, tolerance, self-rule, and democratic responsibility, an "offended viewer" may "avert his eyes," or pursue a political solution. Today's decision represents a welcome step toward restoring this Court's recognition of these truths, and I respectfully concur in the judgment.

Justice GINSBURG, with whom Justice SOTOMAYOR joins, dissenting.

An immense Latin cross stands on a traffic island at the center of a busy three-way intersection in Bladensburg, Maryland. "[M]onumental, clear, and bold" by day, the cross looms even larger illuminated against the night-time sky.

Decades ago, this Court recognized that the Establishment Clause of the First Amendment to the Constitution demands governmental neutrality among religious faiths, and between religion and nonreligion. Numerous times since, the Court has reaffirmed the Constitution's commitment to neutrality. Today the Court erodes that neutrality commitment, diminishing precedent designed to preserve individual liberty and civic harmony in favor of a "presumption of constitutionality for longstanding monuments, symbols, and practices."

The Latin cross is the foremost symbol of the Christian faith, embodying the "central theological claim of Christianity: that the son of God died on the cross, that he rose from the dead, and that his death and resurrection offer the possibility of eternal life." Precisely because the cross symbolizes these sectarian beliefs, it is a common marker for the graves of Christian soldiers. For the same reason, using the cross as a war memorial does not transform it into a secular symbol. Just as a Star of David is not suitable to honor Christians who died serving their country, so a cross is not suitable to honor those of other faiths who died defending their nation. Soldiers of all faiths "are united by their love of country, but they are not united by the cross."

By maintaining the Peace Cross on a public highway, the Commission elevates Christianity over other faiths, and religion over nonreligion. Memorializing the service of American soldiers is an "admirable and unquestionably secular" objective. But the Commission does not serve that objective by displaying a symbol that bears "a starkly sectarian message."

Holding the Commission's display of the Peace Cross unconstitutional would not, as the Commission fears, "inevitably require the destruction of other cross-shaped memorials throughout the country." When a religious symbol appears in a public cemetery—on a headstone, or as the headstone itself, or perhaps integrated into a larger memorial—the setting counters the inference that the government seeks "either to adopt the religious message or to urge its acceptance by others." In a cemetery, the "privately selected religious symbols on individual graves are best understood as the private speech of each veteran." Such displays are "linked to, and sho[w] respect for, the individual honoree's faith and beliefs." They do not suggest governmental endorsement of those faith and beliefs.

Recognizing that a Latin cross does not belong on a public highway or building does not mean the monument must be "torn down." "[L]ike the determination of the violation itself," the "proper remedy . . . is necessarily context specific." In some instances, the violation may be cured by relocating the monument to private land or by transferring ownership of the land and monument to a private party.

GALVES INDIC

Book 4

The Affirmation

N.E. BROWN

MINDSTIR MEDIA

Galveston: 1900 – Indignities
Book 4: The Affirmation
Copyright © 2014 by N.E. Brown. All rights reserved.

Published by Mindstir Media
1931 Woodbury Ave. #182 | Portsmouth, NH 03801 | USA
1.800.767.0531 | www.mindstirmedia.com

Printed in the United States of America

ISBN-13: 978-0-9903626-0-9

Library of Congress Control Number: 2014939487

The Affirmation

CHAPTER 1

Jason Brady had just come home from a ten-day trail ride with six of his friends after delivering a hundred head of cattle to a rancher outside of Buffalo, Texas. Jason lived with his grandparents on a small farm just south of Austin, Texas, and he was anxious to get home. As he got to the top of the hill, he saw the faded, wood-frame farmhouse his grandfather had built, and he gave his horse a swift kick. It was mid-September and he noticed that the yellow, decaying crops needed to be plowed under. It had been a dry summer and the few crops that had survived the drought had already been harvested; it was a never-ending process. Jason had taken over a lot of the chores from his grandfather, who was aging now, and it seemed there was always something that needed to be done. He loved his grandparents, and while he enjoyed getting away from time to time with his friends, he couldn't wait to get home and to his grandmother's delicious home cooking.

Jason's grandmother and grandfather were at the kitchen table when he sauntered in, and he hurried over to the water bucket. He filled the dipper three times and quickly quenched his thirst. He walked around the table and leaned over to kiss his grandmother on the forehead and did the same with his grandfather. They welcomed him and went back to their conversation. They were speaking in German and he noticed a letter sprawled out on the table which was also written in German. Jason never learned the language, but had heard enough of the same words that he could sometimes guess what they were talking about. He recognized some of the words and knew immediately that there had been a death in the family.

"What's goin' on, Grandpa?" he asked.

His grandparents looked at each other and then his grandfather told him to pull up a chair and sit down at the table. "Your father is dead. Someone killed him," his grandfather said. "You need to go to Rosenberg."

"Who's the letter from?" Jason asked.

"It's from a distant cousin of your father. She said your father did some terrible things there and that he was shot with his own gun. You are apparently the only heir, and his property now belongs to you," his grandfather continued.

Jason Brady was only sixteen when he left home and went to live with his mother's parents. His home was in Rosenberg at the time, and he hated his father, Joe Brady. He remembered how Joe constantly abused his mother, especially when he drank. He begged her to leave Brady, but she refused and told him that his father would never let her leave him and that he would find her wherever she went. She was terrified of Joe and hated it when Jason was often caught in the middle.

One day when Jason got home from school he found his father passed out on the couch. He went to find his mother. She was curled up in a ball on the bed and he slowly turned her over. Her empty brown eyes were staring up at him and her face was blue. Blood had dried around her mouth and nose and he knew instantly that his old man had killed her. Jason went running into the living room and kicked at his father, waking him up. "You killed her," he yelled at his father. "You finally killed her. I hate you."

Joe Brady got up and pulled out his Colt .44 gun from his holster and aimed it at Jason. "You can join her if you want. She killed herself. I found her that way when I got home," Brady told him.

Jason hurriedly ran down the dirt and gravel road to town and told the sheriff that his daddy had killed his mother. The sheriff followed him back to the house, and Brady was waiting for them outside. "She told me she didn't want to live anymore and she had been threatening to kill herself. I never thought she would," Brady told the sheriff. There was no way to tell how she died, so the sheriff decided to believe Joe Brady's story. The sheriff knew Brady and his son didn't get along, and besides, Jason was just a kid.

The night after he found his mother dead, Jason's father passed out from drinking. Jason emptied his father's pockets of his cash and threw some things in an old, leather satchel. Before he left, he went into the small room where his mother had slept and took some of her personal things. He grabbed her Bible, her locket, family pictures, and some old letters from his grandparents and walked the three miles to the train station. That was the last time he had seen his father and he never wanted to see Rosenberg again.

According to the last letter Jason's mother received from her parents, they were living southeast of Austin, Texas, in a little town called Seguin. When he got to the train station, he asked for a ticket that would take him to Seguin. The clerk told him he would have to make a couple of changes and that he could check at each depot to find out when the next train going in that direction was coming through. He told Jason that once he got to Houston, Texas, another train would take him to Seguin.

Jason loved his grandparents. They had emigrated from Germany and found relatives who lived in Seguin, and settled there. His mother had met his father at a Saturday night dance when he had come to their town to visit some friends. His mother was seventeen and his father was twenty-five at the time. They married after a three-week courtship and afterwards Brady took her back to his hometown of Rosenberg, Texas. Jason was born ten months later.

Jason was tired after his trail ride, and the last thing he wanted to do was go to Rosenberg. He removed his dirty, grimy clothes and threw them on the floor. He walked across the hall, naked, to the little bathroom and stood up in the tub. He connected a short hose to the water faucet and washed the filth from his body with the cold water. Afterwards, he picked up the homemade bar of soap and sat down in the tub. He put the stopper in the drain and sat there for a while waiting for the tub to fill up with water. The water that came from the well was cold, but he had to scrub ten days of grime from his body, and his long hair was in tangles. His grandmother had heated some water in a kettle on the stove. It was something she always did for him when he needed to take a bath. He put a washcloth over his manhood when she knocked on the door. She placed two kettles of boiling water on the floor, and Jason picked one up and began pouring it into the cold water at the foot of the tub. He began to relax when he felt the warmth penetrating his body.

"You're a treasure, grandma," Jason spouted.

"We love you and missed you," she said, speaking in German.

"Want me to trim your hair?" she asked in English.

"Don't have time for a haircut, and besides, I like it long."

After the tub had filled, he lay still for a while and thought back to when he lived in Rosenberg. He remembered his mother's beautiful smile, but after a few years her smile and happy spirit had disappeared. He had been six years old when he first remembered his father's drunken sprees. His mother would make him go hide in the closet when his father came home drunk. He would listen to his father rant and rave at her and then he would hear her screams.

Jason always felt guilty that he didn't insist that he and his mother leave his father. But he could never convince her to go. Now his old man was dead and he was going to inherit his father's property. How unjust that was, he thought.

Jason's grandmother cried the next day when he left and made him promise to write. They didn't have a telephone, so Jason promised her he would keep in touch. Jason was twenty-four years old and his sandy hair had been bleached to a golden blond from his cattle drives in the sun. His darkly tanned face and deep-set blue eyes made all the girls look twice. He had dimples when he laughed, and even though he was always pushing his hair behind his ears, his curly locks seemed to spring forward and hang in his face. He was almost six feet tall and his muscular body, toned from riding and cattle roping, made him the envy of his friends. He liked to joke, and he had inherited his mother's calm nature. Jason's favorite thing to do was go to the Saturday night dances, and he was smooth on his feet. He had recently met a young teacher whom he liked and had to compete with his friends to get her to dance with him. Other than that, he didn't really have much time for women. He looked after his grandparents and he found no reason to leave them until now.

After boarding the train, Jason put his leather satchel into the corner of his seat and poked at it a couple of times so he could rest up against it. Then he leaned back and tried to get comfortable. He had nothing but bad memories of Rosenberg and he wondered if some of his old classmates might still be living there. There were about twenty in his class, fourteen were boys, and he'd barely finished the tenth grade when he left. Jason finally fell asleep and woke up when he heard them call out his first stop. The conductor told him he should get off and wait for anther train that would be coming through in about thirty minutes. He saw a clock in the train station that said eight o'clock.

Rosenberg, Texas, was a quiet little town approximately thirty-five miles southwest of Houston, Texas, and was the central point for several railroads. It was located in the Brazos Valley just south of the Brazos River. It had been advertised at the turn of the century to have some of the most fertile land in America; however, with the town's location being only a few blocks from the Brazos River, flood waters often spilled over, creating mud-ridden streets. Many of the local people dubbed it "The City of Mud". The sleepy little town boasted a population of one thousand one hundred people, but it always seemed like more because of the location of the Union Depot. It was at the crossroads where railroads would intersect each other and people would often stay overnight to look the town over or take care of business at the local Wells Fargo office.

It was close to midnight when Jason got off the train at the quaint little depot in Rosenberg. He was exhausted. He had hardly recovered from the sleepless nights on his trail ride and now all he wanted to do was find a place to sleep. He stood in the middle of the empty street in Rosenberg and saw a small, electric sign several doors up that said Hotel, Vacancy. He walked in that direction and passed a noisy saloon but chose not to go in. There was no one in the lobby of the hotel and he saw a couple of couches in the waiting area, so he plopped down on one and immediately fell asleep. He woke up early the next morning when a woman poked him in the arm and told him he had to get up.

"Sorry," he said. "No one was here when I came in late last night."

"It's all right," the older woman said, "But if you are going to stay over, you will need to get a room and pay for it."

"Uh, I'll just pay for sleeping on the couch last night. My father's place is just down the road," Jason said.

"Who might that be?" she asked.

"Joe Brady," he answered.

"Well, I'll be darned," she replied. "I haven't seen you since you were a young whippersnapper in high school. I'm Mary Beth Armstrong," and she put out her hand to shake.

"Sorry 'bout your daddy, but he really was a bad egg," she said.

Jason handed her a dollar and asked if that was enough for sleeping on the couch, and she grinned and thanked him.

He was hungry and wondered if the old café was still in the same place. He picked up his bag and started walking towards the other end of town. The place had really grown, he thought. At midnight it had looked like a ghost town, but there were people already shopping and going into the bank. Several women stared at him and smiled when they nodded hello. The place looked different, he thought. He passed Kubena's Boot Shop and the Moers Building before he strolled into the old café and sat at the counter.

"Jason?" the waitress asked and smiled at him. "It's Cathy Rigby, used to be Cathy Liles in school."

Jason smiled at her and asked if any of the others from school were still around. "Not many," she said. "Everybody seemed to head to the bigger cities when we graduated; New Braunfels, Austin, and some to San Antonio. Where have you been?"

"Moved in with my grandparents in Seguin, Texas," he said.

"Sorry to hear about your dad, even though nobody really liked him," she said.

"What would you like to eat?" Cathy finally asked.

"Your breakfast special sounds good," he said as he read it on the chalkboard behind the counter. "And coffee," he added.

Cathy kept eyeing Jason. She had forgotten how good looking he was. She had married a man who was a traveling salesman, and he was gone a lot. She wondered if Jason was married but decided not to ask. There wasn't a ring on his finger now, and his tanned hand showed no signs of a recent wedding band.

Five minutes later the sheriff came in and walked up to the counter and sat beside Jason. "I understand you are Joe Brady's son," he said, looking over at Jason.

Jason saw the sheriff's star on his shirt and smiled at him. "Yes, sir. I got in late last night."

"I hope you aren't here to cause any trouble," the sheriff said.

"And why would I want to do that?" Jason asked.

"Wasn't sure if you and your daddy were close and you might want to seek revenge," the sheriff said.

Jason took several sips of his coffee and finally looked up. "I'm not anything like my old man. I'm just here to claim my inheritance," Jason said. "Is there any law against that?" he asked.

The sheriff smiled and told him that as long as he didn't cause any trouble, he could stay as long as he wanted. "There is one thing I'd like to know," Jason said to the sheriff.

The sheriff motioned to Cathy to fill his coffee cup and then turned to Jason. "What's that?" he asked.

"I'd like to hear the whole story. How it went down and who shot him," Jason said.

"When you're through eating you can follow me to my office and I'll tell you all about it. I guess we owe you that," the sheriff said.

Jason and Sheriff Raymond Wade sat in his office for over an hour while the sheriff told him the details of Brady's second wife's miscarriage and the lady doctor who tried to save her life. Jason wasn't surprised when he learned of his father's drinking and attempt to rape the doctor. He was surprised that a woman could actually overtake him, steal his gun, and shoot him. His daddy was a big man - - at least that was how Jason had remembered him. Jason shook his head and asked if the doctor was a large woman. "Hardly, she's a little thing, but she's not somebody you want to mess with. She came from England and went to medical school in Galveston. She came here about three or four months ago when she saw an ad in the Houston newspaper advertising for a medical doctor for our town. She has four children, but she's not married. Hear she's a widow.

"Well, I guess you want to ride out to your daddy's place. You can use my deputy's horse. I'll ride out there with you and then bring the horse back," the sheriff said. The two men went outside and mounted the horses and rode out to the Brady place. It was pretty much the way Jason had remembered it. There was a winding road that they turned down. The fence was in poor repair and the fields were overgrown with weeds and decaying crops. The house appeared out of nowhere, and Jason dismounted and handed the reins of his horse to the sheriff.

"She shot him over there by that grove of trees," the sheriff said and pointed. "Blood's still on the ground in case you want to go over and see it. They buried your daddy and his wife by your mother's grave in the old cemetery. You know where I am if you need me." The sheriff turned his horse around and rode back into town.

Jason tried the front door and it was unlocked. The place was larger than he remembered. He was still a skinny sixteen-year-old kid when he left, and it felt strange being back. The smell of whisky and cigars filtered through the rooms and he left the door open just to let some fresh air in. The place was dark and depressing and it was hot inside. For some reason all the windows were closed, and as he walked through the house he began unlocking and pushing the windows up. He made his way to the back of the house and opened a door to one of the rooms, and it was dark. He saw a candle in the hallway and took out a match and lit it. When he entered the room, the smell of death almost brought him to his knees. Blood was everywhere, and he gagged and backed out through the doorway. If the sheriff hadn't told him his dad was shot outside, he would have assumed he had been shot in the back room. He wondered what had happened there. Was that where his father's wife had died?

He found it difficult to stay inside the house; after quickly walking through the rest of it, he went outside to get some fresh air. He walked around back to the small corral and barn. There were four horses, two saddles, tack, and some hay. He walked over to the corral and saw that the water tub was empty, so he pumped some fresh water for the horses and went to get some hay. He found a bag of oats and took it out to the horses. They were still drinking from the tub and Jason pumped some more water for them. No telling how long it had been since they had last been fed, he thought. As he headed back towards the house he couldn't help but look over at the grove of trees the sheriff had pointed to. He stalled a few minutes and then headed over to them. He walked down a path through the trees, looking in both directions, and almost walked over the dried, blood-soaked leaves on the ground. A large snake slithered out from underneath and Jason instinctively stomped on its head, taking it by surprise. He lifted his boot again and came down harder on the snake's head, crushing it into the ground. He began kicking it and on the second kick he lifted it into the air so hard it hit another tree ten feet away and fell to the ground as the dead leaves slowly floated around it. He stared at it for a moment and he could feel tears streaming down his cheeks. A second later he began laughing. Was the snake his old man coming back to get revenge? When Jason took a closer look he saw it was a cottonmouth and he realized how lucky he was that it didn't bite him. He breathed out a sigh of relief, and with the side of his boot he scraped other dead leaves and sticks over the blood-stained circle of leaves, wanting any remembrance of his father's passing to disappear. He turned and walked back toward the farmhouse and wondered if he should just leave and go back home. He could meet with the lawyer the next day and turn it all over to him, but Jason was more frugal than that. A lawyer would charge an exorbitant amount of money, and it was money he would rather give his grandparents. Besides, he had the livestock to take care of and he felt he needed to take care of business himself. That would be what his mother would have wanted.

Jason went back to the house and hoped the open windows would help clear out the smell so he could stay the night without being uncomfortable. After the horses had finished eating he saddled up the mare and mounted her. He still had some questions he wanted answers to, and there was only one person who could do that.

CHAPTER 2

Since the fatal night of the shooting, Dr. Catherine Merit had difficulties sleeping at night. Her dreams kept bouncing back and forth from sadness to happiness. She continued to relive the dreadful night that Joe Brady called her because he thought his mail-order bride was having a miscarriage. Brady was drunk and had tried to rape Catherine after she had seen to his wife. When she ran from him, he followed her to a grove of trees where he was stalking her with his gun. Catherine could barely remember what happened, but she did remember that she had fallen to the ground and when Brady unbuttoned his pants and bent down to lift up her dress, she had kicked him and he had dropped his gun. The rest was a blur to her, but she had somehow retrieved the gun and shot Brady in the chest. The last scene was the most vivid in her mind. She was only a few feet away and the blast of the gun shot a huge hole in his chest, causing the blood to splatter back onto her. It was probably one of the worst nights of her entire life. She had killed a man and she prayed God would forgive her.

After bathing and reading a story to her four small children, Dr. Catherine Merit filled her own bathtub and sank into the tepid water. She was agonizing over the events of the past two weeks. She had shot a man in self-defence, but his death continued to haunt her. Her lover, Dr. Samuel Allen, was a doctor at Houston General Hospital, and had come to see her when he heard of her plight. He had brought her out of her depression, and before he left to return to Houston he had proposed to her. She had jumped at the chance to be his wife; but for all the wrong reasons. She was having second thoughts now. She knew he would not be happy living in the small town of Rosenberg, and she had no intentions of moving to the big city of Houston. They planned for Catherine to leave the next Saturday morning and he would pick her up at the train station when she arrived.

Catherine finished bathing and went downstairs to mix up a potion of herbs, honey, and warm milk. She had not been sleeping well and she needed a good night's sleep more than anything. She wanted to have a clear head when she met Samuel. He would not be happy with her revocation of his proposal, and she lay on her bed thinking of how she should break the news to him. Thirty minutes later she finally fell asleep.

The jail cell was dank and musty and Catherine was lying on an old cot. The coils of the springs were biting into her back and she could hear the squeals of the mice up in the rafters. She could see Brady's face clearly as he held a gun to her and tried to lift her skirt. The nightmares had begun and seemed to last forever. The tightness in her throat felt as if someone had put a noose around her neck and she woke up, coughing uncontrollably. The demons sprang out of her head when consciousness brought her back to reality. She sat up and looked around the room.

It seemed the past always became the present when she tried to sleep. She found it hard to swallow, and slowly got out of bed. She wavered for a moment while her eyes adjusted to the dimly lit room, then she walked into the bathroom to get a drink of water. This is absurd, she thought. She was used to nightmares. Her whole life seemed like a nightmare since she had come to America. But tonight the dreams were different; more vivid and very dismal. She knew she could not marry Samuel. He deserved better. Even though he swore he would love her four children as his own, she knew it would be a burden to him. Her children would always come first and she did not feel it proper or right to ask Samuel to be in fifth place. He was a successful heart and lung doctor and he could have his pick of any woman, especially one with no baggage, but still he wanted her. She was flattered and in a way she loved him, too, but she knew in her heart that Samuel would be better off without her. She had too many deep, buried secrets and they would always consume her dreams as they had done night after night. Samuel had knowledge of her past, but not the gritty, evil details of her two years in captivity with a madman who had taken her from her first husband and held her in captivity in Beaumont, Texas. Even she had difficulty putting it all behind her. She was twenty-two years old now and she felt so much older. Still, she had matured and blossomed into an even more beautiful woman and had kept her firm, shapely figure; but she had wisdom beyond her years. She was extremely bright and had graduated in the top five-percent of her class at Galveston's Medical School. While she loved being a doctor, her children were her life and she needed to focus all of her energies on making a living for them and seeing to their education. She knew it would be hard, since women of her generation were supposed to be at home tending to a woman's duties, but that wasn't who she was. She wanted more. She was good with money and even though her medical practice was slow getting started, she was making a small living. She had enough savings to educate all four of her children and her first husband had left her son, Daniel, a small inheritance. Even though she longed to be back in Galveston where her first husband and mother were buried, her life was here now and she had everything she needed. Well, almost everything, she thought. Being a doctor, she knew that a woman's body had needs, too, and she missed being married. She had discovered her own sexuality and enjoyed the marital bed with her two previous husbands, but that was behind her now. Maybe, after she had time to put things behind her, she might marry again; perhaps to an older man, maybe a widower. No one else would have her and her children, except for Samuel. She sighed. Samuel, my sweet, charming, handsome Samuel; she smiled thinking about him. I'll go to Houston and talk to Samuel about the way I feel. Together, we'll decide on our future.

It was Friday afternoon and Catherine was hoping that she would be able to get out of her clinic early, when a knock at the door interrupted her thoughts. The hours were posted on the front door and it clearly said that the clinic closed at two o'clock on Friday afternoons. She was going to Houston to see Samuel on Saturday morning, and she wanted to spend some time with her children before she left. Whoever it was at the door continued knocking and ringing the bell until Catherine went to the front door.

She was surprised when she was greeted by a handsome young man in his early twenties. He didn't look like most of the people who lived in Rosenberg. He was more rugged and tan and she was sure that in the three months she had lived here she would have seen him if he called Rosenberg his home.

Jason took a step back when Catherine opened the door. He was not expecting to see someone his own age who looked like a fairy-tale princess. "I'd like to see Dr. Merit," he said.

"Is this an emergency?" she asked.

"No, but it is important," he said.

"I'm Dr. Merit," she said, but she didn't invite him in.

"I'd just like thirty minutes of your time. I'm Jason Brady. You killed my father," he said.

The blood drained from her face and Catherine turned white. She looked at his hands to see if he had a gun, but he was holding the screen door with one hand and he put out his other hand for a shake.

"What do you want with me?" she asked hesitantly.

"Just wanted to hear your version of what happened. I mean you no harm," he said.

Celli, Catherine's assistant in her clinic, came up behind her and asked if she needed to get Lucas, Celli's husband, and Catherine told her no.

"Come in," Catherine said and pulled the door farther open so he could come in. Celli stood watching. "This is Celli," she told Jason. "She works with me in the clinic." Jason said hello and followed Catherine into the waiting room. "I guess this is as good a place to talk as any," Catherine said. "What do you want to know?"

Jason looked at Celli. "I have no secrets," Catherine said. "She needs to stay."

Jason took a seat and Catherine sat across from him while Celli stood.

"I know my father's reputation, and I suspect he killed my mother when I was sixteen. That's when I left Rosenberg and went to live with my mother's parents in Seguin. I have not been in touch with him for a long time and he never tried to make contact with me. I am his only child and I have inherited his farm. I just want to know what happened, that's all," Jason said.

Catherine looked down at her hands and she felt fidgety and awkward. Her mouth was dry and she felt a sudden sadness come over her. Her fisted hands were in her lap and she stared down, feeling ashamed.

"I've never killed anyone," Catherine said. "I have tried to put it out of my mind, except now I have nightmares about it. Talking about it is very difficult for me, but I'll try," Catherine hesitated for a minute before she began.

"A young woman named Paula Brady came to see me about six weeks ago and she was pregnant. She had bruises and scars all over her body and I suspected she was being abused by someone. She said Joe had paid fifty dollars to her parents and she was sent as a mail-order bride to your father. She told me he became abusive when he drank and would frequently hit her. I tried to help her, but she refused my help. The next time I heard from them was the night your father called and said she was having a miscarriage.

"He picked me up later in his buckboard and took me to his

house. Paula was in the back room and was bleeding badly. I was able to stop the bleeding but she had lost too much blood. I asked Joe if he had hurt her and he pulled his gun on me and threatened to kill me if I said anything. He pushed me to the floor and unbuttoned his pants. I kicked him hard and he fell. I got up and ran from the house. It was dark, and I kept running, but fell." Catherine stopped for a few moments and took a deep breath before she continued. "I heard him calling my name and I pretended to be unconscious. I felt a rock under my hand and when he bent down to pull up my dress I hit him on the head and knocked him over. He lost his gun and I grabbed it. I was holding it and begged him to leave me alone, but he kept coming closer and when he grabbed for the gun, I shot him." Catherine was shaking and crying, and Celli went over and tried to console her.

"Just give me a minute, please," Catherine said. "Celli, could you get me some water, please?" Celli left the room.

"I'm so sorry to cause you any more pain, but I needed to confirm my feelings for him. I hated him and what he did to my mother. You did what you had to do and I'm glad he's dead," Jason said. "I should have killed him myself for what he did. I'm sorry I made you relive that night. I can see you are hurting," Jason said.

Celli came back with the water and Catherine asked Jason if he had heard enough. "I'm sorry, but I don't think I can talk about this anymore," Catherine said, and excused herself. "Celli will see you out."

Catherine went back to her office and walked over to the sink. She splashed some cold water on her face and then took a clean towel from the cupboard and dried her face and hands. Celli came back in and asked Catherine if she was all right, and Catherine shook her head yes. "I'll be fine. He seemed sincere about his intentions. Do you think he really felt that way, or just wanted to find out what really happened? He's so young," Catherine said.

Jason got on his horse and sat there for a few minutes. He could feel Catherine's pain and he hated his old man for everything.

He had been taken aback by Catherine's petite, curvy body and flowing, long hair. She was the most beautiful woman he had ever seen and he decided he needed to get to know her better. She had some kind of a proper accent, but Jason could not place where she might be from. Perhaps given time, he would find out.

Jason stopped at Cumming's Drug Store and picked up some supplies. There were a lot of stares, and when he walked out he ran into Michael Atwood. Michael owned a lot of the real estate in Rosenberg and he and many of his close friends ran the town. His family had owned much of the land that the railroad purchased when it came through. He had also been instrumental in helping Dr. Merit set up her medical practice in Rosenberg. Michael's wife had died a month earlier, and he now had his sights set on Catherine.

"You must be Jason," Michael said. "I heard you were in town. My name is Michael Atwood and I don't believe we have ever met. I wanted to talk to you about your daddy's farm. I wasn't sure if you were planning to stay, or sell it," he said, more as a statement.

"I'm not sure right now. I just got here. I don't even know what its worth or if he owed anything on it," Jason said. "Right now, I just want to get it cleaned up a bit so I can stay here a few days."

"I might be able to help you with that. The value, I mean. I own quite a bit of real estate around town myself and I am familiar with the values," Michael said and took out his calling card, handing it to him. "My office is right over there," and he pointed to it. Actually, Michael had inherited much of his property from his own father, who had died several years ago. He made it a point to buy up land around the county, hoping that someday oil might be discovered on it. After all, oil had been discovered in several surrounding counties, and he wanted to be sure he had his share of the land if it was ever discovered in Rosenberg. For now, his investments had paid off. He was a stockholder in the Wells Fargo Shipping Office and a member of the Masonic Lodge, as well as a respected land developer. He also owned part of the paper mill and cotton gin.

Michael had seen Jason come out of Catherine's office, and he wondered what he wanted. Michael went back to his office and picked up the phone. Celli answered and told him Catherine was in the backyard with the children. Michael hung up the phone and walked the three blocks to Catherine's house. He walked around back and stood at the fence, watching Catherine play a game with the children.

"Good afternoon," he shouted.

Catherine walked over to the fence and greeted Michael.

"I happened to see Jason Brady come out of your house and wanted to be sure everything was all right," he said sincerely.

"He wanted me to tell him what happened the night his father died. He said that his mother had also been abused by Brady and he was sure he had killed her. He was really nice and actually thanked me for shooting him. It was really strange," she told him.

"So, he didn't threaten you?" Michael asked.

"Not at all. As a matter of fact, I feel much better since we talked."

"Could I take you to dinner tonight at the café?"

"I'm sorry, Michael, but I'm leaving for Houston tomorrow and I want to spend this evening with my children."

"Then perhaps when you return we can get together."

Catherine did not answer, but smiled at him and said she would speak with him next week. She knew that after Michael's wife died several months back, he had wanted to spend time with her. His interests were quite clear, but she had no intentions of pursuing a relationship with him. Two widows who lived in Rosenberg had confided in her that they were having affairs with Michael long before his wife had died. He was a powerful man and she did not want to cross him. She also had too many secrets of her own, and Michael was one of the last people she wanted to know about her past. After they talked for a while, Michael went back to his office, determined that next week he would be more open in expressing his feelings for her.

Thirty minutes later, Catherine watched as Alex Cooper rode up to the fence on his horse. She had known Alex for over two years, and they had been briefly married when he was brutally attacked and shot in the head while on a scouting expedition. His injury left him with the loss of his memory of the last five years of his life, and he had asked Catherine for an annulment. She had given birth to their daughter, Emma, seven months later and during that time Alex met Michael Atwood's sister at a sanatorium where he was recovering, and they later married. Catherine did not know of his whereabouts until she moved to Rosenberg and their paths crossed. Every time she saw him, her heart would skip a beat and she longed to run into his arms. She had never stopped loving him and now he and his wife were expecting their own child. Living so close to them made it difficult for Catherine to have feelings for anyone else. That was another reason she couldn't marry Samuel. Samuel was special to her, but she didn't love him the way she had loved Alex. It didn't seem fair; Alex had moved on with his life and they were starting a family. She tried to convince herself that she was no longer in love with him, but she was only fooling herself. She silently convinced herself that if she married Samuel she would finally rid herself of her memories with Alex. That was another reason why she had to decline Samuel's proposal. It wouldn't be fair to him.

Catherine had finally admitted to Alex that Emma was his daughter and her other daughter, Isabelle, was also his. Alex had been treated by an Indian medicine man when he had been shot, and the medicine man's daughter, Mary, and Alex had been intimate while he was recuperating on their reservation. Isabelle had been born, and after the death of her mother and grandfather, she had been taken to Beaumont and left at Alex's old office. Not knowing Alex's whereabouts, Alex's old boss called Catherine and she took Isabelle to live with her and her children. Isabelle and Emma were half sisters and they were now inseparable.

Alex smiled at Catherine and walked up to the porch. He often came by to see his two daughters play, and both he and Catherine had decided it best to keep the true identities of the girls a secret. Alex often had dreams of his and Catherine's short life together and he tried hard to piece together some of the details, but nothing ever made sense to him. Somewhere, deep inside him, he knew he had feelings for Catherine, but he loved Meredith and for now, he didn't want to spoil what he and Meredith had together. After visiting with the children he walked back over to where Catherine was sitting.

"I'm glad you are feeling better. You've been through a lot and you are really a brave woman, Catherine, and I admire you for that." Alex and Catherine looked at each other for a long moment and then Alex turned and left. She watched from the corner of her eye as Alex mounted his horse, Pilgrim. She couldn't help but remember their intimate nights together and longed for him to hold her in his arms. She looked down at the ground and blushed, telling herself that it was a memory that needed to be tucked farther back in her mind. It would only cause her hurt, and she had suffered enough. He no longer belonged to her and was now someone else's husband. She was sorry she had ever agreed to the annulment, but at the time it seemed the right thing to do. She had to move on, and her thoughts turned back to Samuel.

That evening after the children were in bed, Catherine gathered up her clothes and packed them in a small bag. She was apprehensive about seeing Samuel, and worried that he would try and change her mind. He was a wonderful man; if the circumstances were different she would marry him without a second thought. He was the only one who made her feel safe now, and she adored him.

After Jason left Catherine's house he rode out to the old cemetery. It didn't take him long to find his mother's grave. The two graves next to it had fresh dirt piled on top and had not settled into the ground yet. Jason knelt by his mother's grave, kneeling on one knee and looking down. He had a lump in his throat and had to fight back the tears that were clouding his eyes. He hadn't stayed for her funeral because he was afraid if he did, he might kill his father. He vowed he would never be like his father, and when he got up he silently said, I love you mama.

When Jason got back to his place he couldn't help but think about his conversation with Catherine. She really was a beauty, he thought, and he was very attracted to her. Maybe he would stay in Rosenberg a while. It would take some time to sell the property and who knew, maybe he would stay permanently.

Catherine was at the train station early on Saturday morning and paced up and down the depot until she heard the oncoming train. It was an express, so she would be at the Houston station in just under an hour. She still felt tormented. She wondered if she should tell Samuel about Jason Brady, but decided not to because she needed to concentrate on breaking off their engagement. When she got off the train in Houston, she looked up and down the tracks but Samuel wasn't there, and she wondered if there might have been an emergency at the hospital. It was a cool day, so she decided to wait inside the depot.

The night before Catherine had left, Samuel's shift at the hospital ended at midnight. A young nurse he had been dating for the past two-and-a-half months was waiting outside his door when he got home, and he groaned to himself.

"I know you broke up with me the other night but I'm really having a hard time. Could I come in for a few minutes, please?" Samuel was tired and really didn't want to talk, but decided that was the least he could do, so he allowed her to come in.

"I just wanted to talk to you about our break up. I know you said there was someone else, but I wanted you to know that I'll always love you and if it doesn't work out for you, that you can call me," she said.

"I'm sorry you are taking this so hard, Dorothy, but I've known Catherine for several years and this time we are getting married," Samuel said.

"Could I just spend one more night with you? It's late and I live across town. I'm afraid to go home by myself and I don't mind sleeping on the couch," she said.

Samuel sighed and said, "All right, but I've got to get up early so I can meet her train, and you'll have to leave then." Dorothy looked down and shook her head yes.

After he went to sleep, Dorothy rose from the couch, went to Samuel's bedside table and picked up his alarm clock. She pushed the button in and turned off the alarm. She knew Samuel always slept soundly after coming home from a late night shift. When his breathing became deep, she removed her clothing and crawled under the covers slowly so she would not wake him.

Catherine's heart began to beat faster as she thought about seeing Samuel. She knew Samuel wouldn't take no for an answer and in a way she wished he would just take her directly to a preacher and get married. They would just have to figure everything else out after she became Mrs. Samuel Allen. She smiled and felt giddy inside just thinking about it.

Samuel was nowhere in sight and Catherine paced up and down, wondering what had happened to him. She waited thirty minutes and then hailed a carriage. Samuel had told her he kept a key under the flower pot by the door and she could use it anytime. She decided that would be a good place to wait. She would call the hospital when she got inside.

When she arrived at Samuel's brownstone, she walked up to the door, pushed the flower pot aside and picked up the key. When the door opened, she put the key back and walked inside with her bag. The curtains were drawn and the room was dimly lit. She walked to the bedroom and saw Samuel in bed. She smiled, thinking he had overslept, and then she saw movement on the other side of the bed. Dorothy sat up, revealing her naked breasts. Catherine gasped and just stood there, not knowing what to say. Dorothy nudged Samuel's shoulder and he sat up too.

"Catherine," he said, looking at his clock and then Dorothy. "It's not what it looks like. I…" Samuel couldn't think of any way to explain to Catherine what she was seeing. He knew it was bad when he saw Dorothy in his bed, naked.   Catherine removed her engagement ring and threw it at Dorothy, who caught it.

"Give it to her," was all Catherine could say as she picked up her bag and ran out the door.

A carriage was approaching, and she waved at the driver, who stopped. She was in the carriage before he could get off and help her. "Go, just go," she said holding back her tears.

By the time Samuel got out of bed and put his pants on, she was already gone. He stood on the street and looked up and down. His heart was beating fast and he ran his hand through his hair, feeling hopeless. He knew nothing he could say would make Catherine believe it wasn't what it looked like. Samuel stood on the curb trying to get his thoughts together. He loved Catherine more than anything. Maybe he should try and catch her at the train station, he decided.

When he went back in, he said, "Damn it, Dorothy. Did you turn off my alarm?"

She lied and told him no. "You must have forgotten to set it. I was cold during the night and I got in your bed to stay warm. I'm so sorry."

Samuel finished dressing and rushed to the train station. He waited, pacing up and down. He checked on the time for the next train to Rosenberg.

"It's leaving in thirty minutes," the clerk told him.

He sat on a bench and rehearsed over and over in his mind what he could say to Catherine, but nothing he could think of would make it any better. The train to Rosenberg arrived and Samuel paced up and down looking for Catherine, but she didn't come. After it left, he put his hands in his pockets and walked back home, wondering if he would ever see her again.

Catherine had asked the carriage driver if there was another means of transportation to Galveston other than the train. The driver told her that there was a stagecoach company still in operation and only traveled between Houston and Galveston. She asked him to take her there. Catherine couldn't face Samuel right now and she knew he would go to the train station looking for her. She had wanted to go to Galveston to visit her family's graves at the cemetery for some time now, and this was as good a time as any, she thought. The fall weather had set in and she was glad she had brought a sweater.

The stagecoach ride was bumpy and uncomfortable; after it left she was sorry she had chosen this mode of transportation. It felt crowded and she was sitting next to a large man who smelled of body odor. There was another, older man, and one older woman who was probably his wife. The couple sat across from her and the man had long legs, occasionally kicking her when they hit a bump. The man next to her kept falling asleep and his head seemed to always rest on her shoulder. This was the first time she had traveled in a stagecoach; she decided it would be her last. When she went home, she would travel by train through Sugar Land and avoid Houston at all costs.

Catherine tried not to think of Samuel. It hurt too much, and she knew the tears would come in bucket loads later. There would be plenty of time to grieve for him when she got home. She knew she would never trust him again and she reminded herself that it was for the best. It was supposed to be her breaking up with him. She never suspected Samuel had not given up his old ways. At least now she wouldn't need to feel guilty. Their morals and values were too different. She had to move on and forget him. This was probably for the best and he only had himself to blame. Still, it really wasn't easy to accept that your fiancé was caught in bed with another woman. He had lied to her, cheated on her, and she hated herself for being infatuated with his charm and good looks. She couldn't help but wonder why everything seemed to backfire on her. She clenched her fist and tried to look out the window, as it was not the time or place to cry. The trip seemed endless and she prayed God would forgive her for having such evil thoughts about the people who were traveling with her. They were just plain, ordinary people and she had no right to judge them.

CHAPTER 3

When Samuel got back to his house, Dorothy was dressed and waiting for him. He was quiet and she spoke first. "I'm pregnant," was all she said. Samuel looked at her in disbelief. "When I told you it was a safe time, I wasn't sure, and I don't like it when you use those things for protection. I wasn't trying to get pregnant, I just assumed I wouldn't," she confessed. Samuel sat down in a chair and put his head in his hands, staring at the floor.

"Why didn't you just tell me last night instead of turning off the alarm?" he asked.

"I'm not sure. I guess I was afraid you would just marry Catherine anyway. I love you, Samuel, and I want us to be together, at whatever cost. Please don't hate me," she said, crying softly.

Samuel stood up and walked over to her, noticing she had put the engagement ring on her finger. "You're sure you are pregnant?" he asked.

"Yes, I went to the doctor yesterday. He said I was at least seven weeks," she said, sniffling. Samuel sat in his chair for a while and stared at Dorothy. He didn't blame her, but he wished she had just been honest with him. He hated that Catherine's last thoughts of him were of him naked in bed with another woman. His dreams of making Catherine his wife were shattered and he felt he only had one choice.

Samuel was sickened by the fact that he had let this happen. He knew in his heart that the right thing to do was to accept his fate.

Samuel picked up the hand that Dorothy had placed the ring on and kissed it. "Then, will you marry me?" he asked.

Dorothy beamed and screamed yes. Samuel knew he didn't love Dorothy, but she was having his child. He wanted children more than anything but had hoped it would happen when he married Catherine. Fate had a way of changing things. He was as much responsible for the baby as was Dorothy, and he had to forgive her. He could understand her desperation and he knew she loved him. Maybe in time he would learn to love her, too. She was having his baby; the thought of his child growing up without a father was not the way he was raised. That afternoon they went to a little church around the corner and got married.

They stopped at Dorothy's apartment and picked up some of her things and took them to the brownstone. That evening after they made love, Dorothy was curled up in bed next to him and he could hear her soft, even breathing as she slept. For some reason he felt at peace even though it was not Dorothy that he loved. He knew Catherine had been right about one thing. Marriage would have been a constant struggle if he and Catherine had to balance their lives with four children and a failing medical practice in a small town. He liked working at Houston General and he was developing a good reputation. He would have had to give that up for a less secure and simple kind of life in Rosenberg if he would have married Catherine. He knew Dorothy would be submissive and attentive to his needs. He convinced himself it was all for the best. He would focus on her now, and try not to think about Catherine.

When Catherine arrived at the livery stable in Galveston where the stagecoach stopped, she walked over to a waiting carriage. She asked the driver to take her to the cemetery on Broadway, but on the way she wanted to stop and buy some flowers. They stopped at a street vendor and bought several bouquets of fresh fall flowers. The city of Galveston looked different. The streets were fairly busy but not like it had been before the storm. Almost all the vegetation was gone and a slight wind was blowing up the dry sand in the streets. When they got to the cemetery, she walked over to her mother's grave and put flowers at the headstone. John Merit, her first husband, was buried beside her mother, Anne, and so was his sister, Amelia. She had divided up the flowers and put equal amounts at their headstones. Minnie Wyman, her old landlady and friend, was buried across from them, and she put the remaining flowers at her headstone. Catherine walked back to her family's graves and knelt. She took out her rosary and used it to pray for each of them. After she recited the Lord's Prayer and Psalm 23 from memory she looked around and saw the driver patiently smoking a cigarette and staring at her.

Catherine rose and boarded the carriage and asked the driver to take her by her old house. It was the one she and her first husband, John, had built after the fatal storm that devastated most of Galveston three years earlier. The driver told her he would do the best that he could, but many of the streets were blocked off because of the work being done on the new seawall and the city's intention to raise the elevation of the streets north of Galveston Bay to match the seawall's height before gently sloping toward the bay. He also told her of the city's intention to dredge the canal and rebuild the piers on the north end so that the ships could sail back into Galveston's port. For now the railroad and horse-drawn wagons were both bringing equipment into town for the rebuilding of the city.

Galveston was now bustling with a new breed of people. There was a parade of wagons loaded down with support pilings that had been brought in on the train from Beaumont. Workers walked beside the wagons in the event something fell off or the wagon broke down.

When they stopped in front of her old house, the driver told her that it was one of the houses that would be lifted up on stilts five feet and sand would be brought in from the dredged channel to raise the elevation. She found it hard to envision what he was trying to tell her and decided she would pay more attention to the Galveston newspapers. To her surprise, she noticed a sign offering her previous house for sale. Oh, how she longed to be living in it again. She made a mental note to call her real estate agent and ask the price, not that she would be able to buy it or ever hope to return to Galveston. There was a longing inside her to eventually return to Galveston and she did not really know why, except for the memories that seemed to loom at every corner. She was haunted by it. Maybe someday, she thought, maybe someday she and her children would return.

She had asked the driver to drop her off at St. Mary's Catholic Church. When they arrived, Catherine paid him and then walked up the stairs and opened the massive, carved door leading into the sanctuary. She genuflected and made the sign of the cross and walked up to the confessional booth. There were two other people in front of her so she pulled down the kneeling rail and knelt, folding her hands in prayer. A short while later she saw Father Jonathan come from the way of his office. He saw her and nodded with a smile. Fifteen minutes later it was her turn and she walked into the empty side of the confessional booth. She heard soft mumbling and she waited her turn. When the small opening slid up she prayed, "Bless me father, for I have sinned…" Catherine continued confessing her sins and when she finished, she asked if she could consult with him when he was through hearing confessions; he told her to wait for him. He gave her the prayers of forgiveness she was to use as her penance. After she said them, she walked up and knelt before the statue of the Virgin Mary and lit several candles. She saw Father Jonathan walk past her and go towards his office. She finished her prayers, made the sign of the cross, and then followed him.

Father Jonathan had been an old friend of her first husband, John, and they had counselled with him before and after she and John were married. She considered him to be her friend, too, and he had often given her sound advice about her own life.

"I'm delighted to see you again. Tell me about your life, Catherine. Your confession has disturbed me, and I want to hear more. You are like a daughter I never had and I want to help you," Father Jonathan said.

Catherine told him about the past few months since she had left Galveston and moved to Rosenberg. About her renewed encounter with her second husband, Alex Cooper, her secrets from her past, her on-again, off-again love affair with Samuel, and how he had betrayed her; and finally, the murder of Joe Brady and the return of his son, Jason. She felt confused and betrayed. She needed to find a way to bring peace to her soul.

Father Jonathan frowned and thought for a minute. "God often uses the consequence of sin to bring you back to him. The demons you continue to have are of your own making. God has forgiven you, but you must forgive yourself. You must cleanse your soul and ask God to give you strength to allow you to forgive and move forward. It is difficult to be a woman and live in a man's world, but God has given you so much and you have to be grateful for those things. You mustn't give up. You are meant to be a caregiver, Catherine, and God has given you four beautiful children. You are a doctor now, and that appears to be your destiny. Embrace what you have and thank God for those things. In time, you will grow to understand. You must pray and listen for God's answers." Father Jonathan wrote down some scriptures from the Bible and pushed them over to Catherine. "You will find many of your answers in the Bible," he said. Catherine took the note and stood up.

"Before you leave, there is a matter here in my own parish that has given me concern and I would like to discuss it with you if you have a few more minutes," Father Jonathan said.

Catherine sat back down and listened intently. "There is a very powerful man in our parish whose daughter is with child. She is nineteen and has been away at school. They do not approve of the man who got her pregnant and they are considering sending her away to have her child and then put it up for adoption. You had indicated that your children's nanny, Martha, would be leaving soon, and this might be a way that you can help each other. I know this is a strange request, but if you have the room, the young woman could stay with you, help with your children, and you could earn some extra money. Her family would pay you well. They have considered other homes, but have not found one that pleases them. Of course, I would have to get their permission, also."

Catherine thought for a moment and considered what Father Jonathan had just told her. "Do you think the family would approve of me? After all, my past has not been without sin."

"You are a doctor, and you have many gifts, Catherine. I will discuss it with them and get back with you."

They hugged each other and as Catherine walked out of his office, she felt a renewed strength and peace. It was going to get better, she told herself. Catherine put ten dollars in the donation box, made the sign of the cross and left.

Catherine had put the piece of paper with the scriptures in her purse. She would read them later since she had not brought her Bible. One thing Father Jonathan had told her was that she was a woman in a man's world and for some reason it struck her as a challenge. Everything she was trying to do infringed on that. Only men were supposed to be doctors. Women were to be wives and be subservient to their husbands. Women could not make important decisions. And they were to be breeders of children. She knew she could never be a conventional type of woman who would accept mediocrity, and she was not going to apologize to anyone. She had to be strong; her children needed her to be. Father Jonathan's suggestion of opening up her home to an unwed mother was an interesting idea and she decided to face it as a new challenge. Catherine would simply tell the good people of Rosenberg that she was a cousin who had lost her husband.

Catherine decided to stay over and walked the few blocks to the Tremont Hotel. When it came into view she hesitated before crossing the street. She had stayed in that hotel on her honeymoon with her first husband and again when she and Alex were married.

She knew it probably wouldn't be a good idea, but she also knew she had to be strong and learn to live with all of her memories, both good and bad. She waited while another parade of wagons trailed by carrying precious loads of material and small machinery. It seemed so little compared to the enormous task facing Galveston; to build seventeen miles of a concrete and granite seawall. It was overwhelming and would take Galveston years to complete. She crossed the street and was greeted by a young teenage bellboy. He retrieved her bag and helped her up the stairs and into the beautiful formal entryway. She loved this hotel, as it reminded her so much of the hotels in London. She breathed a sigh of relief when she was told there was a room available on the third floor. She smiled and paid the concierge a deposit on the room.

It was just after one in the afternoon when she got settled in her room; it was small but beautifully furnished. She decided to change into a simple dress and her everyday walking shoes and made her way out of the hotel and down the street to a small café. Even though she wasn't hungry, her stomach was growling and she realized she had not eaten all day. Hot tea, soup, and a grilled-cheese sandwich gave her the nourishment she needed before she set out to visit the medical school. While she had no intention of moving back to Galveston any time soon, it was still in the back of her mind that when all of the construction and excavation was done, Galveston would be back to its old heritage and be a marvelous place to rear her children. Maybe by then her past would have been forgotten by those who hated her and she could live out her life in peace.

The medical school was much too far to walk and besides, the workers she had seen were of all nationalities and some of the men looked downright scary. While she was in the café she heard patrons speaking French, German, Russian, and even Italian. She enjoyed hearing the chatter and trying to guess their nationality. Galveston was a melting pot of many languages and people, but there were too many frightening-looking men for her to go out on her own, so she hailed a carriage.

Her heart seemed to beat faster when she saw the medical school. It had been a second home to her when she was studying here. Several of the old dormitory-like structures had been demolished after the horrific storm, and new ones were under construction. When they rode up to the main building, she asked the driver to wait for an hour and she would pay for his wait. The driver seemed pleased, as it would allow him to give his horse a rest and he could take a nap.

Catherine climbed up the stairs and made her way to the dean's office. As she opened the door she was greeted by three distinguished-looking gentlemen who seemed to be as surprised to see her as she was to see the three of them. One was Dean Tom Addison and the other two had been her professors. They exchanged greetings and the two professors excused themselves to return to their respective classrooms.

Her visit with Dean Addison proved to be very productive. He told Catherine that when she decided to move back to Galveston, he would be pleased to make a place for her. Dedicated doctors and teachers were hard to come by these days. All of the new graduates were eager to move to larger hospitals to make the most money. He couldn't promise her a large salary, but it would be enough to support her and her children. Dr. Addison took her hand and winked at her when they finished and told her she was still one of his favorite graduates. "It would please me if you would have dinner this evening with me," he told her.

"I have much to do and I'm extremely tired from my journey. Perhaps on my next return we can do that," she replied, not wanting to offend him. Dr. Addison was married with five children, and it disappointed her that he would even suggest such an encounter. She was sure his wife would not have approved.

The driver was fast asleep when she called out to him. He immediately jumped down and helped her into the carriage. "You can just drop me off at the Galveston Bank," she exclaimed.

She had no intention of going into the bank, but it was down the street from Clay Segal's office and she decided it was time to come face-to-face with one of her demons.

After she paid the driver she walked slowly up to the door. She hesitated and took a deep breath before going inside. The bell rang on the door as she opened it, and a few minutes later Clay Segal walked out of his office with his secretary behind him. His secretary's hair was tousled and her blouse had an open button-hole. She looked flustered and walked quickly to a filing cabinet, avoiding eye contact with Catherine. Clay's face looked sheepish and his mouth dropped open.

"Ca-Ca-Catherine," he stuttered. What a pleasant surprise. Come in." Clay closed the door behind him and pulled out a chair for Catherine to sit in. She stood, not saying anything. "Don't you want to sit down?" he asked.

"I don't intend to stay long," she replied. "What I have to say to you will only take a few minutes." Clay walked behind his desk, wanting to put some distance between them. The expression on Catherine's face told him all he needed to know. It was evident she still harbored resentment towards him.

"I trusted you as John's and my lawyer. What you did to me was shameful, and I just want you to know that I have had enough of you and your evil wife. You egged my house, you told horrible lies about me, and then had me fired from my job at St. Mary's. What's done is done. I'm not the same person you raped and violated two years ago, and if you don't call off your evil wife's harassment, I am prepared to tell her what you did to me and that you are having an affair with your secretary."

The blood drained from Clay's face. He noticed that the door was still ajar; he knew his secretary had heard everything. "Shh," he said, as he walked past her and shut the door.

"Believe me, Catherine, I felt terrible after that day. It was just that I was infatuated with you and something came over me. I know saying I'm sorry won't make it better, but I want you to know that I am remorseful about my actions. I have no control over Carla's hatred for you. I found out that she had paid some hoodlums from another neighborhood to egg your house, and I put a stop to that. I found out what she did at the hospital after the incident. She is extremely hard to manage and has a violent temper. Believe me; I'm sorry I ever married her. She is putting me in the poorhouse. I would leave her, except she is five months pregnant and is now making my life miserable. She didn't want any more children, and she blames me because she has gained fifty pounds."

Catherine bit her lower lip so Clay wouldn't see the smile on her face. He was getting what he deserved, she thought.

Catherine turned around and before she opened the door, she paused and said, "You two deserve each other. I hope you enjoy being miserable together."

"Wait," he demanded. "There is one more thing. Carla sent a letter to a man by the name of Atwood in Rosenberg about you. I don't know what was in it and I didn't ask. I'm sorry if it causes you any pain."

Catherine hurriedly left Clay's office. When she got outside she turned and began walking towards the Tremont. She felt relieved and like a weight had been lifted off her shoulders. She smiled to herself and took in a deep breath. That was one less demon, one she felt sure wouldn't torment her anymore. Unfortunately, Carla had sent Michael Atwood some kind of letter. She couldn't worry about it any longer. Her past was her business and not his. She would no longer be afraid to return to Galveston if things didn't work out in Rosenberg. She strolled down the Strand and stopped in the thrift store and purchased some clothing for the children. She also stopped and ordered some merchandise that would be sent by train to Rosenberg. Wanting to bring the children gifts, she picked out two dolls, two toy cars, and some soap to complete her purchases, then she headed back to the hotel. Christmas was just around the corner and she wanted to get an early start on her shopping.

Catherine noticed a small, out-of-the-way bookstore just before she got to the hotel, and crossed Twenty-Third Street to purchase some books. The Galveston Bookshop was a quaint little shop with rows of shelving that housed hundreds of books. The shop owner was an attractive woman named Sharon, and once she introduced herself, she asked if she could help Catherine find something. "Let me take your packages while you look around. Perhaps I can direct you to the area of books you might be shopping for," she remarked.

"Actually, I want to find some educational children's books," Catherine answered. Sharon walked Catherine towards the back and pulled several books out that were her best sellers. Catherine picked out four books and then noticed the medical books across the aisle. She walked over and found one that had been out of print. "I've been looking for this book for some time now, and I'm delighted to find it. I don't see a price on it," she said, more as a question.

"That is a rare book. There were only two hundred printed, and I was fortunate to have it donated to me. Why are you interested in that particular book?" Sharon asked.

"I'm a doctor, and am familiar with the author who wrote it. He believed that the body was equipped to heal itself in many ways and that your state of mind could determine your longevity. I read parts of it while I was at medical school, but the book was always checked out when I tried to get it. It was later lost or pulled from the library."

Sharon smiled. "I suspect it was pulled from the library. Since you have such a desire to purchase this book, even though it's probably worth three dollars, you can have it for seventy-five cents. It needs a good home. The book caused a lot of controversy and you are the only person who has had any interest in it."

Catherine smiled and thanked her. This was the ending of a day that began with an impossible situation. What a great way for it to

end, she thought. She hugged Sharon before she left and picked up
her parcels, leaving with a smile on her face.

CHAPTER 4

The train ride home gave Catherine time to contemplate all that had happened that weekend; she would not allow herself to be depressed. Samuel drifted in and out of her thoughts as did Michael and Alex. She liked being around strong men and she felt she was their equal, no matter how they each tried to make Catherine feel inferior. Alex had never made her feel that way, and that was one of the many things she loved about him.

It was two o'clock when she arrived at the train station in Rosenberg, and when she walked through the depot she saw Jason Brady. When he saw her he said, "Good afternoon, I hope you had a nice trip. I just came here to wire my grandparents some money. May I see you home?" he asked.

Catherine was still uneasy and not sure if Jason felt any animosity toward her for shooting his father, but agreed. What could he do, she wondered. It was a public street and there were several people around. Jason picked up her bag and parcels and held out a bent arm. She put her arm through it and they walked out into the street. A slight wind had picked up and Jason saw her shiver, so he stopped and took off his jacket and put it around her. They continued walking and making small talk until they arrived at her house.

"Thank you for seeing me home," she said and handed him his jacket.

Jason bowed and said, "It was my pleasure, Dr. Merit."

"Please, you may call me Catherine," she said sweetly. She saw something in Jason's manner that made her feel safe with him. He seemed sincere, and his boyish good looks might have had something to do with that. Jason waited until she had unlocked the door and walked in before he turned and left. He began whistling as he walked back to the depot to fetch his horse. He liked Catherine a lot. She was easy to talk to and her overwhelming beauty would get any man excited. And she excited him.

Martha, her children's nanny, met her at the door when she came in. "I wasn't expecting you until late evening," she said. "I've put the children down for a nap."

"I guess I should have called. Samuel and I have decided not to get married, ever," she said, acting as if it were not important.

"And are you all right with that?" Martha asked.

"Yes, yes I am. I need to stay here with my children. He is better off in Houston and I understand that. I need to get unpacked so I can spend some time with the children," she said as she went upstairs. Catherine stopped at the doorway to the boys' room and then quietly walked up to their beds. Adam had crawled into Daniel's bed and they were sleeping soundly. Her children were her life and she loved them more than anything. She smiled as she saw them sleeping. So sweet and innocent, she thought. She wanted to kiss them but did not want to wake them so she left and checked on the girls, who were in the adjoining room. They shared a double bed, and Catherine marveled at how much they looked like their father. Four beautiful children, she thought, and they belonged to her. This was enough and she was thankful that she was their mother.

Catherine put her things away then walked over and took the scripture note from her purse. She pulled out her Bible and Samuel's letter fell out. She touched it as though it had meaning and she picked it up and kissed it. Goodbye, Samuel, she said softly and put his letter proposing marriage back in the drawer. She thumbed through the pages of her Bible until she got to each passage, reading slowly and trying to understand their meaning. The last scripture was short; Joshua 1:7-8; she must obey the laws as they are written and she had to be strong and courageous. She had found peace and contentment. She placed the note Father Jonathan had given her inside the Bible and put it on her desk. She wasn't tired, having rested on the train, so she went downstairs. There was one more thing she had to do and she picked up the phone. It was mid afternoon, but he answered on the third ring.

"Dr. Samuel Allen," he said.

"It's Catherine, and I want to hear what you have to say," she said softly.

Samuel sighed and felt a lump forming in his throat. "There's no easy way to tell you this, Catherine, but first of all, I'm sorry it ended this way." Samuel told her about Dorothy meeting him the night before and that he had previously broken up with her. She was upset and asked to spend the night on the couch. He told her the rest of the story and finished by saying, "We got married earlier today. I felt it was what I needed to do. I hope you can forgive me. We started out as friends and I hope we can always be friends," he said.

"I would like that, Samuel, and I hope you will be happy together. Thank you for sharing that with me. Goodbye, friend," she said, and she hung up.

Samuel looked at the phone before he put it in the cradle. He was surprised she didn't seem angry and she genuinely appeared to be happy for him. His heart ached for her and he couldn't help but feel better that he had told her the truth and she accepted it. It was over between them and he had to put all of his efforts into his marriage to Dorothy. He hoped it would work out. Dorothy had been in the bathroom, and when she came out she asked who had called. "The hospital," he said, not wanting to hurt her.

A week had passed and Michael Atwood was in his office. He left midmorning to walk to the post office and get the mail. As he walked back to his office, out of habit, he thumbed through it to see if there was anything unexpected. He stopped when he saw a letter to him in what appeared to be a woman's handwriting. He looked at the return address; it was from Galveston, Texas. He opened it with his knife as he walked up the steps to his office. He was already reading it when he slowly sat down at his desk.

The letter was from a woman and it pertained to information regarding Catherine Merit. The letter appeared to have a hostile content, and he looked at the signature. It was signed Carla Beranger Merit Segal. It was the Merit name that drew his attention. She had heard that he was inquiring about the reputation of Catherine Merit. It implied that Carla was John Merit's second wife and that Catherine had been his first wife, but had run off and left John Merit for a drifter named David Brooks. It went on to say Brooks was a murderer, a rapist, and a crook. Apparently Catherine had two children while with Brooks and came back to Galveston after Brooks was hung and told everyone that her two boys were John Merit's children. It went on to say that Catherine had married a second time to an Alex Cooper, but for some reason Cooper had asked for an annulment. Michael grew angrier by the minute and slammed his fist on his desk. Carla went on to say that Catherine had also stolen her wallet while they were both at a local grocery store, but she did not press charges.

Michael picked up the phone and called Alex. When Meredith answered the phone she told Michael that Alex had left on Pilgrim and was headed into town to pick up some supplies. Michael tried to act like nothing was wrong and said he just needed Alex to run an errand for him. Michael went outside and saw Pilgrim tied up across the street at the drug store. He walked over and greeted Alex as he came out the door. He asked Alex to come to his office and that he had something he wanted to show him. Since Meredith and Alex lived in a small house on the Atwood property, Alex did a lot of small jobs for Michael. Michael was Meredith's brother, and Alex always tried to stay in Michael's good graces. Alex knew Michael pretty much ran the small town of Rosenberg and if you were smart, you didn't get on

Michael's bad side. Michael was shrewd and the last thing Alex wanted to do was cross Michael.

Alex sat across the desk from Michael and he could see Michael was angry about something. He threw the envelope at Alex, who picked it up and looked at it. "Go ahead, take it out and read it," Michael ordered. Alex took the letter out and flipped to the back page for a signature. When he saw Carla's name, he looked up at Michael and then he read it.

"You knew Catherine Merit before she moved here?" Michael asked.

"Yes, I did," he answered.

"Why did you have the marriage annulled?" Michael asked.

"As best I can remember, it was after my accident and I told her I couldn't be married to her because she was like a stranger to me. I didn't know she was pregnant with Emma at the time," he said. Michael's mouth opened and he looked angry.

"Go on, where did Isabelle come from?" he asked.

"Isabelle's my daughter, too. The medicine man who took care of me after the accident had a daughter named Mary, and she came into my bed. I recuperated at the Indian reservation for several weeks; I couldn't remember anything, and Mary nursed me back to health, never leaving my side. We grew fond of each other and had talked about getting married. My old boss from Glacier Oil Company finally found out where I was and brought Catherine to fetch me. I went back to Galveston with her, but after a couple of days I decided to leave and go back to Beaumont to try and find out about my past. Catherine offered to have the marriage annulled but did not tell me she was pregnant with Emma. Several weeks later I woke up at a hospital in Houston and couldn't remember anything. That's when I went to Oakwood Plantation Sanatorium. I found out later, after I married Meredith, that something had happened to Mary and her father, and that Mary had given birth during that time to Isabelle. No one knew where I was so they called Catherine. Since Isabelle was Emma's sister, Catherine took her in so she would not go to an orphanage," said a sombre Alex. "I'm sorry you had to find out like this. Catherine and I decided that it was in the past and no one needed to know."

"Is that why Catherine moved here?" he asked.

"No, she had no idea I was your brother-in-law when she answered the ad. She told me that after she had signed the papers and gave you a check that you had told her at lunch about your sister marrying someone from Oakwood Plantation Sanatorium. She felt it was too late to back out of the deal. There is nothing between us, I assure you," Alex said.

"You need to tell Meredith," Michael insisted. "I don't want her hearing about it from someone else. Besides, I don't think it's a good idea for her to see Catherine about her pregnancy. You'll just have to take her to Houston when it's time for her to deliver. Now get out of here."

Alex was relieved that everything was out in the open but felt that Michael was overreacting. He knew Michael was going to come down hard on Catherine, but his concern right now was for Meredith. Alex put Pilgrim in the corral when he got home and went in to talk to Meredith.

Alex asked Meredith to sit on the sofa and he took her hand. "I've been harboring some secrets that have been eating at me for some time now, and I hope you will understand that I didn't tell you because I didn't want to hurt you. You are my life and I love you and I'm going to ask for your forgiveness and understanding when I tell you this story." Meredith could see tears in Alex's eyes, and he looked away for a few minutes. After he got his composure he proceeded to tell Meredith everything, and then told her that Michael had received a letter from John Merit's second wife telling him everything. "It's been difficult for me and I know I should have told you from the beginning, but I wasn't sure I remembered what happened. I could recollect bits and pieces, but everything seemed so muddled and hard to believe. I know I shouldn't blame this on my accident, but I don't think I'm a vindictive person, Meredith, and I never intended to hurt you," he said as he wiped his eyes with his handkerchief. I don't think we should blame Catherine, either, although I know Michael is really angry with her and I'm sure he is going to tell her so. I don't want to lose my girls and I don't want him to run her off. I love Emma and Issy," he continued.

Meredith put her arms around Alex and hugged him. "I was afraid there was something physically wrong with you and I'm relieved you're all right. I'm not upset about Catherine. She seems to be honest, and I've never considered her a threat. I suppose I should find a doctor in Houston to deliver the baby. I still trust Catherine, but if something went wrong, I know Michael would blame her. Thank you for being honest with me," she said. She kissed Alex and invited him to take her to the bedroom. He grinned and picked her up, carrying her down the hall and into their room. Alex slowly undressed her and planted kisses around her protruding belly. They made love and afterwards Meredith's smiling face assured him that everything was well.

Catherine had just seen her last patient and she walked out to put the "Closed" sign up, meeting Michael as he came in the door. She sensed his anger and his stern face caused her to step back. "I need to talk to you right now." He grabbed her wrist, pulling her out the front door. He held on tightly and practically threw her in his car when he opened the door. He threw the letter at her and started the car. "Go ahead, read it," he demanded. Catherine looked at the return address and recognized the letter was from Carla. "Aren't you going to read it?" he asked.

"I already know what it's going to say," she said sternly. Michael drove out of town about two miles and pulled down a dirt road, stopping under a cluster of trees by the Brazos River. He turned off the engine and looked at Catherine.

"What do you have to say for yourself?" he asked.

"What difference does it make? You already believe every

word she's written or you wouldn't be so angry. I'm not a criminal. Everything I've done was for the children. I'm sorry you feel violated."

"Violated? What about Meredith?"

"I'm sorry if I have hurt her. She's been a wonderful friend to me and I never meant her any harm," Catherine said trying not to cry. She was not going to show weakness. Michael was being a bully and she resented it. "Does it please you to be rough with women?" she asked.

Michael gave her a hard look and then started the car. He drove her back to her house and stopped. "Get out," he said angrily.

Catherine got out and walked to the front porch. After Michael drove off, she sat in the rocking chair and began shaking as the tears began to glide down her cheeks. In a way she felt relieved that it was all finally out in the open. She wiped the tears away with the bottom of her white apron. Lucas, her Negro helper, came out and asked if she were all right and said that supper was ready. "Tell the children to go ahead, I'll be in shortly," she said.

The feeling of guilt and emptiness began to slowly bring Catherine down into a lonely place she dreaded going. She knew Michael was a powerful man in Rosenberg, and if he so desired he could convince the townspeople to stop coming to her. She wondered if he were mad enough to do that. She knew her children would be asking for her so she went to her office and splashed water on her face. She took several deep breaths and went to join them at dinner. She smiled when she walked in and blew kisses at each of them.

When Michael got home he poured himself a scotch and went out on the porch. He was angry with himself for having romantic feelings for Catherine and wondered how he could be so stupid as to be drawn into her fabricated life. He really thought she was a saint when he first met her. He drank his scotch down quickly and went in to phone Meredith. He dreaded having to hold her hand through all of this. "Hello, Michael," she said as she picked up the phone.

"Is Alex there, and are you all right?" he asked.

"We are wonderful," she said. "Alex has told me everything and I'm fine. I can tell that you are still angry. Do you want Alex and me to come over?" she asked.

"No, I just wanted to be sure you aren't upset," he said.

"Alex and I aren't going to let this incident grow out of proportion. Alex was still recovering from his accident while all this was taking place. He didn't do it to be malicious. He didn't tell me because he wanted to protect me. I understand that. Everything is fine," she said.

Michael poured himself another drink. Of course he could forgive Alex. Alex could barely remember the last three months and he had no confirmation of any of this other than Catherine's word. The girls could be any man's children. Catherine was probably deceitful to Alex and pulled him into her little lies. He was not going to let her get away with it. He would make her pay. He just had to come up with a plan, he thought.

Two weeks had passed and Catherine had not seen Michael, Alex, or Meredith, not that she expected them to come calling. She managed to keep her mind occupied with her medical practice and the children seemed to use up the rest of her energies. During her office hours Martha, the children's nanny, had told her that Meredith and Alex had come by to see the children and only stayed a little while. Catherine had sent Lucas on some errands and he was back early with empty arms. "Dr. Catherine, the stores say your credit ain't good anymore and they only want cash." Catherine looked displeased and went to her desk drawer where she kept a lockbox. She handed Lucas a ten dollar bill and to let her know if he needed more. She wondered if Michael was behind this.

Michael, Alex, and Meredith continued to have their weekly dinners together, and nothing was ever mentioned again about Catherine. It was as though she had ceased to exist. Michael knew that Alex and Meredith continued to see Isabelle and Emma, but they never brought up Catherine's name. Meredith and Alex had gone to Houston for Alex to have another x-ray of his head injury, and while they were at the hospital, Alex recognized Samuel at one of the counters, talking to a nurse. Alex took Meredith by the hand and walked over and introduced her to Samuel. Samuel smiled and said he was glad to see them. Alex noticed a wedding ring on Samuel's hand and asked, "When did you get married?"

Samuel looked surprised. "A few weeks ago. We're expecting our first child. How is Catherine?" he asked.

"I suppose she's fine. We don't see her much. She stays pretty busy," Alex said.

Samuel said he was glad to see them, but he had to get back to a patient, and left.

On the way back to Rosenberg, Meredith looked at Alex and said, "What do you suppose happened with Catherine and Samuel?"

"I have no idea. Catherine and I haven't spoken more than a few words since Michael got the letter, and that was several weeks ago. If he has a pregnant wife, that could only mean one thing," Alex said. "He must have been courting someone else at the same time and she came up pregnant."

"Oh, no," Meredith said. "That must have been difficult for Catherine to take. She really has been through a lot, hasn't she?"

Alex didn't answer. He felt guilty about avoiding Catherine all this time because he was afraid Michael would get angry again. He decided he would approach her tomorrow and find out.

Alex asked Meredith if she minded if he went to see the girls by himself. "I'm not going to lie and tell you that's the only reason I want to go. Catherine has been a friend to me through all of this and I know she has mine and your interest at heart. She doesn't deserve to be snubbed by us or anyone else."

Catherine saw Alex in the waiting room and was surprised to see him. She finished with the last two patients and then called him into her office. "Are you having problems with your headaches again?" she asked.

"No, in fact they are much better. Meredith and I went to see my doctor in Houston and he says there has been no change. We also ran into Samuel while we were there. He told us he had gotten married, and it wasn't to you. What happened?"

"It's interesting," she said. "Everyone wants to know my business, including you."

"I don't mean any harm by it, Catherine. It's just I was worried about you and wondered what happened. He told us he and his wife were expecting," Alex said timidly.

"Then there, you have your answer," she said.

"Catherine, I'm sorry Michael has given you such a hard time. I know he has a temper, but Meredith and I aren't mad at you."

"You have no idea, Alex," she said, shaking her head. "All my credit in town has been cut off and Celli told me today that Michael is trying to get Lucas to come back and work for him. He told Lucas he would put up the front money for Celli to open up her own clinic. He wants to run me out of town," she said.

"Oh, my God," Alex said. "I'll talk to him."

"No, I don't want you to get involved. You don't want Michael angry at you, too. I'll fight my own battles. I just want you to stay out of my business, please. I'm not going anywhere. I'll just close the clinic if I have too," she said. "I'll be fine and I would appreciate you keeping this between us. I don't want to cause friction between Meredith and her brother. Promise me you won't say anything."

"All right, I promise, but if you need help I want you to promise to come to me. I still have a good amount of my savings and I can give you help with the girls," Alex said.

"Catherine smiled. "You are such a good man, Alex. I'll be fine. I have my own money; from the farm I sold in Beaumont." She walked him to the front door and he reached down and kissed her cheek. He stood looking at her and he knew she was putting up a front. He would have to figure out some way to help her, he thought.

"Take care of yourself," he said.

CHAPTER 5

Lucas had prepared a feast for Thanksgiving, and the entire family was going to sit at the living room table. The main living room was where Catherine seated her patients, but she and Lucas had rearranged the room back to its original use and the table was now displayed with her beautiful china and crystal. She insisted Lucas and Celli join her, the children, and Martha at the table. They were her family now and Catherine wanted it to be festive.

The children were excited because Catherine had told them about Columbus coming to American in 1492 on a ship, and had taught the children about their meeting with the American Indians. They made paper hats and colored most of the morning while Catherine helped Lucas and Celli in the kitchen. Catherine tried not to think about the last three Thanksgivings, which had been filled with hardship and sadness. When she had first come to America, her mother had been killed just before Thanksgiving. The next year she had been violated and brutalized by David Brooks. The next year Brooks captured her again, taken her to Beaumont and held her captive for almost two years. They were the Thanksgivings she wanted to forget. It was all behind her now, and they had settled in to a new home in a new town, and she prayed things would get better. If only Michael wouldn't be so hard on her. She knew she had a troubled past, but Michael was not her judge and jury. She prayed he would let it go.

Martha had given Catherine notice that she would be leaving the week after Thanksgiving. Martha was a dear, caring friend and she would miss her. She had seen Catherine through many of her hardships and stood by her side when she had no one else. She was indebted to her, but Martha was getting up in years and she had an ill sister she needed to look after. It was going to be difficult to see her leave, and she would have to find someone else to look after her children if she wanted to continue to keep her small medical practice open.

Catherine decided it would be too difficult to tell the children that Martha was leaving for good. They were too young to understand. Martha had been their nanny almost all their lives and Catherine knew they loved her. She and Martha decided it would be best to tell the children she was going to visit her sister for a while. Martha had always visited her sister at least twice a year and the children thought nothing of it. Catherine would wait until some time had passed and then explain to them that Martha's sister was ill and she wouldn't be able to return. She hoped by then she would have found a replacement and the children would attach themselves to the new nanny. Daniel and Adam called Martha "Aunt Marty", and the girls simply called her "Amari", which Martha loved. She would miss them, too.

A week after Thanksgiving, Catherine and the children stood on the front porch waving goodbye to Martha as Lucas took her in the buckboard to the train station. Catherine had given Martha a week's severance pay and she couldn't help but choke up when Martha left. She had to look away so the children would not see her face.

Catherine had shortened her hours at the clinic and began closing at one in the afternoon. Celli had been looking after the children, while Lucas put on a white medical coat and helped Catherine see to her patients. He helped her from nine in the morning until half past eleven and then he would leave to prepare lunch. The children usually went down for their naps around half past noon and

Catherine would work straight through until one in the afternoon staying until two o'clock if necessary. She had noticed that Celli and Lucas seemed to distance themselves from her, and decided she should give them a raise. She called Lucas into her office after her last patient and he seemed very nervous.

"I'm afraid I have bad news," Lucas said before Catherine could tell them about the raise. Mr. Atwood is loaning us the money to open up a small medical office at the old Morris house at the end of town. He said he had made a good buy on it and Celli and I can live in the back of the house and use the front two rooms to see patients. It's what Celli has always wanted. She ain't no doctor like you, Mrs. Catherine, but she knows how to do the basic stuff; deliver babies and give shots. Tomorrow is Friday and it is going to be our last day, Dr. Merit. We will be moving out of the carriage house and if you want, we can put up a For Rent sign for you."

"That won't be necessary, Lucas, I'm not sure what I'm going to do," she replied.

When Lucas left, Catherine went out to put a sign on the door that the clinic would close at noon on Friday. It really wasn't a problem; her business had been half of what it usually was and she wondered if that was Michael's doing, also. She had to look on the bright side; her overhead had been cut substantially, except that on Monday she would not be able to see any patients. She would now be a full-time mother. She sighed and decided that was something she could look forward to.

Before she went upstairs to look in on the children, she decided to look up the number for Mark Graham, her real estate agent in Galveston. When she inquired about the house she had previously owned, he told her that the people who had bought it from her had already moved to another city and it was currently in escrow to a Houston family and was going to close sometime in February. He told her if the sale did not go through, he would call her. He was worried that since the city was way behind on raising the street elevations, the buyers might get cold feet because they couldn't deal with raising the house on stilts and having wet sand piped in to raise the elevation while they lived there. It was going to be quite an undertaking and Mark wasn't sure they would actually close on the house. He told her the sellers had been willing to take a loss, as they were already moved. The asking price was $1,500 less than they had paid Catherine when she sold it. She was too late, Catherine thought, but she told Mark to call her immediately if it fell through. "If I did buy the property, do you think you could lease it for me?" she asked.

"Absolutely; they are levelling the streets one street at a time, and numerous residents are looking for temporary housing. Once the work is completed, I can find you a permanent resident. Meanwhile, we can take advantage of the rental market and get you top dollar for rent," Mark replied.

"I am prepared to offer the owners $2,900, which is $1,700 less than they had paid for it in the event it comes back on the market." She knew she was taking a chance, but Galveston would begin growing again after the seawall was finished and the street work was complete. She felt it would be a good investment.

"I'll let them know of your interest, but they won't be able to do anything until the first buyers back out. I'll call you as soon as I know something," Mark assured her.

The next morning she asked Celli and Lucas not to say anything about leaving in front of the children. She handed Lucas an envelope with thirty dollars in it and told him it was their going away present. When he returned, she told him they could leave anytime they wanted to and that he could use the horse and buckboard to move what they needed, and she thanked them again. "I'll probably be selling the horse and buckboard so if you hear of anyone needing it, you have my number."

Catherine walked around back with the children and they played until she saw Lucas and Celli moving out of the carriage house. She moved the children inside to their playroom and found some activities for them to do while she checked in the refrigerator for something for their dinner. There were a lot of choices; Lucas must have cooked ahead for her. She pulled out a meatloaf and turned the oven on. The phone rang, and Catherine wondered who might be calling on Saturday afternoon.

"It's Father Jonathan, and I have some good news. The family would like to send their daughter, Shelby Foster, to come stay with you during the duration of her pregnancy. They will pay you twenty-five dollars a month. If you accept, they will put her on a train Sunday afternoon and she will arrive at ten past three that afternoon."

"That is wonderful news, Father. I will take good care of her. She is aware I have four children and she will be expected to help me, doesn't she?" she said hesitantly.

"Of course, she says it will be good practice for her," he laughed.

Catherine hung up the phone and promised to stay in touch with Father Jonathan. Thank you Lord, she silently prayed.

She looked in on the children and was on her way back to the kitchen when she heard a pounding on the door. She hoped it was not an emergency, but she reminded herself that emergency visits were double on the weekends and the money would come in handy.

"Good afternoon," the man said. "I'm Grady Rylander, and I am with the Houston Chronicle Newspaper. Might I have a few words with you?" The man was short and slightly balding and he was dressed in a suit.

"What is it you want?" she asked.

"I'm looking for Dr. Catherine Merit," he said.

Catherine studied the man for a few seconds before telling him that she was Dr. Merit. "Are you ill?" she asked.

"Oh, no, ma'am. If you will excuse my bluntness, I heard that you recently shot a man who tried to attack you," he said politely.

"What is it to you?" she asked.

"I report the news, and I thought it would make an interesting article in our paper. I would be discrete, of course, and not give your name or town. Could I just have a moment of your time to speak with me?"

"I suppose," she said hesitantly. Catherine looked at his credentials and invited him in. "How did you hear about the incident?" she asked.

"It's a bit unusual to hear about a woman, especially someone as small as you, who could overpower a man twice your size. I thought it sounded like a good story, and I want to hear the details."

"You didn't answer my question. Who told you about it?"

"Well, I don't usually give out my sources, Dr. Merit, but people are talking about it in the streets and I wanted to confirm if the rumor was factual."

Catherine sighed and asked him if he was sure that her name and the town would not be mentioned in the article; he assured her again that it would be kept secret. She told him that now was not a good time but he could come back at one that afternoon. The reporter said he would be happy to.

The children finished their lunch and Catherine took them to their playroom where they laid on their pallets on the floor and Catherine read to them until they fell asleep.

The reporter was on time and Catherine met him at the front door. She gave him a vague summation of what happened, leaving out the part that Brady had tried to rape her. She told him that she made him angry and she ran from him when he pulled his gun on her. The remainder of the details about falling and then catching him off guard by pretending to have been unconscious seemed to her to be enough. He asked her a few more questions and then thanked her and left. Catherine put the matter aside and went about her daily chores.

CHAPTER 6

After Catherine bathed the children and put them to bed, she went downstairs to her office. She heard a knock on the door and Lucas called to her. "It's just me. I wanted to say thank you for the horse and buggy and that everything is out. I fed the horse, but you'll need to tend to him in the morning since we won't be here. We thank you for the money," he said, and left. Catherine walked back into her office and added the word "horse" to her list of things to take care of. She drew a line from the horse to the top. They would take the horse and buckboard to the livery stable in the morning to sell. It would be one less mouth to feed and one less chore, she thought. They could get a smaller buggy later if the need arose, but she knew her practice was going to suffer once Celli opened her doors.

Catherine looked at her ledger. In the four months she had been there she had just about broken even. With the help gone and less food and medicine to buy, she figured she could cut a few more things out of the budget. She looked at her expenses and considered crossing out the telephone. It was a lifeline for many people, and waiting a month or two wouldn't hurt. She hated doing laundry and unless the laundry lady also quit, she really wanted to keep her. The extra income from the rent and her new boarder would make up the void if she continued to cut back where she could. Enough for one day, she thought.

Catherine checked all the doors before going upstairs. She

had never been afraid before, but she always knew Martha was there and Lucas and Celli were close by. When she went upstairs she walked into the boys' room first and found them fast asleep. Daniel had crawled into Adam's bed again, and she smiled when she thought of John. He would be so proud of his son and stepson. Emma and Isabelle were also sleeping in the same bed. They looked like angels sleeping, and she prayed they would never be separated. They were sisters and they needed to grow up together. It was a thought that constantly nagged at her. Issy was not her child, and Alex could take her away if he so desired. Now that Meredith knew the truth, the possibility was there that they might desire to raise her. She couldn't deal with this now. It hurt too much and she needed to concentrate on things she could control.

Catherine woke up several times during the night in a sweat. The dreams had faded away for a while, but now they were back. She was under a lot of stress and that was always when she was most vulnerable. She walked over to the window and looked out. She saw nothing, but she still felt a bit scared. Maybe it was just the dreams, she thought, and crawled back into bed. She woke up again when she thought she heard someone crying. She turned on the light and ran into the boys' room and then the girls' room. They were sound asleep. She decided to sleep in Adam's bed, since it was empty. The crying must have been another bad dream, she thought.

Catherine woke up at six o'clock in the morning and decided to get up even though she knew the children would sleep until at least eight o'clock. She dressed and went to the kitchen. After filling the kettle with water, she looked around the large kitchen and wondered where everything was kept. Lucas had always taken care of that, and she had no idea where the plates or pots and pans were. She walked around and opened all of the cabinets, making a mental note of where everything was. She grabbed the box of oatmeal when she opened the pantry and decided she would prepare that for the children. She continued looking until she found a pot and lid. She fussed at herself for not taking more interest in what was going on in the kitchen. She had relied on Lucas for so much, and it was going to be really hard not having him. More than anything, they had been her friends and she would truly miss all of them. Catherine filled her cup with hot water and placed a tea bag in it. She went out to the front porch and sat in her rocking chair. The sun was just coming up and she pulled her shawl around her as she felt the cool breeze make her slightly uncomfortable. She finished her tea and went back inside. The children would be up soon, so she heated the water again to cook the oats.

After dressing the children and feeding them breakfast, Catherine gathered up their jackets and told them they were going for a ride. They followed her to the stable underneath the carriage house and she helped them get into the buckboard. Catherine fitted the horse in the tack and hitched it to the wagon. So far, so good, she thought. It was close to ten in the morning as she made her way to the livery stable. The blacksmith asked if he could help her. She told him she wanted to sell her horse and buckboard.

"I'll have to check with the owner," he said.

"I was hoping I could leave it. I don't know a lot about taking care of horses," she said.

"How much do you want for it?" she heard a male voice say. She looked towards the back of the barn and saw Jason.

"Oh, hi," she said. "I've only owned it about six months and I paid ten dollars for the horse and twenty dollars for the buckboard. I would gladly take twenty-five dollars for both."

"Sounds fair to me," Jason said.

"Really?" Catherine questioned, not sure he was serious.

"I'm going to buy it for my grandparents. I'm hoping they will come see me soon. I'm on my way to the train station to buy them some tickets," he said and he took out his wallet.

After he paid Catherine she thanked him and told the children to hold hands. They began walking toward town.

"Hey, where are you going?" he asked.

"To town," she answered.

"Town is a half mile away. Put the children in the buggy and I'll give you a ride back."

Catherine smiled at him and Jason lifted the children into the buggy.

"Are you always this independent?" he asked.

Catherine laughed. "I'm the mother of four children, Jason, which one could I depend on?" She laughed, and shrugged her shoulders.

Jason liked her sense of humor. He had never met anyone quite like her. "Where would you like me to take you?" he asked.

"Oh, the general store will be fine," she answered.

"I'm going there, too," he said.

"I thought you said you were on your way to the train station?" she asked.

Jason grinned and said. "I am, but I need something at the general store first."

Catherine couldn't help but smile at him. She loved his dimples and he was certainly a looker, she thought. Catherine told the children to hold hands as they walked up the steps and into the general store. She walked over to the clerk and said something in a quiet voice. The clerk told her to follow him as they walked over to the gun case. He took out three small hand guns for Catherine to look at.

"You probably would feel more comfortable with the little .38 Colt Bisley," Jason said, looking over her shoulder. Catherine turned and looked at him, but didn't say anything. She picked up the .38, felt it, and asked how much it was.

"Eight dollars and I suppose you will want bullets," the clerk said as he pulled out a box. "Eight twenty-five for both of 'em." he said. Catherine opened her purse and handed him a twenty.

Jason was standing behind her with his arms folded, waiting

for her to finish her purchase. After she paid, she took one of the children's hands and herded them toward the front door with her package.

"I'm curious, why do you need a gun?" he asked.

"My help is gone and I want to protect myself, if it is any of your business," Catherine stated.

"Want me to teach you how to shoot it?" he asked.

Catherine didn't answer and kept walking. Jason watched as she slowly began walking with the children. After a couple of minutes, he saw her pick up one of the girls, and then a few minutes later she stopped and put the package in her purse, and then picked up the girl again and then one of the boys. Jason got up on the buckboard and began trotting towards Catherine.

"Going my way?" he asked when he stopped a few feet ahead of them. He reached and took the little girl first and then the boy. Catherine put the other two children in and then climbed aboard.

"Are you sure you want to sell the buckboard?" he asked.

Catherine looked at him and laughed. "Don't tell me you already want your money back," she teased. Jason smiled at her.

When they got to the house, Jason asked if he could come in and get a drink of water. Catherine looked at him suspiciously and said, "I suppose, but if you try anything stupid, you need to remember that I now own a gun."

Jason put up his hands and said, "I promise to be a gentleman."

The children ran into their playroom and Catherine and Jason followed. "I use the kitchen in the back," she said. She walked over and took a glass out of the cabinet. She was glad that she had found where they were the night before. She handed the full glass of water to Jason and he drank half of it. "What happened to your help?" he asked.

"It's not really important. Do you always ask this many questions when you meet someone?" she asked.

"Only those I really want to get to know," he said, and smiled at her.

"Trust me; you don't want to know any more than what I've already told you. I'm pretty much a homebody and I doubt we have much in common to talk about," she said.

"I think you underestimate me," he said.

"I've heard that statement before from another man, and he was just as sure of himself as you are. Thank you for seeing us home," Catherine said as she walked him to the front door.

Jason was even more infatuated with Catherine than ever. She was feisty, interesting, and beautiful. He stopped at the flower store and walked in. "I'll take that group of flowers there," he said as he pointed. Jason filled out the card and asked that they have someone deliver them.

Jason's father had left a sizable estate when he died. The farm sat on sixteen acres and was free and clear of any liens. He had also found a lockbox key hidden at the back of a drawer in his father's house. He took it to the Rosenberg Bank and when he opened the lockbox, there was fifteen hundred dollars cash in it along with a life insurance policy on Paula Brady for ten thousand dollars and one on his father for twenty-five thousand. He had put Jason as the beneficiary for his and also on Paula's policy as secondary beneficiary in case of his death first. Jason opened up his own checking account and put fourteen hundred in it, holding back a hundred. He still had twenty-five dollars that he made from his trail ride, and he felt like a millionaire. Jason was always good with his money. He wired fifty dollars to his grandparents and intended to do it on a regular basis. They had always been good to him and he wanted to take care of them in their old age.

Jason stopped at the depot to pay for two tickets from Sequin to Rosenberg that he was wiring to his grandparents. Before he left, he saw a young woman sitting in the waiting room with a shawl wrapped around her. "What's her story?" he asked the clerk.

The clerk shrugged his shoulders and said she had come in on one of the earlier trains. Jason walked over to her and smiled at her. He wasn't sure if she was Mexican or half Negro and half white, but she looked to be about fifteen years old.

"Excuse me," he said. "Are you waiting for someone?" The girl just stared at him and she looked like she was about to cry. "I could call someone for you," he said.

"I don't have no one to call," she said meekly.

"Where is your home?" he asked.

"Don't got one," she said.

Jason sighed and breathed out. There was a pay phone on the wall, and he picked up the phone and asked the operator to connect him to Dr. Catherine Merit. After putting in two cents, he heard the phone ringing. A few minutes later she answered. "This is Dr. Merit."

Jason told Catherine about the girl and that he thought she might be a runaway. "All right," he said. "I'll wait." Twenty minutes later Catherine walked in with her four children in tow. Jason was standing by the door when she walked in, and he nodded in the direction of the girl.

Jason took the boys' hands and asked if they wanted to play a game. He took them to the corner and took out a spinning top to occupy them. Catherine took the two girls and walked over to the young girl and sat beside her. "My name is Dr. Catherine Merit and I want to help you," she said.

The girl looked up at her and said, "I'm Sadie, just Sadie. Were you at St. Mary's Orphanage when I was younger?" she asked. Catherine couldn't believe what the girl had just asked.

"Oh my," Catherine said. "Were you adopted before the storm?"

"Yes. I was ten years old when I was adopted by a family that needed me to work on their farm not far from Sugar Land. I didn't mind the work, but the lady's brother was mean to me and made me do things I didn't want to do. He threatened to kill me the last time he came into my bed, so when he went to sleep I stole five dollars from his pocket and got on a train. When I got here, I got scared and didn't know where to go."

"Why don't you come home with me and my children, and we'll talk about your future," Catherine said and she took her hand.

"Sadie is coming home with us," Catherine told Jason.

They went outside and climbed onto the buckboard. When they got home Catherine thanked Jason for calling her and he drove off. They walked up to the porch and Daniel ran up and picked up some flowers that had been left. "Look, mama, pretty," he said. Catherine took the flowers and held them while she unlocked the door. When they went in, the children immediately ran to their play area.

"Come in, Sadie," Catherine said. "May I get you something to eat?"

"I haven't eaten since yesterday," she said as she followed Catherine into the kitchen.

Catherine warmed up some leftover food and set it in front of Sadie, who ate all of it while Catherine made sandwiches for the children. "How old are you now, Sadie?" she asked.

"I'll be fourteen in a few months. I was probably nine when I first met you. I remember you because of your accent," she said, and smiled. "I don't want to go back to the orphanage and I'm definitely not going back to the family that adopted me."

"The lady who was helping me take care of my children had to leave, and I desperately need someone to help me with them and some light housework. I'll pay you and give you free room and board. If you don't like it here, you can leave at any time," Catherine told her.

"Really? You would let me live here?" she asked. "I was forced to pick cotton in the summertime and had to do all kinds of chores. The room I slept in was a flea-bitten porch and I had a cot for a bed. This looks like a mansion compared to what I am used to. I'll do it." Sadie was excited, and hugged her. Catherine smiled and hugged her back.

Catherine had almost forgotten about the flowers and picked them up. She put them in a vase and filled it with water. "Are they from your husband?" Sadie asked.

Catherine opened the card and read it. *You really do underestimate me. Your friend, Jason.* She couldn't help but smile. "No, just an old friend," she answered.

"Where is your husband?" Sadie asked.

"I need to feed the children now, so I'll just tell you that my husband died and leave it at that," Catherine said and went to get the children.

"I have to meet someone at the train station at three thirty. Would you mind watching the children while I go and meet her? Her name is Shelby and she is also from Galveston. She is going to stay here for a while, too. I'll tell you all about it later," Catherine said.

Catherine watched as Sadie sat on the floor after lunch and read to the children. Daniel was three and a half, Adam was two and a half, and the two girls had turned one on their last birthdays several months earlier. They took to Sadie immediately, and Catherine stood in the doorway for a while; she couldn't believe her good fortune. She was convinced that the Lord had sent both women to her and she was grateful.

Catherine gave a small wave to Sadie and smiled at her as she grabbed her shawl and set out to walk to the depot. It was cooler than she had first thought, and she pulled her shawl tightly around her. She picked up her step when she heard the whistle of the incoming train. She heard an automobile coming from behind her and she hugged the side of the road when it passed. Michael and another woman were in the automobile and he did not slow down when he saw Catherine. She was not surprised that he would ignore her. At least she wouldn't be bothered with his advances anymore, but she wondered if his hatred would intensify now that he knew her past. There was nothing she could do, and worrying about it would not make it better, so she decided to put it out of her mind.

Only three people got off the train in Rosenberg; a young couple who were met by their parents and a young woman whom Catherine approached. After introductions, Catherine picked up one of Shelby's bags.

"My home is just down the street and I hope you don't mind walking," Catherine said.

Shelby smiled and said she liked to walk. They heard an automobile coming from behind them and they moved closer to the side of the road. It stopped beside them. When Catherine looked over and saw Michael, she wasn't quite sure what he wanted. He got out of the car and asked if they needed a ride. Catherine introduced Shelby as her cousin and they got in Michael's car. When he stopped at her house, he got out and opened the door. Next he took both bags and walked them to the front door. Catherine was almost speechless, but managed to ask Michael if he wanted to come in. He declined and left.

Sadie met them at the front door and told Catherine she had put the children down for their naps. "Adam fell asleep while I was reading, so I thought I should put them in their beds. I hope that was all right," Sadie said. Catherine thanked her and introduced the girls to each other.

"I'll make us some hot tea and we can talk," Catherine said. After she served tea, Catherine gave the girls each other's background and what was expected of them. If they were both in agreement, they would share Martha's old room upstairs and also share in the household duties. Sadie would see to the children and Shelby would help Catherine with her patients and they would take turns with the meals. The rest of the duties would be shared between the three of them. Shelby handed Catherine an envelope and said it was from her father and then thanked Catherine for allowing her to come live with her during her pregnancy. Catherine had not said anything to Sadie about Shelby's baby, and she was glad that Shelby had said something. They heard the children and Catherine asked Sadie to show Shelby to their room while she tended to the children.

The rest of the afternoon Sadie and Shelby took care of the children while Catherine worked in her office and then made dinner. She could see that Sadie and Shelby liked each other and she felt comfortable with them, too. It was hard to believe that both women had just walked into her life when she needed them, and she smiled to herself. God did answer prayers, she thought. After she had helped put the children to bed, she picked up her purse and took out her package. She loaded the gun and aimed it at the window. She decided to put it in her desk drawer at the back, and then closed it. She always kept her door closed and the children were still too young to open it.

Even though there was an open sign on Catherine's front door, she only had four patients on Monday. After she finished seeing them, she walked out on the porch and stood with her arms crossed. She saw Alex ride up on Pilgrim and he asked if he could come in. He couldn't help but notice the empty waiting room. "Where is everyone?" he asked. Catherine shrugged her shoulders.

"Lucas and Celli quit last Friday, and Martha had to go back to Austin to take care of her ill sister. I guess it is best there are no more patients," she said. Alex could see the hurt in her eyes and he wondered if Michael had a hand in this. "The children are in their playroom, if you want to go back there. I have a new girl, Sadie, and I told her about you so just introduce yourself and make yourself comfortable." Alex watched her walk back toward her office. He felt the need to hold her and tell her everything would be all right, but he couldn't risk getting that close to her.

Catherine sat in her office and picked up the note that Jason had left with the flowers. She smiled, went to the kitchen and picked up the flowers. She carried them back to her office and bent over to embrace their fragrance. They reminded her of her first husband, who always brought her flowers. She wondered what her life would have been like if John had not died. She heard the front door open and close; she walked to the front and opened the door. She saw Alex leaving, and she felt sad. Here she was, raising his children alone. She knew he had regrets, too. She was standing in the doorway looking out when she saw Jason coming towards her house. She stepped back, not wanting him to think she was watching him, and she closed the door. A few minutes later she heard a knock. She waited an appropriate length of time and then opened it. "Good afternoon," he said. "I came to ask you if you would go to the dance with me this Saturday night."

"Dance? I didn't know there was a dance," she answered.

"They have it once a month in an old barn. It's behind one of the saloons," he said.

"Is it safe?" she asked.

Jason laughed. "'Bout as safe as any other place, I guess. I went last Saturday night and there were mostly family people there. You can get a beer and most people seem to be having a good time. How about I pick you up at seven thirty? If you bring a big enough purse, you can bring your gun, if you're worried," he said, and grinned.

Catherine pursed her lips and thought. She sighed and finally said, "This isn't a date, is it?"

"Not if you don't want it to be," he answered. "I do like to dance a lot, so you better wear your dancing shoes," he teased.
"All right, then, dance partners," she said. "And by the way, the flowers are beautiful. Thanks." Jason gave a slight bow as he turned to leave. Catherine stood on the porch and watched as Jason mounted his horse. He grinned and tipped his hat as he rode off. As she watched the trail of dust behind them she couldn't help but wonder if she was doing the right thing. What am I getting myself into, she asked herself and smiled. Maybe it would get her mind off of her problems. Jason seemed sweet enough and she was beginning to think he was a gentleman and not a man after revenge. She needed a night of fun, and she loved to dance.

CHAPTER 7

The remainder of the week was slow, with four to five patients arriving every day. She hoped things would pick up after Michael got over his anger. Still, she thought it odd that he had stopped to give her and Shelby a ride. Maybe he was just curious. Shelby was pretty and she had not started showing yet. Michael was unpredictable, and who knew what his reasons were. At least he was trying to be cordial, she thought.

Sadie and Shelby were wonderful companions and Shelby caught on quickly. Catherine told her she would make a good nurse; it pleased Shelby. Neither had spoken about the baby and Catherine felt that in time, she would open up about it.

That night after the children were put to bed, Catherine made some hot tea and invited Sadie and Shelby into the downstairs family room to visit. Catherine tried to tell them as best she could about how she came to Rosenberg, and Shelby opened up about her dilemma.

Shelby had finished Ball High School in Galveston and decided to go to the University of Texas in Austin. She had just begun her freshman year when she met a young man who was twenty-two and was working at the bookstore across the street from the campus. He had asked her out on several occasions and she was drawn to him. After they dated for a few weeks, he told her that he loved her; then one thing led to the next and he had talked her into having sex with him. He moved away when she told him she was pregnant. She had wanted to go to nursing school, but her pregnancy happened and her parents were embarrassed for her. She was excited about coming to live with a female doctor and hoped that she might learn something while she was here.

Sadie had been adopted when she was ten by a family with seven other children and all of them had to work on the farm. Sadie spent many long hours in the hot sun picking cotton and sugar cane, and helping with the wash. She said she never had time to think about herself and they did not let her go to school. She had learned to read and write at the orphanage before she left. When the woman's brother came to live with the family about six months ago he began tormenting Sadie, and had raped her in the barn on several occasions. After he violated her the last time, she stole some money from his pants pocket when he fell asleep and she left on the next train that came through. That was how she came to Rosenberg.

Catherine hugged both of the girls and told them how happy she was that God had brought both of them to Rosenberg. She told Shelby she could borrow any of her medical books to read and she would teach her how to assist with the patients. Sadie liked playing with the children; Catherine also gave Sadie some books to read. It seemed like everything was falling back into place and while the patients were not plentiful, with the cutbacks Catherine had made, she thought everything would be fine.

Saturday night finally came; Catherine felt comfortable leaving Sadie and Shelby with the children. The two girls seemed to care a lot for the children. Jason rang the doorbell at seven thirty sharp and he looked quite handsome. His hair looked like it had just been washed and he had on a new shirt and leather jacket. Catherine liked what she saw. "Wow," Jason said. "You are gorgeous." Catherine smiled as she took his hand. He helped her up on to the buckboard and thanked her again for selling it to him. "My grandparents are supposed to come in on the afternoon train Monday, and it will be perfect for them to use. They're going to spend Christmas with me," he said. "My grandma is a great cook, and I look forward to it every year."

Catherine became solemn when she thought about Christmas coming up. It was not one of her favorite holidays, and she always seemed to get depressed. "Did I say something wrong?" he asked when he noticed she looked sad.

"Oh, no, I just realized, I've got to go grocery shopping myself. I didn't realize it was so soon," she answered.

Jason smiled at her and said, "Time does fly by, especially now."

When they arrived at the dance barn, there were horses and carriages everywhere and they could feel the excitement. "I guess word is out that there is a band playing out of Houston," Jason commented. Jason paid the twenty-five cents a person charge and made their way to a table for two not far from the band. "Is beer all right with you?" he asked.

While Jason went for the beer, Catherine saw Alex and Meredith come in; behind them was another woman, on the arm of Michael. The woman looked to be closer to Michael's age and she appeared very matronly. Catherine looked away, but noticed they went across the dance floor and sat directly across from her. They didn't notice her until they had all sat down. She was relieved when Jason came back to the table with their beer. A few minutes later the band began to play. She had just taken a sip when Jason grabbed her hand and pulled her up.

The song was a fast foxtrot; she was amazed at Jason's ability on the dance floor. He was twirling her around and she couldn't help but laugh. She was surprised she could keep up with him and then people began clapping as they danced. She caught a glimpse of Michael leaning over and saying something in Alex's ear. Alex looked at her with a grim expression. She decided she was not going to let them put a damper on her fun evening. She would just pretend they were not there. When the dance was over, everyone clapped and then the band played a slow number. Jason pulled her tightly into his arms and held her close as he swayed to the music. She was beginning to feel uncomfortable, and when the dance was over, she said she needed to take a break and she walked back to their table with Jason following her. He had noticed her tighten up when the band played a slow number. He had also noticed Atwood and his friends talking about them, and Atwood never seemed to take his eyes off Catherine.

He smiled at her when they sat back down but she didn't return the smile. "If you feel uncomfortable, we can leave," he said softly. "I didn't mean to embarrass you."

"Oh, you didn't, I, uhh, I just haven't danced in a while and I'm not used to people staring at me," she tried to explain.

"If they're staring, it's because you are the most beautiful woman at the dance, and I mean that seriously," he said. Jason finished his drink and said he was going to get another. Catherine sat looking down at her drink, wishing she had just stayed home. She looked up to see if Jason was coming and saw him standing at the bar talking to another young girl. It didn't surprise her. He was extremely good looking, and any young girl would find him attractive. She saw Michael watching; a few minutes later he said something to his lady friend and then got up, walked over and asked her to dance. She was taken aback but got up, and he pulled her into his arms. "Just so you know; it was Celli who wanted to open up her own shop and she needed Lucas to help her. I had nothing to do with them leaving," Michael insisted. "I know you think I had something to do with it, but I didn't. I'll admit that I was angry when I found out about you and Alex, but that's behind us now. Both Alex and Meredith thought I should apologize to you, but I have nothing to apologize about," Michael continued. "I stopped the other day to pick you and Shelby up because Shelby's father is an acquaintance of mine and he asked me to keep an eye on her. I wanted to meet her."

Catherine looked up at him but didn't say anything. The dance ended and he walked her back to her table. Jason was back and stood up when they approached. "Thanks for letting me dance with your lady friend," Michael said, and he turned and went back to his table.

"I didn't know you knew Michael Atwood that well," Jason said.

"He helped me buy my house when I moved to Rosenberg," she answered.

Catherine began to relax a bit and they stayed and danced throughout the night. Several other men had asked Catherine to dance, but she declined. She would have liked to dance with Alex and at one time, when she was dancing a slow dance with Jason, she had shut her eyes and pretended it was Alex she was dancing with. When she opened them, Alex and his party had left. Jason sensed her mind was somewhere else; he suggested that they leave.

Jason walked her to the door and Catherine took out her key and unlocked it. When she turned back around, Jason put his arms around her and drew her to him. He kissed her softly at first and then he became more passionate. She pulled away from him and thanked him for a lovely evening.

"I think you need to go. It's not that I don't find you attractive, Jason. Any woman would love to be in my place, but I am not the right woman for you. Please just be a friend. I want nothing more." Catherine went in and shut the door.

It was mid-December, and Catherine was dreading the upcoming holiday. It brought back too many memories. People and places she wanted to forget. Samuel had been on her mind lately, too. She remembered their romantic weekends together. He was a wonderful lover and she missed that part of their relationship. He always made her feel safe, and she missed their intimacy. She knew she had to somehow get herself out of her slump, so she decided it was time to bake her first turkey. Finally, Catherine thought, something to keep her occupied. She started making a list of things she needed to do and also made a grocery list. She had pulled the decorations down from the attic earlier that week. She decided to go to the grocery store and have them deliver a small tree to her house so they could decorate it that night. She grabbed her knapsack and jacket and ran to tell Sadie and Shelby where she was going. She stood in the doorway and listened as Sadie read a story to the children from one of the new books she had bought. When Sadie looked up, Catherine told her she was going to the store. Sadie smiled and nodded her head yes. Shelby was upstairs cleaning.

Catherine walked to the general store, picked out a five-foot tree for them to deliver to the house and bought a few groceries. She was halfway home when she heard an automobile coming, but she did not look around. It could only be one person, since Michael had the only one she knew of outside the city of Houston. When he approached her he stopped and opened the door.

"Get in," he shouted to her. Catherine stood her ground and their eyes met. "Please," he said more tenderly, "Just get in."

Catherine did as he ordered but didn't say anything. Michael took her groceries and set them on the backseat. After revving up the engine, Michael made a U-turn in the road and spun off in the other direction. They rode in silence until they got to a fork in the road and Michael turned down a gravel road towards an old abandoned barn. He pulled behind it and stopped. Catherine waited, wanting him to speak first, but he looked at her for a few minutes and then gently took her hand. She watched as he pulled it up to his lips and kissed it and then he moved closer to her. She knew she should be afraid, but for some reason she wasn't. Her heart began to beat at a rapid pace and she swallowed, not sure what she should do. Michael slowly approached her like a lion approaching his prey. She knew she should open the door and run, but she felt paralyzed. She put her hand on the door handle and willed herself to open it, but couldn't. He had some kind of mental hold on her and she felt unable to move. She felt herself becoming aroused by the way he was looking at her. His sultry eyes and forward mannerism made her feel sexy. While she often felt like she hated Michael, she wondered what it would be like to kiss him. "I think this is a mistake. You should take me home now, Michael," she said softly.

Michael smiled at her and said, "You've been flirting with me and tormenting me since we met. Why don't you let me help you relax?" Her body seemed to shut down. She kept telling herself that Michael was a gentleman and wouldn't force himself on her.

She watched as he slid closer and pulled her face toward his, kissing her with a passion that sent chills down her spine. While they were still kissing, he gently unbuttoned the front of her dress. Catherine pushed his hand away and he grabbed hers and forced it behind her back, kissing her neck as he held her against the seat. She wanted to scream but he met her mouth passionately with a kiss and she felt paralyzed and unable to move.

"You mustn't do this," she whispered.

He used his other hand to unbutton the remaining buttons on her dress and when he reached the bottom button he moved his arm up her back and around her neck, pulling her closer to him. He began kissing the back of her ear and moved down her neck. Catherine gasped and tried to pull away, but she had nowhere to go. His closeness shot tentacles of warmth through her body. She moaned and closed her eyes. Michael was intoxicated with her sensuality and was encouraged that she stopped trying to pull away. He grabbed her buttocks, pulled her under him on the seat and began kissing her breast softly. He did it slowly, enjoying her sweet smell and soft, delicate breasts. She was so beautiful; his arousal escalated. Catherine moaned as he slowly placed his wet mouth on her nipples and began to suckle gently. She couldn't believe how good it felt to be in a man's arms again. Why was he so irresistible? Michael moved back up to her mouth and kissed her, forcing her mouth open with his tongue. He was on top of her now and she wanted to plead with him not to go any farther, but her body ached for intimacy and she longed for the closeness of him inside of her. Michael moved his hand to the bottom of her dress, pulling it up, and she felt him unbutton his pants. She began to stiffen and wanted to stop, but couldn't.

"Michael, you have to stop," she whispered. She was telling him no, but her body wanted more.

"I want you so much, Catherine, and I can feel you want me, too."

Before she could say anything, Michael was searching her mouth for her tongue again and his passionate kisses aroused her. It surprised her that she wanted more, and she knew he did, too. She wanted to stop him but couldn't. Michael wasn't the kind of man to force himself on a woman, or was he, she wondered.

"Please, Michael, we have to stop," she said louder. "Please stop. No, don't stop." The unique pheromones of his fragrance made her insides ache and sent her libido spiralling.

It had been months since Catherine had been with a man and she wasn't sure if it was Michael's strong, unrelenting masculinity or if she was just sexually vulnerable at the moment. Whatever it was she couldn't stop him, didn't want to stop him. She knew it was wrong and that she was sending mixed signals to him. God help me, she silently said to herself. When he reached down and kissed her breast again she responded by pulling his face up to hers, allowing his tongue to enter her open mouth once more. Their tongues mated and their kisses grew more intense. He would stop there, she thought. Michael moved quickly, pulling at her clothing, and his hands found their way down to her undergarments. He pulled them off and moved her legs apart with his knee. His fingers began fondling the valley between her legs and she arched her body closer to him. When she became more passionate, Michael couldn't wait any longer and moved his erection inside her. Catherine gasped in a momentary shock. She was breathing hard and she was unable to move. Michael was on top of her and he was having his way with her.

No, this wasn't right, she thought, but she couldn't stop. Not now. She pulled him to her, moving with him as she felt him inside her. She wanted him too, and she hated him for making her feel this way. He had finally conquered her, taken her dignity away, and she let him. She screamed as she gave in to her desires, not wanting it to end.

Michael was intoxicated with her sensuality and he gave a soft growl when he found his release. When it was over, Michael felt pleased with himself. He had been waiting for this moment since he had first met her. He knew it was only a matter of time that she would let him have her. He slowly sat up and he felt exhilarated. Catherine looked up at him and he gave a satisfied smile. She blinked back her tears and for a moment she found it hard to breathe as she tried to catch her breath.

Catherine tried to put herself back together and grabbed her undergarments off of the floorboard where they had fallen. She opened the car door and got out. She didn't want to look at Michael again and she didn't want him to see her cry. She wavered as she walked behind the automobile, trying to put her undergarments back on. Stunned and visibly shaken, she sat down on the side of an old broken-down piece of machinery. She hated herself and she hated Michael for taking her the way he did. Why couldn't she stop him? Why didn't she stop him? The tears began sliding down her cheeks and she prayed he would just drive away and leave her there. She was extremely embarrassed and she felt like she was in shock. She lowered her head and put her hands up to her face, feeling the warmth of her tears as they began trickling down her cheeks. She wasn't sure if she could ever look at Michael again.

Michael watched and waited. He was enjoying the aftermath of his conquest. After a few minutes he finally got out of the car and walked over to her. "Are you all right?" he asked. "I didn't hurt you, did I?"

She didn't look at him. She didn't want to get back in the car with him, but they were miles from town and she didn't even know where she was. She got up slowly and Michael followed her, opening the door for her to get back in the automobile. Michael handed her his handkerchief and she took it without looking at him and dabbed at her eyes. They drove back into town and neither spoke. She could feel Michael glancing in her direction, but pretended not to notice. He asked her where she wanted him to take her. After taking a deep breath she finally said home, and Michael could barely hear her. When Catherine got out and closed the door, neither said anything. Michael headed for home; and he had to admit that there was a small part of him that felt guilty. She had allowed him to take her, and he was surprised by that.

Catherine was in a state of disbelief and walked toward the kitchen. She began putting the groceries away that she had bought earlier. What had possessed her to let Michael have his way with her? Was she no better than a common harlot? She was afraid she could never look at him again. She felt a pain in her gut when she thought of what Alex would say if he knew. She was in agony and she had brought it all on herself.

Catherine had gone through the motions of pulling in the Christmas tree and setting it in the corner of the living room. She left it and quickly ran up the stairs to her room and flung her bathroom door open. After closing it, she fell to the floor and covered her face with a towel. She had no idea how long she wept. Shame had filled her whole body, and she prayed for God's forgiveness.

After Michael left Catherine, he began feeling remorseful. He hated the way she avoided him after they had been intimate. He had not intended to bed her, but she was just so beautiful and he had been dreaming of having her since the day he met her. He had only wanted to break the ice with a few kisses, but she kept sending mixed messages and then, when she kissed him back, he could not stop himself. He remembered her asking him to stop, but when she kissed him back it was as though she was telling him she wanted him, too. Never had he been with a woman who responded to his lovemaking the way she did. She was everything he could ever want; sensual, mysterious and beautiful.

CHAPTER 8

Michael was on his way home, deep in thought about his rendezvous with Catherine, when he saw his handkerchief on the floorboard and without thinking, he bent down to pick it up and then put it to his face. When he finally brought himself back to reality, it was too late and the last thing he saw was the tree.

Catherine got up, washed her face and went back downstairs. Earlier she noticed a sack of fresh vegetables that had been left at her door and she went outside to get them. Maybe a patient had come and left them, she thought. Catherine busied herself in the kitchen and after she put her groceries away she walked into the waiting room that they sometimes used as a dining room. She had to stay busy. She didn't want to break down and cry again. The large formal dining table was up against the wall and had reading material on it. The twelve chairs were lined up around the side of the walls where the patients sat and waited. Catherine picked up the literature from the table and then pulled it out, centering it under the crystal-embellished chandelier. She pulled out each leaf of the table and then moved the chairs around it. Seven people will fit comfortably, she thought. The sideboard had been moved to the hall and the ball feet had castors under them so it could be rolled. She moved it back into the dining room. Now it looks like home, and I'm going to use my antique china again on Christmas day, she said to herself. She was beginning to get her mind off what she had done; and then she heard someone at the door.

It was Lucas. "Come, come quick," he shouted, "Mr. Atwood's had a bad accident." Shelby was standing behind her and told her to go. "I was on my way back into town when I found him," Lucas continued.

Catherine gathered her medical bag and got in the wagon with Lucas. They drove about a mile towards Michael's house when she saw the wreck. His automobile had missed the curve and struck a tree. Smoke was still coming from the engine. Michael was lying on the ground beside the road, and when they got closer she could see he was bleeding. Lucas and Catherine rushed to his side and she took out her stethoscope. His heartbeat was strong and it looked like he had a dislocated shoulder. He was barely coherent and Catherine asked him to follow her finger as she moved it from side to side.

"Where do you hurt?" she asked him.

"I jumped out before it hit the tree and I landed on my shoulder," he said in a raspy voice. "I may have cracked a couple of ribs. I'm not sure."

"Did you hit your head?"

"I don't think so," he said and groaned. "My back doesn't feel too good, though."

Catherine turned to Lucas and told him that he needed to find a long board and some strapping. If he had broken anything, she needed him to be secure when they put him in the wagon. Lucas left to go to Michael's farm. Catherine asked Michael if he could move his legs, and she watched as he moved both of his legs and then his arms and hands. He grimaced when he tried to lift his arm, but there was some movement. She breathed a sigh of relief and took some clean gauze, wiped the blood from his cut lip and checked his head for any other injuries.

"Michael, I need to give you a shot that will help take some of the pain away. Will that be all right?" she asked.

"You're not going to get back at me for taking advantage of

you, are you?" he tried to laugh.

Catherine looked at him sternly and said, "I'll wait until you are healed before I get out my gun and shoot you," she said with a half smile.

Michael smiled back at her and grabbed her arm. "I'm sorry if I hurt you, Catherine. That wasn't my intention. I've desired you from the moment we met. I promise I'll never do that again."

The needle had pierced his arm and his speech was getting slower as the medicine began to take effect. Catherine held Michael's hand as she sat beside him on the ground for the thirty minutes it took for Lucas to return with Meredith and the material Catherine told him to fetch. Alex was ahead of them riding Pilgrim.

Catherine explained that she had given Michael a shot for his pain and that he would probably sleep for a while. The three of them managed to slide the board under Michael with the least amount of movement, and then they strapped him to the board. Catherine rode in the wagon with Michael and Meredith back to Michael's house, and his houseboy came out and helped carry him in and put him in his bed.

Catherine asked Meredith to get some whiskey and then politely told everyone to leave the room except for Lucas. They needed to pull Michael's arm back into its socket and she knew it would be painful. Catherine and Lucas worked together to make sure that they only had to do it one time. Michael screamed out and Catherine held the whiskey up to his mouth. Michael gulped it down. Together, Catherine and Lucas wrapped a tight corset of bandages around Michael's midsection and shoulder and he grimaced with pain as they had to slowly move him around.

"You need to stay in bed for a few days. Lucas will stay with you. I've shown him how to give shots and he will give you another one in a couple of hours." Michael grabbed Catherine's hand, pulled her down to him and then motioned for Lucas to leave the room.

"I want to make this right, Catherine. Marry me."

"You're in no position to marry me or anyone else right now, Michael. You just need to concentrate on getting well."

He continued holding her arm. "Then will you forgive me?" he asked.

"Michael, can't we get past this and just forget this ever happened?"

"What if I don't want to forget?" he pleaded.

Catherine didn't answer as she pulled away, picking up her medical bag. "Have Lucas come and get me in the morning. You are going to be sore, I'm afraid, and you'll be in pain for a few days. Once you feel like getting out of bed, I want you to go to Houston and get some x-rays. I'll be back to check on you tomorrow."

Michael watched as she left the room. He wanted her, and not in the way he had taken her earlier. He wanted her forever and he was going to marry her.

Alex drove Catherine back to her house. They stopped and looked at the wreckage again. The full moon reflected off the side mirror of the wrecked automobile, and Alex commented that he wondered why Michael had driven so fast around the curve. "He's always careful; he must have had something on his mind to have just totally missed the turn. I must admit he hasn't been himself lately."

Catherine didn't answer back. She wondered if she might have been on Michael's mind. She knew Michael was going to pursue her. Once Michael got his grip on something, he wouldn't turn it loose, and she knew it. She should have known better than to let him take her the way he did. What she was thinking, she wondered.

"I asked you a question, Catherine," Alex said, staring at her.

"I'm sorry, what was it?"

"Do you think he will recover from his injuries?"

"Yes, assuming he didn't suffer a back injury. His ribs are fractured and his shoulder dislocated from his arm. It will take weeks, but he should be fine. He needs to be taken to Houston for x-rays as soon as he is able," Catherine said.

Alex helped Catherine down from the buggy and walked her to the door. "You might have Lucas pick me up sometime tomorrow morning. I'll need to check on him and leave some more medicine for his pain."

"Are you all right? You seem to be distracted. Is there something bothering you?" Alex asked.

"I'm just tired. It's been a long day. Take care of yourself, Alex."

He watched her as she entered the house and it was clear to him that he still cared about her. He felt an attachment to her and the need to take care of her made him want to go to her and hold her.

Catherine checked on the children; they were in their pyjamas, playing with Shelby and Sadie. She went upstairs and collapsed on the bed. It was the week of Christmas and Michael was almost killed. Why was it that it seemed bad things happened during this time of year, every year? She let Michael have her and she felt guilty. Now he was laid up in bed with who knew what. She was angry with Michael, but she was as much to blame. She wanted to bury her head in her pillow and cry, but instead she got up and went to spend time with the children.

Catherine spent another restless night. Her bad dreams were endless and when she woke up she thought she heard Michael calling her. She listened carefully and sat up in bed. She heard the whistle from the midnight train and then fell back into her pillow. She stared into the dark, feeling herself sink back into a drowsy, deep sleep. She felt like she was floating and then someone grabbed her and pulled her into a ravine. It was a place she had not seen before and she tried to crawl out, but something had grabbed her leg and pulled her back. When she looked down she was staring into Joe Brady's eyes; he was grinning at her. She tried to kick herself loose, but he grabbed her other leg and pulled her into the cavern. It was dark and the ground was cold and wet. She tried to scream but couldn't, and then he had his hands around her neck; she was choking. Catherine was gasping for breath and tried to swallow and when she woke up, Sadie and Shelby were standing over her trying to comfort her.

"Shh, everything is all right, you just had a bad dream." Sadie had brought a wet washcloth over and the light from a candle reflected off of Sadie's brown eyes. Catherine took the cloth and put it over her face.

"I'm fine now. I'm sorry I woke you. I guess I must have had a nightmare," Catherine said softly.

"Would you like for one of us to stay with you?" Shelby asked.

"No, thank you. I'll be fine now. You two go back to sleep."

Both girls left the room and Catherine took in a deep breath. She rubbed her brow and sat with her head in her hands for a while. She felt cold so she pulled the covers up around her as she put her head back on her pillow. When she finally woke up, daylight was streaming through the curtains and she blinked as she reached over and looked at her timepiece. It was eight thirty in the morning.

When Catherine had dressed and gone downstairs, Daniel ran up to her. "Mommy, Lucas is here."

"Mr. Atwood had a really rough night and he needs you to come and check on him," Lucas said, apologizing.

"Let me check on the children and then I'll come," Catherine answered.

Sadie and Shelby were in the kitchen feeding the children and said they would take care of things. Catherine went into her office and retrieved some medicine and her doctor's bag. Lucas helped her into his buggy and they were at Michael's house in twenty minutes.

Michael was irritable and sweating when Catherine arrived, and she could see he was in a great deal of pain. She took out a vial and put a needle into it. "I think we should call Houston General and ask them to send an auto ambulance for you. I don't want you to get pneumonia, but if you do, they'll be better able to treat you there."

Michael grabbed her arm and pulled her to him. "Please come

with me. I need you," he pleaded. "Meredith and Alex will stay here with my kids and they can check on yours as well. Please tell me you'll come. Please."

"We'll see. I need to go make the call to Houston General and see how quickly they can be here," Catherine said, and left the room. Alex had been standing in the doorway and followed her into the living room where the telephone was.

"Meredith and I will look in on the kids if you can go," Alex said. "I know you don't want too, but I don't think he will leave without you."

When Catherine hung up the telephone she turned and told Alex and Meredith that it would be a little over an hour before the auto ambulance could get there. "I'll need to go home and pack a small bag. The injection that I gave Michael should keep him calm for a least a couple more hours."

"I don't know how we can ever thank you for everything you have done," Meredith said. "I know Michael will pay you well." After she saw Catherine's face, she realized that she should not have said anything about payment. She knew Catherine wasn't there for the money. She was their friend.

"I'll stay with Michael until all the tests are done and the doctors have stabilized him. I'll call you and give you updates on his condition."

The auto ambulance was well-equipped and the two nurses who came with it told Alex that the hospital had purchased two of the auto ambulances several months earlier and that they were lucky to have one come this far. "Not many of the county folks can afford it," one of the nurses said. Catherine gave the two nurses information on Michael's condition and joined them inside the ambulance once Michael had been placed inside.

After they arrived at the hospital, Catherine asked that Dr. Samuel Allen be called. She was concerned that Michael might have pneumonia. She knew the rest of his ailments could be treated, but pneumonia was another story.

Dr. Samuel Allen was pleasantly surprised when he saw Catherine in the emergency room. She acted professionally and filled Samuel in on Michael's condition. Samuel sent him to the x-ray room to have his lungs x-rayed as well as his ribs and shoulder. Michael had awaken and insisted that Catherine go with him. Samuel looked at her, and then told Michael that she was not allowed to go into that part of the hospital. Michael protested as they wheeled his gurney away.

"What was that all about?" Samuel asked.

"I think he is scared. He's never been sick before, and I guess he wants to be in control."

"Come with me," Samuel said as he pulled her by the hand.

Catherine followed as Samuel pulled her across the hall and through two other doors. He finally stopped in a back corner and pulled Catherine to him. He put his arms around her and hugged her tightly. When he reached down to kiss her, she turned her head away.

"I guess I deserve that. I've really missed you." They stared into each other's eyes for a few moments and then Samuel said, "Giving you up was the hardest thing I've ever had to do in my life." Catherine could tell he was sincere. Samuel sighed and then punched the mattress of a folded up roll away bed with his fist. They both laughed as Samuel leaned his head back on the wall and looked down at her. "You're killing me, Catherine, and I feel like I'm dying a slow death. I really miss you."

"I'm sorry, Samuel, but what we had is over and we both have to move on. Your wife needs you now. Being pregnant makes your absence from her even harder for her. You need to concentrate on your marriage."

Samuel watched as Catherine turned and left the room. He knew she was right. She was always right, but he still loved her. He would always love her.

Catherine was sitting in the waiting area when Samuel

motioned her to follow him. "Thanks for the advice. Still friends?" he asked. She smiled and shook her head yes.

"You were right," Samuel said. "He's in the early stages of pneumonia and I'll start his treatment right away. His shoulder seems to be back in place just fine and three of his ribs are fractured. Time should heal all of that. He needs to stay in the hospital until he is over the worst. Will you be leaving soon?" he asked.

"I'll stay the night, and then probably go home when Michael's condition stabilizes," she answered.

The hospital personnel were really helpful to Catherine and gave her all the privileges they gave all the doctors. After Michael had settled into his room, Catherine called Meredith and filled her in on Michael's condition. Then she checked in with Shelby, who assured her that she and Sadie had everything under control.

"I'll try to be home in a couple of days and I'll definitely come home before Christmas," Catherine told Shelby. "Do you mind taking the decorations out of the boxes and helping the children decorate the tree?" she asked.

"When the children saw the tree they were so excited we put the lights on and will finish it after their naps," Shelby said.

"Jason Brady invited all of us to his house for Christmas dinner. His grandparents are here and he says his grandmother loves to cook. Would it be all right if we go? He said he would pick us up in his buckboard," Shelby said excitedly.

"Well of course," Catherine answered. "That sounds like fun and I'll be looking forward to it." Actually, she breathed a sigh of relief. She had not completed her shopping for their Christmas meal and she knew she would be exhausted when she got home.

When Catherine hung up the phone, she reflected on what Shelby had said about having Christmas dinner with Jason. They are a perfect match, she thought; Jason and Shelby. Wouldn't that be something? Catherine heard Michael calling her name, so she quickly went to check on him.

"Please stay with me. I need you here," Michael said as he took her hand and pulled her closer to him.

"Michael, I'll stay, but only on a professional level, just to make sure you are well-taken care of."

"Fine, then charge me whatever you want. I need you here," he said sternly.

"Please don't be angry with me. It's not about the money. When you are feeling better I'll tell you why we can't be together. It just would never work," she pleaded.

Michael pulled her to him and he kissed her softly on the lips. "Whatever it is, Catherine, we can work through it." He was slurring his words and she gently pulled away without saying anything. She knew the medicine he had just been given was making him sleepy, and she saw no reason to continue with the conversation.

Samuel had told Catherine there was a small hotel called the Midtown Hotel just a block from the hospital, and she left to check in. It was quaint and older, but for now she just wanted a bath and a change of clothing. On the way back to the hospital she stopped at a diner and had some soup and hot tea. When she got back to Michael's room, he was just waking up. A nurse brought in a tray of food for him and she turned the crank on his bed so he could sit up and eat. Catherine helped him cut up his meat since his left arm was in a cast. "Is there a chance I may have gotten you pregnant?" he whispered to her. Catherine stared at him, surprised by his remark. "I didn't have any protection with me when we, you know what I mean."

He waited for Catherine to say something. "I suppose that could be a possibility, but I hadn't stopped to think about that. Your accident happened so quickly."

"You would have to marry me, then. I mean, if I got you pregnant," Michael continued. Catherine thought back to when she had last bled. She figured she should start in a few days. Surely she couldn't have gotten pregnant, or could she, she wondered. Catherine bit her lip and looked away.

"I'm just saying that if we made a baby together, I want to do the right thing. I can tell by the look on your face that that could be a possibility, right?" Michael asked hopefully.

Catherine still didn't look at Michael. She was embarrassed now and worried. "If you are through eating, I'll take your tray," Catherine said.

"Dammit, Catherine, look at me," Michael insisted. She turned and their eyes locked. "I want to marry you. Why are you so hardheaded?"

"I don't love you, Michael, and besides, any man who seems to get close to me gets hurt. My first husband, John Merit, died; Alex was shot after we got married, and now you and your automobile accident. Isn't that reason enough?"

"Catherine, you had no control over any of those things. None of that was your fault. I was tired and in a hurry to get home when I missed that curve. I'm not going to lie and tell you I wasn't thinking of you, because I sure as hell was. But I did that to myself, not you."

"I've checked into a hotel down the street and I'm very tired. I'll check on you in the morning," Catherine said and leaned over and kissed his cheek.

Samuel ran into Catherine in the hall when she was leaving, and he stopped her. He could see despair in her face. "What's wrong, Catherine? I just got off. Have a drink with me," he said as he led her down the stairs and out the door.

They stopped at a small saloon around the corner, and Samuel ordered wine for the two of them. "Are you going to tell me, or do you want me to start guessing?" Samuel asked.

"Michael wants me to marry him and he won't take no for an answer," she said as she sighed.

"That wouldn't be all bad. He has lots of money, Catherine, and he would take care of you and your children. It's a real opportunity for you," he said as he touched her hand on the table.

Catherine sighed again. "I don't love him. I still love Alex," she said, looking down.

"I don't love Dorothy, either, but I'm making it work even though I still love you. It's kind of a mess. Neither of us has really gotten what we wanted, have we?" he said sympathetically. Catherine smiled and wiped away a tear with her napkin. She looked up at Samuel.

"I didn't say that to hurt you, Samuel. I'm just trying to be honest."

"I know that. You've always been honest with me, but I can't help but think you loved me, too. At least a little bit," Samuel insisted.

"You are right, Samuel. I've always had a thing for you," she said as she smiled at him. "Michael's such a strong man and I feel like he suffocates me. He's controlling and he has two children of his own," Catherine said.

"Maybe that's what you need, Catherine. Let him take care of you. You said you wanted lots of children. With his two that would give you six and you can still have more," Samuel tried to convince her. "I worry about you, Catherine. It's not safe for you in that big house. You need someone to look after you."

Samuel was still holding her hand and he squeezed it. Catherine looked down and then up. You are truly a wonderful friend, Samuel, and I'll think about it. I keep feeling like I'm running away from something, and I'm not sure what it is."

"You have suffered nothing but pain since you came to America, Catherine. You've got to stop running. Marry Michael. Let him take care of you and the children. You deserve to have the best of everything."

"What about you, Samuel?" she asked, and he smiled at her.

"I'm going to try and make my marriage to Dorothy work. Surely if I try hard enough, I'll grow to love her. She's going to be the mother of my children and I'm looking forward to being a father. I make a good living and we are going to buy a house soon. No family is perfect." He looked down at his empty wine glass and said,

"Dorothy is expecting me soon, so I guess I better go. I'll be back at work day after tomorrow. Will you still be here?"

"It depends," she answered. "If I decide to marry Michael, I'll be staying," she said, grinning. They hugged and Samuel kissed her on the cheek as they parted ways.

Catherine went back to the hospital. If she was going to even consider Michael's proposal he needed to hear the whole story.

CHAPTER 9

Michael was sitting up in bed talking with one of the doctors when Catherine stopped at the door. Michael waved her in with his good arm and introduced her to the doctor who was looking after him.

"Michael has been telling me what a good job you have done looking after him, and I must concur with him. You've done an excellent job putting him back together," the doctor said. They all laughed and the doctor left the room.

"I wasn't sure you were coming back and I'm glad to see you," Michael said softly. "I know I come off as a charging bull sometimes, Catherine, but I do have my tender moments."

"There's a lot you don't know about me and after you hear it, you may want to take back your proposal," she said, looking at him. She walked over and took his hand and kissed it softly. I know I'm stubborn and I've built this wall around me, but I have my reasons."

Catherine spent the next hour telling Michael about her life since she arrived in America; her mother's death at the hands of David Brooks; the arranged marriage to John Merit and how she fell in love with him. She left nothing out. She told him of her life with David Brooks in Beaumont and how Alex had attempted to help her and why she refused his help. She told him how she watched as the posse hung David from a tree in their front yard.

"You don't have to go on, Catherine. I can see how much it hurts you to talk about it," Michael interrupted.

Catherine took a deep breath. "I am not proud of my past, Michael, and I'm trying very hard to make a life for myself and my children now. I'm not sure I'm good enough to marry anyone. I hope you understand that."

"Why don't you let me decide that?" Michael put his hand behind her neck and pulled her closer to him. He kissed her softly on the lips and then intertwined her hair with his hands, drawing her body up to his. He took a deep breath and smelled her hair. "Oh, Catherine, I want you to be my wife. Marry me, please."

Catherine moved her face down to his lips and kissed him. At first it was a gentle kiss and then she crawled up on the bed and put her arms around him. "I'd like to think about it for a couple of days if you don't mind," she whispered.

"Take whatever time you need," Michael said.

"Excuse me," the nurse said as she walked in. Catherine sat up abruptly and she and Michael laughed.

When Catherine finally left to return to her hotel, Michael felt relieved that Catherine had not totally rejected him. He knew he had not been the perfect gentleman with Catherine, but he was going to make it up to her. He really felt bad that he believed the ridiculous lies Carla Segal had told about her. Catherine had been treated cruelly since she arrived in America and he was going to make sure he protected her and made her life a lot easier. Even though his shoulder and ribs were beginning to throb, Michael felt a calm come over him. He was breaking down Catherine's wall and he knew it was just a matter of time and she would be his. He reflected back to the day of his wreck and what had really caused it. He had bedded his share of other women, but Catherine was different. He had never had any woman respond to his lovemaking the way Catherine did and it excited him just to think about it. He fell asleep and dreamed of the day they would be together.

Michael was discharged two days later and Catherine had made arrangements for their transportation to the train station. Before she went up to Michael's room to get him she stopped at the emergency room where Samuel was working. "I didn't want to leave without saying goodbye and thank you. Michael and I have made peace with each other, and I told him I would think about his marriage proposal."

"That's great," Samuel said with a grin. "We need to stay in touch."

"We will, and you have to let me know when the baby comes," she said with a smile.

Samuel kissed her on the forehead and watched as she disappeared around the corner. He had a lump in his throat and he had to go outside to get some fresh air. He wished he didn't love her so much. He bit his lip to keep the tears from clouding his eyes and then he took a deep breath and went back inside to his patients.

Michael and Catherine settled into a large, private room in the Pullman car. It had a bed in it, but Michael said he wanted to sit up so he walked over and sat down by Catherine after giving the porter a tip. "I've ordered us some coffee and hot tea if that pleases you," Michael said.

"That's wonderful, thank you," she answered.

After the train pulled away Michael began telling Catherine about his unhappy marriage to his first wife. "At first, everything seemed to be great, but I had no way of knowing about her mood swings and deep depression. One minute she was happy and the next, sad. After a while nothing I did pleased her. Then she started drinking. I found out later that drinking runs in her family. Her mother had died young, too," Michael said, and then became quiet and just looked out the window.

"You have two beautiful children and I can see you love them very much," Catherine said as she tried to lighten the conversation.

"They are everything to me. Meredith and Alex have been helpful in looking after them. You are a great mother, Catherine. I've seen you with your children and you love them as much as I love mine. The children get along well together and I know we could make it work as a family. I won't rush you, but I have to admit, patience is not one of my virtues." Michael started to say something else, but didn't.

"If I were to marry you, how would you feel if I kept the clinic open two or three days a week? I could bring the children into town when I come to work and Sadie and Shelby can look after them. Would you have a problem with that?" she asked.

Michael stared out the window trying to find the right words. "Of course, I would prefer that you be a full-time mother to our children, but I suppose I could live with that, at least for a little while."

"I've always been a full-time mother to my children, Michael. They are happy and well-adjusted, and I spend a lot of time with them," Catherine answered back.

"It will be different when we are married, Catherine. I don't want to have to make an appointment with you if I want to spend thirty minutes with you in the middle of the day. I have needs, too," Michael said.

Catherine could feel the tension growing and Michael had not said anything she didn't already know. "I spent almost two years in captivity being at the beck and call of a monster. I had no rights. I was told when I could go to the bathroom and when I could eat. He made me sleep with him whenever it pleased him. I can't be in a marriage where I am suffocated and made to feel like a prisoner," she said in a stern voice.

"Is that what you think of me?" Michael said in an angry tone. He grabbed her arm and turned her to him. Catherine could see his anger and hurt in his eyes and she froze, waiting for him to hit her. She put her hand up to her face and looked down. Michael slowly released her and sat back down.

"I apologize for the remark I just made. I didn't mean to offend you. That was not my intention," she said softly and wiped a tear from her eyes. Michael reached for her and pulled her to him.

"I would be a good husband and take care of you, Catherine. You don't need to hide behind a wall of fear. I can be insensitive at times myself and I promise I will work on that. I want to make you happy," he said, and then kissed her hard and long.

They sat in silence for a while and then the conductor called out the Rosenberg stop. "We're here," he said and stood in the doorway waiting for her. Catherine picked up her purse and bag and left in front of him. She was still apprehensive about their plans of marriage, and she just needed a little time to sort things out.

Lucas was waiting out front of the station and helped Michael and Catherine into the buckboard. Lucas chatted about how well Michael looked and the fact that he was absolutely certain that a storm was coming. When they stopped in front of Catherine's house, Michal turned to her and said, "Will you and your family join us tomorrow for Christmas dinner?" he asked her.

"Jason Brady's grandparents are in town and we have already accepted their invitation. I'm sorry, Michael." He leaned over and kissed her; she could see the disappointment in his face.

Catherine watched as they drove off and then slowly turned and went into the house. She was tired and emotionally drained. Michael was a complicated man and she knew a marriage to him would be a constant state of turbulence and heartache. She might be more willing to be the kind of wife that most men wanted if she were in love with Michael. But there were times she felt as though she hated him. He was arrogant and always had his way with everyone. What was she thinking when she told him she would give his proposal consideration? Catherine stopped and bit her lip when she realized she had not started her period. She took a deep breath and let it out. She had a lot to think about. A baby would change everything.

Lucas helped Michael get settled then asked if Michael needed him to stay. "You go on. Tomorrow's Christmas. You need to be with your family," Michael said.

Meredith and Alex were in the living room waiting when Michael came in, and Meredith sensed that Michael seemed angry about something. "Are you feeling better?" she asked Michael.

"Yes, I'm just tired and I think I'll just go rest," he said and went to his room.

"Something is bothering him. He seemed so upbeat yesterday when we spoke on the telephone. What do you think happened?" she asked Alex.

"You know your brother better than anyone. What do you think it is?"

"I'm not sure, but he talked a lot about Catherine yesterday, and how helpful she was. Maybe they had a disagreement," Meredith said.

Alex didn't answer. He knew Michael had set his sights on Catherine and he knew she was not the least bit interested in having a relationship with him. At least that was how he saw it.

Catherine's stomach had begun to feel woozy and she felt like she had to throw up. She dropped her bag on the floor and rushed upstairs to the bathroom. She barely made it in time when she began throwing up. Afterwards, she sat on the floor in the bathroom with a washcloth up to her mouth. Sadie came in and asked if she could help. Catherine motioned her away. "Whatever I have, I don't want you or the children to catch it," Catherine said as the bile began to come back up into her throat. "Just take care of the children and keep them out of my room, please."

Sadie finally left when Catherine motioned with her hand for her to leave. The nausea was agonizing and she continued to gag as she tried to vomit. She pulled a towel off the towel rack and put it under her head as she lay down on the floor. She closed her eyes and tried to take slow, deep breaths. She wondered if she could keep some castor oil down, but didn't feel like going downstairs to get it. Another spell hit her and she tried to empty her stomach, but it was useless. She had not had very much to eat in the last two days, so she couldn't blame it on bad food. It didn't feel like the nausea she had had from her pregnancies and she closed her eyes tight and prayed she wasn't pregnant. She wondered if God was punishing her for being so hard on Michael. Why couldn't Michael leave her alone, she wondered. She felt exhausted from the constant dry heaving and she tried to pull herself up to the faucet to get some water but she fell back on the floor and fell asleep.

The storm clouds had hovered over Rosenberg for several hours and then the sky began to rumble and crack, and giant bolts of lightning flashed with a violent force, causing the electricity to go out in the entire town. The rain came down in bucket loads and drenched everything. The noise woke Catherine up and then she felt nauseated again. She heard one of the children crying and she tried to crawl out of the bathroom. She was shivering from the cold and she felt helpless.

Someone came in the bedroom with a kerosene lamp and she was grateful for the light. Sadie set it on the floor as she got to the bathroom and saw Catherine on the floor. "Are the children all right?" Catherine gasped.

"The thunder scared them a bit, but Shelby and I made a tent downstairs in the children's playroom and we are eating dinner underneath it. They are fine," Sadie said. "Let me help you into bed." Together, Sadie helped Catherine take her dress off, put on her nightgown and get under the covers of the bed. Sadie put another blanket on top of her when she saw Catherine was shivering.

"Could you go downstairs and bring me my medical bag?" Catherine asked. She was still holding the towel up to her in case she threw up again. Sadie returned with the bag and a glass of water.

"Tell me what you need and I'll get it," Sadie said.

"I need to give myself a shot so I'll stop vomiting, and sleep," Catherine said as she searched for the medication in her bag. Sadie helped give her a shot in her leg and then Catherine fell back on the bed. "I won't be going with you to Jason's tomorrow. Just plan on taking the children. I'll be fine. I really need to sleep now. We'll wait until later in the day to give the children their Christmas presents. They are wrapped, but I want to be there with them."

Catherine slept until almost noon the next day and when she woke up she had horrible cramps. When she made her way to the bathroom, she discovered she had started bleeding and she was relieved that she wasn't pregnant. She felt light-headed and went back to bed. She heard the door open, and Shelby asked how she was feeling.

"Dreadful," Catherine said. "But I'll be all right. I just need rest."

"Jason is on his way and we will be leaving soon. I'll bring you back something to eat," Shelby told her.

The electricity had come back on in the early morning and by the time the sun came up the storm clouds had disappeared and it promised to be a beautiful Christmas day.

The phone rang several times while Catherine was trying to sleep, but she didn't feel well enough to go downstairs. All she wanted was to be left alone.

It was close to six o'clock in the evening when Catherine felt someone shaking her and asking her to wake up. She turned over and saw Michael standing over her. "Why are you here?" she said in a whisper, not sure how he got in.

"Shelby called me earlier and said you had been ill and I was worried about you. She left the front door open so I could check on you." Catherine tried to sit up and Michael pulled her pillow up so she could lay back on it. He walked over and picked up a chair and set it down beside the bed. "I've brought you some soup. Do you feel like trying some?" he asked. She shook her head yes, but didn't look at him.

"I must look awful," she said as Michael put a small tray in front of her with the soup and a spoon on it. She reached for the water on her bedside table and he helped her get it.

"You look like you don't feel well, but you are still beautiful," he answered. "I'm sorry you came down ill. What do you think it was?" he asked.

"I'm not pregnant," she answered.

Michael looked away and then turned back. "That was not why I was inquiring," he said, and Catherine could tell she hurt his feelings.

"Forgive me, Michael, I'm not myself today."

He smiled at her. "Apology accepted."

Michael watched as she sipped the soup and her pale face began to slowly show her natural color. Catherine finished most of the soup and Michael took her tray and set it aside. "Promise you'll call me if you don't improve. I would be happy to take you to Houston General if you feel the need arises."

"I think I'm going to make it. The soup was wonderful, and I really appreciate your bringing it, Michael."

Michael bent down and kissed her on the forehead and left.

A few minutes later Shelby came in and told Catherine that they were riding up in Jason's buckboard when she saw Mr. Atwood leave. "I hope you don't mind that I called him. I was so worried about you."

"No, I appreciate your concern. Did you and the children have a nice day?" Catherine asked.

"Yes, the meal was wonderful and Jason's grandmother sent us home with lots of leftover turkey and dressing. When you feel like eating again, I'll prepare it for you." Shelby hesitated and then said, "You aren't interested in Jason, are you? I mean, I really like him and he asked me to the dance this Saturday night. I told him yes, but I won't go, if you really like him."

Catherine smiled. "Jason is a really nice man, but I'm not taken to him, if that is what you mean. He is very sweet and I think you would have a nice time. Does he know about the baby?" Catherine asked.

"Yes. He came by the house after you left for Houston and he's been stopping by almost every day to see me. Are you sure you don't mind?"

"Shelby, I have four children and I'm not in a position to be romantically inclined toward any man," Catherine said as she smiled.

"Not even Mr. Atwood? I think he is sweet on you."

Catherine laughed. "No, not even Mr. Atwood."

The next morning Catherine was feeling better and when she heard the children get up, she called them down to open presents. She had tried to tell them the story about baby Jesus and how the wise men had brought gifts to Mary when he was born, but she knew they were still too young to understand what Christmas was all about. When she finished her story, the children immediately tore into their presents. She was glad it was Sunday because she wouldn't have to see patients and she could spend the whole day being a mother.

The next day Lucas had picked up Michael and took him to his office. Michael was going through his older mail and then picked up the Houston Daily News. It was dated the day before Christmas and he had not read it because of his accident. He glanced at the headlines and quickly read the news that interested him. When he turned to page four, the name, Dr. Catherine Merit, seemed to jump off the page when he saw it. The article mentioned her name and that she had shot a man in self-defense in the small town of Rosenberg. Michael groaned when he read it. He knew the publicity would not be good. The article said she was a widow with four children and lived alone. He gave a deep sigh. It was an open invitation for some drifter to come to Rosenberg in hopes of finding a wife. Just as he was about to leave and go to Catherine's house to show her the paper, the sheriff came in.

He told Michael he was concerned because the local gossip had made its way to several towns via the railroad, and that men of every age were showing up at the saloon asking questions about Dr. Merit. He was worried for her safety. Michael showed the sheriff the newspaper.

"It's only going to get worse," Michael said. The sheriff shook his head. "I'd like for you to go with me to Catherine's house and tell her what you just told me," Michael added.

Catherine was reading the children a story when she heard a knock on the door; she asked Sadie to answer it. When Sadie returned and Catherine looked up she saw Michael and the sheriff standing in the doorway.

"What is it?" she asked.

"We need to discuss an important matter with you, Catherine, in private," Michael said.

Catherine handed Sadie the book and asked the men to follow her to the waiting room. Michael showed Catherine the newspaper article and the sheriff told Catherine the same thing he had told Michael. Catherine looked down at the floor and her fists were clenched in her lap.

"You, the girls, and your children aren't going to be safe here," Michael said.

"When the man from the Houston newspaper interviewed me, he promised he would not give my name or the town where I lived. I trusted him," she confessed. "I don't want to leave my home," she said, trying to hold back her tears. Catherine was frightened, but she took a deep breath and said, "I have a gun and I'm not afraid to use it," she said.

"So do you plan to shoot every man who comes calling?" Michael asked.

She sighed again, letting out a long breath. "Of course not. What I meant was that I'm capable of protecting my family if I have to."

"You need to give this some more thought, Catherine," Michael said.

"I will," she said and stood up. Both men stood up and she walked to the front door and opened it. Michael was exasperated with her but decided to leave before he said something he would regret. He stopped just as he got to the door.

"You know you can call me for anything, Catherine. Promise me if you get scared you'll call me or the sheriff."

Catherine nodded her head yes and stood at the door with her arms folded. Both men bid her goodbye and left. She wondered if the two men had exaggerated then decided to go on about her day.

It was late and Catherine had already put the children to bed. She hadn't said anything about the article to Sadie or Shelby because they would worry. Before she went upstairs, she checked all the doors and made sure the locks had been secured on all the windows. Catherine went to her desk drawer and took out her gun and bullets. She loaded the gun and then went upstairs to her room and placed it under the other pillow on her bed. She lay on her bed staring out the window, wondering how she could have been so naive as to believe the reporter. She was beginning to doze off when she heard a loud pounding on her front door. She carefully took her gun from under the pillow and laid it down beside her while she slipped on her robe. Clutching the gun to her breast, she made her way down the stairs and stood frozen at the bottom when another pounding began.

"We need help," someone said in a slurred voice while laughing.

"Yeah, doc, let us in," she heard another voice say.

Shelby had started down the stairs; Catherine motioned to her to stay put. Catherine slipped into the living room and picked up the phone. When the operator answered Catherine told her she needed the sheriff to come immediately to her house because two men were trying to break in. The operator told her to stay on the line while she tried to reach the sheriff. She heard the phone ringing in the background and a few minutes later the operator told Catherine that it was a busy night in town and she thought the sheriff might be very busy.

"Would you please keep trying?" she asked. She was getting

scared now, and decided to try something else.

"You need to leave now," Catherine shouted through the door. "I've called the sheriff and he is on his way." She heard one of the men curse to his companion and shortly thereafter she heard the sound of galloping horses. She sighed with relief.

Sophie was at her side now and the two women hugged each other. Sophie went back to bed but Catherine was wide awake now and her heart was beating at a rapid rate. She sat down on the couch and pulled her robe around her. She was chilled and she began to shake. She stared at the door for a while and was startled when the phone rang.

"Catherine, are you all right?" Michael asked. She sighed with relief when she heard his voice. "The sheriff just called and told me you had reported that two men tried to break into your house. He told me when he got there he walked around it several times and he saw no one. Do you want me to come over?"

"Yes," she answered. "I would like that."

Twenty minutes later she heard a soft knock on the door. "Catherine, its Michael."

Catherine put the gun on the coffee table and ran to the door. When she opened it she threw herself into Michael's arms and held on to him. It surprised him, but he responded by putting his good arm around her and stroking her hair.

"It's all right. I'm here now, and no one is going to hurt you." Michael was tall and well-built and he rested his chin on top of her head as they held on to each other.

"Oh, Michael, I've never been so scared. Thank you for coming," she said almost in a whisper.

The room was dimly lit but when his eyes adjusted he released Catherine and walked her over to the couch. "Tell me what happened," Michael said tenderly.

"They just kept pounding on the door. One man was slurring his words and I could tell they had been drinking. He said it was an emergency and to let them in. I told them I had called the sheriff and they finally left."

She was sitting close to him on the couch and he had his arm around her. He could feel her heart beating and she was shaking. Michael wanted to scold her for not heeding his warning, but he knew if he was going to get Catherine to accept his marriage proposal he needed to be kind and gentle with her. Make her see that she needed his protection; that she needed to marry him. He would set down the rules once they were married.

"Why don't you go upstairs and try and get some sleep? I'll stay downstairs and sleep on the couch," he suggested. "I doubt they'll be back but you can't be too sure."

"I'm not sleepy right now. I'll stay with you for a while and then go up."

Catherine felt safe in Michael's arms and she was seeing a softer side to Michael that she had not seen before. She soon fell asleep in his arms. Michael settled back in the couch and put his legs and feet up on the coffee table. There was a blanket lying over the top of the couch and he pulled it over and tucked it around Catherine's body. He nestled himself into the couch and soon fell asleep.

Catherine woke up early the next morning and she could hear Michael's soft, easy breathing as she slowly eased herself away from his body. It was the first time in a long time she had slept through the night without waking. She smiled as she watched him sleeping and wondered if perhaps she should tell Michael she would marry him. She at least would give it serious consideration. She also knew she and her family could not stay in the house alone.

CHAPTER 10

Catherine was in the kitchen when Michael joined her. He set her gun on the table and suggested she keep it out of reach of the children. She smiled at him and poured him a cup of coffee. When he sat down at the table, she put the pot down and sat in the chair beside him.

"Thank you for coming to my rescue last night," she said and bent down to kiss him on the cheek. She sat down beside him and reached across the table to pull her teacup closer. Out of habit she twirled the tea bag around while waiting to see what Michael was going to say.

Michael took a sip of his coffee; when he put it down he reached for Catherine's hand and pulled it up to his face. He kissed it softly and looked into her eyes. "I know we have had disagreements and I do respect your opinions. I've never met anyone quite like you before and I'm sorry if I have appeared arrogant and opinionated. It's just how I was raised. I have been given a lot of responsibility and I've always thought that it was the man's obligation to provide and take care of the family. I realize that your unfortunate circumstances have caused you to be placed in a man's role, but you don't have to do that now, Catherine. I would like to do that for you. I'm asking you one more time to marry me."

Catherine looked down at her cup, nervously twirling her tea bag around. She wanted to say yes. She needed to say yes, but still her gut feeling was that a life with Michael would always be in turbulence. She had to have more time. She put her hands in her lap and took a deep breath. She was uneasy and was trying hard not to feel intimidated by Michael. In some ways he reminded her of David Brooks. He was strong, possessive, and demanding. She knew everyday life with him would be a challenge and she had her four children to worry about. How would Michael react if Adam had a difficult day or the girls got on his nerves? Adam could be a real handful sometimes and she knew he would wear on Michael's patience. Michael had told Catherine when she first moved here that when his son was twelve he was shipping him to a military school in Virginia. She had noticed that while Michael was a good father, she rarely saw him with his own children.

"I don't want to rush into anything, Michael. I'm aware that being a woman alone with four children makes me vulnerable, but I don't want to get married because I'm in fear of my life. I need more time," she answered.

"You are exasperating at times, Catherine, and I don't want you to marry me just because you need to feel safe. Nor do I want to wait around like some lovesick school boy waiting for an answer to go to the prom. You need to make a decision. I have been seeing another woman and she would marry me in an instant. Don't be sorry you let me go."

Michael got up from the table and the chair fell backwards, hitting the floor. He bent down and picked it up, giving Catherine a hard glare. "I won't ask again." Michael stormed out, and when Catherine heard the front door slam, she jumped. She felt sick at her stomach and her hand began to shake as she tried to pick up her cup. I'm not going to let him intimidate me, she told herself.

It was still too early for the children to be up and Catherine tried to calm her nerves when Shelby came in. "I thought I heard Michael earlier," she said more as a question.

"Yes, he was here, but he had to leave," Catherine answered.

"Is everything all right?" she asked.

Catherine hesitated. "I don't seem to have a very good record where men are concerned," she answered. "Michael asked me to marry him and I couldn't give him an answer," she replied.

Shelby walked over, put her arms around Catherine and hugged her. I know you have to follow your heart, but perhaps you could grow to love him," Shelby suggested.

"I wish it were that easy. He's an extremely complicated man and I think I am much too set in my ways now," Catherine said.

Shelby sat down next to her. "Jason has asked me to marry him."

"That is wonderful news," Catherine said, excited for Shelby.

"He wants us to get married as soon as possible because he wants the baby to have his name."

"Oh, I'm so happy for you both."

"I won't leave you empty-handed. I plan to come back every day and help you in the clinic, and Jason said he didn't mind my working for you part-time. You won't have to pay me because you are teaching me so much, and you will still have Sadie to help you in the evenings," Shelby said.

"Don't worry about me or the clinic. You and Jason will have a wonderful future together," she added. The doorbell rang and Shelby told Catherine she thought it might be Jason because he told her he would come over and discuss it with them. Shelby went to the door and a few minutes later came back to the kitchen with Jason.

Jason and Shelby talked with Catherine about their plans for the future, and that if it were all right with her, they wanted to get married the next Saturday at noon. Catherine suggested that Shelby call her parents and give them the news and that she would be happy to tell them what a fine man Jason was. Before Jason left, Catherine asked him for a favor. She told them about the reporter and the article in the paper and about the two men who had come the night before. He suggested that he sleep in the living room over the next few nights just in case someone else decided to come by; Catherine was relieved.

Michael drove the short distance back to his office. He had always kept extra clothes there and he had a back room with a small bed and some of his personal items. He did a quick shave with cold water and cursed when he nicked his chin. He was obsessed with Catherine and in his lifetime he had never wanted anything so badly. He decided to wait a few days and thought it best to ignore her. She would come around, he thought. He had everything a woman could desire. Wealth, a beautiful home, stability, good looks, and he considered himself a great lover. What woman wouldn't want him?

Michael had just finished changing when he heard the front door open. When he walked out he was greeted by Alex. "I stopped by the house earlier and your housekeeper told me you went to Catherine's house because of an emergency and didn't come home. I hope everything is all right."

"A couple of men tried to break in last night. Seems that article in the newspaper was an open invitation to get a look at the brave doctor." Michael was irritated about Alex's interest in Catherine, but wanted to hide it. Alex had been married to Catherine, and even though it was only for a short period, maybe Michael could gain some insight into how he should proceed. "They were gone by the time I got there and she asked me to stay the night." Alex stiffened when he heard the last remark but tried to remain passive.

"Well, you did the right thing. She needs someone to look after her," Alex said.

"I've asked her to marry me," Michael said matter-of-factly.

"When's the wedding?"

"Not sure. She didn't give me a definite answer, and I'm glad. She comes with a lot of baggage and we both decided we needed to give it some time."

Alex didn't answer back. He was sure Catherine would never marry Michael, and once she got to know him better she would realize how demanding and selfish he was.

"I need some coffee," Michael said. "We can talk some more at the café."

Talk some more, Alex wondered to himself. It wasn't as though Alex was his best friend. They tolerated each other because of Meredith, and that was it.

They both ordered breakfast and sipped on their coffee. "Tell me, Alex, do you remember much about being married to Catherine?"

Alex didn't look at him. He actually had no memory of their marriage together, but in the short time he had gotten to know her again, he had concluded that she had many fine qualities and was extremely compassionate. She had also surrounded herself with a shield of strength and determination. He knew little about her captivity with David Brooks in Beaumont, but he knew enough to ascertain that no man was going to tell her what to do. Marrying Michael would be like living with a keg of dynamite. It could explode at any time.

"No," Alex answered curtly. He would not tell Michael anything, even if he did remember.

Alex decided it was time to change the subject and began talking about the two new stallions Michael had purchased in Houston from a breeder. Michael wanted to try and dig some kind of response from Alex about Catherine, but decided enough had been said.

Later that evening when Alex returned home, Meredith asked if he had seen Michael.

"Yes," he remarked. "We had breakfast together. He told me he had asked Catherine to marry him."

"Really, what was her answer?"

"She didn't give him one. Seems they both agreed to give it a little time. I would be surprised if she said yes," Alex said.

"Why do you think that? Michael would make a wonderful husband. She would be lucky to be his wife."

"What I meant was that she gave me the impression that she disliked your brother intensely. After all, he has been very unpleasant with her at times, especially when he found out about our brief marriage," Alex said, defending his remark. Actually, he was terribly bothered by the fact that she would consider being Michael's wife and he would see them together almost every day.

"They are both strong willed," Meredith said, "But I'm sure they are capable of finding a common ground. I'm sure Michael is in love with her."

"I don't think Catherine is in love with your brother," Alex said in a matter-of-fact tone. He knew he had upset Meredith by his comment; he went over and wrapped his arms around her, kissing her on the cheek. She didn't respond, and Alex turned her around and tilted her chin up towards him. "My God," he said. "You are so beautiful when you get mad at me."

"Don't think you are going to try and use your charm to make it better. I know you think Michael is arrogant and controlling, but he has a lot of responsibility and he has tripled the family's trust fund. We live in one of his houses, don't forget."

"I thought our house belonged to the trust fund and you were a fifty percent owner?" Alex retaliated.

"I am, but Michael looks after it as well as the rest of my money," she said. Alex's jaw dropped and she knew she had hit a nerve. Alex had been paying Michael rent ever since they moved into the house, but he guessed Meredith didn't know that.

"My apologies," Alex said, and went outside. He and Meredith rarely argued and he felt badly that it had to happened now while she was pregnant and in a delicate condition. He had already made up his mind that once the baby came he would go back to his old job. Clarence Henry had told him it was his when he was ready. They always needed experienced scouts and Clarence considered Alex one of the best. He would have to hold his tongue and not say anything until after the baby came, he thought. There was no need to worry Meredith. He had been Michael's errand boy long enough, and Michael made sure Alex didn't forget that he had what Michael called "a free ride."

He was also bothered by the fact that Catherine would be miserable being Michael's wife. She had no idea what the real Michael was capable of and he knew she would be unhappy being his wife. It was not up to him to tell her that, though, and if he did and Catherine backed out, Meredith would never forgive him. He heard the door open behind him.

"I've brought you a fresh cup of coffee," Meredith said, smiling at him. Alex smiled back but didn't say anything. She wrapped her arms around his waist and said, "I accept your apology."

Catherine was busy putting the Christmas decorations away when the phone rang. Mark Graham wished her a happy new year and told her that the buyers had backed out of the house deal because the street was being leveled and the streets were still not finished. He asked if she were still interested. Catherine had previously written a letter offering a price to the sellers if the buyers did back out, and he told her that if she still wanted to exercise her right to purchase, he would draw up the papers according to her letter and they could close on Wednesday. Catherine told him she was definitely interested in following through with the purchase; she was beginning to get excited now. When Shelby came in, she had a bouquet of flowers in her hands.

"They are beautiful. Jason is so thoughtful," Catherine said.

"They aren't for me," Shelby responded and set the bouquet of roses on Catherine's desk. Catherine took the card out of the envelope:

> *Forgive my rude conduct yesterday when I left. You did not deserve it.*
> *Yours, Michael.*

Catherine smiled.

"Michael sent them," she responded to Shelby.

"He won't give up, you know. I've heard that no one tells Michael 'No'," Shelby warned.

"He is determined," Catherine said and sighed.

"I need to go to Galveston Wednesday to take care of some business and I'm closing the clinic Friday, so you can have the day off. Oh, Shelby, I'm so happy for you and Jason. He will be a great husband and father. What did your parents say when you called them?"

"Of course, daddy thinks I'm making another terrible mistake. Mother has always been supportive, but doesn't think she can talk father into coming. She's happy that I won't have to give my child away or raise it alone. Not that I was ever going to put it up for adoption. I love my baby. He is part of me. Thank you, Catherine, for taking me in and being a sister to me. I don't think I could have done this by myself." The two women hugged each other for a long time before parting.

They heard the doorbell ring as someone came in and Shelby went to greet them. A tall, intimidating, unshaven man was standing in the waiting room and bloodstains were on his upper torso and shoulder. Shelby asked the man to wait while she got the doctor then ran back to Catherine's office. After telling Catherine about the intrusive injured man, Catherine took her gun from her purse and put a towel over it, cupping it to her breast.

"Call the sheriff and tell him about the man. I'll stall him," Catherine said.

While Shelby made the phone call, Catherine asked the man to come into her exam room and take a seat. She walked back to the doorway leading into her office. It had a separate lock on it and if she needed to make a quick exit she could run in and lock the door before he could cross the room.

"I'm Dr. Merit, what happened to your arm?" Catherine was trying not to act afraid.

"I set up camp up by the river last night and was taking the saddle off my horse when someone shot me. It spooked my horse and he ran off. Whoever shot me went after my horse and neither came back. It was dark and I couldn't see, so I just settled in for the night and this morning I walked into town to find a doctor."

The man was certainly intimidating, Catherine thought, but for some reason she didn't think he was there to hurt her. His story seemed genuine. "Let me help you get your jacket and shirt off," she said.

He hesitated. "I've never met a lady doctor before. You obviously aren't from around here. You have a foreign accent."

"I moved here several years ago from England, but I studied at the medical school in Galveston." The man began taking off his jacket with Catherine's help. She picked up her scissors just as Shelby came in the room. "This is my assistant, Shelby." The man nodded at Shelby.

"This may hurt when I cut away your shirt. The blood has dried, causing the shirt to stick to the wound, but I'll try to be gentle."

"I'm not afraid of pain. Do what you have to do."

"What's your name?" Catherine asked, just as the front door bell rang. Shelby went to check and returned with Sheriff Raymond Wade. The man looked up at Catherine. Even though his size and appearance were rugged, his soft hazel eyes gave an appearance of gentleness.

"We've had some trouble lately and I asked Shelby to call the sheriff. He needs to find who shot you and took your horse," Catherine assured him.

"My name is Trent Mathews and I'm an oil scout for Humble Oil Company. My papers are in my satchel that I left out front." Trent told the sheriff the same story he had told Catherine.

Trent had been shot in his shoulder; it was a through and through bullet, and Catherine was relieved she would not have to surgically remove it. Had the bullet stayed in his shoulder overnight infection would have already set in, making his chances of recovery less likely. He continued his story and said he never saw the bandit's face. The shot had knocked him to the ground and he wasn't sure if he had blacked out or not. It stunned him and he was afraid if he moved the man would have shot him again so he lay still until he heard him gallop away.

"There have been a number of people complaining of a horse thief, but no one has seen his face. You always work alone?" the sheriff asked.

"We usually go out in pairs, but my partner's wife was having a baby so I sent him home to Houston two days ago. Figured I could finish up my business in these parts and head back to Houston at the end of the week."

"Mind if I check your papers in your saddlebag before I leave?" the sheriff asked.

"Help yourself. I've got nothing to hide."

Trent grimaced when Catherine swabbed iodine around his wound. "How much pain are you in?" she asked.

"Enough that I won't be able to sleep. Only got a few hours during the night."

"You need to be in a hospital but Rosenberg doesn't have one. Sometimes we have to improvise. There is a room upstairs in my carriage house. It's not fancy, but it's clean and you can stay up there until you are well enough to travel. I need to give you a couple of shots, and the bandages will need to be replaced in a couple of hours. I can look in on you and it would be closer than the hotel up the street. Fortunately it missed a main artery or you would already be dead," she said.

"That would be mighty nice of you to give me a room. I have an expense account with my company and they will take care of the bill," Trent said.

"Let me take care of the stitches and then get you bandaged up. When I'm finished, I'll show you to your quarters and I can administer the medication when we get up to your room. It will make you sleepy and I want to be sure you are in your bed before giving you anything." When Catherine finished, she wrapped bandages around his wound and then went to the closet and brought out a man's robe.

When Trent stood up he towered over Catherine's petite body and she had to look up and stretch her neck as she stood close to him. She gently helped Trent into the robe and asked if he could keep his arm close to his side so it wouldn't move or if he preferred, she would make a sling for him.

"No sling," he responded.

"Unfortunately, you won't be able to use your right arm for a week or so."

Catherine couldn't help but notice Trent's muscular physique and an older wound about two inches long just above his waist. He had several days' growth of hair on his face and his dark hair hung down an inch below his ears. He reminded her of Alex when he would come back from his scouting expeditions. She guessed Trent was in his mid thirties.

"I apologize about my appearance, and I'm left-handed," he said. "I wasn't expecting to meet two lovely ladies in my travels."

"We see all kinds," Catherine said, smiling. "Going to the doctor isn't something people usually plan. They are either sick or have had an accident. There is no need to apologize. If you feel like it right now, you can join me in the kitchen and I'll make you something to eat."

Trent followed behind her while Shelby stayed to clean up. Catherine went into the kitchen and pulled a chair out for Trent to sit down.

"I'm guessing you haven't eaten in a while, so if you don't mind eating with my children and I, I'll make us some breakfast. Trent watched her.

"I know you don't do this for all of your patients. I'm sorry to put you to so much trouble; I don't want to keep you from your work," Trent said, almost embarrassed.

"There are no patients in the waiting room right now. They usually begin showing up late morning, and I haven't had breakfast myself."

Daniel came in rubbing his eyes. "Mommy, what's for breakfast?" he asked, and then he noticed Trent and stopped.

"Daniel, this is Mr. Mathews. He is a patient here and he is going to have breakfast with us."

A few minutes later Adam came in and walked right up to Trent. "Who are you?" asked an inquisitive Adam.

Trent grinned at Adam. "I'm Trent Mathews; who are you?" Trent's voice was husky and it scared Adam, who ran around the table and clung to Catherine's leg.

"This is Adam, my second son."

"They are a couple of fine looking boys," Trent remarked, and then he looked up at Sadie as she came in the room holding Emma and Isabelle. Trent pulled the robe tighter around his hairy chest; he felt a little embarrassed.

"This is my friend, Sadie, and she is holding Emma and Isabelle, my two daughters."

"You have four children?" he said, surprised.

"Yes, I got married when I was sixteen," she laughed.

Sadie put the children in their respective chairs and fetched the milk. Thirty minutes later everyone was seated at the kitchen table enjoying toast, eggs, bacon, and grits. Catherine poured Trent a second cup of coffee and then sat down. All the children bowed their heads and held hands with the adults while Catherine said the prayer. Trent wanted to ask where the man of the house was but thought it best to ask Catherine in private. He had noticed that there were no smoking pipes or holsters anywhere, and he couldn't see anything that would indicate that a man even lived in the house.

When they finished, Catherine suggested that Trent follow her up to the carriage house. "You have some beautiful children, Dr.

Merit. Mind if I ask where their father is?"

"I'm a widow. Sadie is an old friend and helps me look after the children. Shelby is also a friend and helps me in the clinic. Please don't think that just because there is not a man around that I'm an easy target. I manage just fine."

"I didn't mean anything by my question; I apologize if I've acted inappropriately. I was merely curious."

When they arrived upstairs, Catherine's mood had changed. "The sheets are clean and there are fresh towels in the bathroom and running water. There is a chamber pot behind the door and the outhouse is around back of the house. Please have a seat on the bed and I'll give you your shots. Catherine's demeanor seemed to have changed from being warm and friendly to purely professional, and Trent didn't know what to make of it. He suspected that the memory of the loss of her husband must have triggered something, and he felt bad for her.

Catherine administered the shots and said, "You'll begin to get sleepy in five to ten minutes, so I'll leave you alone. You need to rest now," she said, and went over to add another log to the potbellied stove. She had sent Shelby up earlier to start the fire so the room would be warm for Trent.

"Dr. Merit," Trent said softly as he stood up. Catherine turned and looked at Trent. He was taken aback by her beautiful features and he found it hard to breathe. For some reason he forgot what he was going to say. He was feeling sleepy and lethargic.

Catherine could see he looked confused, and walked back over to him. She pulled the covers back and knelt down to remove his boots. When she finished untying his boots, she pushed him back on the bed by his shoulders, removed his boots and lifted his feet up under the covers. She started to loosen his belt but Trent grabbed her hand.

"I can finish," he said as he finally breathed out. Catherine smiled down at him. He was holding her hand and wouldn't let go.

"Is there anything else you need? I'll be back to check on you in a couple of hours."

Trent didn't want her to leave and they stared at each other for a few minutes. He finally let her hand go and said, "My business card is in my satchel and I would appreciate you calling the main number on it and let them know I'll be out of commission a day or two and, if you don't mind, could you bring my things to me when you come back?"

Catherine smiled and nodded her head yes. "Try and get some sleep now; you need your rest."

Trent watched her leave; when he heard the door slam downstairs he turned and looked out the window and watched her walk across the yard and into the house. She was a magnificent creature, he thought. He had been to a lot of places and had bedded his share of women. He had even been married for a while to a pretty little lass, but never had he encountered a woman as beautiful as Catherine. Catherine's face was still vivid in his mind when he dozed off to sleep.

CHAPTER 11

Several patients were waiting for her when she went back to her clinic. It was almost two o'clock in the afternoon when she finished seeing all of them, and she quickly washed her hands and went into the kitchen to heat some soup and make a sandwich for Trent. What was she thinking when she suggested he stay in the carriage house? She must have felt sorry for him -- or was it because there was something about his deep-set, warm eyes that drew her to him. Maybe it was his similarities to Alex. Whatever it was, he should be fine in a couple of days; he would be gone and she would probably never see him again.

She set the tray down on the upstairs landing and gently opened the door. When she peeked in, Trent was sprawled out naked on top of the covers. She was mesmerized by his body. His feet extended over the end of the bed and she estimated his height to be at least six feet four inches tall. He was facing away from her or she probably would have shut the door immediately. His wide upper torso gently curved into his tight thighs and she decided he could have been a model for one of her medical books. He was a beautiful specimen of a man. She stood longer than she should have, staring at him, because Trent reached down and pulled the sheet up over his legs and buttocks. Catherine blushed and shut the door so fast the noise even made her jump. She felt the heat rise up to her face and she decided to wait a minute before she knocked on the door. She had been caught peeking and she wondered how she could ever face him. Maybe he would still be groggy, she hoped.

She tapped on the door several times before Trent said come in. She opened the door and picked up the tray. Trent was smiling at her when she finally looked up at him. It tickled him that even a lady doctor enjoyed looking at a naked man's body. He only wished that it was under different circumstances.

"I thought you might be hungry. I had more patients than I usually do, and it was two o'clock before I realized it." Trent sat up in bed, making sure his vital parts were covered. Catherine set the tray on a table beside him and poured him a glass of milk.

"I called your office and talked to a sweet lady by the name of Agnes Harper and told her about your accident. She was concerned, of course, but I assured her you were being taken care of and would be back in Houston in a few days. If you continue to improve, you could probably go home in a day or two. It's an express and you would be there in less than an hour."

"Do you always take control of everything like this, or do you just want to get rid of me?"

"I suppose it's a little of both. I have to go to Galveston on business the day after tomorrow and I didn't want to give Shelby and Sadie more work than they can handle."

"I appreciate your honesty."

"You'll need to see a doctor when you get to Houston. They'll need to take out the stitches eventually. If you don't have a doctor, I could give you a recommendation."

"It's been a while since I needed a doctor, but I could probably get a name from my company," Trent said.

"I've brought some more medication for you to take when you wake up," she said. "Are you still hurting?"

"No, the pills will be fine," Trent lied. "Is there an afternoon train today? I could be ready to leave anytime. I feel like I might be a burden to you."

"Oh, Trent, I'm sorry if I made you feel that way. I guess I just have of lot of things on my mind right now. Forgive me. I like that you are here. It's a nice diversion. I don't have many male friends to talk to, and you make me feel like a woman and not a doctor."

"Would you be willing to come back later and help me shave and clean up a bit? Regardless of what I look like right now, I prefer to look more clean-shaven."

Catherine smiled and tilted her head to the side. "I'll be happy to, as long as it's above the waist," she said, blushing. When she left, Trent watched her out the window again and before Catherine got to the kitchen door she stopped and looked up at the window. She saw Trent smiling at her; she smiled back and went into the house.

Trent ate his food but decided not to take the two pills Catherine had left him. He knew he might not ever see Catherine again once he left and he wanted to enjoy whatever time he could with her without being groggy. His shoulder was aching, but the pain was bearable. He was beginning to feel warm in the room so he got up and walked over to the woodstove and opened the damper so the logs would burn out. There were some extra logs sitting beside the old potbellied stove; he wondered who had chopped the wood since there were no men around. In fact, he wondered who had made the fire to begin with since it had already been started and the room was warm when they first went in. He began to feel a bit nauseated and retired back to the bed, lying on top of the sheets. A few minutes later he began sweating and then his body began shivering. Trent moved under the covers and closed his eyes. He passed out a few minutes later.

Catherine sent Shelby up to Trent's room when supper was ready, and she returned telling Catherine that Trent didn't answer the door.

"Go ahead and sit down with the children and eat. I'll go check on him."

Catherine grabbed her medical bag from her office and ran to the carriage house. She banged hard on the door and heard Trent moan. She went in to find him barely coherent, and shaking. She took another blanket from the closet and covered Trent, then went back to add logs to the fire. The embers were still red hot and the flames caught quickly. It took her several minutes to prepare and administer the shot. Her own hands were shaking and she took several deep breaths to calm herself. She noticed the pills sitting beside the table and wondered why men never listened to directions. One of the pills was an anti-infection pill that she had purchased from a Chinese doctor when she was in Houston. She had read that the pill was very effective for infections and purchased the bottle for emergencies. One of the shots she gave him was also an anti-infection serum she had purchased from the same doctor. She watched as Trent's eyes rolled back and he fell asleep again. She had never had a patient die at her home and she prayed Trent would pull through. Apparently the bullet had done more damage than she thought and he must have been in a lot more pain than he let on. When he pulled through she would make sure he understood what pills he absolutely needed to take. She knew he would sleep for several hours and she left to return to her family. After the children had been put to bed, she prepared some food for Trent and took it to him.

She entered his room cautiously, as it was dark. She took her lantern over and set it on a table beside his bed. He moved and opened his eyes. Catherine put her hand to his head and he asked how long he had been out.

"About four hours. You've come down with a fever. Do you feel like eating?" she asked.

Trent leaned up on his elbow and asked for some water. Catherine tucked another pillow behind him and he sat up while she poured him a glass full. She could tell from his cloudy eyes that he was still not feeling well, but he didn't complain.

"You won't be able to leave anytime soon; you're much too weak."

"Sorry about that. I don't want to be a burden. If you could just help me to the train station in the morning I'll have someone meet me."

"I don't think so, and you're not a burden. You need another day of rest. If you are better in twenty-four hours, your train on Wednesday leaves thirty minutes before mine. I'll see you get there and I'll call someone at your office to be sure and meet you at the train station. You will need to go straight to the hospital. I'll call ahead and give the doctor there an update on your condition. It's possible some of the bullet fragmented and could still be in your shoulder. They have an x-ray machine that will tell if it's there."

Trent sighed then grimaced when he turned to put the glass on the table. Catherine touched his forehead and shook her head. "You still have a fever. Try and eat something if you can.

"Meatloaf; it's my favorite." Trent ate only half the food before he stopped and said how delicious it was but that he didn't think he could finish it. "You are an incredible woman, Dr. Merit, but I'm sure I'm not the first man to tell you that. It was my lucky day when I came here. Thank you."

Catherine smiled and didn't say anything. She saw Trent look towards the bathroom. "I'll bring the chamber pot to you and go outside. Stay close to the bed," she said as she brought the pot with the lid to him. He waited until she went downstairs to relieve himself. He felt dizzy so he covered the pot and lay back down. She knocked ten minutes later and went in. Catherine straightened the bed and picked up the chamber pot.

"I'll be back soon and check on you. Can I bring you anything else?" she asked. Trent shook his head no.

Catherine made a quick change into a clean, loose-fitting dress, grabbed another blanket, her medical bag, and the clean chamber pot and went back to Trent. She had told Sadie and Shelby she was staying in the carriage house that night so she could keep an eye on Trent.

Jason had arrived earlier prepared to sleep in the living room in the event other intruders tried to get in. Shelby had told him about Trent and he had assured Catherine before she left that he would keep an eye on the family and make sure they stayed safe.

Trent was asleep when she came in and she went back downstairs for more firewood. She had also brought her Bible with her and she pulled another chair up to Trent's bed so she could use the light from the lantern to read by.

Catherine hated to wake Trent, but it was time for his shot so she rubbed alcohol on his arm, causing him to wake up. He smiled at her but didn't say anything and watched as she methodically took the needle and pricked his arm. He drank some more water and fell back asleep. It was probably midnight when he woke again. The lantern had been turned down low and he saw the empty chair. He tried to move and realized someone was in the bed with him. A closer look melted his heart when he saw Catherine sound asleep on top of the covers, lying next to him. He adjusted his body, moved his left arm under her head and pulled her close to him. He breathed in her floral lilac scent and closed his eyes, absorbing her sweet, delicate smell. There was something special about Catherine and his only wish was that he had met her under different circumstances. He slowly drifted off to sleep again and when the morning sun drifted slowly through the window, Trent opened his eyes. Catherine was no longer there.

He wondered how she managed to maintain such a busy schedule and he felt guilty that he was part of that problem. Taking care of four children, mentoring and doctoring the sick, looking after him; he decided to try to get up and get dressed. Trent stood up slowly and the room began to spin. He fell back down on the bed just as Catherine knocked on the door. Trent covered himself and told her to come in.

"I've brought you breakfast. How are you feeling?"

"Not too good. I don't seem to have much strength," he said. "Is that normal?"

"You have an infection, and for now all you can do to get better is stay in bed and take your medicine," she answered.

"I know you have better things to do than look after me," Trent protested.

"If you aren't better by tomorrow, I'll make a quick trip to Galveston, take care of my business there and be back by mid afternoon. Shelby's fiancé, Jason Brady, has already agreed to look in on you while I'm gone. Shelby can give you your shot and get your lunch for you," Catherine said.

"I'll never be able to repay you for your kindness, Dr. Merit," Trent said sincerely.

"Just get better," she said smiling. "And please call me Catherine."

"Thanks for staying with me last night," Trent said.

"I tried to be quiet. I didn't know you knew I shared your bed. I was going to sleep in the chair, but I couldn't get comfortable."

"It was nice, waking up and seeing you beside me. You're beautiful when you sleep," Trent said and smiled. "Could you read me a couple of psalms from the Bible?" he asked.

Catherine picked up her Bible and sat in the chair beside Trent's bed and opened her Bible. She began reading Psalm 3:1 and continued till she finished that verse. She smiled when she looked up and found Trent sound asleep. She silently prayed he would pull through.

Her day was going to be hectic and since no patients had arrived yet, she decided to make a quick trip to the bank to get the funds she needed for the closing on her house. It meant that she would have to walk past Michael's office and she hoped he would not see her. The transaction took about thirty minutes and she was nervous and anxious to get back home. Just as she got up to leave, Michael came into the bank.

"Morning, Catherine; is everything all right? You look stressed," he said condescending.

"Uh no, everything is fine. How are you?" she asked and hoped she wouldn't get into any lengthy conversation with Michael.

"I'm doing wonderfully. Could you join me for some coffee?" he asked.

"I'm afraid I have patients waiting and I need to get back to the clinic, but thank-you anyway," she said and walked past him, not looking back.

Michael stood and watched her leave. It frustrated him that she was so hardheaded. If she married him, she wouldn't be stressed and she wouldn't have to work. How could he make her see that? He was curious to find out what business she had at the bank and why it took thirty minutes. The bank president was a good friend of Michael's and was happy to tell him that Catherine had withdrawn a sizable amount of money. She had told the president that it was for a business deal. She had the cashier's check made out to herself. Michael's curiosity had really been tested now, and he was determined to find out what Catherine was going to do with the money.

Catherine was relieved that no patients were waiting for her when she returned. She wanted to spend what little time she had with her children before lunch. She decided to check on Trent first and she quietly opened the door. She walked over and sat in the chair, watching him sleep. His rugged appearance was almost appealing. She tried to picture what he might look like with a shave and haircut. He was only covered to the waist and she noticed that his bandage had come loose. She tried to reattach it without waking him, but Trent woke up and was watching her when she looked up.

"I need to change your bandage," she said sweetly. Trent pushed himself up and Catherine fluffed his pillow and put another one behind him. She had placed a kettle of water on the stove when she had first come in; she walked over and picked it up, pouring some of it into a bowl and adding some cold water to it. After she cut away the old bandage she cleaned the area with warm water and dabbed it dry with a clean cloth.

"Your wound seems to be healing nicely," she said. "It's beginning to dry up, which is a good sign. It means that the infection is going away. I think you should stay a couple more days. You don't need to travel until you feel up to it. Maybe Thursday or Friday you'll feel better."

Trent wanted to argue with her, but he liked being under Catherine's care. She was intoxicating and he was sure she was an angel. Not only did she look like one, but she was gentle and kind; when she was in the room with him all he wanted to do was look at her.

When Catherine finished putting a clean bandage on his shoulder and wrapping it around his arm, Shelby came upstairs to tell her Michael was in the house and wanted to talk to her. Catherine put the towel, her gauze, scissors, and medication back in the basket she had brought upstairs with her and suggested Trent should get some rest.

After Catherine left, Trent walked over to the side of the window and peeked out. He saw a well-dressed man in a suit standing on the porch. Shelby walked past Catherine and Michael and went into the house. Trent couldn't hear what they were saying, but he suspected there was tension between them. Michael put his hands on his hips and was looking down at Catherine from the porch. She was standing at the bottom of the steps with the basket in her hands, looking up at him. He was saying something to her and Catherine was shaking her head, no. When she scurried up the steps, he grabbed her arm and tried to pull her closer to him. Catherine dropped the basket and seemed to freeze in place like a statue. It was obvious she was rejecting his advances. Michael finally released her and stepped back. He said something to her and then turned and left abruptly through the side gate.

Catherine stood with her back to the carriage house and slowly walked over to a chair and sat down. A few minutes later she burst into tears. After she composed herself, she got down on her knees and crawled over to her basket and began putting the scissors, gauze, and other items back in the basket. When she picked up the towel her eyes went to the carriage house window. Trent had ducked back and she had not seen him watching her. She was relieved. She didn't want Trent to see the way she had broken down -- not that it really mattered anyway. He would be leaving soon and she would never see him again. Tears began to fill her eyes again and she used Trent's towel to wipe them. Trent watched through the curtain as she took several deep breaths and went into the house.

It was one o'clock that afternoon when Catherine returned to Trent's room. He pretended to be asleep when she set the tray beside his table. She sat down in the chair and stared out the window. She was deep in thought when Trent took her hand and squeezed it. "Looks like you need a friend," he said. Catherine smiled at him.

Michael had demanded that Catherine tell him why she had taken so much money out of her account. He was a director of the bank with access to this information, and he said he was concerned someone might be blackmailing her. When she told him she wasn't being blackmailed and that it was a business investment, he was furious that she did not discuss it with him. It ended badly, she thought, but it didn't concern Trent, even though she would have liked to tell him.

"How are you feeling?" she asked.

"Much better, thanks to you. I hate to be blunt, but is Michael your boyfriend?" Catherine's smile left her face and she turned away.

"I hope you like ham and green beans," she said, ignoring his question. He didn't answer; he knew he touched a nerve. He started eating from the plate of food Catherine had handed him and didn't say any more.

"Michael is sort of a friend," she began to say. "He pretty much runs the town and he isn't used to being told no. He's asked me to marry him, and I've refused. I don't ever want to get married again -- to him or anyone else -- and I can't seem to make him understand."

"Forever is a long time," Trent said.

"It's a long, unpleasant story, Trent, and I am not up to elaborating why I feel the way I do. Let's just say I have everything I could ever want or need and I just want to be left alone," she said.

She turned and stared out the window again and Trent felt like she was a million miles away. He wondered what had happened in her short lifetime to make her feel the way she did. He wanted to take her in his arms and tell her everything was going to be all right, but he hadn't earned that right yet and he didn't think she needed one more man pursuing her right now. Whoever or whatever had hurt her was embedded deep inside her, and he felt that all he could do right now was to try and win her trust.

"You are a strong woman, Catherine, and you should follow your instincts and your heart. You are in a difficult situation, though. You're beautiful, smart, and you obviously carry a lot of responsibility. You are always going to have men taunting you, pursuing you and wanting to marry you. It's a fact of life," Trent said. "God made man to be the hunter and women their prey. It's an uneven society and I can feel empathy for you. It's not fair, but unfortunately it will always be that way. There will always be a Michael coming after you. The best advice I can give you is to find a man who is willing to be your equal and allow you to think for yourself. Then marry him. You'll find a balance that way, and you won't have to worry about being pursued."

"And what about you?" Catherine countered back. "Why are you alone?"

"Because I choose to be. My first wife left me because I was never home. I'm married to my job and I'm always gone," he answered.

"So it's all right for a man to be unmarried and alone, but not a woman," she said.

"I know it's a double standard, but it's the kind of world we live in."

Catherine thought for a minute and then said, "If you could find a woman to marry who didn't care if you were gone all the time and didn't demand anything, would you get married again?" she asked.

Trent laughed and said, "So far, I've never met a woman like that."

Catherine smiled, picked up Trent's dirty plate and put it on the tray. She retrieved the needle and vial she had brought with her. "It's time for your shot," she said. Trent studied her and wondered what was going through Catherine's mind. When she left, Trent pondered the conversation they had. She was different, and like no other woman he had ever met. He wished there was something he could do for her, but he couldn't change the world and for sure, he wouldn't be able to change her. He knew one thing; he wanted her for himself, but he didn't think she could be easily persuaded into another relationship or into his bed. He liked challenges, and finally fell asleep dreaming of having his way with her.

CHAPTER 12

Catherine had wired Mark Graham the afternoon before she left, telling him she would be on the nine o'clock train and could he arrange for her to have a carriage waiting for her. After she boarded the train the next morning, she situated herself into a seat in the far corner at the back of the train. It was on time and pulled away from the station fifteen minutes after its arrival.

She sighed as she thought about Trent. She had taken him his breakfast earlier than usual that morning and gave him his necessary shots. She knew one could cause him to sleep several hours, and Jason had promised to look in on him later in the morning. She couldn't help but think about their conversation the night before. Trent had not told her anything she didn't already know. She lived in a world of prejudices and men ruled. It was a lesson she had learned the hard way.

While she stared out the window at the dreary, decaying meadows and falling leaves, she decided that she needed to stop at a jewelry store before her eleven o'clock appointment that morning. She was going to buy herself a wedding band. Her plan was to tell everyone, including Michael, that she was engaged to an old friend who lived in Galveston and that once all of the ground excavation was complete on her old house, she and her children would be moving back.

Catherine had weighed her reasoning carefully. While Carla

and Clay Segal still lived in Galveston and knew all of her secrets, Michael was more of a threat to her now. His overpowering personality and determination to marry was causing her extreme mental anguish and for some reason she was afraid of him. Galveston was much bigger, and she would simply weave herself into the fabric of the city and stay out of Carla and Clay's way. On the other hand, Rosenberg was much smaller, and everyone knew everyone else's business. Whenever she would go into town she had to walk by Michael's office, and he was resilient and determined. She was afraid he might try and get her alone again; she had let down her guard once and she was now paying the consequences. She had become extremely tense just thinking about it, and was glad when the conductor called out the Galveston stop.

After she stopped at the jewelry store, she proceeded to the lawyer's office to sign the papers purchasing her house and another paper allowing Mark Graham to handle the leasing of the house. He had found a family to rent it for six months while the excavation and leveling of their street was completed. They would pay her forty-five dollars a month for renting it, even though there was no furniture in it. Mark had agreed with her that the house at the price she purchased it was a really good investment and she would have no problem making a profit when and if she ever decided to sell. He told her the founding fathers of the city were going to see to it that Galveston flourished again. The additional money was a blessing to her and surely in six months she could find a buyer for her house in Rosenberg. She finally completed the closing, and her horse and carriage was waiting to take her back to the train station.

She was in a hurry to return to Rosenberg, concerned about Trent. She liked him and he was easy to talk to. She smiled when she remembered him telling her that he liked having her fall asleep next to him. It was an impossible situation, and she knew Trent would be getting better and most likely be leaving soon. The last thing she needed was to become attached to a man who lived thirty-five miles away, and besides, she knew very little about him. He was a bit mysterious. When you asked him a question he often answered it in brief words, leaving you wanting him to tell you more. He wasn't demanding at all and seemed to appreciate the slightest courtesies. He was the total opposite of Michael, and she was glad for that. Michael used up all her energy and seemed to suck the life from her being. After her last encounter with him on her back porch, she knew she had made the right decision when she refused to marry him. He would be constantly looking over her shoulder and he would probably want to be in control of her money, too. She still suspected Michael was seeing the two widows whom he had been having affairs with for the last two years. She prayed she could last the next few months in Rosenberg with Michael's constant demands.

The train was on time and she made her way to a window seat at the back of the train. She had brought a pen and paper with her and she carefully addressed an envelope to the dean at the medical school. She chose her words with caution and advised him that she would like to be considered for a teaching position at the medical school the next fall. Her preference would be to teach at night, which would allow her to be home in the daytime with her children. However, she would be willing to take whatever position was available. Catherine believed she could leave her home before dark and then she would make arrangements for a carriage to pick her up and bring her home when the last class was over. Her plan seemed simple enough. Even if there were no positions available, she could always get a part-time job at John Sealy Hospital. She didn't date the letter because she wanted to make sure she had a buyer for her own house before she mailed it. Her thoughts went back to Trent; she wondered if he had a girlfriend. He was much too good-looking not to have at least a mistress. The thought saddened her, but encouraged her, too. There had to be other men like Trent in the world. She would take her time and find just the right man; a man who wouldn't make so many demands on her and would love her with complete tenderness. Someone directly opposite of Michael would be perfect, she decided.

Catherine twirled the small gold band on her left finger around several times and wondered what her life would have been like if her mother hadn't been murdered by David Brooks. She had tried unsuccessfully to forget about her own two-year abduction by David and her tortured life with him. It was as though she had been sent to a living hell. But for now, she had other demons to face. Michael was her pursuer now, and he was much more discrete about it. He was a fox in sheep's clothing and everyone in Rosenberg admired and respected him. She prayed her plan would work. If she could convince Michael she was going back to marry another, then he would stop pursuing her. The question was, would he believe her story? She knew when she stopped at the jewelry store and spent ten dollars on the gold-filled wedding band that she was being foolish, but it made her feel better -- and besides, it might keep other men from bothering her. She remembered when they came to America her mother, Anne, had continued to wear her small wedding band to keep strangers away.

When Catherine got off the train Michael was waiting for her. She stepped off slowly and he approached her. "Shelby told me what time you were coming back," he said as he picked up her satchel. She said you had business in Galveston."

Michael grabbed her hand and began walking with her. He felt the ring on her finger and lifted her hand up closer to take a better look and then he looked at Catherine.

"I'm engaged," she said, "And I'm sorry, Michael. It's a man I've known for a long time and we've been writing letters to each other since I left. We're getting married next spring."

Michael knew she was lying. There were no letters. One of his jobs, being on the city council, was to oversee the small post office and keep up with the new regulations. Roy Jackson, the postmaster, saw Michael every day when he came to get his mail. Michael had told Jackson about Catherine's newspaper article and that it would be best if he looked through Catherine's mail every day to see if there were any suspicious letters. Other than a couple from a priest in Galveston and catalogs from companies in Houston and Galveston, there was no other mail.

"So what was the money for that you took out of the bank?" Catherine became upset again because Michael was interfering in her financial matters but decided to tell him the truth. One lie today was enough, she thought.

"I bought a house; the same one I used to own. It had come back on the market and it was a good investment," she said, not looking at him. Michael stopped and looked at her for a long time.

"So, you are leaving Rosenberg. What about your daughters' father? Alex won't be happy about you taking them to another town," Michael said.

"I'm not planning to leave right away, but someday I would like to return to Galveston, Michael, and neither you nor Alex can stop me from going."

"What's his name?" Michael asked. "Your future husband."

"You don't know him. He's not from around here," she said and reached for her bag. Michael moved it out of her reach.

"I'll see you home," he answered. They began walking towards Michael's office.

"My house is in the other direction," she protested.

"I am expecting someone, and I need to leave a note on my door. It will only take a minute," he rationalized. Catherine felt hesitant, but so far Michael had not acted too angry, and she felt she owed him that.

Michael unlocked the door with his key and opened it, taking a step back so Catherine would go ahead of him. After they both went inside, she heard Michael click the lock shut after he closed the door. She turned and started to say something, but Michael reached for her and she ducked and ran behind his desk.

"Michael, please, please unlock the door and let me go home."

He began approaching her slowly, and she realized she had blocked herself behind his desk and there was no exit. A large file cabinet was barricaded beside his desk and the wall. Before she could think, Michael had her up against the wall and had wrapped his arms around her body and he had each hand on the wall, supporting himself as he towered over her small frame. There was nowhere she could go.

"You've taunted me, Catherine, flirted with me and even had sex with me. Do you really think I'm going to just let you shut me out because it doesn't suit you? I don't think for one minute you've conveniently found another man to marry. I think you are lying to me. He bent down to kiss her but she turned her head. A few seconds later, Michael had cupped her chin with his hand and forced his mouth upon hers.

There was a loud pounding on Michael's door; he closed his hand over her mouth and told her to be quiet. "Michael, it's Alex." and there was more pounding. Catherine's heart was beating faster and faster and she wanted to scream but couldn't. They both stood frozen in place. He continued to hold her still until he was sure Alex had left.

"I'm not through with you, yet," he whispered to Catherine. "I'll have you again, I promise." He walked over to the door and opened it. Catherine gathered her things and practically ran out the door.

When Alex left, he walked across the street and waited inside the boot store. When he saw Catherine run out the door, he went after her. "Catherine," she heard Alex call. She was close to tears but stopped, not looking at him. "Are you all right? Did Michael do something or say something to hurt you?" he asked.

She took a deep breath and tried to calm herself. "No, I was just in a hurry to get back home," she said.

Alex took her satchel and said, "Let me see you home."

They walked in silence. It was obvious something had happened at Michael's office, and it was apparent Catherine did not want to talk about it. When they got to Catherine's front porch she turned to Alex.

"I bought my old house back in Galveston and at some point I'm going to be leaving Rosenberg. Michael is determined to make my life miserable, and I don't know how long I can stand it. I know you have a right to see your daughters, but Michael won't take no for an answer. I hate him, Alex," she said. Alex walked her up the stairs to her house and they went inside and sat in the living room.

"I do understand, Catherine. As soon as the baby comes I plan to go back to my old job. I've had enough of Michael myself. I'll still come home on the weekends to be with Meredith and the baby. Meredith and I will need a bigger house. If you decide to sell your house, I might be a buyer."

"I'll take that into consideration," she answered. "I promise you can still see the girls anytime, Alex. I want them to know you as their father."

"Catherine, I'll help you any way I can. I haven't told Meredith I'm going back to work. I want to wait until after the baby comes, so I hope you won't say anything."

"Of course, I won't. I told Michael I was getting married to someone in Galveston, but he doesn't believe me," Catherine said.

"Did Michael hurt you, Catherine? I saw you come out of his office. You were with him when I knocked on the door."

"No, but I'm glad you interrupted us. Our discussion was beginning to heat up. Thank you." She stood up and Alex sensed she was ready for him to leave. "We'll talk again when I have more time," she said as he left.

Shelby and Sadie were with the children in the back of the house, and Catherine went to find them. They were all asleep on pallets they had made on the floor. She smiled at them and then took her bag upstairs. A few minutes later she was knocking on Trent's door. She went in and found him asleep. She tiptoed over and sat in the chair beside him. He was innocent of any knowledge about her past, and yet she felt like she had known him for years. His being there gave her a warm feeling and she knew she would be sad when he left. She got up and walked quietly over to the window and stared out. Trent woke up and watched her.

"Did things go well in Galveston?" he asked.

She smiled and answered, "Yes, as a matter of fact they did. Thanks for asking. Did you get your shots?" she asked.

"Jason and Shelby brought me lunch and stayed while I ate it. Then Shelby gave me my shot. Jason invited me to the wedding on Saturday, but I told him I would probably be leaving soon." When he finished talking he waited to see what Catherine was going to say, but she just looked down. He could tell she was unhappy about something but she hadn't said anything, so he decided to say nothing.

Catherine started to leave the room and then turned and asked, "Is there anything else I can do for you?"

"What I'd really like is a shave and a haircut. Jason seemed to have a lot on his plate and I felt like he was in a hurry to return to his farm to get it ready for their wedding, or I would have asked him."

Catherine smiled. "Do you mind if it's after dinner? I haven't seen my children since yesterday and I'd like to spend some time with them."

"I'm in no hurry," he said laughing, trying to get Catherine to laugh. "I'd do it myself, but I'd probably cut myself. I'm still a little weak."

Catherine gave him an incredulous look and then laughed. "I'll see you at suppertime," she said, and left.

It was after supper when Catherine came back with a basket of towels, comb, scissors, shampoo, and a large kettle of hot water. Trent was wearing his robe and was sitting up in bed.

"I had to read the children a story before putting them to bed," she explained.

"Do you ever stop and take time for yourself?" Trent asked.

"Unfortunately, private time is a luxury I can't afford. I am alone late in the evenings when the children are asleep," she said as she dragged a chair over to a table and filled the empty bowl with hot water. She began taking out the straight razor, scissors, and a comb.

"You do know how to use that thing, don't you?" Trent asked, looking at the straight razor.

Catherine laughed. "Of course; I used to shave my husband during his illness before he died. I was quite good at it," she mused.

She patted the chair and Trent got up and walked over to it and sat down. She slid his robe gently from his shoulders and put a towel around him. After she had finished shaving Trent, she stood back and looked at him for a long time.

"Is something wrong?" he asked.

"No, it's just that you look so much younger than I thought. You are quite handsome, but I'm sure you already know that. Why don't you come to the sink, and I'll wash your hair."

Trent smiled, as he was enjoying the attention as well as Catherine's innocent chatter. With Trent's beard gone, she estimated he was around thirty or even maybe younger. She was a good judge of a person's age.

When she finished, she walked him back over to the chair and dried his hair with a towel. She began cutting the hair around the back of his neck and her soft fingertips touched the side of his ear and then again as she brushed hair from the side of his neck, causing him to become aroused. She accidently dropped the comb into his lap and instinctively went to pick it up when she noticed his bulge under his robe. She hesitated and drew her hand back. Trent reached for the comb and handed it to her. He sheepishly looked up at her, took her hand and put the comb tenderly into her palm then pulled her down on his lap. It surprised her, but she didn't jump up. She sat there for a moment before she looked up at him. She reached up and kissed his cheek. Trent was just as surprised as she had been, and he wanted to enjoy the moment. He would have liked to have taken it farther, but he knew her brief kiss was her way of telling him no. Catherine slowly got up and finished Trent's haircut, carefully trying not to arouse him any further.

"I couldn't help but notice you have a new ring on your finger," he said.

"It's a promise ring," she answered.

"Who's the lucky man, Michael?"

"No, I'm afraid I've created a monster," she confessed. "I thought if I bought myself a ring and told Michael I was getting married to an old sweetheart, he would leave me alone. How stupid was that?"

"Desperate times sometimes call for desperate measures," he answered. "What are you going to do?" he asked.

"Well, I bought a house in Galveston and I'm planning to move there when all of the excavation is finished, but it's taking a long time and I'm afraid Michael isn't going to let up. His presence is much too great here in Rosenberg and at first I thought if I were nice to him that he would take no for an answer and just be friends. But it doesn't matter what I do or say, Michael is determined to have his way and frankly, I'm tired of fighting with him. I almost married him last month, thinking that I could make it work. But now that I've gotten to know him better, marriage to Michael would be a death sentence. His first wife committed suicide in a sanatorium and I can understand why." She stopped and looked away. "I'm sorry; I shouldn't be telling you all of this. I know you won't say anything to anyone, at least I hope you don't. But still, you don't need to hear about my hardships. I'll manage."

"If it helps to talk about it, I really don't mind. It's the least I can do. You've done so much for me and I've done so little for you. If there was something I could do to help you, just say the word. You saved my life and I'd like to repay you somehow."

Catherine walked Trent back to the bed and she sat in the chair next to him. She didn't know why, but she asked Trent if he would like to stay until Sunday and go to the wedding with her. "I will have your clothes laundered, and I'm sure Jason can loan you a shirt for the wedding."

"I always carry a couple extra in my saddle bags. I guess I was lucky the thieves just wanted my horse. Nothing would give me greater pleasure. Will Michael be there?"

Catherine laughed then and said, "No, thank goodness. They hardly know each other."

Trent took her hand and looked at it, turning it over and then bringing her fingers to his face. He slid her hand down the side of his face and he closed his eyes, inhaling her scent. When he looked up he noticed Catherine had also closed her eyes. When he kissed her fingertips she opened her eyes and smiled at him tenderly. She moved closer to him and stroked his hair gently then combed her fingers through his dark, smooth hair. He pulled her face to his and gently kissed her mouth; his insides began to ache with longing and desire for her. It wasn't a passionate kiss, but it was all he needed to assure himself that he wanted her. He needed her, too. He wondered if she had played this game with Michael and caused him to be obsessed with her. Whatever the reason for her flirtatious actions, he certainly wasn't going to turn her down. He also knew that if he was going to bed Catherine, it needed to be her idea. Trent released her and she slid back into her chair. Catherine bit her lower lip and looked down.

She was lonely and she felt a strong connection to Trent but she caught herself. "I'm sorry I let you kiss me."

"I'm not," he answered. "You didn't like it?"

She sighed. "Oh, I liked it all right, but I'm not the kind of woman to have sex with a stranger, and I didn't want you to get the wrong impression. It was a wonderful kiss."

"I guess it's been a while since you've been intimate with a man?" he said more as a statement. "Catherine, as a doctor you must know that women have the same needs a man does. Its better when you love each other, but--" he stopped talking when Catherine got up to leave. She began picking up her scissors and razor, and started tidying up the mess she had made when she cut his hair. Trent watched.

"I'm sorry if I said something offensive. That wasn't what I meant to do," he said softly.

"Apology accepted. I know what you were trying to say and I need to leave before I change my mind and stay. We would both regret it," she said as she walked out the door.

Thirty minutes later she came back into his room. "I didn't think I would see you again tonight," he said.

"You need your shot," was all she said as she rubbed alcohol on his arm and injected the medication with the needle. She read her Bible to him, picking up where she had left off the night before. When she finished, Trent was sound asleep and she walked around the bed and lay down beside him. Tears trickled down the side of her face onto her cheeks. As though he knew she needed him, Trent put his arm under her neck and drew her to him and kissed her on her forehead. He pulled her closer to him and they fell asleep in each other's arms.

"No, please let me go. I want to go home. Please," Catherine was crying out in her sleep and Trent gently woke her.

"Shh, you are having a bad dream. It's all right. I'm here and no one is going to hurt you," Trent assured her. He pulled her close to him and she cried for several minutes before she stopped. She started to get up, but Trent pulled her back to him.

"Stay with me, please."

Catherine was embarrassed, but moved closer to him. She rested her head on his good shoulder and fell back to sleep. Trent lay awake for a while, wondering what Catherine's life had been like. He knew very little about her except that she was a widow with four children and he knew she was lonely. She was running away from a man she disliked and she was trying to make sense of her life. She had so much responsibility for a woman her age. He guessed she couldn't be more that twenty-three or -four. He felt compassion for her but he knew there was little he could do for her. He lived in a different town and he knew long distance romances rarely worked. Besides, he was already living with another woman and he had never gotten a divorce from his first wife. The woman he was living with was also married to someone else and neither knew where their respective spouses had gone. It was a convenient relationship for both of them and until he had met Catherine he found no reason to make any changes. Mary Belle, his current lady friend made no demands on him. She was always glad to see him when he would just show up. Sometimes weeks would pass before she would even hear from him. She was a few years older than Trent, had a nice body, and was always a willing partner in bed. But something was missing in their relationship and they both knew it. Maybe it was just habit that they put up with each other. Maybe he should count his lucky stars that he even had someone to come home to. He breathed in Catherine's lovely lilac scent and kissed the top of her head. Catherine was everything Mary Belle wasn't; beautiful, compassionate, and smart. For four years now he had settled for a woman like Belle, as he called her, because it was easy and she made no demands on him. But he also knew she wasn't faithful. He had come home early from one of his trips and found Belle in bed with another man. He didn't make a scene as he felt he had no right to. Belle apologized the next day and said she would never do it again, but since that day, Trent felt differently about her. He no longer felt guilty when he left to go to work and he was especially careful not to get her pregnant. She had ruined the possibility that Trent would ever marry her, and she knew it. Trent had fallen asleep again and before daylight Catherine left his bed.

CHAPTER 13

The morning light crept in the window and Trent opened his eyes. He felt better and went into the bathroom to wash up. His shoulder was aching and he wished the pain would go away so he wouldn't have to take the shots. Maybe he could convince Catherine to just give him the pills. He stared at himself in the mirror. His hair was perfectly cut the way he always liked to wear it and even he had never given himself such a close shave. He rubbed his hand over his chin. When he heard the door open and close, he grabbed a towel and wrapped it around his waist. He peeked out, saw Catherine and walked into the room holding his towel around him.

"I wasn't expecting you for a while, but I'm glad to see you."

Catherine handed him his robe and turned around so he could put it on. Trent sat on the bed and drank the glass of fresh-squeezed orange juice Catherine had brought. After he finished his juice, Catherine changed the dressing on his wound and told him it was healing nicely. She seemed distant and quiet. Trent didn't know what to make of it and then asked her what time it was. She told him it was around eight thirty in the morning.

"You said there was an express train at ten o'clock in the morning and I think I'll try and make it," Trent said.

Catherine was surprised by his sudden need to leave, but in a way she was relieved. Trent had been a nice diversion but she was feeling an attachment to him and if he stayed a few more days it would be harder to see him go.

"I'll go get your clothes and bring them to you. Promise me you'll see a doctor right away. I'll write down the name of a good doctor who will see to your health."

Catherine left, and Trent walked to the window and watched her. He saw the hurt in her eyes when he told her he was going to leave. He had hoped she would talk him out of it, but she didn't. He had been there four days yet he felt like he was leaving his best friend.

A few minutes later he saw Catherine coming out of her house; one of her sons followed her out, crying "Mama." Catherine turned and bent down. She ran her fingers through his curly blond hair, bent down and kissed him. He put his arms around her neck and she picked him up and took him back into the house. She returned a few minutes later with Trent's clothes.

"There is no way I can thank you. I'll leave my company calling card for you to send the bill," Trent said, taking the clothes. Catherine handed Trent a piece of paper with Dr. Samuel Allen's phone number on it. She also handed him a small paper candy sack with some pills in it.

"It's important that you take the medicine in this bag. The directions are in there. Dr. Allen is with Houston General and he will see you get the care you need. After you see Dr. Allen, ask him to call me and I'll give him an update on your condition. Promise me you'll go straight to Houston General. You are still not out of the woods," she said. Trent assured her he would. "When you are dressed, come down to the kitchen and have some coffee. Your train doesn't leave for forty-five more minutes."

Catherine was stirring the oatmeal when she saw Trent through the glass window in the door. She opened it for him and looked up into his blazing hazel eyes as he towered over her. She pulled out a chair for him to sit in and poured coffee into an empty cup. "Would you like some oatmeal? It's easy and the children like it," she said in an apologizing manner.

"Oatmeal is fine," he answered. One by one the children came to the table. Their chattering had stopped when they witness Trent's intrusion on their ritualistic breakfast of oatmeal. He smiled at them and only Adam was brave enough to speak. "You the man someone shot. Does it still hurt?"

Trent laughed. "As a matter of fact, your mama took all the hurt away. You should be proud of her."

Adam grinned at his mother. Adam continued asking more questions and Catherine made a gesture to him, putting her finger over her mouth to try and quiet him. He stopped to take a few bites of his oatmeal and then belched. "Schuse me," he said softly.

Shelby joined them for breakfast and Catherine told her that after she walked Trent to the train station she had permission to leave so she could get ready for her wedding.

"You are coming to our wedding?" Shelby asked, looking at Trent.

"I have intruded on Dr. Merit's privacy long enough. It's time I return to my home in Houston," Trent answered.

Catherine and Trent walked in silence to the train station. Trent held his right arm close to his body to prevent movement and he carried his saddlebag in his left hand. Catherine offered to carry it, but he refused. The train was five minutes early, so Catherine walked Trent to it. "Promise me you'll go straight to the hospital," she said.

"I promise," he said looking down at Catherine.

It was difficult, but Catherine stood on her tiptoes, put her arms around Trent's neck, pulled his face down to hers and kissed his lips. She had opened her mouth slightly, enveloping his thick, pink lips, and he opened his mouth and met her tongue with his. It was the sweetest, most enduring kiss he had ever experienced, and she shivered.

Catherine slowly pulled away and said, "Until we meet again." Trent smiled and boarded the train.

Catherine walked back over and stood by a bench with her

arms folded, watching as the train pulled away from the station. Trent had found a seat by the window and watched as the train passed by her. She looked sad, but forced a smile and gently waved her hand. Trent smiled and waved back, wondering if he would ever see her again.

On the way back from the train station, Catherine heard a horse galloping up behind her. She moved over closer to the side of the road and looked back. It was Sheriff Raymond Wade. He got down off his horse and tipped his hat. "Afternoon, Dr. Merit. We caught the thief who shot Trent Matthews and he's in jail. They are keeping his horse at the livery stable until he is well enough to fetch it. He'll need to stop by the jail and give us a statement. I know he said he didn't see his face, but maybe seeing him will jar his memory."

"He just left on the train back to Houston, but I'll let him know so he or someone from his company can get it," Catherine said. The sheriff tipped his hat again and mounted his horse.

It was two o'clock when the phone finally rang. Catherine had been anxiously waiting, hoping that Trent had followed her instructions to go straight to Houston General.

"Catherine," she smiled when she heard Samuel's familiar voice. It had been a few months since she had spoken to him and she was surprised at herself when she realized she missed him so much.

"Samuel, it's good to hear from you."

"I've seen your patient, and his x-rays show it was a clean wound. He told me you had taken good care of him. His wound is healing nicely. We are going to keep him overnight just to be sure. What are those pills you sent him back with?" Samuel asked.

Catherine was hurt that Samuel didn't even ask how she was and acted totally professional with her. She replied, "They are antibacterial and healing pills I purchased from a Chinese doctor in Houston."

"Well, like I said, he's going to stay overnight and be released tomorrow. I appreciate the referral. You take care, now," he said, hanging up the phone. She had heard his name being called over the loudspeaker and wondered if he was extremely busy, or if his friendship with her no longer mattered. She hadn't spoken to him in a while and he was going to be a father soon. Still, she felt slighted; like he had suddenly turned on her and now she was alone again with no one. She had meant to ask Samuel to tell Trent that his horse was at the livery stable in Rosenberg, but his abruptness took her off guard and she forgot. She went to her office and picked up Trent's calling card.

Catherine introduced herself again when Agnes Harper answered the phone at Humble Oil Company. Agnes was pleasant and informed Catherine that Trent had called her and she had called Trent's girlfriend to inform her that he was in the hospital. They would see to everything on their end. Catherine relayed the conversation she had with the sheriff and Agnes assured her that it would be taken care of.

When Catherine returned the receiver to the phone she sat down and looked at Trent's card. Trent hadn't said anything about a girlfriend to her, but then she had only asked if he had been married. She sighed, feeling relieved that Trent was an honorable man and had decided to leave. She knew they both felt a connection to each other but he must have wanted to stay true to his girlfriend. It pleased her that there were still men who had morals and stayed true to their monogamous relationships.

Trent wasn't happy when he returned from the x-ray room and found Mary Belle waiting for him. He wondered how she knew he had gone there. Dr. Samuel Allen entered the room and gave Trent a good report, but said that he wanted to keep him overnight just to be sure the infection was gone. Trent had wanted to talk to Dr. Allen in private about Catherine Merit, but Mary Belle would not take the hint to leave. She watched over him like a mother hen. Catherine had told Trent she had known Dr. Allen for several years and had met him at

St. Mary's Hospital. He figured he would be able to find out more about Catherine's past from Dr. Allen.

When Trent woke up the next morning he quickly dressed himself. He had just finished tying his shoes when Mary Belle came in. She had sensed a change in Trent's demeanor towards her. He had been irritable and curt with her the night before, but she decided he was still in pain from his injury.

"I could have gotten home on my own. You didn't have to miss work," he snapped at her.

"I wanted to be here for you," she said softly.

Trent decided he would wait until they got to her house before he told her he was moving back to his old place. He still paid rent on a small room in a boardinghouse and would often go back there after his trips in order to clean up and change, but he still had a lot of things at Mary Belle's house.

Dr. Allen came in and gave him a prescription for some medication. "I'm not sure what those pills are Dr. Merit gave you. I don't have any information about them, but I'm sure she has done her research on them and they have obviously helped you. Understand that I'm not responsible if you have a bad reaction to her medication. It's entirely up to you to take whatever pills you want, but I can only be responsible for what I give you. I don't recommend you take them both at the same time. Choose one or the other," he remarked and left.

"You need to get rid of those pills that lady doctor gave you. If Dr. Allen doesn't know what they are, there's no telling what's in them," Mary Belle whined. Trent gave her an incredulous look but didn't say anything.

When Trent got back to Mary Belle's house, he went to the closet and took out an old suitcase and opened it on the bed. Mary Belle watched as he emptied the two drawers he used and took the remainder of his things from the closet they shared. He heard her sniffling and stopped to look at her.

"It's been over for a long time," he finally said. "You and me;

I guess finding you in our bed with another man affected me more than I realized."

"I told you I wasn't in love with him. I only love you, Trent. Please don't leave me like this," she whimpered.

"Then look at me and tell me it was just a one-time fling," he said. She looked away and didn't answer. "I thought so," he said, closing his suitcase.

He took a key out of his pocket and laid it on the table when he left. He felt a weight lifted from his shoulders when he got into the street, and wondered why he had hung around so long. There was one more thing he had to do. After he dropped off his belongings at his rooming house he stopped at a lawyer's office down the street from his own office. He had met the man a couple of times at a business luncheon and he seemed intelligent enough. After the men shook hands, Trent told him he wanted to get a divorce from his wife whom he had not seen in years and he had no idea where she lived. The lawyer told him it would take a month or two. Notices had to be sent out to her last known address, and published in the newspaper. Trent paid him a retainer of twenty dollars in cash and told him to get on it.

"Trent," Agnes Harper said, surprised to see him, "You were supposed to be at the hospital."

"Doctor released me," he answered.

"Wonderful; and I got some good news to tell you. They caught that terrible man who stole your horse and he's in jail. The thief, I mean. Your horse is at the livery stable in Rosenberg. I was going to send one of our men after it tomorrow," she said.

"Don't do that," Trent said.

"Well, the sheriff wants to talk to you anyway, so I guess it would be best for you to go get him yourself; when you are up to it, of course. Makes no difference if the horse is at our livery stable or theirs, as long as he is being tended to." Agnes got up and gave Trent a hug.

"Sure glad it wasn't your time," she said. "I been prayin' for ya."

Trent walked down the hall to one of the back offices. It was just a hole in the wall, but it was private and had a telephone in it. Catherine had also written down her phone number and he asked the operator to place the call for him. A young woman answered: "Dr. Merit's office, Sadie speaking."

"Hi, Sadie, this is Trent Matthews; I was wondering if Dr. Merit was free?"

"Hold on," was all she said.

He really didn't know what he was going to say to her, but he just wanted to hear her voice.

"How are you, Trent?"

"Much better, thanks to you. Dr. Allen kept me overnight and said you had done a great job on stitching up my wound and taking care of me. He said the infection was gone. He wasn't familiar with the medication you had given me and gave me another prescription, but I'm taking your pills and not his. He said to choose one or the other, and since I got better so fast I decided to keep taking yours."

"I agree; you shouldn't take both medications. Did Agnes tell you what the sheriff said?"

"That's one of the reasons why I called. I thought I would come back Sunday on the morning train, and I'd like to see you. I'll get a room at the hotel," he said.

"You can stay in the carriage house but I have to warn you, I haven't had time to clean it up."

"Good, I'll do that for you. It's the least I can do. See you about half past ten?"

"Yes, I'll be looking forward to it."

When Catherine hung up the phone she felt a twinge of excitement. Trent was coming back. She sighed, wondering if she would be able to resist his beautiful body. He had a girlfriend, she remembered, and that was all the resistance she needed. But it was nice to fantasize about being with someone. Just having someone to hold her would be nice. She smiled to herself and went about her day.

The small wedding ceremony was intimate and there was no doubt in her mind that Jason and Shelby were very much in love. Jason's grandfather was best man; Catherine stood beside Shelby and wished that her own family would have cared enough to come. Sadie wore one of Catherine's dresses and acted as the bride's maid. It was heartwarming, and Shelby looked beautiful in a pale-pink gown Catherine had loaned her. It was a gown Catherine had worn when she was first pregnant with Emma. Rose, Jason's grandmother, had made a headband and used old lace and fresh flowers as decorations, and Shelby looked beautiful. Afterwards, Rose had prepared an enormous feast. Shelby and Jason had decided to take the late afternoon train to Galveston for their short honeymoon. Catherine had recommended they stay at the Tremont and had counseled Jason on how to arrange his accommodations. Shelby had hoped that Jason would be able to meet her parents for lunch the next day. Her mother had agreed and assured Shelby that her father would be there no matter what.

The children were exceptionally good throughout the ceremony and lunch, but she could see that Adam was getting tired and a bit irritable so she held him in her lap on their ride home.

Catherine and Sadie spent their time straightening up the house and Catherine left during nap time to go to the grocery store. She didn't think Michael would be at his office on Saturday afternoon, but in any event she was going to make sure she was not alone with him. When she got home she took clean sheets upstairs to the carriage house and made a quick bed change. She swept the room and brought up more firewood.

Sunday morning Catherine heard the whistle blow on the incoming train and she couldn't help but be a little excited. Trent was easygoing and his presence was intoxicating. He was probably one of the most interesting looking men she had ever seen. She had just put a roast in the oven when the doorbell rang. Catherine took off her apron and checked her hair and face in the mirror. She pinched her cheeks tightly hoping it would give them some color, and then put a big smile on her face.

Trent grinned widely when Catherine answered the door. He leaned down and kissed her on the cheek once they got into the house. She blushed and took his hat. "How's the shoulder?"

"Still a bit sore, but it's healing nicely." Trent followed her through the house and out the back door. "How was the wedding yesterday?"

"It was just beautiful. I'm sorry you couldn't make it." When they entered the room, the fire had already taken the chill out of the air.

"I thought you were going to let me clean up the place. It's immaculate."

"I had a little extra time and it didn't take that long," she answered. "I'll let you get settled. There is an empty chest of drawers and you can put your things in there. The closed door here is the closet." Trent smiled at her and she suddenly felt like a love-struck teenager. She turned to look at Trent one more time before she left. "I, uh, just make yourself comfortable and you are welcome to join us in the house anytime."

Trent hung up a few of his clothes and took off his gun and shoulder holster so he would be more comfortable. He didn't always travel with a gun when he rode the train, but since his accident he decided it couldn't hurt to have it in case of an emergency. He looked at himself in the small mirror and ran his hand through his hair like a comb. For some reason he had butterflies in his stomach. It surprised him that Catherine affected him that way. He had forgotten how beautiful she was. Today, she did not have her hair pulled back and tied. It was hanging freely over her shoulders and it fell loosely down her back. He liked it that way, he decided.

Catherine was in the kitchen preparing lunch when he came in and offered to help. She gave him the knives and forks and suggested he could set the table. They bumped into each other a couple of times, and by the third time it became funny and Trent spun her around on the floor like he was dancing with her. They laughed and teased each other. Everything seemed so normal, and Catherine couldn't remember laughing so much. She teased Trent for being a gentle giant and he teased her about being his guardian angel. After the food was placed on the table family style, Trent commented that she had enough food to feed an army.

"I usually cook extra on Sunday so we can have leftovers."

"Roast beef, sausage, potatoes, corn, and green beans," Trent said and licked his lips. He backed away when Catherine brought the rolls out of the oven.

"Would you like to call the children while I fill the glasses with milk? They are just through that door," she said pointing to it.

He nodded his head and left. The children came running into the kitchen with Sadie and Trent. Adam was in Trent's arms. "Look, Mommy, I'm taller than you," Adam said proudly.

They held hands and bowed their heads while each child said their own individual prayer. Trent couldn't help but notice how patient Catherine was with her children. They were rambunctious but yet well-mannered. Trent had never spent much time around children, but he marveled at their innocence and questions.

"Your mom is really a great cook," Trent said to the children.

"Yeah, except sometimes she burns stuff," Adam added.

Everyone burst out laughing. Catherine's two daughters seemed to have a conversation all their own. Trent found it hard to understand them. They still spoke in baby talk and each time one of them said something Catherine would translate what they said. He found it fascinating.

Trent helped Catherine clean up the kitchen while Sadie put the children down for their naps. She had made coffee and put two cups on a tray. She had made hot tea for herself but knew Trent preferred coffee. They went back into the living room to visit and drink their beverages.

"Dr. Allen is a busy doctor. They were paging him constantly and I guess he must work night and day. I don't think he left the hospital the whole time I was there," Trent commented.

Catherine explained that most doctors worked in twenty-four and sometimes forty-eight hour shifts without sleeping.

"You get used to it. When I worked at the hospital in Galveston, we were so busy we worked constantly and the time would fly by."

"What made you want to become a doctor?" Trent asked.

"For some reason, after my mother was killed, I just knew I wanted to go to college. The sisters at the orphanage encouraged me," she said. "I was really quite good in math and science, and I fell in love with learning all I could about the human body."

"Wait a minute," Trent said. "Your mother was killed and you were put in an orphanage?"

Catherine refilled their cups and proceeded to explain how she and her mother had come to Galveston from England after her father, brother, and sister died. She briefly told Trent about David Brooks and his infatuation with her mother. She became sad thinking about it and then asked Trent how he had become an oil scout.

"My dad worked for an oil company and insisted I go to college and follow in his footsteps. He worked more in the fields erecting the rigs, overseeing the men who did the actual work, and reporting back to the higher-ups. My older brother worked with him. They both worked for Humble Oil until they were killed in a terrible accident on the job. I was in college. My mom died shortly thereafter of a broken heart. She was frail and sick a lot and she just couldn't get past their deaths."

Catherine touched Trent's hand and told him she was sorry.

"Looks like we have both had our share of sorrow," he said.

They talked about everything until Isabelle came in and told Catherine she had wet her panties. Catherine hugged her and excused herself to get Isabelle clean panties. Trent looked around the beautifully furnished living room and wondered how Catherine kept up the house, took care of the children, and had a medical practice. He knew Sadie helped with the kids, but still he couldn't help but be impressed with Catherine's ability to juggle so many things.

Catherine motioned for Trent to follow her and they went to the back room, which looked like a school room. It had a blackboard, a bookcase filled with books, and a large table with scissors, colors, and paper. He watched as they make more animals out of paper and clothespins. He sat at the table with them and also tried to cut out an animal. The children laughed when Trent couldn't put his fingers through the holes of the scissors. Trent put the scissors down and began tearing strips of newspaper, making a chain of circles and interlocking them together with paste to make a long chain. The children watched and began copying him. When they had finished, it was almost six feet long, and Trent made a corral out of the chain. Afterwards they collected all of the homemade animals and put them inside the corral. They had taken a box and put it by the corral; the box served as the barn. Each child would take a turn and talk about what kind of animal they had made and why, and then they had to make the kind of sound the animal made. Everyone was having a great time giggling and laughing when each one made the sound of a pig or a horse. It had been a beautiful day filled with laugher, fun, singing, eating and being a family. Catherine had just finished washing her last dish when Trent put down his cup towel and came up behind Catherine. He put his arms around her waist and bent down and kissed the side of her neck.

"If this is what family and home is all about, I think I've been missing something. It's been a wonderful day. Thank you for including me," Trent said. Catherine pulled Trent's arms closer around her and he grimaced as the pain shot through his shoulder.

"I'm sorry. I forgot about your shoulder," she said, turning around and facing him. He stood a good twelve inches taller than she stood and he bent down as he tilted her chin up. She met his lips as she stood on her tiptoes. Their kisses became more passionate and needy but finally Trent released her.

"I'll be leaving early in the morning to start working again. It's all around Rosenberg, and I'd like to rent the carriage house during my assignment if you don't mind. I don't expect you to cook for me or do anything extra. I'll be coming and going, but each time I come back I'll knock on your door and let you or Sadie know I'm here. Would that be all right?" he asked.

Catherine was so surprised that Trent's attitude had suddenly changed. Now he was discussing a business transaction. She hesitated, trying to take it all in. "Yes, of course," she said.

"I pay seven dollars a week in Houston. Is that acceptable to you?" he asked.

"Yes, it's more than enough."

Trent thanked her again for the wonderful day and told her he would see her in a day or two. He could tell by Catherine's lack of words that he had surprised her. He knew he could have gotten her into bed -- if not tonight, the next -- but he didn't want to take advantage of a lonely young woman who was hungry for a relationship. He wanted more; he wanted her to love him. He didn't want to bed her without a commitment and he knew it would take some time.

CHAPTER 14

The next morning Catherine was up early; she looked out the kitchen window and saw a glow from the lantern in Trent's room. She had not slept well the night before and she was glad Trent had not pursued her yet she felt terribly rejected. She should have been the one to say no, but she wasn't given that opportunity. She reminded herself again that Trent had a girlfriend and she wondered why God continued to test her. She was Eve waiting for Adam to hand her the apple, and she was hungry for it. And yes, last night she would have probably taken a bite of the apple. Forgive me, Jesus. I'm so weak, she silently prayed. She looked up when she heard Trent knock on the door.

"Good morning. Are you always an early riser?" he asked.

"It's the only time of the day I can get anything done around here. Would you like some coffee before you leave?" she asked, getting a cup and saucer from the cupboard.

"Sure." Trent took off his hat and pulled out his chair.

"Are Mondays usually busy at the clinic?" he asked.

"Sometimes; it will be this morning because I was closed last Friday."

Trent smiled at her and sipped his coffee. They made small talk and laughed about the fun they had on Sunday and then Trent got up, thanked her for the coffee, and left.

Once again, Catherine felt a sense of rejection, and busied

herself getting breakfast ready for the children. Trent was constantly in her thoughts, though. He had flirted with her, encouraged her, and now he rejected her. She shrugged off the idea that he just didn't like women. He obviously did, since he had a girlfriend. Her thoughts continued to go back to Trent off and on during the day and she struggled to put him out of her mind.

Catherine was surprised to find Meredith in the waiting room when she opened the clinic. It was Shelby's first day back and she was eager to help Catherine with her patients. Shelby appeared to seem happy, but Catherine felt something was just not quite right. "Why don't you show Meredith into the examination room and I'll meet you there," she asked.

Catherine greeted Meredith and inquired how she was feeling and she replied, "I'm feeling very well, but I have some concerns that I hope you don't find difficult to talk to me about, I mean since you and Alex were once married, but my belly is getting full and I was wondering if I should let my husband continue to be intimate with me," she said awkwardly.

Meredith looked at Shelby, who acted a bit embarrassed, and Catherine said, "Shelby and Jason just got married over the weekend."

Shelby put her hands on her belly and looked down at the floor. "Do you mind if I listen? My honeymoon was difficult because I, too, was concerned about being intimate with Jason. He was so sweet and gentle, but I felt terrible that I couldn't relax, so we didn't do anything."

Catherine smiled and turned to Meredith. "As long as you don't feel any pain, being intimate should be fine. Have you ever tried getting on top of him?"

Meredith blushed and looked away. "Alex had mentioned that, but I'm afraid it might hurt."

"God made man and woman to be intimate with each other, Meredith, and there is more than one way to make love. All of it can be very pleasing and you should not be afraid. Just take it slowly and if you find it hurts, you can stop. Alex seems to be a very patient man and," Catherine stopped when she began to visualize Alex making love to her on their wedding night. "I think I hear one of the children crying," Catherine said and excused herself.

Meredith watched as Catherine went upstairs. She wondered if Catherine still had feelings for Alex and she wondered if she and Alex had explored different ways of making love. She knew Catherine would remember, but Alex probably didn't. Yet, she was uncomfortable about her and Catherine's conversation. She turned to Shelby and the two girls began discussing their relationships with their husbands. They were both laughing when Catherine returned fifteen minutes later. They had both decided they would take Catherine's advice. After all she was a doctor and she had four children. Meredith asked Shelby and Jason to come for dinner Wednesday evening and Shelby was delighted. Catherine smiled as Meredith left. She was happy the two couples were getting together.

That evening Meredith prepared Alex's favorite dinner and began giving him sensual looks at the dinner table. Alex reached over and took her hand. "Is something on your mind?" he asked.

"I spoke with Catherine today and she told me it was perfectly safe to continue our intimacy and she gave me some suggestions as to how we could make it better," she said, feeling embarrassed.

"I didn't know it could get any better," he said, smiling back at her. "What did she suggest?"

"I would rather show you than explain it," she answered.

"I'm game," he said, smiling. Meredith got up from the table and walked around behind him. She wrapped her arms around his shoulders and kissed him on the neck. When she kissed him behind the ear she saw the goose bumps appear on his neck.

"She suggested I get on top," she whispered.

Alex immediately got up and picked her up in his arms. The bedroom wasn't very far, and when he stood her up beside the bed to start undressing her, she kissed him passionately on the mouth and began undressing him.

Shelby greeted her husband with a smile and told him she had a surprise for him after dinner. He hugged her and told her how much he loved her and that he was the happiest man in the world.

Their honeymoon had been a disaster. Shelby froze every time Jason touched her in their wedding bed and lunch with her parents was even worse. Shelby's father lectured her on her irrational decisions and told Jason he would never be good enough for his daughter. Jason took everything in stride, but Shelby began to withdraw from him after her parents left and they took the next train home. Jason had slept on the floor that night, not wanting his grandparents to know he had failed as a husband. He had been patient, but thought he might talk to Dr. Merit in a few days if the situation didn't improve.

After Shelby and Jason helped his grandmother clean the kitchen, Jason joined his grandfather by the fireplace and waited for the women to join them in the living room. They visited for a while and soon the older couple retired to their room. Jason looked at Shelby and asked what she wanted to talk to him about. She joined him on the couch.

"You have been a wonderful husband, Jason, and I'm sorry I was self-conscious and afraid on our wedding night. I want to make it up to you. I spoke with Dr. Merit today and she told me it would not hurt the baby and that we could do whatever felt right. Could we maybe, you know," blushing as she tried to finished her sentence.

Jason put his arm around her and they kissed. He picked her up in his arms and took her to their bed. She pulled the covers back before Jason laid her down, and they slowly began removing each other's clothes. Jason had also felt awkward. While he wasn't a virgin, he had only bedded a couple of women and the sexual encounters were over in a few minutes. He and his grandfather had had several talks over the past week and his grandfather had given

Jason pointers about how to please his wife. He was cautious and gentle with Shelby as they removed each other's clothing, giving each other soft kisses and touching each other in appropriate places. He felt Shelby begin to relax before he tried stroking her abdomen. He bent down and kissed her protruding belly and jumped back when he felt the baby kick. They both laughed, removing any tension there might have been between them. She pulled Jason's hand between her legs and their lovemaking became more passionate. It wasn't long before Shelby gently eased herself on top of Jason's erection, and the two eagerly consumed one another until they both fulfilled their needs. Jason knew he had pleased Shelby. She had collapsed on the bed beside him and began kissing his neck and nudging herself closer to him. He thought he had died and gone to heaven. In his young life, he had never felt such gratification and it was apparent Shelby felt the same way. They both fell asleep, peacefully holding each other, and Shelby got up in the middle of the night to use the bathroom. When she returned, she began stroking Jason's immediate arousal and they had sex again; this time it was more passionate, more erotic, and more satisfying.

The next day when Jason dropped Shelby off at Catherine's office, he told her to thank Dr. Merit. "I will do no such thing," she grinned, "I think she will know when she sees my happy face. Besides, I'm an hour late."

Catherine didn't comment when she saw Shelby come in. Catherine was with a patient and Shelby proceeded with helping her. After the patient was gone, Catherine couldn't help but smile at Shelby. She was happy for her and the two women hugged.

"I was going to talk to you before my honeymoon, but Trent was taking up all of your extra time. I brought it all on myself. But it's fixed now. Jason couldn't be happier and neither am I. Thank you so much, Catherine," she said. "It was magnificent."

Catherine went into her office and left Shelby to clean up. She was happy for her, but still she ached silently when she remembered her first night with John Merit. She, too, had been apprehensive and after she had read the books about men's and women's anatomy, her fears went away and hers and John's intimacy was wonderful. She wondered if she would ever be intimate with a man again. In the beginning she thought sex was a wife's duty and it was inappropriate to enjoy it. She was glad she could help both Shelby and Meredith with their fears. She hadn't spoken to Meredith, and again became sad when she thought about Meredith and Alex having intimate relations together. Alex had been a wonderful gentle, yet passionate lover to her in the short months they had been married. Both he and John Merit had taught her the wonderful gift of intimacy; and then there had been Samuel. Oh yes, Samuel, she sighed. Their lovemaking had been more erotic, and she leaned her head back and she felt herself become aroused thinking about her sexual encounters with Samuel. Being a doctor, he was totally uninhibited and they had had sex on the floor, in the bathtub, and even standing up. She smiled to herself and then put her head down on her arms on her desk and began to cry. The day she had let herself go and had sex with Michael was the beginning of a horrible nightmare. He felt like she belonged to him after that and she knew getting away from him was going to be difficult. Her thoughts were interrupted when Shelby knocked on the door and told her another patient was waiting. She checked her appearance in the mirror and pinched her cheeks to bring the color back. After taking a deep breath and walking out, she came face-to-face with Alex.

"I stopped by to see the children and I asked Shelby to tell you that you had a patient. I hope you don't mind." Shelby had left the room and Catherine asked Alex how he was feeling.

"I'm feeling great, thanks to you. Meredith told me she had a talk with you yesterday and I wanted to thank you." Catherine looked down and blushed. Even being a doctor, it was sometimes hard to remember, when certain matters were being discussed, that she was not only a doctor, but a woman. She had been brought up not to discuss matters of such a nature with men and it was especially awkward with Alex, since he had no memory of their intimacy when they were married.

"I still have not told Meredith about our visit regarding my old job. The baby will be here in a couple of months and then I hope she'll be open to moving out from under Michael's thumb. You had mentioned selling the house and I'm hoping you will let me have the first chance at buying it. Knowing Michael, he'll probably try to buy it back himself just so I can't."

"Of course, I give you my word. I will be taking most of the furniture with me since the house I bought has none. I'll be leaving some of it though, but I'll make a list for you. Thank you for understanding why I have to leave. I'll put the figures together. I purchased the house and property at a good price, but I spent a good deal of money on repairs and improvements. I don't care whether I make a profit."

Alex walked over to her and put his hands on her shoulders, bent down and kissed Catherine on the cheek. "You are an incredible woman, Catherine, and I hope you will find the happiness you deserve." She didn't move when Alex released her and left. Here she was, once again, in need of something more.

Trent had left on Monday and didn't return until after lunch on Wednesday. Each night before he returned Catherine would go out on the back porch and look up at his window. She still couldn't understand why she was so drawn to Trent. Perhaps it was his rejection of her. Did she just want what she knew she couldn't have, she wondered. Was that the reason Michael felt so possessive of her? She was in the kitchen when she happened to glance out the window and saw Trent carrying his saddle bags upstairs. She watched and hoped he would not turn around and see her staring. Saturday was Catherine's twenty-third birthday and she felt sad because it meant Trent would probably be going back to Houston. She wondered if their kiss the other night was their last. She had put a ham in the oven earlier and she opened the oven door to check on it. She closed the oven door and walked over to hang her apron up on the hook by the backdoor, and saw Trent. She broke into a smile immediately, and when he came in it was all she could do not to run into his arms.

"I hope I didn't scare you when you looked up," he said. "I saw you were busy."

"It's all right," she said. "I was just checking on a ham I had put in the oven. Will you be staying for dinner?" she asked.

"If that's an invitation, I accept."

"When do you plan to go back to Houston?" she asked.

"I still have to complete some work, so as soon as I finish that, I'll go back."

"Oh," Catherine said. "But you'll be going back to Houston for the weekend?"

"I'm not sure," he answered. He was certainly being evasive about her questions, she thought, and guessed that maybe his girlfriend lived somewhere else. She decided she had asked enough questions, and it really wasn't her business anyway.

After dinner that evening Trent helped Catherine with the dishes again but kept his distance. After he had left to go to his room, she saw an envelope on the table with her name on it. She hesitated for a few minutes before opening it. There was forty dollars in it with a note that said *thanks for everything*. She sat down in a chair and stared at it. Her eyes filled with tears and she crumbled the money in her hand and threw it across the table. Catherine tore the envelope and note into small pieces. She continued to pick up the pieces and tear them in half once more until it became a game. She pulled a chair over to some cabinets and stood up in the chair. There was a bottle of scotch on the top shelf; she reached for it and then took out a glass. She sat at the table, staring at the bottle and empty glass. She rarely drank but for some reason tonight she just felt like having one. She decided to tuck the children in before she poured herself a glass. She wasn't going to get drunk, but darn close to it, she thought.

She returned to the kitchen after the children had gone to bed and lit a small candle. After turning off the overhead light she sat down at the table and poured herself a drink. The small pieces of paper she had torn up were still scattered over the table and she began scooping them into a pile. She finished the first shot of scotch and poured herself another. She began to relax as the effects of the scotch made her warm and giddy, and then she blew lightly on the pile of scraps and they scattered again. She slowly scooped them up again, giggling as she did. She jumped when she heard a soft knock on the window. Trent had been watching her from outside for the last five minutes and decided he needed to go in before she got drunk.

"Do you often drink alone?" he asked.

She sat up in an erect position and said firmly, "Yes, when I feel like it."

"Mind if I have a drink, too?" he asked, then went over and retrieved a glass from the cabinet.

"Suit yourself."

"Looks like you have some kind of game going on. Don't let me stop you," he said.

Catherine took another drink and scooped the pieces of paper toward her. She picked up two of the larger pieces of paper, tore them in half and then blew the pile away again. Trent watched as her eyes fixated on scooping the pieces back into a pile once more. She took another drink and then picked up the bottle of scotch to pour herself another. Trent grabbed her hand and took the bottle from her. She stared up at him. Trent wasn't sure why she was intent on getting drunk, but he didn't like what she was doing to herself.

"Why are you here, Trent Matthews?"

He looked at her, not sure how to answer. "What do you mean?" he asked.

"It's a simple question, why are you here and not with your girlfriend back home?" Catherine wanted to take it back the minute she asked the question, and looked away.

"First of all, I don't have a girlfriend and like I told you, I have work here."

Catherine looked down at the pile of papers on the table. Now Trent was a liar. How stupid was she to think he might a different? Catherine stood up quickly and announced she was going to bed -- and immediately passed out. Trent caught her before she fell to the floor. He took her into the living room and laid her on the couch. He stared at her for a long time and wondered what had happened to make her start drinking. He had been gone almost three days, and it could be anything. Maybe Michael had something to do with it. Then he remembered her saying something about him going back home to his girlfriend. And tearing up the envelope and letter he left for her, what was that all about?"

Trent went back to the kitchen and noticed the two crumpled-up twenties lying on the floor. He straightened them out and laid them on the table beside the torn-up paper. He finished the drink Catherine had poured him. He thought about just leaving right then, but he was tired and figured he would try and get a couple hours sleep and head back to Houston in the morning. Oh, what the heck, he thought. The scotch tasted good, so he poured one more drink. He looked up and saw Catherine standing in the doorway.

"I'm sorry," she said. "You must think I've lost my mind, but I assure you, I've never done this sort of thing before. Today I just felt overwhelmed." Catherine walked over, picked up a dish towel and wiped her eyes with it. She saw the money on the table and picked it up. She folded the twenties and stuck them in her pocket. "Thank you for the money. It's more than enough. Please lock the backdoor when you leave. Good night."

Trent was overwhelmed, too. If he were smart, he would get his things and go to the local hotel. A lonely widow with four children was a big responsibility and he was becoming attached to her. Through all her self-made barriers and showing everyone that she could do it alone, she was beginning to fall apart. Could he just leave her like this or risk staying and fall in love with her only to be rejected like Michael. It wasn't his nature to walk away from trouble and even if he decided not to stay he couldn't leave her like this. He decided to wait until the next morning and make sure it was just as she said it was; a bad day. If she was all right in the morning, he figured he would just go back to Houston and see if Toby's wife had had their baby.

Catherine woke early the next morning with a throbbing headache. Not only did her head hurt, but she cringed when she remembered how foolish she had acted the night before. Trent probably thought she had gone crazy. She made coffee first and then put her kettle of water on the stove to make her some hot tea and honey. She took two aspirin and walked over to the table where the small pieces of paper still sat; remnants of her irrational actions. Catherine swept them into the trash can. She put the bottle of scotch on top of the ice box and was tempted to just pour it out, but decided to leave it. She noticed the light coming through the upstairs window of the carriage house and was glad Trent had not left yet. She wanted to apologize for acting so foolishly.

She cracked eggs into a bowl for scrambled eggs and put some bacon on to fry. If this was the last time she was going to see Trent, she wanted him to see her as a normal woman taking care of her family, not the drunk she was the night before. She laid bread out on a pan to toast in the oven and then heard a tap on the window. When she looked up and saw Trent, she smiled and opened the door for him. In spite of her throbbing headache she acted as if nothing had happened. She asked Trent if he had slept well and said that she would have breakfast ready shortly. Trent watched as she went through the motions of pouring his coffee into a cup and returning to the stove to turn the bacon.

"How are you feeling this morning?" he asked.

"Great," she said cheerfully. "You know, I was thinking that if you decided to stay in Rosenberg over the weekend, I mean, the children and I would be happy to have you join us. I'm not much on birthday parties, but I'll be twenty-three on Saturday and I thought I would have a little party for me and the children. I understand if you have to get back." She was rambling, and stopped herself before she said something she would be sorry for.

"Would you like for me to stay?" he asked in his low, husky voice.

"Yes, I would," she said. Trent got up from the table and walked over to the stove.

"I'd love to Catherine," he said, and put his arms around her and hugged her. "You've got to stop running away from your feelings." Catherine turned and put her arms around his waist, hugging him back.

"So you really don't have a girlfriend?" she asked.

"Not anymore. I've been living with a woman for the past four years but when I went home last week I broke up with her. You made me see things differently, Catherine. My relationship with Belle was simply a convenience. A few months back I came home and found her in bed with another man; she convinced me it had only happened once, but I felt differently about her and I guess I just stayed out of habit. We were still both married to someone else."

Catherine's jaw dropped open and she stepped away from him. Trent turned off the burner because the bacon had begun to burn. "Hear me out, Catherine.

"My wife left me for another man five years ago and left a note that she was heading West with an old flame. I was angry for a while and didn't go after her or try to find her. I met Belle and she told me her husband had left her for another woman. Neither of us wanted to get married again so we didn't try to find our spouses. As time went by we just settled in. She was always waiting when I came back from my trips until I came home early this past summer and found her in bed with the preacher. She finally admitted they had been carrying on for some time. I contacted an attorney to try and get a divorce, but he said it might take at least a month."

Catherine was resting up against the table with her arms folded, listening and trying to understand Trent's situation.

"I've always been a one-woman kind of man and I don't like sleeping around. I don't want to hurt you, Catherine, but I'm doing the best I can to fix what I needed to fix a long time ago. I'll understand if you want to take back your invitation."

"Thank you for your honesty. When you said you didn't have a girlfriend, I thought you were lying to me and trying to take advantage of me. I'm sorry I didn't believe you. Agnes said that your girlfriend was at the hospital with you so I made some assumptions."

"She did show up at the hospital, and after I was released and went home with her I packed up my things and moved them back to my boarding house. She begged me to stay, and cried. I felt bad that I didn't even feel sorry for her. In fact, I never felt so relieved about anything. You are a strong woman, Catherine, and you turned down an offer to marry a wealthy man and live a life of luxury, but you stayed true to yourself. I admire that about you and it made me realize that I shouldn't settle for less than what I want. Whether anything happens between you and me, Catherine, you've taught me a lot about relationships and I thank you for that."

"Do you still want to stay after my foolish actions last night?" she asked.

"None of us are perfect, and I'm not proud of the way I acted. I told myself the only way I would stay would be if you asked me. You never asked me. You asked me if I was going back to Houston and I told you I didn't know. Then when you brought up the girlfriend and I told you I didn't have one, you assumed I was lying. We're both proud and have a stubborn streak. I'll work on mine if you'll work on yours."

Catherine was staring at the floor and Trent walked up to her and tilted her mouth up to his. He bent down and his mouth consumed Catherine's sweet, luscious lips, kissing her with a sweetness that made her melt. Trent thought it was the most wonderful kiss he had ever experienced and he knew he was hooked.

Catherine was almost in a trance when he let her go. Her mind totally went blank and she was at a loss for words. Her head had stopped throbbing and she felt a calmness flow through her body. Trent was staying; she slowly broke into a smile.

"We have a lot to talk about," she said as she poured Trent another cup of coffee.

CHAPTER 15

Trent left after breakfast and told Catherine he wouldn't be back until Friday. She didn't want Trent to go, but she tried to act unconcerned. He seemed to be a man of few words but she had learned so much about him in the last hour that she felt more content than she had felt in a while. She had put up her guard because she felt threatened by men. David Brooks, Joe Brady, Michael Atwood. They had all left a lasting impression on her that sent chills up her spine. They had all taken away her dignity and she was determined to get it back. She had to at least give Trent a chance. Allow him to get close to her. She dreaded having to bring up her past but she knew that he had to know about everything before they carried the relationship any farther. Would he stay after he heard about the indignities she'd endured? Catherine sighed and decided she needed to pray harder. Beg God to forgive her for her weaknesses and give her strength to move forward.

Catherine confided in Shelby that Trent would be back to spend her birthday with her family, and Shelby invited them to come for dinner. "Rose, Jason's grandma, loves to cook and Jason really liked Trent," she told Catherine. "Jason will come and pick you up around four thirty on your birthday."

"Oh, that would be great," she said and hugged Shelby.

Thursday and Friday were busy with patients and in between times of administering medicine to children who had colds and fever in the clinic, Catherine tried to clean up her office. She was excited Trent was coming back. She was finally letting down her guard and she had to give him a chance. He was everything she could desire in a man. Patient, caring, understanding, and downright handsome, she thought.

When Trent didn't return on Friday, Catherine went up to his room after she had put the children to bed. The room seemed empty and the fire in the stove had gone out hours ago. She looked around the room and saw he had left nothing and she stopped breathing. She felt her throat tighten up. She had cleaned his room the day after he left and she guessed she didn't realize that he had left nothing there. She sat down on the bed and smoothed his pillow with her hand. How could she have been so stupid? He never intended to come back. The reality of it all began to be an open book to her now and she fussed at herself for believing that Trent might be different. Catherine got up and walked over to the window to look out and saw the key she had given Trent to use. It was the key to the carriage house and it was lying on the window sill; his final farewell to her. He wasn't man enough to tell her to her face he wasn't coming back. So be it, she thought. She pulled her shawl tightly around her shoulders and walked back over to his bed and lay down on it. She felt she was in a sinking ship and she was drowning, and she wondered how she had gotten to this place. Betrayal, emptiness, and a hollow feeling filled her heart. She did want to find love again. Someday her children would be grown up and gone and then she would have no one. She needed something to look forward to and she remembered her house in Galveston. Six months at most and she would be back there. She should have never left. She swore she would never let fear get in her way again. She would stand up to Michael and the Carla's of the world. She knew there were good people out there and she would make new friends. Catherine fell asleep on the bed and woke several hours later. She was shivering from the cold and when she sat up in bed, she remembered she was in the carriage house. She quickly ran down the stairs and into her house, bolting the back door and walking quickly through the house checking windows and doors to make sure they were locked. She ran upstairs and checked each of her children's rooms and they were all sound asleep. She ran to her bed, almost out of breath, and collapsed on it. She reached for her gun under her pillow and held it to her chest. Calm down, she said to herself. Everything will be all right. She put the gun under the pillow next to hers and curled up in a ball. Sleep finally took her deep in the same cavern she always found herself in, looking up at the tall rock walls, trying to crawl out -- and then the water began spilling onto her head. She was gasping for breath and woke up again. It was a full moon, and she could see shadows dancing around in the room. A wind had picked up outside and the limbs on the trees were being blown side to side, making the shadows look like they were coming after her. She walked over to a chair she kept by the window and sat in it. Why did love have to hurt so much, she wondered.

Trent had worked his way back towards Houston because he wanted to drop his maps off at his office and get some nicer clothes from his room. He also wanted to do some shopping before he headed back to Rosenberg. Agnes delivered the bad news when he got to his office. His partner's wife and child had died in childbirth and the funeral was Saturday. Toby Butler, Trent's working partner, had been like a second brother to Trent. They often finished each other's sentences. Trent left to go find Toby, but stopped at the train station to send a telegram to Catherine.

Partner's wife & child died. Funeral Saturday. I'm sorry and I hope you have a happy birthday.

Trent

Michael was in his office when the young errand boy came in. "Mr. Guthrie at the station said you might want to read this before I take it to Dr. Merit's office. He thinks there may have been a family member of Dr. Merit's die and that you might want to give her the news."

It was all over the town of Rosenberg that Michael had been seeing Catherine. Michael gave him a tip and thanked him. "I'll see she gets the message," said Michael.

After the boy left, Michael tore the envelope open and read it. It had come from the Houston station and Catherine had told him she had no relatives. He vaguely remembered hearing the man's name who had gotten shot and was treated by Catherine, but after thinking about the conversation with the sheriff, he recalled the name -- Trent Matthews -- and that he worked for Humble Oil Company in Houston. Michael picked up a box of matches by his wood stove and struck a match, lighting the corner of the paper. He watched it burn for a minute and then tossed it into the black potbellied stove. He opened the damper so it would burn fast and smiled to himself. He picked up his pen and took out a plain piece of paper. *Don't come back. I'm marrying Michael. Catherine.* He had printed the note he was going to send to Trent, and smiled to himself. That would take care of any hope Trent may have had of pursuing Catherine. He walked to the train station and asked the clerk to send the message to Trent Matthews in care of Humble Oil Company in Houston, Texas. He explained that one of Dr. Merit's patients had taken to her and was now harassing her. Michael left the station with a smile on his face. If he wasn't going to have her, no one would. He just had to figure out a way to keep Catherine in Rosenberg.

Trent accompanied Toby Butler on the train ride along with two caskets that were housed in the luggage area of the train. Trent felt badly for Toby. He had been married less than a year and he knew Toby had loved his wife. The son she had borne never came to life and after she fell asleep she never woke up. They were taking Toby's wife to her hometown of Maxwell, Texas, just southeast of Austin. He knew it would take a day or two, but he felt like Toby needed him and he hoped Catherine would understand. In his heart he knew she would. He wanted to tell Toby all about Catherine, but he didn't think it the time or the place to do it. He was there for Toby and not the other way around. Toby decided to stay in Maxwell and spend a few days with his in-laws and Trent took the train home later that day. He got into Houston at eleven thirty that night and decided to call Catherine the next day. He finally fell asleep at two o'clock the next morning after taking a couple of the pills Catherine had given him.

It was close to noon when he woke up, and he cursed to himself. He hurried to get dressed so he could go to his office to use the phone. He never had a phone put in his small apartment because he had no need for it. His office was only a few blocks away, and he sprinted down the side of the empty streets, anxious to talk to Catherine. Agnes kept a row of shelves next to her desk with the different employees' names on it so they could easily grab their mail and phone messages. Out of habit, Trent grabbed the papers from his box and went back to the tiny room in the back to make his call. The telegram caught his eye, and as soon as he sat down he slit it open with his knife. Trent stared at it for a long time. He stopped breathing for a few seconds and then he looked at the time it had been sent. It was dated the same day he had sent his, but later in the afternoon. He hadn't talked to Catherine since he had left on Wednesday and he had sent the telegram on Friday before noon. It only took Michael two-and-a-half days to talk her into marrying him. He found it hard to believe. She had been so adamant about disliking the man and had told him "marriage to Michael would be a death wish."

Trent sat back in his chair and put his hands behind his head. He stared at the ceiling for a while and then put his hand in his pocket, where he had put Catherine's birthday present. He took the box out and held it in his hand. When he lifted the lid the small angel on the gold chain sparkled as it caught the light. He knew the minute he saw it that he wanted to buy it for Catherine. She had been his guardian angel. Trent snapped the lid back down and put it back in his pocket. He had bought it in Rosenberg and figured he would return it the next time he went through there. He had no one else to give it to, and besides, it had been a special present for a special woman. Trent left his office, put his hands in his pockets and started walking. He wasn't in love with her, he told himself. Love is something that grows after getting to know someone. He was definitely infatuated with her. He convinced himself that by the time Monday came and he went back to work he would forget about her. It started raining and Trent turned up the collar on his coat and started walking. He noticed an older Chinese couple go into a café and he headed up the street towards it. When he got there the sign read: Wong's Chinese Café. He really didn't care for Chinese food, but he hadn't eaten and he was sure he could find something on the menu to eat. Maybe the rain would stop while he ate, he thought. The menu was in Chinese and it finally hit him that he was in Chinatown. He saw a waitress carrying a plate of food past him and told her he would have what they were having. Fifteen minutes later half of a duck with rice was sitting in front of him. He peeled off the skin, not sure if you were supposed to eat it, and found the dark meat underneath rather tasty. At least it was filling.

Trent was soaked when he got back to his room and he took everything off and stood under the hot shower, trying to wash away the last three days of grit and grime. He washed his hair and the whole time he was doing it he kept seeing Catherine scrubbing his head and shaving him. He wondered how long her image was going to continue to override his thoughts. He dried off, walked over to his bed naked and stretched across it. Trent looked at his wound and picked up a small pair of scissors he used on his hair. He looked down and began snipping the stitches and pulling them out one by one. He felt he needed to rid himself of anything that reminded him of Catherine. He had put the box with the angel in it on the side table by his bed so he wouldn't forget to take it back. He picked it up and took the chain out, held it up and watched as it danced around in the air as he examined it. He smiled when he pictured Catherine's face when she would have opened it. He had called her his guardian angel and she called him her gentle giant. What was wrong with him, he asked himself. Long distance romances never worked. He decided to write Catherine a letter. He couldn't let her have the last word, he decided. He needed to tell her how he felt and that he understood why she was marrying Michael. He really didn't, but it sounded good. He finished the letter and signed it, *Yours, Trent.* He found a hotel envelope he had picked up in some town and put the letter in it. He licked it and was disgusted by its taste. He addressed it to Dr. Catherine Merit, Rosenberg, Texas, and then looked at the hotel address. The hotel was located somewhere in a place called Hawthorn, Texas, and he remembered he and Belle had stayed there last year when they went to visit her sister. He put the letter on his bedside table so he wouldn't forget to mail it. For some reason his arm was throbbing again and he took the last two pills out of the candy bag she had given him. The last of the pills and the last memory of Catherine, he tried to convince himself.

Catherine made excuses for Trent and tried to act as if she didn't care. She concentrated on her work in the mornings and spent time with the children later in the day, and at night after the children were asleep she would go up to the carriage house and sit in the chair by the window and read her Bible. The evenings were long and she decided after her birthday she wouldn't go back up to the room in the carriage house again.

Michael called her the morning of her birthday and said he wanted to come by. He wouldn't take no for an answer. He acted as if he had done nothing wrong, and wanted to come by and give her a present. Michael arrived several minutes later and Catherine reluctantly let him in. He bent down and kissed her on the cheek.

"How did you know it was my birthday?" she asked.

"I know pretty much everything that goes on in this town," he answered. "I know you have been angry with me, Catherine, and I've come to apologize. I want us to be friends. I could certainly make your last few months in Rosenberg a lot nicer," he said. "Please look at me."

Catherine showed him into the living room and sat down, looking up at him.

"I'm afraid I have given you a bad impression of me and that's not who I am. If we could just get past everything that has happened and start over, maybe we can make some sense of this. I don't like that you are afraid of me. I promise I will never hurt you."

Catherine looked down at her hands and felt uneasy, not sure how to answer him. He handed her a small box with a purple bow on it. "Happy Birthday," he said.

She slowly took the box and opened it. She gasped when she saw the beautiful cameo pin that was surrounded by a rope of gold. "It's beautiful," she said. "It's much too extravagant," she continued.

Michael took it out of the box and pinned it on her blouse. "It suits you," he said. "It magnifies your beauty." Catherine smiled and blushed.

"Now that's the Catherine I remember," he said as he picked up her hand and kissed it. "I'd like to take you to dinner this evening."

"I've been invited to Shelby and Jason's for dinner, but thank you, and Michael, thank for the present. I know we have had a lot of tension between us, but you have to let go. I'm not your chattel and you have to respect my wishes."

"Agreed," he said. "I hope you have a pleasant day," he said, and left.

After Michael had left, Catherine stood in the hallway totally puzzled. He was like a lizard that kept changing colors. At least for now, she thought, he was pleasant enough; but she did not trust him and would make sure they were never alone together.

Several weeks had passed and when Trent's letter arrived at the Rosenberg post office, the postmaster put the hotel envelope aside, proud of himself that Catherine wouldn't be harassed by some foolish suitor. When Michael came to pick up his mail it was handed to him along with his mail.

"I'll check into the matter," Michael told him, and gave him two dollars.

Michael wasted no time opening the envelope when he got to his office.

My dear Catherine, as you know, I am a man of few words but I am perplexed by your telegram advising me that you are marrying Michael. I felt we had a strong connection and wanted you to know that in the event you change your mind I will be here for you. I pray God will give you guidance.

Yours, Trent

Michael took the letter and envelope and wadded it into a ball. He turned the damper open and threw the paper into the burning stove. It exploded into flames a few minutes later and he watched it burn. He smiled to himself and walked over to a drawer and took out a tiny box. When he opened it the one-and-a-half karat diamond ring glistened when it hit the light. It had cost Michael $350.00. There was no way she would be able to resist such a beautiful ring. Michael put it in his pocket and waited until he was sure the children were down for their naps. The front door was still unlocked and he reached up to stop the bell from ringing before he opened the door all the way. Catherine was in her office looking at her books and was startled when she looked up and saw him standing in her doorway.

"Forgive the intrusion," Michael said. "I just want to talk to you for a few minutes." Shelby had seen him go into Catherine's office but decided to stay out of the way. Michael scared her, too, and she felt badly that he wouldn't leave Catherine alone. She left to help Sadie with the children but left the kitchen door to the playroom open in case she heard Catherine calling.

Michael closed the door and sat across from Catherine. He

took off his hat and smiled at her. "I've never had anything affect me more than having you avoid me the way you have these past few weeks. I've acted inappropriately and it has humbled me more than you can imagine. I'd do anything if you would reconsider and give me a second chance. Michael took out the box and opened the lid, placing it on top of the books she had been working on. Catherine stared at it but didn't say anything for a brief moment. She inhaled a deep breath as if she were going into a fire and then spoke.

"It's beautiful, more beautiful than any ring I've ever seen. It has nothing to do with the way you have treated me, Michael. I know you have a temper and you are arrogant; I understand that is who you are. The fact is I do not love you and I have no intentions of ever getting married to anyone. I just want to be left alone so I can be a mother to my children and live my life in peace. Is that asking too much?"

Michael picked up the ring and snapped the box shut. "You'll be sorry someday, Catherine, that you didn't marry me." He got up and left.

Catherine sighed with relief that he didn't stay any longer. She buried her face in her hands and prayed this was last time he was going to bother her.

CHAPTER 16

Several weeks had passed and Trent and Toby were busy mapping an area just southwest of Houston. They were only about five miles from Rosenberg and Toby suggested that they go there and sleep in a hotel room. At least there would be running water there, he told Trent.

"We'll see," Trent said.

Toby had noticed that Trent seemed preoccupied. Toby dominated the conversation each night around the campfire, talking about his wife and how he missed her. Trent rarely said anything but always listened to Toby as he confessed his love for his wife and how he wasn't sure if he would ever find love again. He finally asked Trent why he seemed so preoccupied. Trent finally told Toby about Catherine and how she had taken care of him. After she had invited him to come back on her birthday, and he'd agreed, he'd received a telegram telling him she was marrying a man she hated. He told Toby he moved out of Belle's house and back into his apartment.

"You're in love with Catherine," Toby said.

Trent gave him an incredulous look and said he barely knew her.

"What if she changed her mind and didn't marry that Michael guy? You can't give up, Trent. You got to give it one more shot. We can be there in thirty minutes if we ride hard," Toby said.

"I don't know," Trent said. "I wrote her a letter and told her to call me if they broke up or she changed her mind. I've not heard back from her."

"Come on," Toby said as he kicked his horse and took off in a fast gallop.

Trent had to ride hard to catch Toby, and then it became a race. They slowed down when they got to the edge of town. When they got to Catherine's house, Trent dismounted and tied his horse to the fence. He took a deep breath and looked up at Toby.

"I'm not so sure this is a good idea," Trent said.

Toby nodded toward the house and smiled at him. Trent walked up to the door, rang the bell and waited. No one came to the door.

Catherine was busy in the kitchen when she thought she heard the doorbell. She waited to see if she heard it again. When she didn't hear it again, she finished what she was doing and went to the door. She looked out the window and didn't see anyone but then opened the door cautiously and looked out. She saw the backs of two men on horseback in the street as they passed the train station, and she was glad she had not opened the door. She tensed as she wondered if the two strangers might come back later. She thought of calling Jason but she had to learn not to depend on others. Maybe one of them needed a doctor -- not that she would have invited them in. She went back inside and closed the door.

Catherine helped get the children ready for bed and read them a story. After she had put them down she went downstairs to the front door and made sure it was locked. She started back up the stairs when the phone rang, and it startled her. She hesitated but didn't answer it. Five minutes later she dialed the operator back. Since Rosenberg was a small town, the operator knew all the residents' voices and their respective phone numbers. Many of them shared a party line, but since Catherine was at the opposite end of town and the phone line was put in when she moved there, no one else shared her line. "I was wondering if you could tell me who made that call, Mrs.

Blankenship."

"Well, he didn't give a name, but he was calling from the hotel," she said.

Catherine suggested that if the caller tried to put the call through again, to just pretend she was ringing but not to put the call through. She suggested there was a prankster in town and did not want to be bothered.

After Mrs. Blankenship hung up, she rang the sheriff's office and told Sheriff Wade that someone staying at the hotel was bothering Dr. Merit and he might want to look into it. The sheriff called Michael immediately and after getting instructions, he told Michael he would take care of the problem and left.

Sheriff Wade walked into the small hotel and looked around. He walked over to the desk and asked to look at the register. The young woman turned the book around so he could read it. "Are they up in their rooms?" he asked.

"No, I heard one of the men say they were hungry and headed down to the café," the young girl said.

The two men were seated at a small table by the window and Trent saw Sheriff Wade as he walked past then come into the café. Trent acknowledged him and introduced him to Toby.

"You back working in these parts again?" the sheriff asked. Trent said that they were, and had heard that they had caught the man who shot him.

"Yep, I did. I sent him over to Harden County where he was wanted for murder. He'll get a short trial and then they'll hang him. Don't need men like him around here," Sheriff Wade said.

"I guess you heard the good news?" Wade asked Trent.

"Not sure I know what you are talking about," Trent said.

"That lady doctor who treated your gunshot wound got herself a big engagement ring from Michael Atwood a few weeks ago. Recon they'll get hitched sometime in the near future," he said, smiling at Trent. "She's damn lucky a man like him would marry a widow with four little kids. He could have his choice of any lady in Texas, but he took a shine to the good doctor. Yep, I've been invited to the weddin."

Trent and Toby looked at each other. "Been good talking to you, Sheriff," Trent said and continued eating.

Toby waited while the sheriff left. "That was peculiar," Toby told Trent. "Why do you think he took it upon himself to tell you she got a ring?"

"No matter," Trent said. "It's done."

The men finished eating in silence. Toby wanted to stop at the saloon but Trent said he wasn't in the mood and he thought he would get something at the general store before it closed. Trent didn't really need anything but he just wanted some fresh air.

February was usually cold and windy, but the wind had settled down and there was a gentle breeze chilling the exceptionally warm day. Trent knew the general store was probably closed and he walked down to it and around to the back of the store. He didn't want anyone to see him and the sun had already gone down, leaving just enough light for Trent to find his way to the back corner of the carriage house. He ducked behind it and looked around the corner. He could see Catherine in the kitchen and she was alone. His heart was beating fast and he took a few breaths of the cool air, hoping it would help him come to his senses. Something just wasn't right and he always relied on his sixth sense. Trent didn't want to scare her, but he didn't know how else to get her attention. He quietly made his way to the back door, picking up a large rock on the way. He threw it hard against an old water can that the wind had turned over.

Catherine jumped when she heard the noise. She ran to the cupboard and grabbed her gun. Trent had unscrewed the light bulb on the porch and was standing just to the right of the door when Catherine came out with her gun. Trent grabbed it, pulling her to him and cupping his hand over her mouth so she wouldn't scream.

"It's me, Trent."

Catherine struggled to get away from him and he released her. Catherine was shaking, but she ran into Trent's arms and they held each other for a long time.

"You scared me to death," was all she could say once she got her composure. "How could you do that to me?"

Trent bent down and kissed her long and hard. She struggled at first but finally gave in to him and began kissing him back. Their kisses were ardently sensual and they were both out of breath when he finally released her. She almost fell backwards, but Trent caught her.

"Forgive me," he whispered, "but I didn't know what else to do. You didn't answer my letters and when I called earlier you didn't pick up. I had to see you one more time, Catherine."

"What do you mean I didn't answer your letters?" she asked.

"When I got back to Houston that Friday, I stopped at my office to leave some maps and I found out my partner's wife and child had died, and I had to attend the funeral a hundred miles away on your birthday. I sent you a telegram and then I got yours telling me you were going to marry Michael." Catherine gasped, not believing what he was telling her. "I also mailed you a letter and didn't get a reply. My partner, Toby, and I were working just outside of Rosenberg and he suggested I talk to you in person. I must admit, I was hesitant to come, but now that I'm here, I'm glad I came."

"I never got a telegram and I never sent you a telegram telling you Michael and I were getting married," Catherine finally said.

"When Toby and I were at the café this evening, Sheriff Wade came in and told me Michael had given you a big engagement ring. Is it true, Catherine, are you going to marry him?" Trent asked.

Catherine started crying. "No," she whispered, "He tried to give me a ring, but I didn't take it. When I didn't hear from you I couldn't understand why you would tell me all those things and then just never hear from you again. I kept punishing myself because I thought maybe the night I got drunk that after you left, you decided you didn't want to get involved with someone like me." Catherine began to tremble and she had goose bumps on her arms.

"Why don't we go inside and sort this thing out?" he asked.

Catherine sat at the kitchen table almost in shock. Trent saw the scotch bottle on top of the ice box and took it and two glasses to the table. He poured them both a shot.

"He's evil," Catherine said. "He runs the town and everybody in it. He has to be behind all of this. The telegrams, the missing letter, and now the sheriff hunting you down and telling you Michael and I were getting married. Oh, Trent, I'm so sorry to bring this upon you. If you were smart you would leave now and never look back. I'd never forgive myself if something happened to you."

Trent could see Catherine was tormented and scared, but he certainly wasn't afraid of Michael or anybody else. "Take a drink of scotch and try and relax," he told Catherine. "I've come up against men like Michael before and they can be vindictive, but they are all talk. He may be a powerful man in these parts, but I'm not afraid of him."

Catherine looked away, her eyes clouded with tears. "You have to leave," she said. Trent gave her a questioning look. "I," she stopped and then said, "You need to get as far away from me as you can. I'm not good for you, Trent. You have to leave now." She didn't make eye contact with him and he knew she was terrified of Michael and he understood why. Trent would have to leave soon and she would be alone and vulnerable to Michael's abusive ways.

He wasn't in any position to act like a gallant hero and offer to take her away with him right then. He knew she wouldn't go. She had planted roots here and she had four small children and a fourteen-year-old who depended on her.

"Catherine. I understand why you are scared, but between the two of us we can figure out a way to safely get you and your children to Galveston and away from Michael. I won't make any demands on you or expect you to give me anything in return. I just want to help you. When I leave in the morning Michael will assume his plan worked and that we won't be seeing each other anymore. He'll let down his guard. Come to Houston this weekend and tell everyone you are going away for a day or two of shopping and we'll talk about this."

Catherine didn't answer.

"I'm going to leave you now, but tomorrow I'm going to make a reservation at the Roosevelt Hotel in Houston for Friday night. There's a train that arrives from Rosenberg at four o'clock in the afternoon and I'll be at the train station waiting. If you aren't there …" Trent stopped and took a drink of his scotch. "If you aren't there I'll never try to contact you again." Trent reached over and took her hand and brought it to his lips. He felt like Catherine was a million miles away. "Did you hear what I said?" he asked softly. She didn't answer, but got up and walked over to him and stood looking down at him.

She knew she could easily fall in love with Trent. He was the nicest human being she had ever met. "I'll be on the train," she said, and he pulled her onto his lap. They held each other as though their lives depended on it. Catherine stood up and took his hand and pulled him out the back door. He followed her up the stairs to the carriage house. Catherine shivered from the cold and Trent picked her up and carried her over to the bed. He pulled the sheets back and then tugged at her apron, taking it off of her. He lay down beside her, kissing her softly and then more passionately. They stared into each other's eyes as though they were trying to tell each other how much they needed to be together.

"Are you sure you want to do this?" he asked.

Catherine silenced him with a kiss and began unbuttoning his shirt. She snuggled closer to him, planting soft, wet kisses on his neck and chest. She helped him take off her dress and then Trent pulled off his shirt. Their need to fulfill each other's desires was overwhelming and their passion for each other was taking them to a place of no return. Between kisses, Catherine managed to unbuttoned Trent's pants. He had already removed his boots and together they managed to totally disrobe each other in a matter of a few minutes. They began exploring each other's bodies with their hands and they both needed to fulfill a hunger that had built up inside their bodies. Trent lowered his head and kissed her hard, pink nipples, making a soft groan of gratification. Catherine kissed his neck and moved her hand below his waist, touching him softly. She had lost all control over her mind and she had begun to lose all sense of reality. She didn't care about anything at the moment except loving Trent. She tried to move his arousal inside her but he gently took her hand away.

"I didn't bring protection," he whispered. "Let me."

Trent moved his hands between Catherine's legs and gently massaged Catherine and she arched her body up to feel his strong fingers caressing her sweet spot. She felt as though her body was on fire and she called out his name. "Trent!" Her body was riddled with tremors of satisfaction. Her nails dug into Trent's back, willing him not to release her. Her tremors echoed through his own body and he forced himself not to explode his seed all over her. He managed to pull himself away from her as he released his arousal. It was the hardest thing he had to do. He wanted her just as much as she wanted him, but he was concerned for Catherine's well-being. Catherine clung to him and buried herself under his arm and began to weep. Trent pulled her to him and pulled the covers up. She fell asleep in his arms and Trent lay still, wishing he never had to let her go. He had denied himself the chance to feel her womb consume him and he wanted to consume her, too, and he prayed he would get that chance. He knew in the morning she would regret that she had been intimate with him, but she wouldn't have to worry about a pregnancy. Trent knew all her pain and feelings had to erupt eventually, and bringing her to an ultimate orgasm was the medicine she needed. Trent bent down and kissed her on the forehead. He let her sleep for a while before he woke her up.

"You know I can't stay here, but I didn't want to just leave you without you knowing that I have no regrets and I hope you don't, either. This was the most wonderful night of my life, and I promise you that it's your decision if you want to see me again. I'll be waiting at the train station."

Catherine watched as Trent's statuesque body got out of bed and dressed. He smiled at her when he bent down to kiss her. "Are you going to be all right?" he asked. She smiled up at him and shook her head, yes.

Trent didn't want to leave Catherine, but he knew if he stayed the night someone might see him leaving in the morning and he didn't want Catherine to be vulnerable. He had a full day of work ahead of him the next day, and he had to get a couple of hours' sleep. Toby was sound asleep when Trent let himself into the room. He took off his boots and slept on top of the bed with his clothes on. The two men woke up within a few minutes of each other.

"Did you see her?" was all Toby asked. Trent smiled and said, yes.

The two men stopped at the café for some coffee and breakfast. They knew they probably wouldn't eat again until nighttime. Very little was said about Trent's meeting with Catherine. Toby knew in time Trent would open up. Trent was very private about his affairs, and Toby respected that about him. Trent had lived with Belle for over six months before he had told Toby about her. It was who he was and Toby understood that about him.

Trent glanced at Catherine's house as they walked their horses through the street. It was only seven o'clock in the morning, but Trent was hoping to get one more glimpse of Catherine. He didn't see her but she saw him. She had been sitting in her chair in the upstairs window hoping to see him before he left. She moved away from the window when the two men approached and looked out the corner, not wanting him to see her. She watched until the men had left her sight. Friday, she thought. She hoped she could get Jason and Shelby to stay Friday night and Saturday. One night, just one more night with Trent was all she wanted and then, she told herself, she would never see him again.

CHAPTER 17

The next two days seemed to drag by. Shelby said she and Jason would be happy to stay over and help with the kids and would probably just take them to their house on Saturday morning because Toby's grandparents, Rose and Charles, loved having the children. She told Catherine if she wanted to stay over Saturday night, too, to just call them and let them know if she was staying over. Catherine had started closing the clinic on Fridays unless an emergency came up. It gave Shelby time to spend with her husband and Catherine could get caught up with her books.

Catherine spent the entire day with her children and when they were put down for their naps she went upstairs to bathe and pack her bag. She was beginning to get cold feet and she promised herself she was just going to get away from everything and try and relax. Still, Trent was in her every thought. She appreciated the fact that he was concerned she might get pregnant and he treated her with so much compassion. She had started her period the morning he left and by Friday it would be safe. Her excitement seemed to escalate. She had just gotten out of the bathtub when Sadie came in and told her Emma had begun throwing up. Catherine put on her robe and went into the girls' room. Sadie was cleaning the floor and Catherine picked Emma up and took her to the bathroom to clean her up. She vomited again on Catherine's robe and started crying.

"Shh, it's all right sweetie, mama's here."

Thirty minutes later Isabelle began vomiting. Catherine set towels on the floor with Emma on one side of her and Issy on the other. Catherine told the girls she was going to get them some medicine and they both began screaming. Catherine told Sadie to take the boys downstairs and keep them away from the girls.

"It is probably contagious," Catherine said as the girls alternately vomited into the chamber pot.

A while later the two girls fell asleep up against Catherine. She kissed them and prayed she wasn't the cause of their illness. It was apparent to her that God didn't want her to go to Houston and she hated that the girls were God's way of telling her it was wrong. She thought of Trent and how strong-willed he had been not to give in to his desire for her. She, on the other hand, had no willpower and she hated herself for it. She felt badly that she wouldn't be at the train station and it hurt, thinking of how disappointed he would be. Everything happens for a reason, she told herself.

Jason and Shelby arrived and Sadie told them about the girls. Shelby went upstairs to see if there was something she could do.

"You can fetch my medical bag, a teaspoon, and make some hot tea and honey. Put some ice in it to cool it down and bring it upstairs, with two glasses. When they wake up they will be thirsty and need nourishment," she told Shelby.

Trent was waiting at the train station in Houston when he heard the whistle blow and he bit his lips trying not to smile. He was sure Catherine would walk off the train in a few minutes and he would have her to himself for the next twenty-four hours. The train had three Pullman cars that carried the passengers and the other cars carried mail and freight. He walked towards the first Pullman car and watched anxiously as the conductor stepped down and placed another step for the passengers to make an easier exit. His eyes danced back and forth between the three passenger cars and then up to the windows to see if he could find her. His heart began to beat faster as the remaining passengers got off the train. He walked up and down by the three passenger cars, almost tripping over a little girl because he was frantically trying to find Catherine. He apologized to the little girl's mother and moved farther back so the passengers could retrieve their baggage. He saw a tall woman waiting by a bench appearing as if she was looking for someone. He stood watching sweethearts kissing and families waving goodbye to loved ones as they boarded the train heading east with a New Orleans destination. He was still standing and staring at the train as the whistle blew and it began chugging its way down the tracks. The tall, young woman was still standing by the bench waiting. For a minute their eyes caught one another and Trent tried to smile and nodded his head in a friendly gesture.

As the train disappeared, the smoke stack blew out black, billowing smoke and the smell from the fumes made it hard for Trent to breathe. He put his hands in his pockets and he walked away. He had gone by the hotel earlier that day and prepaid for the room. He had registered as Mr. and Mrs. Lawrence Smith. He didn't really want to go back, but he had put roses in the room and he had hidden the box with the necklace under one of the pillows. When he got to the Roosevelt he decided to go into the bar and have a couple of drinks. He was sitting at the end of the bar drinking a shot of whiskey when a tall, young, willowy brunet sat down next to him and ordered club soda. Trent didn't look at her; he was deep in thought when the woman asked him a question.

"Excuse me, but are you staying in the hotel?"

"I have a room if that's what you mean," he answered curtly.

"I saw you when I got off the train. Did your friend not make it?" she asked.

"No," he answered, looking straight ahead.

"I was supposed to meet someone myself, but he didn't show up. He told me he would make me a reservation here at the hotel."

Trent looked at her for the first time. When she sat down, he assumed she was a prostitute looking for a man for the night. The woman sitting next to him was anything but that. She was tall, probably no more than twenty, had wiry, curly dark brown hair, a very plain face, and was wearing a brown dress with a green jacket over it. The hat she was wearing was hanging lopsided and she looked very forlorn.

"I checked at the desk and they didn't have my name or his name registered. I don't have any money or a place to sleep. You look like a nice man and I hate to ask you for help, but I've come a long way," she said softly.

Trent put a dollar on the counter and told the bartender he was paying for both drinks and took her arm. He picked up her small bag and escorted her up to the third floor; when they got to the door she hesitated.

"I hope you don't think I'm uh, well, that I'm a woman of the night," she shuddered.

Trent smiled at her. "No, I don't think that at all," he answered back.

She gasped when she walked inside the lavishly furnished room. "Oh my, the room is so beautiful -- and the flowers." She stopped when she realized he had probably bought them for whoever he was waiting for. Trent walked over to the bed and without messing it up he reached under the pillow and took out a box. He walked over and handed it to her.

"I won't be needing this anymore, either," he said, handing her the box. Trent took out his wallet and took out a ten dollar bill, giving it to her along with the key to the room. "I've already paid for the room tonight. I hope you find what you are looking for," he said and left the room.

"Mister," the woman said. Trent turned and looked at her, waiting for a further response. "I'm sorry your friend didn't make it, either." Trent gave her a half smile and closed the door.

CHAPTER 18

Several weeks had gone by since Trent had left. Catherine had thought about contacting him, but each time she told herself it was best not to complicate his life anymore. She figured by now he had forgotten about her and moved on, perhaps rekindling the romance with his old girlfriend. At least he had someone to go back to, if that were his choice.

Shelby's baby was due soon and she was looking forward to its arrival. She and Shelby had grown very close and Catherine was happy for her and Jason, but she knew once the baby came, Shelby would not be able to help her on a full-time basis. When she went into town that morning, she posted a notice on the outside of the small courthouse. The note simply said she needed a respectable, motherly type of woman to care for her four children, and to apply in person. Her intentions were to allow Sadie to help her in the clinic and teach her the necessary skills to become a nurse. Two hours later her waiting room was full. Catherine asked how many people were there for an illness and only one person's hand went up. "I'll have to see my patients first and then I'll visit with the rest of you afterwards. If you do not care to wait, you may come back tomorrow. No one left. After Catherine saw her patients she began seeing the ladies one by one who were interested in the nanny position. There was only one man in the waiting room and Catherine asked his name and why he was there. He told her his name was Martin Boudreaux and introduced his wife, Emily, sitting next to him.

"We would both like to discuss the job that is available," he said. Catherine asked them to come into her office.

"When we moved here three months ago from New Orleans, we heard they were hiring at the paper mill but when we got there all the jobs were filled. We checked at the cotton gin too, but they had no openings. We are from France and speak fluent French. Emily's mother came with us, but she died on the ship before we got here. We were quarantined and lived in a small shack with other people, waiting to make sure we did not have the fever or something else. They kept us in those close quarters by the shipyard for over six weeks and rationed food sparsely. After we got out, they told us our trunks were lost and we were put out on the streets with nothing but the clothes on our backs."

Catherine couldn't believe the horrible way they were treated, and listened intently.

"We had enough money to take a train to Houston because we couldn't find employment in New Orleans. Someone on the train was from Rosenberg and said our chances might be better here because of the paper mill. We have been here three weeks and our money is drying up," Martin continued. "We have been living in a room down by the livery stables and I have been doing odd jobs there, but it's not enough. We saw your notice and here we are. I'm a good cook and Emily is, was, a good mother. We lost our little girl when she was five. We heard you used to have a couple who lived in your carriage house and we were hoping both of us could come work for you."

Catherine's heart went out to the couple, but she was a bit apprehensive because they had no references. She told them she would let them know the next day. After the couple left, she interviewed the remaining ladies in the waiting room. There was only one she felt would be able to care for her four children; the lady was a widow with two grown children. She told her she would get back with her the next day. Catherine liked that the lady had a telephone and could be reached if there were an emergency.

Catherine was finding it hard to make a decision. She felt like the couple would be a good fit since Martin could cook and look after the maintenance of the house, but she had no way to check them out. She decided to call Jason and see if he could check with the man at the livery stable to see if he knew anything. Jason was pleased to help her and said he would find out what he could. That evening Jason called her back and said that Jake at the livery stable gave Martin praises for everything he did and would like to keep him, but he could only use Martin part-time and they needed something more stable. Catherine thanked Jason and asked him if he would contact Jake and tell Mr. and Mrs. Boudreaux to come back the next day.

Catherine knew that Shelby's pregnancy was making her tired and she was only working about four hours a day, but she called her in the next morning and told her about the couple from New Orleans. Shelby encouraged Catherine to hire them and that it would be nice to spend the next two or three weeks at home getting ready for the baby. She wanted what was best for Catherine also, and knew that the additional work Catherine had taken on because of Shelby's condition was beginning to be too much for Catherine.

The Boudreaux were waiting when Shelby finished talking to Catherine. "I'm afraid I can't make you any promises as to how long I will employ you because my plans are to move to Galveston in the next six months. For now it would give you a roof over your heads," Catherine said.

Catherine told them both what would be expected of them and how much she could pay, and said if they accepted they could start immediately. The Boudreaux were eager to start and after Catherine gave them the key, she introduced them to her four children and Sadie.

"I've tried to keep the room above the carriage house in good order, but you will probably want to spend the day cleaning and putting your personal things inside. I will get with you when the children are down for their naps regarding the remaining duties you will have."

Catherine was relieved that she could take cooking and cleaning off of her list of things she needed to do. She was far behind in her book work and reading, and she felt like a great weight had been lifted from her shoulders. It would be nice to be able to freshen up her language skills. During their conversation she asked them questions in French to test their skills and was amazed that they were able to understand her. It had been a few years since she had spoken French and she had to struggle with some of the words. It would be a nice change, she thought.

The Boudreaux's abilities far surpassed anything Catherine had expected. Martin had painted the room above the carriage house and repaired everything that needed repair. His cooking skills were amazing, introducing new dishes to her and the children every day. The children loved Emily and she had begun teaching them French. If Martin wasn't cooking he was cleaning and taking care of the house. He told Catherine as soon as the weather permitted he would start on the outside.

Catherine took no chances, though. Until the Boudreaux proved themselves, she kept her jewelry and important papers in a box which was hidden in a trapdoor she had discovered in her office. Each afternoon after her office was closed; she walked the three blocks into town and made deposits each day, keeping only what she needed for groceries and sundry items.

Catherine was slowly and mechanically going through the routine she had established early on, seeing patients four and a half days a week, taking care of her children, and trying to stay away from Michael. She had seen him on occasion driving down the street with an attractive young woman, and she was hoping he had moved on and given up the idea that Catherine would ever marry him.

There wasn't a day that went by that she didn't think about Trent and their night together, and she hoped and prayed that he had forgiven her and moved on with his life. So be it, she thought. Things happened for a reason and she felt that Trent would be happier with someone with fewer problems, someone who could be a real wife to him. He was handsome, and she was sure he would find someone else. After dinner each night after the children had gone to bed, Catherine couldn't help but think about their last night together. She knew Trent wouldn't be back. He had told her if she didn't show up at the train station he would never bother her again. She knew he was a man of his word. Perhaps when the time was right down the road, there might be another man like Trent who would come along and sweep her off her feet. Silly girl, she would tell herself. Things like that only happened in fairy tales.

Every Sunday afternoon Catherine would walk to the train station to fetch a Galveston Gazette. She was an avid reader and she read the paper from cover to cover. It was important for her to keep up on the progress taking place in Galveston. She marveled at the fact that the sand and water that was being removed from the new channel was being pumped into the neighborhoods to raise the elevation after each house was raised on stilts. She had read that there was a terrible mosquito problem and home owners had to walk on platforms that had been built to cross the streets because the streets were constantly soggy and often flooded. It was hard to imagine that this was even possible. However, it also meant she probably wouldn't be able to move into her home before the fall semester so she could start teaching. It seemed there were frequent setbacks, and she prayed for patience.

The next month seemed to fly by and Catherine had just finished reading a story to her children one afternoon when she heard the phone ring.

"It's Alex; Meredith is in labor and she's having difficulties with the delivery. Celli is here now and she doesn't seem to know what to do. Meredith has been in labor for over six hours, and I'm worried," Alex said. "Something is just not right. We need you,

Catherine. Michael's leaving his office right now and will be waiting out front for you."

Catherine told Sadie and Martin where she was going and went to get her medical bag. She hesitated when Michael opened the door to his automobile. They hadn't spoken more than two words to each other in over a month, but since it was an urgent matter, she knew Michael had no choice but to take her directly to Meredith's house.

When Catherine entered the house, Celli and Alex were in the bedroom with Meredith. "The baby has not dropped into the birth canal and Mrs. Meredith, she been pushing and pushing and nothing happens," Celli told Catherine. "She passed out once and then I woke her up, but it's not good." Catherine ran to the bathroom and washed her hands quickly and returned to Meredith's room.

"I think it would be best if you left now, Alex," Catherine said politely to him. Celli moved away so Catherine could take over.

"Meredith, try not to push anymore. I know it will hurt, but the baby is in the wrong position and I will need to try and turn him. When was your last birthing pain?" Celli told Catherine it had been five minutes and the last was about eight minutes.

"Then I need to move quickly," she said.

Catherine turned the baby with precision care and slowly moved the cord away from the neck as Meredith felt the next pain.

"Push," Catherine said. "Push hard."

Meredith strained and pushed as hard as she could, and screamed.

"Good, it's moving now. On your next contraction give me another push."

Two minutes later Meredith screamed again and pushed the baby out. Alex and Michael were in the living room when they heard the cry of a baby and Alex couldn't wait another minute. He rushed into the room and watched as Meredith grinned up at him. He grabbed her hand and kissed her.

"It's a boy. We have a son."

Celli took the baby and washed him with a warm sponge. Catherine saw to Meredith's needs and congratulated the couple.

"What's his name?" she asked Meredith.

"Elliott, after Alex's father," Meredith said.

Catherine smiled and said it was a lovely name. Catherine had never known Alex's father's name, and it made her feel empty inside. They were never married long enough to find out those little things that couples spend months talking about the first year. In fact, her time with Alex was so short; it was hard to remember much of anything about their short marriage. Catherine excused herself and told Alex to call her if Meredith or the baby needed anything. She left the clean up to Celli. Catherine washed her hands and picked up her medical bag to leave.

CHAPTER 19

The February breeze was chilly and she started walking towards town. Catherine sucked in a deep breath and pulled her coat tighter around her body. There was still enough daylight and she figured if she walked fast she would be back home in about an hour. It was a sobering feeling as the north wind bit into her skin. She set her bag down on the side of the road and buttoned her coat. The nagging winds were tearing at her skirt, but she just wanted to be alone right now. She willed herself not to cry. Alex and Meredith seemed so happy and she had not had that experience when she had Alex's daughter, Emma. She had almost died after she gave birth. She remembered Samuel delivering her baby and she wondered when his child might be arriving. She had almost made it to the road when she heard the engine on Michael's new car rev up. She just wanted to be alone and not have to deal with Michael. She knew she was being foolish, but she didn't care.

Michael was surprised that Catherine had already left and only stayed a few minutes to see the baby and he went to look for her. Meredith had called Michael in to see her son and he asked who had taken Catherine home. They looked at each other, but no one answered. Michael went outside and looked up the road and realized that his driveway made a thirty-degree turn to the road and the fields had not been tilled yet. The decaying weeds were preventing him from seeing Catherine so he got in his automobile and drove up the road. She stepped to the side and hid in between two haystacks, hoping he wouldn't see her; but he was driving slowly and stopped when he noticed her out of the corner of his eye.

"Do you know how ridiculous you are trying to avoid me? I'm not going to hurt you," he said.

Catherine hesitated, but walked around to the side of the car and got in. "I'm getting married next month," he told Catherine. "I'm marrying a young widow from Houston who loves me very much."

"Good for her," Catherine remarked.

"I was hoping we could just be friends, Catherine," Michael said.

"Tell me one thing, then. Was it you who sent the telegram to Trent Matthews in Houston?"

Michael hesitated, but said, "You should thank me for that. He's a married man, Catherine. He would have only caused you grief."

It was all Catherine could do not to scream at him and after a few minutes she said, "I would appreciate you staying out of my life from now on." Nothing more was said and she jumped out of Michael's car as soon as they drove up to her house.

Catherine was shaking when she went into her office and closed the door. She hated Michael for his controlling ways. Martin tapped on the door and asked if she were all right. "Yes, I'm fine. I just need a few minutes alone," she answered. "The children are hungry and we are waiting dinner for you, Dr. Merit." Catherine got up from her desk and joined them in the kitchen.

"Meredith had a baby boy," she announced.

Daniel looked up at Catherine and said, "You mean the baby doesn't live in her belly anymore?"

The grown-ups tried not to laugh and Catherine said, "That's right. You'll get to see him in a couple of days."

"Is Miss Shelby's baby going to come out soon, too?" Adam asked.

"I expect it will be coming soon," she answered.

Catherine looked around the table and marveled at how her family was beginning to change. The children loved their new nanny and were also becoming attached to Martin. She had also noticed that in the past few weeks her patient list was growing and she was seeing five to ten patients each day. One of her patients told her that she had come highly recommended. Catherine assumed that Michael's new love interest had diverted his attention away from her and she was pleased by that. For the first time in several months good things were happening to her.

Two weeks later Jason called Catherine and told her that Shelby's water had broken and said he was bringing her to the clinic for Catherine to deliver the baby. When they arrived at the clinic, Sadie escorted Shelby and Jason to a back room that Catherine used for emergencies. When Catherine finished with the patient she was seeing, she went to examine Shelby. Shelby told her the contractions were about thirty minutes apart.

"It might be several hours before the baby is ready. Sadie or I will be back frequently to check on your progress," Catherine said.

Jason's grandparents had come with them and Catherine took them back to the kitchen where she had coffee and a kettle of water brewing.

"Make yourselves at home, please. Martin, my helper, will get you something to eat or anything else you might need," she said and went back to her patients.

Three hours later, Shelby delivered a six pound, three ounce baby girl. The family was ecstatic and when Catherine asked Jason what her name was going to be, he said, "Mary Beth, after my mother," he beamed. The family stayed and had dinner with Catherine and her family and after making sure the baby was fit, the Bradys left to settle in their new bundle of joy.

Catherine was exhausted by the time she took her bath and crawled into bed. The daytime was easy to get through, she thought, but the night time had become her enemy. She could easily fall asleep, but an hour or two later she would wake up and stare at the shadows lurking in her room. No matter how late she went to sleep or what she ate or drank, sleep usually wouldn't come for hours. She was comfortable with her routine now, and for the first time since she arrived in Rosenberg she was making a good enough living to be able to save some of her wages. Still, Galveston kept calling. Lately her nightmares were of her mother and her tragic death. Not a night went by that David Brooks didn't show up, taunting her, raping her, filling her head with the demons she fought and tried to resist. In one dream, David Brooks and Joe Brady were taking turns burning her with cigarettes. Maybe in time, she thought, they would fade away. She tried to think about more pleasant things and her thoughts brought Trent into her arms. He was quite a mysterious man, intriguing and well educated. Even though he used his words wisely, his soft manner and quiet demeanor spoke unsaid words that made her feel comfortable and safe with him. She prayed he had forgiven her.

The next afternoon after Catherine had made her deposits at the bank, she saw Alex approaching on Pilgrim. Alex got down and tied Pilgrim to the hitching post. "Mind if I walk you home?" he said as he fell into step with her.

"How are Meredith and the baby?" she asked.

"They are great, thanks to you. You saved their lives. Meredith and I will forever be indebted to you. I'm glad you were here for her."

Catherine smiled and said she was glad it all went so well and that she was happy for them.

"I talked to Meredith and she is open to the idea of moving into town. She had always loved her uncle's house. She thinks I should talk to Michael first, but regardless of what he says, I want to buy it."

Catherine told him how much she had in it but since she had made such a good buy in Galveston she would take five hundred dollars less. She told him that the work on the streets in Galveston was moving slowly and that it would be months before she could leave. Alex told her time didn't matter and he would have the attorney draw up the papers when she was ready to sell.

"Have you mentioned to her that you were going back to work?" Catherine asked.

"No, but I'm going to soon. I've spoken to Clarence at Glacier Oil Company, and he told me that Humble Oil Company was in negotiations to buy out the company and it would mean that the offices would relocate to Houston," Alex said as they got to the house. "Houston would be a lot closer than Beaumont and I'm sure I won't have to work more than 100 miles from home. I guess the girls are taking their naps?" he asked.

"Yes, but you can stop back in thirty minutes or so and see them," she said.

"Meredith sent me on an errand and will be expecting me back soon, but I'll stop by tomorrow and see them. Maybe we'll bring Elliott by if Meredith is up to it," he said.

Catherine watched as Alex walked back to town. The world couldn't get any smaller, she thought. What were the odds that Alex would end up working for the same company Trent worked for? She was convinced God had a sense of humor. She knew one thing, Trent and Alex were a lot alike and she marveled at their similarities. Perhaps one day she might see Trent again, and she smiled at that possibility.

Catherine continued to keep up with the street elevation progress in Galveston, and Mark had written her to let her know that her street was next and it would be a mess if she moved in before it was finished. He suggested that she wait at least until the end of the year and assured her that the tenants were having to also wait and would be delighted to stay in the house. He told her about the terrible mosquito problem and that residents had to use walkways up on stilts to maneuver around the neighborhoods. He told her that even after the fill had been pumped onto her street it would be months before it dried enough for people to be able to use the streets. She decided not to let Mark's letter dampen her spirits. She could stay in Rosenberg as long as she needed to and now that Michael was no longer pursuing her, she didn't have to leave.

For some reason Catherine began thinking about Samuel, and tried to think back to when she had first found out Dorothy was pregnant, because she figured her due date was somewhere the middle of March. She hoped Samuel had accepted his fate and that he was happy being married to Dorothy. She had remembered thinking that Meredith, Dorothy, and Shelby were all within a month to six weeks of delivery. She decided to pick up the phone and call Samuel, even though he was extremely short with her the last time they spoke.

Samuel had not known a lot about Dorothy when they married. She was in her second year of nursing school when they had met at the hospital. She was pleasant enough when they were dating, but after they got married she seemed to be a different person. Her mood swings were volatile and she was extremely lazy. Samuel liked things neat and tidy and there were constant arguments about the messy town house. She said that the brownstone was too small and that if they had a larger home, there would be ample room to put things. They spend most of their free time shopping for a new house, but nothing seemed to please her. Samuel thought she was in her seventh month and commented to Dorothy that she looked more like she was just a month away. They had already ruled out twins. Still, Samuel couldn't help but wonder if the baby was really his. Time would only tell and he decided to say nothing more until the baby was born.

Catherine waited until Samuel came to the phone. "If you are terrible busy, you can call me later," Catherine said.

"No, I'm just coming off my shift and I was just about to go home. How are you?" he asked Catherine. "Are you Mrs. Atwood now?"

"No, Michael is engaged to another, thank goodness," she answered.

"I'm not surprised," he said. "You really didn't want to marry him, anyway."

"I was just thinking about you and when the baby was coming and decided to call you and find out, friend to friend, of course. You were very short with me the last time we talked."

"Yea, sorry about that. The emergency room was packed and I really couldn't talk" Samuel assured her.

"I understand; like I said, I was just thinking about you and wanted to make sure everything was all right."

"My work is great, but my marriage needs some work." He wanted to tell her that he suspected he really wasn't the father of their child and that Dorothy had let it slip one day that she had been seeing her old high school sweetheart prior to dating Samuel. He knew she wasn't a virgin from the beginning and he had accepted her word that the baby was his. Now he was having reservations. "Look, I need to get home. I'll call you back soon, I promise. Take care, Catherine, it's a cold, cruel world out there."

"You have been a wonderful friend, Samuel, and I hope things work out for you."

Catherine could sense his unhappiness and felt badly for him but there was nothing she could do. It would probably be best if she just forgot about him. He had obviously forgotten about her.

One month later, Dorothy woke Samuel up at four o'clock in the morning. He had only been home a few hours and had fallen into a deep sleep.

"What is it?" he asked.

"I think my water just broke."

Samuel sat up in bed and he felt the wetness on the cold sheets. He knew she was at least a month early but didn't say anything. It only took him a couple of minutes to dress. He walked to the closet to get Dorothy's small suitcase and when he opened it to

put her things in it, he noticed it was already packed. He knew
Dorothy wasn't a planner and was surprised the suitcase seemed to
have everything she needed. He walked back to the bed and asked if
she was having any pains.

"A couple," she said meekly.

"How far apart?"

"Maybe thirty minutes," she answered.

"Get dressed. We'll have to walk since the trolleys aren't
running."

Samuel held on to Dorothy's arm as they began the seven-
block walk to the hospital. The air was cold and fresh and it felt good
on his face. He knew it was too early for her to deliver and he doubted
the baby was premature, but he would give her the benefit of the
doubt and not say anything until the baby came.

Three hours later he was in the birthing room when Dorothy
gave birth to a five pound, six ounce baby boy. Samuel was
overwhelmed and held the baby, examining it to make sure he was
healthy. Tears filled his eyes as he tried to estimate how many months
had passed. He gave the baby to one of the nurses and left the room.
He was sitting outside in the waiting room as his friend and fellow
colleague came out and asked if everything was all right.

"Yes. Just a bit overwhelmed," he answered.

Dr. George Benton had worked with Samuel for over a year
and they had shared a strong bond. He knew Samuel had been married
less than eight months and the baby was full-term. He didn't say
anything because he just assumed Dorothy got pregnant while they
were dating.

"Dorothy is asking for you. They took her to a private room.
Number 305," he said.

Samuel got up slowly and walked down the hall. They had not
even talked about a name, but at this point he really didn't care.
Dorothy had screwed up his whole life. He wondered it had all been a
lie and he had fallen for it.

She could sense something was bothering Samuel and asked him what was wrong.

Samuel scratched his head and told her that the baby was full-term but she delivered three weeks early.

"Was there anyone else before me? I need you to tell me the truth," he said. "How many were there?" Samuel asked. Dorothy looked away and didn't answer. "How many," he said louder.

Dorothy began crying and said, "Only one," in a soft voice. "But I know it's yours, Samuel. It's our baby, yours and mine. I'd like to call him Samuel, Jr. if that's all right," she said more as a question. They had not discussed names before now and he hesitantly told her Samuel was fine.

It was nine o'clock in the morning when Samuel walked over and picked up the telephone. Catherine was in her office and picked up on the second ring. She listened as Samuel told her he had a son. "I'm so happy for you, Samuel," she said. "It's what you always wanted."

"Almost," he said. "What I wanted was a child with you, Catherine." Catherine was at a loss for words but finally told him that she wished only the best for his new family. She felt his hurt and wished too that things could have been different. Their parting words were cautious and carefully spoken as they hung up the phone.

CHAPTER 20

Catherine went into the kitchen to prepare some hot tea when she heard a soft knock at the back door. When she opened it, Meredith was bundled up in an overcoat and the baby was swaddled in a thick blanket. Catherine took Elliott from her so Meredith could take off her coat.

Catherine pulled the blanket away from Elliott's face and smiled at the sleeping baby.

"What a beautiful child," Catherine said. "How about having tea with me?"

"That sounds great," Meredith answered. They could hear the children laughing and giggling upstairs. "It sounds like they are all happy," she said.

"Yes, thank goodness," Catherine replied.

Catherine set two cups of hot tea on the table and waited. She could sense Meredith had something on her mind.

"Alex wants to go back to work," she finally said in a hesitant voice. "He said he was tired of being Michael's errand boy and he wanted to pay his own way."

Catherine put her hand on Meredith's and patted it. Catherine knew how she felt. She had not wanted Alex to go back to scouting when they were married, but that was the kind of man he was. She knew she had to choose her words carefully.

"Men, especially men with strong character, like Alex, feel

they have to make their own way in the world. Alex needs to feel like he is taking care of you and Elliot. Perhaps you could encourage him to try and be home on the weekends. Surely his boss could find something for him to do that wouldn't drag him all over the countryside," Catherine said.

"I know you are right. I could sense Alex's anxiety when Michael would order him around. I just didn't want to get in the middle and I was hoping Alex would adjust. I guess he hasn't. Oh, Catherine, I don't want to lose him."

"You aren't going to lose him. If he will agree to be back home a couple of days each week, then over time you will get used to his being gone. Actually, it's unusual for a husband to be around as much as Alex has been. You might suggest that he try it for six months and then ask him if he would be willing to discuss it further at that time if you feel it is not working out. I know you and Alex are very close, but sometimes absence makes the heart grow fonder and it might make you even closer. I think it would help if you could at least show him that you are willing to give it a try. Maybe on occasion you could spend a weekend in Houston with him. I would gladly take care of Elliott for you," Catherine said.

The baby woke up and began chewing on his fist. Meredith opened her blouse and Elliott hungrily suckled on her breast. Catherine watched in awe. She felt slighted by the fact that she would probably never have another child, but tried not to think about it.

They continued to talk for a while and then Meredith left. Catherine worried about Alex going back to work, too. What if he had another accident and he lost his complete memory? What if he got shot again and died? She shook her head and tried to clear her mind. Alex was no longer hers and he never would be, she scolded herself.

When Alex returned to his home the next evening, he told Meredith he had a long talk with Michael and Michael understood that Alex wanted to return to his old job. He assured Meredith that he would be working close to home and would be home on the weekends. He also told her he had spoken to Clarence, his old boss, and it was agreed the Alex could set his own hours and that he would be working in pairs for safety purposes. Meredith confided to Alex that she had spoken with Catherine and while she was not completely happy about his leaving, she would try it for six months.

The next morning when Meredith woke up she found a note from Alex.

You looked so peaceful sleeping, my love, and I hated to wake you. I will be careful and will be home soon.

Love, Alex.

She wept when she read it.

The April winds in Texas were soothing to Alex and after he arrived in Pasadena, Texas, he felt he needed to give Pilgrim a rest. He figured they were another two and-a-half hours to Liberty City, Texas, and he was making good time. It had been a while since Pilgrim had been on the trail and Alex was worried he would tire easily. Alex always wore a hat to keep the sun from burning his face, but he could feel the heat radiating through his skin even though the temperature was only about fifty-five degrees. He left Pilgrim under a small, covered corral next to an old livery stable that used to be a way station for stagecoaches and he walked through town until he found a general store. He purchased a jar of cow udder cream and then stopped in at a small café. He ordered the breakfast special and picked up a local newspaper to read while he sipped his coffee. It was a small paper with local news on the front, but the inside page was filled with information about the cities in south Texas that were flourishing because of oil. He counted six small towns between Houston and Beaumont. On his trip he had noticed some small drilling rigs and knew that it was just a matter of time before the countryside would be cascading oil rigs over every hill. After he finished his breakfast, he gave Pilgrim another drink of water and pulled himself up on his saddle. He took out his udder cream and covered his face with it, gently rubbing it into his skin. He was tired, but the open space rejuvenated his self-esteem and he looked forward to the future in anticipation.

Alex left Pilgrim at the stables in Liberty City, Texas, and removed his saddle. He took his saddlebags and walked the three blocks to the Lindy Hotel. He had been through here a couple of times but had never stayed the night. The room was clean and had a bathroom with a shower. He pulled off his boots and emptied his saddlebags on the bed. He stared at Meredith's picture for a while and then picked it back up and tucked it into the bottom of his saddlebag. As Alex was taking off his suit and vest he felt something in his vest pocket. When he pulled it out it was the picture of Catherine that he had kept but had forgotten about. He stared at it and then reflected on Catherine's face. Did she feel the same way Meredith did when he left her the first time, he wondered. Had he caused her that much pain? Yes, he had felt drawn to her and they had become good friends while he was in Rosenberg, but he loved Meredith. He still couldn't remember his previous life with Catherine. Alex was exhausted and decided to go see Clarence the next day. He called the front desk of the hotel and asked that they send up a ham sandwich. He hadn't slept well the night before so when he finished his sandwich, he showered and then crawled under the covers naked.

When Alex woke up, the sun was shining through the curtains in the window and he grabbed his pocket watch. It was seven o'clock; he jumped out of bed. He was up half the night and finally had fallen into a deep sleep around two o'clock in the morning. When he went outside, he was surprised that Liberty City was mostly just a railroad station and a few stores. There were a couple of boarding houses, a saloon, a café, and a small train depot. A deep well had been discovered in Hardin and most of the oil companies used Liberty City, Texas, as their headquarters, since the train stopped here. Clarence was at the back of the café seated at a large table when he saw Alex come in.

"Welcome back." Clarence introduced Alex to a younger man in his middle twenties by the name of William Berks.

"Will," he said. "My friends call me Will."

A few minutes later they were joined by two more men. Alex did not know either of them but couldn't help but notice the tall, clean-shaven man. He had seen him before but couldn't remember where.

"This is Trent Matthews and Toby Butler from Humble Oil Company," Clarence said. "The papers have been signed and the merger has taken place. Humble's headquarters are in Houston and we will be operating from there from now on. For the next couple of weeks you will be traveling between Sour Lake, Liberty City, Beaumont, and maybe Humble -- just north of Houston. Trent and Alex will partner up and Will and Toby will be a team. Since Trent and Alex were both shot out on a routine mapping expedition, working in pairs will be safer. Trent and Alex looked at each other but neither said anything. Humble's men will take the lead and bring you two up to snuff on how the company wants things done. You can learn a lot from each other, and I hope you will be comfortable working with each other."

Clarence handed Trent and Toby their leather pouches with the maps and the instructions of where they were to survey and talk to the land owners. "At the end of the week you'll meet me back at Humble's offices in Houston. There will be new instructions and I will be sending Trent and Alex north to work on the Humble, Texas properties at that time. After you have read over your orders, you men need to head out and I'll see you back in Houston on Friday."

Clarence left and Trent motioned the waitress to fill their coffee cups. He took the papers out of the pouch, looked at them for a few minutes and then handed them to Alex. Toby did the same thing. After they had finished reading their instructions without saying a thing, they took their last sip of coffee and got up to leave. Each man mounted his horse and they headed out in pairs in opposite directions.

"Got the supplies you need?" Trent asked Alex. Alex nodded his head yes. Each man had a gun holstered around his hip and they also carried a rifle in their saddle.

Alex and Trent made a lot of progress the first few days. They usually made their camp on the outskirts of the closest town and sometimes they would get permission from an owner to stay on their property to set up a camp near their house. Trent and Alex talked very little about their personal lives. Camp talk was mostly about the property they had surveyed and the maps. By nightfall they were both tired and ready for sleep. Alex never had difficulty falling asleep. He would simply wake up two hours later and then have trouble going back to sleep. This was probably the hardest week he could ever remember. His mind was always on Meredith, Elliott, or Catherine.

On their last night before returning to Houston, Alex and Trent worked until the sun had gone down, which was around seven thirty. Tired and exhausted, Trent suggested they make their camp in a grove of trees several yards from a small, winding creek. They watered their horses and bent down to fill their canteens with water. Not wanting to prepare their dinner, leftover rabbit, beef jerky, and a can of cold beans was the evening meal. They made a small fire and each took out a tin cup, filled it with water and set it close to the fire. Trent took out a small can of tea bags and put one in his cup and offered one to Alex. Trent spoke first.

"How long ago has it been since you were shot?" he asked Alex.

"Almost two years," Alex said. "What about you?"

"About three months ago," Trent said. "They caught the man who shot me and took my horse. Heard they strung him up a while back because he was wanted for killing a couple of men."

They each took a drink of their tea and Alex commented that he still preferred strong coffee, but it was too much trouble. "Guess no one has figured out how to put coffee into these tea bags."

Both men laughed. Alex opened his saddlebags and took out his picture of Meredith. He had done this every night and would stare at it for a long time. He returned it to his saddlebag and then looked in his vest pocket, took out another picture and looked at it. Trent had assumed the first picture was of Alex's wife. Alex went to put the picture back into his vest pocket, but dropped it. The gentle night breeze caught the picture and it glided towards Trent's foot. Trent reached for it and before he could hand it to Alex he caught a glimpse of it and then handed it to Alex. It surprised him that the woman in the picture was the spitting image of Catherine. His curiosity got the best of him.

"Beautiful woman," Trent said. "Who is she?"

Trent thought that maybe Catherine was Alex's sister.

"She was my first wife," Alex answered.

Trent gave him a curious look.

"I was married to her for a couple of months when I got shot. The bullet went through my scalp and I lost part of my memory. I tried hard to remember how we met and got married but I just couldn't. Still can't. There were some other extenuating circumstances, so we decided to have the marriage annulled. I didn't know she was pregnant with my daughter until a year or so later when she moved to my town in Rosenberg after I had met and married someone else. Meredith, my wife now, just gave birth to our son, Elliott. This is the first time I've been away from them and it sure is hard." Trent tried to smile and shook his head like he understood. "What about you? Got a family?" Alex asked.

"No," Trent said. "Had wife for a while, but I was never home much so she ran off with someone else. That was six years ago and I'm still trying to find her so I can get a divorce."

The two men laid their heads back on their sleeping bags and looked up at the sky. Alex was thinking about going home to Meredith and his son. Trent was trying to understand what Alex had just told him. He had been married to Catherine and one of her daughters was his. She had three other children. Catherine had told him her first husband had died. Then who was Isabelle's father, he wondered. He didn't usually ask a lot of questions about people's personal lives, but he couldn't help but ask Alex one more question.

"The woman you were married to, did she ever remarry?"

"No, and it's not because she hasn't had the opportunity. I think she almost married a doctor from Houston, but apparently he was seeing someone else and he got her pregnant so they got married." Alex laughed. "My brother-in-law would marry her but she keeps telling him no. I don't think she will ever remarry," Alex said, looking up at the stars.

"Why do you think that?" Trent asked.

"I'm not sure," Alex said, pondering the question. "I hope she finds someone. From what I've heard, she's had a difficult time since she came to the United States. She needs someone to take care of her; not that she's needy, but I often visit my daughters at her house and I can just tell she is lonely."

Trent had to catch himself before he asked about Issy, and had to think about the question. "Did I just hear you say you had more than one daughter with her?"

"Isabelle, my other daughter, isn't hers. That's another story in itself. Catherine took her in when Isabelle's mother died because I had disappeared and Isabelle was Emma's sister. I'll tell you about that another time. I've probably said more than I should."

Neither man fell asleep for a while. Both stared up at the stars and tried to sleep. Trent could hear Alex's soft, easy breathing finally, and after he was sure Alex was asleep he walked down to the creek. The half-moon gave him just enough light to find his way to a big rock. The croaking frogs began jumping into the water as Trent sat down on the rock. He was trying to sort out in his mind why Catherine had not been on the train and to this day had not tried to contact him. He decided to wait a while before he told Alex that he knew Catherine and that she had saved his life. He shook his head, trying to grasp the fact that the man he was partnered up with had once been married to her and they had a child together. As hard as he had tried over the last three months not to think about Catherine, something or someone always brought him back to the five days they were together. Belle had tried hard to patch up their relationship and Trent had spent a couple of nights with her, but each time he did he swore it would be his last.

They made their way back to Houston on Thursday evening and left their horses at the livery stable. They met at Humble's offices early the next morning to be briefed about the wells and when the men parted they agreed to meet for dinner Sunday evening at six o'clock to look over their orders and plan the next week's work.

CHAPTER 21

Grey Wolf still lived on the Indian reservation where he grew up. He had married his childhood sweetheart, Mary Windsong, but he knew Mary did not love him when they married. She had been in love with a white man named Alex Cooper, whom she had nursed back to health after he suffered a gunshot to his head. She had allowed Alex Cooper into her bed and she became pregnant. When Cooper did not return to marry her, Grey asked Mary's father for her hand in marriage and he convinced Mary to marry him. Mary had died in childbirth and Grey Wolf's hatred for Alex Cooper was undeniable. He vowed revenge and after several failed attempts at trying to end the life of Mary's daughter, Isabelle, he took her to Beaumont and left her at Alex's old office. He still mourned for Mary and was always looking in every town he came to for Alex Cooper. Grey Wolf had purchased a peddler's wagon and frequently traveled to different towns selling the leather goods and trinkets the Indians made on the reservation. That was why he was in Liberty City the day he saw Alex.

Grey had stopped at the general store late one afternoon when he saw two men on horseback riding out of town. He ducked behind a building and swiftly ran down the back of the buildings until he reached the end and stopped. He waited and then stretched his neck around the corner of one of the buildings. It was him, he was sure of it. He was still riding the same horse; Grey pulled back and carefully watched as the two men rode by on their horses. He smiled to himself and thought that Alex Cooper must be working in Liberty City. Grey knew he had some planning to do. He had dreamed of the day when he would find Cooper and take his life. He was sure it was him. The next time he would be prepared to follow them. Right now he was expected back at the reservation to pick up more wares. It was not time. He would wait for the spirits to give him a signal.

Alex caught the train back to Rosenberg, expecting to get there around three o'clock. He missed Meredith terribly and was anxious to get home. He had called ahead and she was waiting for him at the train station. Catherine had offered to keep Elliott for several hours while Meredith picked up Alex in the buckboard. It was a bit cold to have the baby out in the elements and Meredith was not very skilled with driving the buckboard. When Alex got off the train he hugged Meredith a long time and then kissed her. They had a couple of hours before they were expected back at Catherine's house at seven o'clock that evening and they made good use of their time together.

Catherine had heated the bottle and picked up Elliott while Sadie read a book to the children on the living room floor. Adam came over and watched, patting Elliott with the tenderness one would not expect from a boy at three and a half. He was totally infatuated and watched as the baby suckled on the bottle. Catherine pushed his curly locks away from his face and he smiled up at her. Elliott was a good baby and was a delight to care for. He would often just lie on a blanket and kick his feet, moving his arms in constant rhythm. Elliott looked a lot like his father and in a way she had wished Elliott was hers. She loved cuddling and feeding the baby, and she hoped one day she might have another.

She thought of Trent and what a wonderful father he would be. Maybe she was too hard on herself; she knew she had probably made a mistake when she didn't call Trent back and explain why she didn't come. Michael had come between them and she realized that

Michael had actually won. He did everything to keep them apart and yet now she no longer had to worry about Michael. He was going to marry another. She wondered to herself if she was too late and she prayed Trent hadn't gone back to his old girlfriend.

Catherine picked up Elliott, went to the kitchen drawer and took Trent's calling card out. It was not even four o'clock in the afternoon and maybe he was still at his office. She dialed the number and Agnes answered. "Humble Oil Company."

"Could I please speak to Trent Matthews," she asked.

"He's left for the day," she answered. "Sometimes he comes in on Saturdays and gets caught up on his paperwork. I can leave him a message, but I can't promise he'll get the message anytime soon."

"That's all right. This is Dr. Catherine Merit in Rosenberg and I just wanted to find out if he had fully recovered from his injuries. You can just tell him I called." Catherine hung up the phone then realized she had not left a phone number. She wondered if Trent still had her number but decided she wouldn't call back. If he was still interested, surely he could figure out how to call Rosenberg and put the call through.

Catherine picked up the phone and dialled the operator. "Mrs. Blankenship, I might be getting a call from a friend who may have lost my phone number, and I want to be sure you will put the call through," Catherine said. "His name is Trent Matthews."

"Of course," she answered.

After Agnes hung up the phone she tore off the sheet of paper with Catherine's name on it and stuffed it into Trent's mailbox, sliding it under a pile of other letters and papers. All the mailboxes were full with correspondence from the new company and piles of papers each employee had to sign. Trent had noticed the full box before he left and decided he would go through it on Saturday.

Trent had grabbed a sandwich on his way back to his room. He couldn't wait to take off his dirty clothes and get cleaned up. He was standing in the shower washing his hair and the memory of

Catherine washing and cutting his hair came back to him. Ever since Alex had told him about some of Catherine's past, he couldn't stop thinking about her. He wondered what she would do if he just showed up in Rosenberg again. He decided that wasn't a good idea but wasn't sure if he tried to call her now whether the call would go through. He dried off and sat on the bed. When he heard a light knocking on the door he quickly slipped into his pants and opened the door a crack.

Belle was standing outside with a bottle of whiskey in a brown bag. Belle was the last person Trent wanted to see right now, but he was a gentleman so invited her in. Belle put her arms around him as soon as he closed the door; she tried to kiss him. He tried to pull back but she grabbed his groin and began massaging him. Trent tried to back up and fell on the bed. She knew Trent's weaknesses and began rubbing him and kissing him until she felt his arousal. She smiled to herself and began taking off her clothes. She knew Trent didn't love her, but she knew he was a man first and that after five days without a woman it wouldn't be hard to get him aroused. Trent was a wonderful lover -- at least he had been in the past. Today he was different. He was no longer making love to her, he was just having sex. When Trent finished, Belle had tears in her eyes. He wasn't the same man anymore and she knew she had lost him. Belle quietly got out of bed and dressed. Before she left she turned and looked back at him.

"I won't be back," she said, and she shut the door behind her.

Trent lay in bed staring at the ceiling, and hated himself for letting Belle get him aroused. He had always been a good lover and made sure Belle had enjoyed their intimacy as much as he had. He had been rough with her tonight and treated her like she was a prostitute because she had acted like one and had brought it upon herself. Trent knew what he had done was not right but it was the reason she probably was gone for good. It was finally over between them and at least for that he was glad.

The next morning after breakfast Trent made his way to his office, remembering there was lots of mail and correspondence he had to go through. While Agnes was a fairly good receptionist, her filing skills were terrible. Half of the items in his box belonged to someone else and he spent the next thirty minutes sorting through it. There were scraps of papers that he put into a separate pile. Some were from callers and others were just bits and pieces of information scrawled on scraps of paper. The small office was warm; when he opened the window to let some air in, a gust of wind blew half of his piles off onto the floor. Trent cursed under his breath and got down on the floor, trying to get them all back into one pile so he could pick them up.

He got up and closed the window then bent down to retrieve his papers. He had the pile in his hands when he noticed a scrap that had managed to sail under his desk. He picked it up and wondered how long it had been down there. He sat back down and still had the scrap of paper in his hands. When he looked at it he saw the words: *Friday, 4:15. Catherine Merit called to see if you had recovered from your injuries.* Trent breathed out and then took in another breath, holding it for a few seconds and then relaxed, breathing out again. He bit his lower lip and smiled to himself. He wondered why after all this time she decided to call. Trent opened his top drawer and began digging through it. He had carried Catherine's phone number around for days before he finally took it out and put it into his desk drawer. At least that was what he remembered. He gave up looking for it and picked up the phone.

"Could you please put a call through to Dr. Catherine Merit in Rosenberg, Texas? I don't have the number," he told the operator. After hearing the operators speak to each other on the telephone, he finally heard the phone ringing.

Catherine was in her office when she heard the phone. Her heart almost skipped a beat and she prayed it was Trent.

"How are you, Catherine?" Trent said after she answered.

"I'm doing fine. It's really good to hear from you. I owe you an explanation," she said.

"I'm listening," was all Trent could think of to say.

"I would rather tell you in person. Perhaps we could have lunch tomorrow in Houston. I could be there by eleven o'clock if you could meet me at the train station," she said.

Trent didn't answer immediately, remembering the last time when she was supposed to come and she didn't show up. "I promise I won't stand you up again," she said.

"All right then, I'll see you at eleven," Trent said. He hung up when Catherine hung up on her end.

Catherine knew Trent was a man of few words and it didn't surprise her that he had little to say. But he didn't say no, and at least she would be able to explain why she didn't come. She told Martin, Emily, and Sadie that she was going to Houston for the day on Sunday. She said she needed to pick up some medicine in Chinatown and would be home by six o'clock Sunday evening.

That night Catherine went through her closet looking for something to wear. She pulled out her spring ecru dress that she had worn for Samuel. It was probably a bit early to be wearing the pale colors, but the matching shawl would make it look more complete. She had made herself a potion of honey, herbal tea, and some additional herbs that she hoped would help her to sleep. She was excited for the first time in a long time and she prayed that Trent had not gone back to his girlfriend. She remembered him telling her he was a one-woman kind of man.

Trent was finishing up in his office and carefully took the note Agnes had left him about Catherine, folded it and put it in his pocket. He picked up the phone book and looked up the number for Barron's Restaurant. It was an elegant new restaurant that had an indoor atrium and an aviary filled with beautiful birds. He had heard they served a fabulous brunch complete with chefs making crepes and omelettes using your choice of ingredients. He made a reservation for two and told the concierge there would be a large tip if he gave him the best table in the house. He spent the next hour going through his papers, signing what needed to be signed and trashing the remainder.

Trent stopped at the store on his way home to get some cleaning supplies. He hadn't cleaned his apartment in weeks. There wasn't a lot to do since it was so small, and he didn't think he and Catherine would go back to his room, but it was motivation enough for him to dig in and at least change the sheets and straighten it up a bit. It would keep him busy, and he needed to stay busy.

He heard the whistle of the incoming train and decided to wait inside. He didn't want Catherine to think he was anxious. Let her think he had just gotten there. Actually he had been fifteen minutes early.

He was standing by the window looking at the train and his eyes danced from one car to the next. When a petite woman exited the train, his mouth opened and he stared at the most beautiful woman he had ever seen, and realized it was Catherine. She was stunning. Her hair hung softly over her shoulders and part of her hair was tucked neatly up inside a cream-colored hat that had small ostrich feathers curled back around her head. He quickly opened the door and went out to greet her. He took off his hat and bent down, kissing her lightly on the cheek.

"You look beautiful," he said with a smile.

Catherine's eyes sparkled as he bent down and kissed her. He took her arm and led her to a waiting carriage.

"I took the liberty of making a reservation for brunch. It's a fairly new restaurant and I have heard good things about it," Trent told Catherine.

They chitchatted, making small talk about the children, and Trent held Catherine's hand the whole way. She was thrilled he didn't appear to be angry or holding a grudge.

The restaurant was exquisite and Trent knew Catherine was impressed. He was impressed, too, as the concierge showed them to a table that was perfectly situated among flowering trees and a glassed-in aviary. There was a bubble of glass that arched over the entire restaurant, and birds flew freely behind cages that housed them in a natural environment. Trent gave the waiter a large tip and thanked him.

"This is amazing," Catherine said. "I never knew that a place like this existed."

The waiters were all dressed in tuxedo-like uniforms and the tables were elegantly set with European fine china and water goblets. Trent smiled as he watched her take it all in. A waiter came over to their table and offered to fill one of the glasses with Champagne. Trent nodded his head yes. They each took a sip and then a second. It was the finest Champagne either had ever tasted.

"You aren't going to try and get me drunk?" she teased.

"A man can only hope," he teased back. "This is your day, Catherine. You can make it what you want." They looked at each other with a hunger in their eyes and Catherine licked her lips and smiled.

"What I want is for you to forgive me for not calling you. The girls came down sick an hour before I was to get on the train. I couldn't leave them. I knew I should have gotten word to you, but I had convinced myself there was a reason for everything and it wasn't meant for us to see each other. I have to admit I was scared of what Michael was capable of doing. He's engaged to another now, and I don't have to fear him anymore. Can you ever forgive me?"

"Of course, I do," he said. "I don't want you to worry or be sad today. I just want you to relax and enjoy. You take too much responsibility for things you shouldn't. How long has it been since you did something just for you?" he asked. Catherine thought, but couldn't remember.

She smiled and looked down at her hands. Trent picked up his glass of Champagne and held it up, waiting for Catherine to pick up hers. She finally did and Trent said, "Today is a new day for you, Catherine, and I want you to enjoy it."

Their glasses clinked and they took a sip, smiling at each

other. For the next couple of hours they were treated like royalty. The food was delicious and they laughed and talked about everything. They decided that nothing negative would be brought up in the conversation. A lot of their conversation was superficial, but they found a lot of things, happy things, to talk about. They were immediately drawn to each other and neither wanted the day to end. Trent paid the exorbitant bill and left a nice tip. It was worth every penny, he thought to himself.

"When do you plan to return to Rosenberg?" he asked.

"I told my family I would be home by six o'clock," she said.

"Then I need to have you at the train station to catch the four forty train. We still have two hours. Is there anything special you want to do?" he asked.

"I really hate to ask you this, but I'm out of some of my medicine and I can only buy it in Chinatown," she answered.

Trent whistled and a carriage pulled up. After they boarded, they sat beside each other and Trent continued to hold her hand. Catherine talked about how many species of birds they had to find to fill the aviary at the Barron. The driver was listening and told her there were over sixty different species and they were mostly from Brazil and South America. He told them the Barron Restaurant was owned by an eccentric Australian who spent money like it was free. He went on to tell them about the difficulty they had putting the clear glass over the restaurant and that they had brought in a special glass cutter from France to cut each individual piece. He told them that emperors and dignitaries frequently rented the entire restaurant for their entourage, spending thousands of dollars.

"The Australian wasn't so dumb after all," the driver said. They all laughed.

They finally made their way to the heart of Chinatown, and Trent asked the driver if he could wait thirty minutes and then take them to the train station. They were gone almost an hour, but the driver had fallen asleep and was still where he had left them off. They made it to the train station with fifteen minutes to spare.

"I can't begin to tell you what a wonderful day this has been, Trent. I really hope, I mean ..." she sighed. Trent cupped her chin in his hand, forcing her to look at him. She didn't hesitate as she met his lips, and they kissed. They heard the whistle blow from the incoming train and Trent smiled down at her. They were both too timid to say what they really wanted to say. Trent knew if he was going to have any kind of relationship with Catherine it would have to be her idea so he decided to let her speak first.

"I hope we can do this again soon," she said, smiling. I had a lovely time."

"I hope so, too," he said.

Trent held Catherine's hand as they walked toward the train. Catherine was sure Trent was going to leave her hanging and she hated not knowing.

"Trent, be honest with me," she said and hesitated. She knew she had Trent's full attention. "Do you want to see me again?" she asked waiting and hoping he would say what she really wanted to hear.

"Nothing would please me more than to see you again, Catherine." She put her arms around his neck and they clung to each other. Their final kiss was long, hungry, and passionate and neither wanted to let go.

"All aboard," the conductor yelled.

When Trent released her she quickly stepped up into the train. Trent stepped back smiling at her and watched as she sat down by the window. He walked over to the open window as Catherine leaned out. Trent took her hand and reached up to kiss her goodbye once more as the train began to move away from the station. She blew him a final kiss and Trent reached out like he was catching it and pulled his fisted hand to his heart. He continued to watch as the train disappeared down the tracks.

Catherine was almost giddy when the train pulled away from

the station. She had never really been courted before and if this was how it was done, it was the most romantic thing she could imagine. She put her hands to her warm, blushing cheeks and she smiled. Tears of joy were beginning to fill her eyes. How could she not fall in love with this man? He was everything -- and then she stopped, realizing that he had spoken nothing about his previous girlfriend. It didn't matter, she convinced herself. He told her he wanted to see her, and she was sure he was as smitten with her as she was with him. It would be a long week she thought, but she felt sure he would call her.

Later that evening, Catherine was in her office alone after she had put the children to bed. Martin and Emily had finished cleaning the kitchen and gone up to the carriage house. Catherine was still deep in thought about her day with Trent. When she heard the phone ring, she jumped up and ran to answer it.

"I just wanted to make sure you made it home all right," Trent said.

She breathed a sigh of relief. "Yes, I'm all settled in, thank you."

"I'm not sure where my next assignment is going to be, but I expect to be out-of-pocket for a couple of weeks. You said you had a couple working for you now and that they are living in the carriage house. I know Rosenberg's a small town ..." Trent didn't finish his sentence.

"I'll come to Houston," she broke in. "I mean, I don't mind the train ride. I rather enjoy it."

Trent smiled to himself. Catherine was trying to act like a lady but he knew she was attracted to him. No woman had ever kissed him the way she did, and no woman had ever given herself to him the way she had their last night in the carriage house.

"Wonderful," he answered.

They said goodbye to each other. Two weeks, she said to herself. Just two more weeks. She didn't want Trent to think her forward, but there was no way she wanted Trent to meet Michael if he came to Rosenberg, and she felt free when she was in Houston. It had been such a wonderful day and she wasn't going to ruin it by thinking negative thoughts. Trent was right. She had to be more positive.

CHAPTER 22

Trent had just enough time to go home and pick up his leather pouch before he met Alex at the Baxter Hotel. It was an out-of-the-way, small hotel, but it was clean and in a nice part of Houston. Trent had told Alex about it and they met in the lobby. They decided to look over their orders for the week so they could decide the route they needed to go. A few minutes later Clarence joined them. "Sorry to do this, fellows, but I need you to go back to Liberty City first thing in the morning. We've got a few irate home owners who didn't understand some of the paperwork Will and Toby had them sign and while you are there I need you to box up what's left in the office and ship it back to the Houston office. Looks like we might have a big well about to come in outside of Humble, and I need these loose ends taken care of. I'd do it myself, but they want me in Humble tomorrow. I'll see you men in Humble by the end of the week. I'm afraid you'll have to stay and work through the weekend."

The two men had dinner and decided to leave at seven o'clock the next morning and head to Liberty City, visiting with a couple of landowners on their way. The assignment looked easy enough. Trent and Alex didn't take long to form a bond. They had similar work ethics, got right to the point and did their jobs efficiently. Trent was a year older than Alex, who was thirty-two. Trent was thirty-three. Both of their mothers had died at a relatively early age and they had strong, influential fathers who had also died. They both looked up to each other and they were both extraordinarily handsome. Neither rambled on or used unnecessary words. They were smart, direct, and to the point. The men had a great deal of respect for each other and to their knowledge had no enemies to speak of. Unfortunately, Alex did.

Grey Wolf had been watching and waiting for Alex to return. Grey had returned to Liberty City the night before, leaving his peddler's wagon behind on the reservation. He had ridden his horse and had been anxiously waiting all day Monday in hopes of seeing Alex. The pair rode through town at half past two in the afternoon and tied their horses to the hitching post while they went into Glacier's temporary offices. Grey was waiting across the street, cutting away at a piece of wood that, when finished, would look like a toy wooden gun he planned to sell. When the men finally came out he studied Alex and Trent. He could see they both had a single holster and gun on their hips and each carried a rifle on their saddle. Grey knew he could take out Alex with a single throw of his axe to Alex's head. Trent was another story. He hadn't expected they would be traveling in pairs. He decided to wait until they made camp somewhere and take them by surprise during the night. The two men loaded up boxes onto a small buckboard and unloaded them at the train station. After they took the buckboard back to the livery stable, they stopped and purchased some supplies at the general store, mounted their horses and headed northwest.

Grey watched as the men finished their business and left town. Grey stayed a good distance behind them and made sure he wasn't noticed. There were still three hours left of daylight and Grey figured they would make camp on Lazy Bend Creek. It was a favorite watering hole of travelers and it was not uncommon for other campers to be in the vicinity. Grey would be able to blend in and they would assume he was setting up camp for the night just as they were. Grey was in hopes no one else would be around. While Grey often wore the traditional Indian dress, he was in plain leather pants and a work shirt he had bought at the general store. He had his hair tied back in a ponytail with a leather string. His axe and rifle were on his horse along with his bow and arrows, which he kept in its sheath. This would be easy, he thought. He would wait until almost midnight, when they would be in a deep sleep, and attack the big man first, taking him out with his axe, and then slit Alex's throat with his knife. Both weapons were recently sharpened and would cause immediate death.

Just as Grey had thought, they made it to Lazy Bend Creek before dark and the men dismounted and removed the saddles from their horses. Grey dismounted several hundred feet away and waited for the men to water their horses. Grey was patient, and soon he smelled the smoke from their campfire. It was getting dark and the quarter moon shed enough light so he could go to the creek and water his horse. Afterwards, he tied his horse to a small tree limb and began his approach towards the men. The glow from the fire made them easy targets, but Grey wanted every advantage. He had a clear shot, but he didn't want to leave any witnesses behind and if there were other campers in the area, he would give up his position. He wanted it to be clean and there would be nothing left that would indicate that the murderer could be an Indian. He planned to remove his axe, and the knife would leave a clean cut. He felt confident and excited that he would soon have his revenge. There were many horse thieves and bandits who would be blamed. Grey would chase the horses away; he wouldn't take them even though he could get good money for them. If he was caught with the horses, they would assume he had killed the men. No, he thought, he was much smarter than that. All he wanted was revenge. Alex Cooper had to pay, and Grey would see he got his due.

Trent and Alex wanted to get a head start on the next day and decided they would travel until sundown and be able to make Humble by noon the next day. They had purchased bread, cheese, and dried beef and planned to eat lunch in Humble.

"Not sure whether I'm being paranoid or just cautious, but I have a feeling someone might be following us," Alex said in a quiet voice to Trent.

"I have the same feeling," Trent agreed. "Think we should take turns sleeping?" Trent asked.

"I think we should tie the horses up close to where we are sleeping. Pilgrim has keen senses and he will alert us if he hears or sees anything. He is a light sleeper and so am I," Alex said.

"Good idea," Trent said. "I'm a pretty light sleeper, too."

The two men didn't talk a lot. Trent laid out his bedroll and untied his holster from his leg and removed it, laying it to the side of his bedroll. He knew that whoever might be out there would probably wait until they had fallen into a deep sleep and he had no intention of doing that. He checked his gun, making sure the bullets were all in the chambers. There could be more than one and he wanted to be ready. He tried to analyze the situation. If there was more than one, why didn't they just aim their rifles at them and shoot? Maybe there was only one and he was planning to sneak up on them when they fell asleep and slit their throats with a knife. Trent noticed a small log, reached over and rolled it close to his bedroll. Alex watched and gave him a gentle nod of approval. Alex got up and poured the leftover coffee they had brewed on the fire and crawled under his blanket next to his saddle. He, too, had his gun underneath his blanket. He heard Trent doing something and figured he was making his bedroll look like someone was sleeping in it. For some reason neither of the men were greatly afraid but since both had been shot before, they were more cautious and alert.

Trent had memorized most of the surroundings before they put the fire out. He knew that whoever might come after them would come from the east since it was thick with brush and forest. Alex's bedroll would be the most vulnerable since it was closest to the brush and trees.

Trent whispered to Alex that he was going to crawl between two bushes which were only a few feet away from Alex. A few minutes later he said, "I'm in place and will take the first watch."

Trent was able to hide within some dense thicket and he settled in with his gun in his lap. He could barely see Alex, but he could hear his deep breathing. Trent had lots of time to think and it wasn't hard for him to find something to occupy his mind. He relived the whole day he had spent with Catherine and then the last night in the carriage house. Thinking about her beautiful body and the sweet smell of her perfume was captivating, and he imagined himself being married to her. Trent figured he had been taking his watch for several hours when he looked up through a clearing and noticed the moon had moved behind a large tree. He became more alert when he heard one of the horses move. Trent listened intently. He heard a thump and then he saw the shadow of a man with his arm up and a knife in his hand as he approached Alex. Trent squeezed the trigger on his gun, firing it three times. He heard a scream and then a thud. Alex was on his feet instantly and Trent came out of the bushes. Alex kicked the knife away from Grey's hand and both men stood in a guarded position to see if there were any other attackers.

Alex took out a match and lit it, bending down to pick up some brush and put the match to it, adding some kindling of twigs and more firewood. A few minutes later the fire's flames gave off enough light to show a blank expression on the Indian. They both looked at Trent's bedroll and saw an axe embedded deep into the piece of wood Trent had covered with his blanket. Trent walked over and felt for a pulse on Grey's neck and shook his head, indicating he was dead.

"Have you ever seen him before?" Trent asked.

"Yes, I have," Alex answered. "Wasn't he standing across the street from our office when we rode into Liberty City?"

Trent took a closer look and said, "Looks like him. I guess we should take him back to Liberty City in the morning and talk to the sheriff. He might know who he is. Sure hate to lose a whole day, but I'm not much on leaving a dead man."

"Glad we had each other's back," Alex said, "or we might

both be dead."

Neither of the two men got much sleep the rest of the night. They were up early. They rolled Grey in a blanket and tied him to the back of Alex's saddle. They had only gone a few hundred feet when they saw a horse tied to a small tree limb. They found the bow and arrow and blanket Grey had left, so they took Grey and tied him to the pinto and headed back to town. They made good time and made it in just less than two and a half hours. The sheriff came out when he saw them tie up outside his window.

The sheriff walked over and moved the blanket from around Grey's head. "What happened?"

"He tried to kill us," Trent said. "We suspected someone was watching us, so I took the first watch. He put an axe in my bedroll thinking I was asleep, and then went after Alex with his knife. I shot him three times. Do you know who he is?"

"His name is Grey Wolf. He usually comes in a peddler's wagon from the reservation to sell trinkets and wares the Indians make. He's gotten into trouble a couple of times but he's never tried to kill anyone. Guess there's a first time for everything," the Sheriff said.

People were beginning to crowd around, and the sheriff saw a young Indian boy who sometimes traveled with Grey.

"You," the sheriff pointed at the young boy. "Come here." The young Indian hesitated but walked forward. "You know anything about this? You better start talking, or I'll make sure you and your half-breeds never show your faces around here again," the sheriff demanded.

"Grey blamed this white man for his wife's death."

Alex asked, "Who was his wife?"

"Mary Windsong," the young boy said.

Everyone looked at Alex. "I'd rather talk to you in private," Alex said to the sheriff. Alex followed the sheriff inside and came out fifteen minutes later.

"All right, everyone needs to go take care of their own business. Grey Wolf got what he deserved," the sheriff said as he handed the reins of Grey's horse to the Indian boy. "Take him back to your reservation and I don't want to see any of your kind back here in a long time. Now get out of here."

Alex and Trent left a while later and neither said anything. Trent was curious but he knew Alex would tell him when the time was right. He could see Alex was deep in thought and disturbed by the whole thing. Trent was bothered by it, too. He had never killed a man before, and even though Indians had little status in the communities they were still human beings. He knew he would never forget the stone-cold look on the Indian's face. It finally hit him that Grey was wearing war paint.

It wasn't until evening that Alex finally told Trent the whole story of how he came to know Mary Windsong and how after Alex had gone to the sanatorium Mary must have married and given birth to Alex's daughter. He had been told that Mary died in childbirth.

Alex turned to Trent, "I owe you my life. If you hadn't shot him I'd have a knife in my gut."

"Could have been the other way around. Had you been on the first watch, you would have saved my life," Trent said. "So your daughter is now living with Catherine?"

"Yes. Catherine was afraid I was going to take her away when we met up again. But I couldn't do that. Emma and Isabelle are really close and Catherine is a good mom. I didn't want to bring any more hurt upon her. I knew she took it really hard when I left her, and for that I'm sorry," Alex said.

Trent wanted to ask more questions but decided he had heard enough. He didn't care what Catherine's past was, and if the occasion arose and she wanted him to know about her past it would be her decision. He felt he had already crossed the line by not telling Alex he was seeing her. The more he thought about it the more he realized how awkward it would be if he and Catherine developed a relationship together so he decided to say something to Alex.

"I don't usually talk about the women in my life, but this is really an unusual situation," Trent said, knowing he had Alex's full attention. "I met Catherine a while back when I was shot up by the Brazos River. She patched me up and let me recuperate in the room over the carriage house." Trent stopped and decided he had said enough.

"I heard about that incident, but I didn't know it was you," Alex said. "It really is a small world, isn't it?" Trent nodded and hoped Alex wouldn't ask him a lot of questions.

"You said you don't usually talk about the women in your life; are you and Catherine seeing each other?" he asked.

"She came to Houston last week and we had lunch together, that's all," Trent said.

"She's a very unusual woman, Trent. My brother-in-law would do just about anything to get her to marry him. She swears she'll never marry again, but I wish you luck. I can't help but worry about her a bit since that article was in the Houston paper about her killing a man," Alex said. He had Trent's full attention. Alex told Trent the story of the night she had shot Joe Brady. "I guess I shouldn't be telling you all these things about her, but if you do decide to pursue her, do it with caution. She's been hurt an awful lot and I do hope she finds someone. I wish you luck," Alex said.

Alex hadn't told Trent anything he hadn't already figured out himself or could have read in a newspaper. It was obvious Catherine had built a wall around herself and her family. Actually it was more like a fortress, he thought. Trent was deep in thought when Alex asked him if he planned to see her again.

"I'm planning on it, but you obviously have known her longer than I have and she might tell me no. It wouldn't be the first time," he said, poking the fire with a stick. "Women sure are complicated," Trent said.

Alex laughed, "Wait until you get married. Unfortunately you have to keep playing these games so they always think they have the upper hand. Meredith is a strong woman just like Catherine, and she really keeps me on my toes." Alex took out Meredith's and Catherine's pictures and looked at both of them. "Meredith is everything to me and I can't wait to get back to her and my son. I'm not sure why I keep Catherine's picture in my vest pocket, but maybe I was just waiting for the right man to give it to. Here," he said as he handed Trent Catherine's picture. "Maybe it will bring you luck. She needs a man like you."

Trent was touched and he knew somewhere hidden deep in Alex's mind he really cared for Catherine. "Thanks, I'll keep it safe," Trent said, taking the picture.

CHAPTER 23

It was a long two weeks for Catherine and Meredith. Catherine had no idea who Alex' partner was until she was having tea one afternoon with Meredith and the baby.

"What did you say Alex's partner's name was?" Catherine asked as she stopped and held in her breath.

"I'm pretty sure he said Trent Matthews. He was paired up with him since he works for Humble Oil Company and the companies merged. Alex said he was a real gentleman and just as knowledgeable as he was. I'm so glad they are working in pairs." Meredith noticed that Catherine went quiet, and asked if she had said something disturbing. "Do you know this Trent Matthews?" Meredith asked.

"Yes, I treated him a while back when he was working in our area. He too had gotten shot, and I took care of him for a few days. You are right, it's nice they are working in pairs and can watch out for each other."

After Meredith left, Catherine couldn't help but wonder how things were falling into place. What were the odds that Trent and Alex would meet, much less be traveling partners. She wondered why Trent had not said anything to her, but realized that it was because Alex would never say anything about Catherine's past to anyone. At least she thought he wouldn't. She decided not to worry about it.

That evening Trent called Catherine. "I'll be back in Houston Thursday night and I've decided to find a new place to live. I've been staying in a one room efficiency apartment and it's all right for sleeping, but I need more space. I was wondering if you might come to Houston this weekend and help me look. I'll be happy to get you a room at the Roosevelt unless you would rather stay somewhere else."

"I think I could arrange that," she said, trying to sound like it was unimportant. "I could probably come in on the morning train that arrives at ten o'clock on Friday if that works for you."

"It's perfect," Trent said. "I'll get some things lined up and will get us a carriage for the day. How long would you like to stay in Houston?" Trent asked.

"Two would be great. I'd like to do some shopping on Saturday if that's all right."

"Then we'll make it a weekend," he said, smiling to himself.

Catherine hung up the phone and felt her excitement escalate. She wished she wasn't so attracted to Trent. He would make a wonderful friend. What if she fell in love with him and he didn't fall in love with her? She took in a deep breath. I need to let myself go a bit, she thought. Nothing is perfect, and she was going to spend three beautiful days with a handsome man. What more could any woman want?

Catherine had lost several pounds over the last few months and the dresses she had seemed to hang like feed sacks on her. She should have already done the alterations herself, but she kept putting it off, thinking she wouldn't need them for a while. She would take them to the alterations lady the next day, and ask if she could at least alter one of her favorite dresses.

Wednesday was really busy and she decided she would just have to make do with what she had. Later, when she stopped at the bank, she would look at the general store and the church thrift shop. Finally the last patient left and she hurried to get her purse. She kissed the children goodbye and told them when she got back she would read them a story.

She stopped at the alterations shop first. Esther was a very good dressmaker but usually just did alterations. Catherine noticed a beautiful, teal-green satin dress hanging up with a darker corresponding green jacket hanging behind it.

"Oh my," Catherine said. "This is so elegant."

"I have to send it back to New York. The lady who ordered it said she found something she liked better and doesn't want it anymore," Esther said. "Would you like to try it on?"

Catherine flipped the tag over and saw it was a size smaller than she usually wore, but she couldn't resist giving it a try. She went into the dressing room and made a quick change.

"Oh my goodness," Esther said. "It's stunning on you, and it fits perfectly." Catherine turned and looked at the back of the dress in the mirror and turned to see the front view again.

"How much is it?" Catherine asked.

"It's six dollars," Esther said. "But I will let you have it for five if I don't have to return it to the store. They always charge me a restocking fee if I return something, and it would save me the postage."

Catherine had eighteen dollars she was going to deposit at the bank and decided she had not bought herself anything in a long time and she wanted it. She would be frivolous, she thought, and then said, "I'll take it."

Catherine left three dresses for Esther to take in and left with a huge smile and a shopping bag. She couldn't remember ever being so excited about anything.

When Catherine walked into the bank, Michael was coming out with a lovely young woman who looked to be Catherine's age. She moved aside so they could pass, but Michael stopped to introduce the woman. "This is Elaine Cummings, my fiancée," he said.

Catherine couldn't help but smile with relief. "It's my pleasure. I'm Dr. Catherine Merit," she said. Both ladies were polite and proper. "When is the wedding?" she asked.

"Her father owns a chain of drug stores in Houston, so we are getting married there in two weeks," Michael said.

"I'm very happy for you," Catherine said and excused herself.

Catherine woke early Friday morning and decided to wear an outfit that was less dressy than the one she had purchased. She wanted to wear some good walking shoes if they were going apartment hunting and the new dress she had purchased would be saved for Saturday. She was touched that Trent wanted her to help him find a new place to live. It was confirmation to her that he had not gone back to his girlfriend. She was smiling to herself, too, because Michael had found himself an innocent young woman to marry. She almost felt sorry for her. The poor girl had no idea what she was getting herself into, and Catherine certainly wasn't going to say anything.

She was waiting inside the depot for her train to arrive when Michael and Elaine walked in. Elaine noticed Catherine and started walking towards her. Michael reluctantly followed.

"Hello, Catherine. Are you traveling to Houston today?" she asked.

"Yes, I have some business there," Catherine answered.

"That's wonderful. We can sit together and you can catch me up on Rosenberg's society." Catherine looked at Michael, who was glaring at her.

"Why yes, that would be nice," Catherine said.

"Maybe I should escort both of you ladies to Houston. I don't have much on my schedule today and I would be honored to do that," Michael said.

"Oh, Michael. It's an express and besides, since I'm going to be living in Rosenberg, Catherine and I could become really good friends," Elaine said.

"I promise I'll speak kindly of everyone in Rosenberg," Catherine said, smiling. She enjoyed watching Michael squirm. Actually, she had no intentions of saying anything bad about Michael. No one wanted him to get married more than she did, and then he would be out of her life for good.

"Well then, I'll see you to your train." Michael took both ladies' arms and walked them out to board the train. Michael gave Elaine a long kiss and escorted her on first and then pulled Catherine back. He leaned down and whispered, "Don't say anything you might live to regret." Elaine came back looking for Catherine and saw them talking.

"I'm so glad the children are well now. Your daughter really gave me a scare," Catherine said out loud and removed Michael's arm from hers. She smiled as she boarded the train.

Elaine took a window seat and Catherine scooted in beside her on the bench. "I'm delighted that we have some time to visit. It's hard, moving to a new town and not knowing anyone."

"How long have you known Michael?" Catherine asked.

"My father and Michael have been friends for years. I've always looked up to him. We got reacquainted a couple of months ago when Michael attended a society ball. He has been courting me and writing the sweetest letters. After he got permission from my father to marry me, he took me to a wonderful new restaurant called the Barron and that's where he proposed. I was really taken aback, but I know he'll make a good husband and I've met his two children as well as Meredith and her husband, Alex," Elaine said. "What does your husband do?"

"I'm a widow," she answered.

"Oh, I'm sorry, I didn't know. You are wearing a wedding band and I just assumed you were married."

Catherine had been looking out the window and turned to Elaine. "I have discovered that by wearing a wedding band I am not as easy a target. It's safer and discourages would-be suitors."

"Yes, I can understand that, except I live in the safety of my parents' home and my father can run them off with one look," Elaine commented. They both laughed.

They continued to make small talk and Catherine guarded her words cautiously. There were a lot of things Catherine disliked about

Rosenberg; the constant flooding in the streets after a rain, the small town gossip and until now, Michael. But Catherine kept her opinions to herself.

When Catherine got off the train, Trent was waiting for her and she longed to run into his arms, but Elaine was not far behind, so she introduced them.

"Well, you didn't tell me you had a handsome friend waiting for you." Catherine was taken aback by Elaine's flirtatious manner.

Trent had rented a carriage for the day and offered to give Elaine a ride.

"Oh, that is so kind of you, but, oh, there he is now, my father," Elaine said. She made the necessary introductions and gave Catherine her phone number. "I doubt you will have extra time, but you can call me if you find yourself without something to do. I'll be sure and send you both a wedding invitation," she said, and left with her father.

Trent took Catherine's arm and led her over to where his horse and carriage had been tied up. "Is she anyone I should know?" Trent asked Catherine when they got into the carriage.

Catherine laughed. "That girl is Michael's new fiancée, and we just happened to be on the same train."

Trent gave her an incredulous look. "The world is getting smaller by the minute," he said.

"What do you mean?" she asked.

"I was going to save it until later, but I guess now is as good a time as any to tell you that I'm working with Alex Cooper," Trent said.

Catherine was silent for a while as they made their way through the streets. Trent waited for what seemed like forever before she said something.

"Then I guess he told you we were married for a short while," she said in a disappointed manner.

"Yes, he did, Catherine, but I can assure you that Alex and I are gentlemen first and he was very brief in his comments. Besides, I really don't care what your past is. It's your business, and I'll make no demands on you with regard to it. Trent was holding the reins to the horse but released one of his hands, taking her hand and placing it on his knee and then smiled down at her. She returned the smile but Trent could tell Catherine's demeanor was guarded. They rode in silence for a while and Catherine's hand rested on his knee.

A while later they pulled down a street by a row of town houses that reminded Catherine of the one Samuel lived in. Trent pulled the carriage over to the side and pulled a board up to lock the wheels. He put his arm around Catherine and turned her toward him. He bent down and planted a soft, tender kiss on Catherine's mouth. She gave a soft sigh and kissed him back.

"All better?" he asked. She smiled at him and felt giddy inside. He was the sweetest man, she thought, and her worries subsided.

A man was standing outside the town house and turned to unlock the door when Catherine and Trent walked up. The man gave Catherine a suspicious look but introduced himself. Trent introduced himself and Catherine. They entered a common hallway and then the landlord unlocked the interior door to the apartment. It was dark inside because the electricity was turned off. The man walked over and drew the curtains back.

"Not much in here, like I told you, just the basics; a bed, chest of drawers, table and two chairs, and that couch over there. You can buy anything else you need. Oh, and there is an icebox. Ice is delivered Monday, Wednesday, and Friday."

Trent held Catherine's hand and walked over to the kitchen area, which had two small burners, an oven, and a long table that extended out and divided the kitchen from the small living room. Trent released Catherine's hand and walked around the bed and into the tiny bathroom which had a stand up shower in the small bathtub, a toilet, and a sink.

"If you sign the papers today, you can have it for eighteen dollars a month," the man said. Trent walked over and looked out the small window into the street. He saw a streetcar stop across the street; he liked that transportation was so close to the front door of the town house.

Trent looked at Catherine and she smiled at him. "I think it could be fixed up really nice," she said. "It's spacious and in a good part of town."

Trent smiled and said, "All right then, I guess I'll take it."

The landlord took a piece of paper out of his pocket and filled out some information and had Trent sign it. It was a three-month lease and that was fine with Trent. If anything developed between him and Catherine, three months would be long enough. If not, he would stay there and renew his lease even though he knew the landlord only wanted a three-month lease so he could go up on the rent upon its expiration. Trent was given two keys. One opened the main door to a hallway that led to three more apartments and the other key opened his apartment. There were four mailboxes; the landlord told him his apartment number was 3-A, then turned and showed him which mailbox was his.

When the landlord left, Catherine and Trent went back into the apartment and gave it a closer look. "If you want, we can pick up some cleaning supplies and I'll help you clean it," she said.

"I didn't bring you all the way to Houston to be my cleaning lady," Trent laughed. "I didn't expect I would like the first one I looked at, but it's got everything I need so I didn't want to tire you out tramping all over Houston. This was my first choice because I can walk to my office and I can catch the trolley to the train station."

"Since you won't let me help you clean, let's go ahead and move your things since you have the carriage for the day," she suggested.

Trent walked over and put his arms around her and looked down at her. "You sure you don't mind? We could probably do it in one trip. I've already boxed up most of the stuff and packed my clothes. I have already given notice and I have to be out of the place on Monday."

"Then, best we get going," she said.

They spent the next hour putting the few things Trent owned in the back of the carriage and under the front bench. It was tight, and Catherine had to sit close to Trent because they had to put a box on the front seat, too. Trent took one last look around his old apartment and knocked on an adjoining door. An elderly woman came out and he gave her the key. They were at the town house thirty minutes later. Catherine had noticed one of the smaller boxes was open and had some cleaning supplies in it. She took them out and proceeded to start cleaning the bathroom. Trent was busy hanging up his clothes in the closet and when he looked around he didn't see her.

"Catherine," he yelled. He opened the front door and walked out. His first thought was that she had simply left. He opened the front door to the street and didn't see her. When he turned around and walked back inside his town house he walked right into her, causing both of them to fall to the floor. He managed to twist around her so he would take the brunt of the fall and she fell on top of him. They both began to laugh and then Trent grabbed her and hugged her.

"You gave me a start," he said. "I thought you had left me."

Catherine wove her fingers through his hair and gave a half smile, biting her lip. They looked into each other's eyes as though they were searching for an answer. Trent couldn't wait any longer. He kissed her with a passion and desire he had never felt before. He swept the hair from her neck and began nuzzling her with his kisses. His sweet, breathy kisses lulled her into a languid state and she let out a soft sigh. Trent finally fell back beside her and stared up at the ceiling. He thought he was going to die if he couldn't have her. But not yet, he told himself, not now. He let out a huge sigh and rolled up, leaning on his elbow staring down at her. She said nothing and did nothing. God, she was so seductive, so alluring, and so beautiful. He got up and reached his hand down to her. She grabbed it and pulled herself up.

"Regardless of what you say, I'm going back to clean the bathroom," she teased.

Trent watched her leave the room and a minute later he heard the water running. Trent took some sheets out of another box and made the bed. He topped it with a blanket and threw the two pillows on top. He never had a bedspread but it would have to do for now. Trent took out his pocket watch and looked at it. Catherine had also finished, and walked out drying her hands with a towel.

"It's almost one thirty, and I bet you are hungry. We can go by the hotel and check you in so you can leave your bag," Trent said.

"We can do that later. My bag will be fine here," she said. "Actually, I'm ravenous. Give me just a minute," Catherine added and walked back towards the bathroom. "I need to pin up my hair. It sort of got messed up," she smiled.

They decided to walk the two blocks to a café Trent had eaten at once before. They found a small table in the back and Trent waited for Catherine to be seated before he pulled out his chair.

"It's a relief to have that out of the way. Now we can spend the rest of the day doing whatever you want," Trent said. Catherine looked up at Trent, taking in his broad, muscled shoulders, and for a moment losing herself in the thought of his holding her and bedding her. She relaxed and smiled at him.

"I like being with you, Trent," she said smiling. "Do you mind if I ask you a question?"

Trent leaned forward with anticipation and took her hand. She placed her other hand on top of his. "You did say you had broken up with your girlfriend, didn't you?"

Trent smiled. "Yes, and I also told you I was a one-woman kind of man. Does that scare you?" he asked. Catherine looked down and shook her head, no.

"This is different," he said. "I guess I've never really courted a woman before and I must admit it's a bit awkward. I'm very attracted to you, and I don't mean I just want to take you to bed. I like being with you. I feel like I've known you a long time and I know that sounds crazy."

The waitress came over and took their order, interrupting their conversation. After she left, Catherine said, "I feel the same way. I didn't think for a minute that you were just interested in me sharing your bed and since Michael is out of my life, I'm open to the possibility of getting to know you better." Trent wanted to jump across the table and kiss her, but instead he took her hand and kissed it.

"So, you really don't care if I have a terrible past and have four children?" she asked.

"No, it doesn't matter what you have or have not done, Catherine. I'm a good judge of character and I've seen how you are around your family."

"I'm not very good at relationships, Trent, and I don't want to give you the wrong idea. I do find you very attractive and I enjoy your company. What if I told you I had killed a man," she said.

"So have I," Trent said. "And I bet it was for the same reason. You had to, or they would have killed you first. I'm not shocked by anything, Catherine. You need to take back what it is you've lost. You don't seem to think you deserve to be happy."

Trent could see the hurt in Catherine's eyes and he knew he had struck a nerve. She was close to tears.

"You have no idea what I have lost. It hasn't been easy for me, losing two husbands and trying to raise four children by myself. I have to take them into consideration as well. I know I am independent and set in my ways; you have to understand that I can make no promises."

"You have obviously been hurt by someone or maybe several people, but whatever it is, you aren't going to shock me or run me off. You were not responsible for whatever it was that has caused you to feel you don't deserve happiness. I want you to put everything aside, Catherine, and live for today. You have such a great future ahead of you and I want to be a part of it."

Catherine tried to smile, but she had spent years accepting the indignities she had suffered and feeling that she was not worthy of happiness.

Neither could finish eating their food, and Trent paid the tab. They got back in the carriage and said very little until they got to the livery stable and returned the horse and carriage. They took the trolley back to Trent's new apartment. Trent hated himself for what he had said. He had spoiled their weekend and he prayed Catherine would not want to return home.

CHAPTER 24

When they walked into the town house, Catherine walked over and picked up her bag. "I'm sorry, Trent; I guess I'm not ready for a relationship. I think I need to go back home."

"I'm sorry I hurt you, Catherine. That wasn't my intention. It seems like every time I start getting close to you, you back away. Is that what you really want? Maybe I'm presumptuous, but I think you want to be with me, too."

Catherine set her small satchel down and sat on the couch.

"I guess I'm afraid of falling in love again. I'm not very good at it and the men seem to always leave me for one reason or another. I know I am a bit mixed-up when it comes to relationships. My children are my life and I have to think of them first. You are a very kind and considerate man and I like you a lot and I want to continue seeing you, but I can't make any promises." She chewed her lip and looked up at him.

Trent walked over and rummaged through a box until he found what he was looking for. He took out two glasses and a bottle of wine and set it on the table in front of Catherine. He opened the bottle and poured them each a glass of wine. He looked at her tenderly and sat down beside her; he picked up one glass and handed it to her. They sipped on their wine and talked, but Trent felt like she was drifting into a quiet world all her own. He pulled her closer to him and held her in his arms and she soon drifted off to asleep.

Trent had dozed off, too, and when he woke up Catherine was gone. He stood up, walked over and knocked on the bathroom door. When there was no answer he opened the door only to find the room empty. He turned on a light and saw that she had also taken her satchel. Trent cursed under his breath, locked the door to his apartment and caught the trolley to the train station. When he walked into the depot, Catherine was sitting in a chair looking down at her folded hands. The train was pulling in.

Trent walked over and sat down beside her, taking her hand in his. "I'm a patient man, Catherine."

She stood up when the porter called for people to board the train to Rosenberg. Trent stood up too. "Goodbye, Trent," she said and walked out the door.

Trent followed a few feet behind her. If this was the last time he was going to see her, he would embrace the last few minutes of her beauty. He watched as she stepped up on the platform and into the train. His eyes darted up and down the car she had stepped into, hoping she would take a window seat. Just one more look, please God, let me see her just once more. He stepped out of the way of a man carrying a suitcase and swept the car with eager eyes. The train was moving and he felt like someone had knifed him in the stomach. He put his hands in his pockets and just stared as each car pulled past him. He almost jumped onto the last car, but decided he needed to give her some space. The caboose was the last car, and he turned and watched it heading out. He started to leave and saw someone several yards away on the other side of the railroad tracks. He stood watching. He stopped breathing for a second, and then he went to her.

She rushed into Trent's arms and held him tight. She began softly crying and clutching him. "I really have no idea why you want to be with me, but if you will be patient, I'll give it a try."

Trent grabbed her and kissed her. When he finally released her, he grabbed her satchel and said, "Come on. I just ran out of my patience."

The trolley had just arrived when they got to the street. Catherine sat down on the crowded bench and looked up at Trent, who was holding onto the leather strap above her. Trent was looking down at her and each time their eyes met they both smiled in anticipation.

It was dark when they got to the town house and Trent clicked on the light. They stood kissing for a while and slowly Trent began unbuttoning Catherine's dress. She was captured by his intensity and her body ached to be close to him. For some reason all her fears were gone and she knew she had to put her trust in Trent, forget about everything in her past, and give him a chance.

Trent reached over and turned off the light. He picked up Catherine and carried her to the bed and after pulling the blanket back, he laid her down and untied her shoelaces and removed her shoes. She pulled at his shirt, wanting him to kiss her again; her body ached for the joy of what was to come. He pulled away, took off his boots and turned to her, kissing her with a fierceness that made his knees grow weak. He removed her dress and pantalets and began removing the rest of his clothes. His hot, throbbing body covered hers and he could feel her soft breast rise up to meet his chest as she quietly whimpered. He kissed her neck and she searched his body with her trembling hands, pulling him closer to her.

Trent gently moved her legs apart with his knee and slowly began kissing her breasts, her navel, and then he nuzzled himself into the sweet, alluring scent between her legs. She arched herself up as he teased her with his tongue. She called out his name and softly screamed, don't stop. Trent knew he couldn't wait much longer and he tore open the packet with his teeth and slipped on the protective cover.

He mounted her in the missionary position and gently eased himself inside her. She was small, and he tried to gently push himself inside her, not wanting to cause her any pain. She rose up and pushed herself onto him and met him thrust for thrust and the overwhelming ritual of their ancient mating took them into a world that seemed not to exist. Catherine fought to breathe and then screamed out, not wanting Trent to stop.

She closed her eyes and felt like she was in a cocoon swaying in a cloud. She had lost herself in the experience of the moment and she felt a bond with Trent that would never be broken. Their rhythm sped up, and her body was aching, knowing that her throbbing release would soon come. Her last gurgling moan told Trent that he had fulfilled her erotic desire and he thrust himself deeper inside her losing all consciousness of the real world, and the lights began to explode in his head as he finally gave in. He rolled over beside her and pulled her close to him.

After Trent regained his composure he rose up and put his arm under his head, staring at this beautiful creature that had brought him so much pleasure. Disheveled strands of Catherine's hair had fallen across her eyes and he gently used one of his fingers to move it away. She opened her eyes and smiled at him. Catherine was still marveling in the fascination of her deep orgasm. She couldn't remember ever feeling one so deep, so long, and so pure.

She took his hand and moved his index finger into her mouth and gently teased it with her tongue. He had one of his legs draped over her and she felt the enormous muscle between his legs come to life. She saw the gentleness and love in his eyes and she pulled his face closer to her and gave him a long, succulent kiss that sent tingles down Catherine's spine. He searched her mouth with his tongue and he pulled her on top of him. She spread her legs and straddled him. Her pink, luscious nipples hardened again and she arched back when he embraced her breasts with his hands, softly teasing them with his fingers. She whimpered and rolled her head back.

Trent felt the warmth between her legs and he teased her with his fingers until she thought she couldn't wait anymore. Trent reached over to the table to grab another rubber and she took it from him. She opened it and placed it on him and then placed him inside her.

Trent's rugged groan only excited Catherine more. They began moving together and she fit him like a glove. The momentum of their rhythmic moves penetrated throughout their hungry bodies until they both exploded like an erupting volcano, each feeling the deep aftershocks of their tremors. Catherine fell on top of Trent and he could feel her heart beating rapidly and then she slowed her breathing and gently rolled off. Trent moved with her, holding her, not wanting to ever let her go; they held each other for a long time.

They wanted to confess their love for each other but neither wanted to say it first, so they lay in silence, a peaceful and loving silence. For now all the turmoil in Catherine's life was gone and in its place was a deep love for a man whom she hoped she could spend the rest of her life with. She had loved before but it was always with trepidation and uncertainty. Trent was strong enough for both of them and if he asked her to marry him, she wouldn't hesitate. She would go anywhere with him as long as she had her children.

Trent lay next to Catherine and her slow, easy breathing melted his heart. She was asleep now, content in his arms. Trent rarely cried, but he had to fight back a tear when he thought that he had almost lost her. He decided that when they went shopping the next day he would buy her an engagement ring. He was divorced now and there was nothing stopping him. He smiled to himself and then wondered what he would do if she said no. He would be patient. They had come this far and he was sure she felt the same way he did.

He was looking down at her when she woke up thirty minutes later. She smiled up at him and said, "I know there isn't any food in the house or I would cook you the most wonderful meal."

"I was just thinking of going out and getting something. What did you have in mind?"

"Surprise me," she said.

"Promise you'll still be here when I get back?" he said teasingly.

"You are stuck with me for the next two days," she giggled.

"I suppose you would like some wine with that order," he said more as a question.

"Hmm, sounds good," she said as she stretched her arms over her head.

Trent bent down and kissed her hard and got up. "If I don't leave now, I may never leave."

While Trent was gone Catherine got in the shower and washed her hair. She had brought her own soap and enjoyed the pounding of the water on her head. She felt as though her life had taken a complete one hundred and eighty degree turn, and she had never felt so happy. She knew very little about Trent except that he was an oil scout but his kind, easygoing spirit overwhelmed her and it just felt right.

Trent returned an hour later with wine, fried chicken, mashed potatoes, gravy, and corn. It looked like a feast. She had put on her nightgown, and a lace robe fell off one of her shoulders as she picked up her glass of wine. Her wet hair hung in clusters of curls around her beautiful face. Trent couldn't take his eyes off the open neckline of her gown showing the crease of her soft, luscious breasts. "You are so beautiful, I can hardly take my eyes off of you," Trent said.

They talked and laughed as they dined on their country dinner, sipping their wine and engrossing themselves in the pleasure of each other's company. When they finished eating, Trent poured their wine glasses full again.

"Do you mind if I ask what changed your mind at the train station?"

Catherine sighed and took a sip of her wine and then let out another sigh.

"You were right when you said I was running away from something. When I saw the look on your face when I got on the train, I realized I was running away from me; my fears, my past, and now you. You were a future I didn't think I was worthy of and you made me realize that I would always be running away unless I stopped to embrace what was before me. I really want to be with you and I would be doing both of us an injustice if I didn't at least try. I'm in love with you, Trent Matthews."

Catherine bit her lip and looked down. There, she had said it, and she prayed he wouldn't reject her.

"Tell me again," Trent said. "Tell me you love me again."

She looked up and saw him smiling at her, "I do love you; I really do."

Trent almost knocked over the table when he got up. He picked Catherine up from the chair and swung her around, kissing her and holding her. "I love you too, Catherine." He put her back down on the floor and got down on one knee, holding her hands. "Will you marry me?"

Catherine knelt down in front of him and put her arms around his neck. "I do want to marry you, Trent Mathews. Nothing would please me more."

They made love several times during the night; every time the intensity of their love grew stronger. They slept until after nine o'clock and Trent woke first. He sat up on his side with his hand holding his head, just staring at her. She had said yes, and all he could think of was how he could get her to the preacher before she changed her mind.

Catherine finally woke and stared up at his handsome, rugged face. She sighed and closed her eyes again. "I should have asked you one question before I said yes," Catherine said.

"You can ask me anything, but I'm not going to let you change your mind. A promise is a promise," he said.

She giggled and then became very serious and bit the bottom of her lip. "You do believe in God?" she asked hesitantly.

"Of course, I believe in God," Trent answered back. "I was raised Catholic; but I have to admit I haven't set foot in church for a long time."

Catherine screamed and stood up on the bed. Trent watched her in amazement; she was acting like a little girl. He started laughing when she began jumping up and down on the bed.

"So, you're all right with my Catholic upbringing?" he asked.

"I'm also Catholic. We can get married by a priest," she said, getting even more excited.

Trent laughed and said, "If that's what you want. I'll have to go to confession first and it's been quite a while since I've done that. He grabbed her hand and pulled her down on top of him. He slid her nightgown off of her and started kissing her neck, but she pulled away.

"I don't want to be intimate with you anymore," she said. Trent looked puzzled. "I want us to get married first."

"Then I suggest you get yourself dressed. The Catholic church is a block away."

Trent took a quick shower and shaved while Catherine dressed. He had wrapped a towel around himself when he walked into the bedroom. Her beauty was almost overwhelming. She looked like an angel, he thought.

"You really are beautiful," he said. "I know I keep telling you that, but every time I look at you it's like I'm seeing you for the first time."

Trent quickly dressed while Catherine did her hair. Catherine had put coffee and a kettle of water on the stove earlier and they sat at a small table and ate pastries and drank their beverages.

Catherine had dressed in the new ensemble that she had purchased the day before she left Rosenberg. The hat she had worn was a pale ivory color and she had placed a green flower on top of the rim to pick up the green in her dress. She was lovely.

"I love you, Catherine," Trent confessed again. "You've made me a very happy man."

CHAPTER 25

Trent stopped at a jewelry store first, and together they picked out matching wedding bands. As they approached a floral stand, Trent walked over and asked Catherine what kind of flowers she liked. She looked carefully at several different ones and finally picked up a ready-made bouquet of spring flowers. There were six pale-pink roses and an assortment of small flowers and baby's breath. She beamed as she held them up to her nose and took a whiff. Trent paid for them and grabbed her hand. "Let's do this," he said.

Mass had already ended when they stood in front of St. Joseph's Cathedral. Trent opened the heavy, inlaid door to the chapel. They both touched the holy water with their finger tips and made the sign of the cross. The priest and an altar boy were putting away the chalice and cloths they had used for Holy Communion. When the priest heard the door close, he turned and watched as Catherine and Trent approached him.

"We would like for you to marry us, Father," Trent said.

"When would you like for me to perform this ceremony?" he asked.

"Uh, we would like to do it today, if you could work us in," Trent said.

"And why all the hurry?" the father asked.

Catherine is only in Houston for two days and I leave for work out of town on Monday. We were just hoping we could do this today," Trent said.

"Very well," the priest said. "When was your last confession?" he asked.

This time Catherine spoke. "Father, neither of us have been very dutiful in our Catholic obligations and we would like for you to hear our confessions first."

"So, both of you are Catholic?" he asked.

"Yes, Father, we are," Trent said.

"Very well then, I was going to catch up on my paperwork this morning, but apparently performing the union of matrimony trumps that. Who would like to be first?"

Trent spoke first. "I guess I should, because my penance will be much longer than Catherine's."

The priest turned to the altar boy, who was busy folding up the kneeling rails. "Please go to the rectory and get two rosaries from the gift shop area." The boy eagerly left. "I'm assuming you did not bring your rosaries," he said, looking doubtfully at Catherine and Trent. They were holding hands and Trent squeezed Catherine's. They both shook their heads, no.

"Very well, follow me," the priest said, walking toward the confessional. Catherine walked up to the statue of the Virgin Mary and lit seven candles, kneeling before it and praying for her deceased family and Minnie Wyman, a good friend who had also died. She was deep in prayer when Trent touched her shoulder. She made the sign of the cross and walked back to the confessional. Trent pulled down the kneeling rail and the altar boy walked over and handed him a rosary. Trent bent his head and began to pray. He smiled as he began saying his penance. The priest must have felt sorry for him, because Trent was expecting a longer penance. A short time later Catherine joined him, and the altar boy handed her a rosary. Trent and Catherine finished praying at the same time. When they looked up, they saw the priest and altar boy waiting for them at the front of the church.

The priest whispered to them to kneel before him and they did.

Speaking in Latin, the priest said a few words and then made the sign of the cross. After several more prayers in Latin, he motioned for the young altar boy to bring him the communion chalice and wine goblet. Catherine and Trent took communion and said their silent prayers. When they finished, the priest raised his hands indicating for them to stand up. He leaned down and asked Trent their names and then proceeded to ask each to repeat the vows after him. Catherine and Trent exchanged rings and then the priest pronounced them man and wife. After they kissed, they were invited into the priest's office to sign the necessary papers and pay for the rosaries.

Catherine and Trent mechanically signed the papers, and Trent gave the priest two twenty-dollar bills and asked the priest to give the altar boy another gift of five dollars. After they said their thank you, the couple left. They stopped outside the church and Trent took Catherine into his arms and gave her a long kiss. Several people stopped and one man whistled. They started laughing as they ran down the church steps. Trent walked Catherine over to a bench in a small alcove off to the side of the church. It was a peaceful area surrounded by wisteria bushes that were just starting to bud. He turned to her and looked long and lovingly into her gentle hazel eyes.

He looked away for a minute and clenched his lips. Tears came to his eyes and he breathed in a deep breath. Catherine's eyes were beginning to fill with tears, too, and they took each other into their arms and held tightly.

"Catherine," Trent began to say, "I promise I'll do everything in my power to make you happy, to love you and your children for the rest of our lives, and I will lay down my life to keep you safe. You have made me so happy." He sniffed and took out his handkerchief and handed it first to Catherine and then she dabbed his teary eyes.

"I promise to always love you, Trent. I'll do the best I can to make you happy," she said.

"You already have," he answered.

They walked back to the town house and while Catherine put

her things in her satchel, Trent packed his own bag. He had picked her up and carried her inside the apartment when they arrived, but he told her the place wasn't good enough to spend their honeymoon in so he was taking her to the Roosevelt Hotel.

Catherine couldn't help but smile as she waited for Trent to check them in as Mr. and Mrs. Trent Matthews. It was then she realized that Merit also began with an "M" and the small hand towels she had with the initials "CM" could still be used. It was such an random thought at this time, but she felt almost giddy. She was Mrs. Trent Mathews and she had never felt so happy. It was as though when she said yes to Trent she was saying yes to herself, that she had a right to be happy. She was still daydreaming when Trent walked over and kissed her on the lips. She smiled up at him.

"Ready to see our room?" he asked.

The elevator stopped on the seventh floor and the bellman took both of their satchels to Room 706. Trent tipped the bellman and told him he would see to the bags. Trent opened the door and then picked Catherine up and carried her into the luxurious suite. He kissed her before he set her down. He walked back and brought in their two satchels.

"Are you hungry?" Trent asked.

"We can order something up later," she said smiling.

"What would be your pleasure?" he asked.

Catherine thought for a minute and then said, "We could make a baby."

Trent looked at her. "You want more children?" he asked.

"Yes, of course. I want to have your child."

Trent picked her up and swung her around the room with a big grin on his face. "I was afraid you wouldn't want any more children since you already had four."

"You do want to have children, don't you?" she asked.

Trent carried her over to the bed and laid her down. "More than anything," he said. "Nothing except being married to you would make me happier."

They slowly undressed each other and crawled under the covers. Trent could see the desire in her eyes and her sultry look invited him to take her. He wanted to tease her first, make her ask him for it. She reached up and pulled his mouth to hers and she whimpered when he searched her mouth for her tongue. He pulled back and she twisted her fingers in his hair, pulling him back to her and she poured all her overwhelming love into a sensual, long kiss. The palm of his hand slid down her back tracing her spine, and she pushed herself up against him and wrapped her leg over his thighs. His gaze moved down the front of her body and he started kissing her breast and suckling on her nipples. Her moans were alluring and he knew if he didn't slow down he wouldn't be able to stop himself. The smell of her lilac scent was driving him crazy.

Trent turned her over on her stomach and traced her spine with his fingers, circling her buttocks and moving his hand between her legs. He whispered to her to get up on her knees and when she did he came behind her and circled her body with his arms, exploring the sweet tenderness of her body. He moved his fingers between the folds of her clit and began massaging her. She screamed out, "Ahh, oh, Trent."

A few seconds later he pushed his arousal deep inside her and she pushed her hips back and leaned forward. This seemed to enhance the sensation of this lascivious position. Their animal instincts gave way to the ritual mating. Catherine reached up and grabbed the back of his head and the thrusts became more intense, more demanding until they both relinquished themselves to the lustfulness of their desires.

They fell onto the bed together and Catherine clung to Trent's body, lost in her own peaceful gratification. Trent pulled her closer to him and shivered. Catherine felt the tremors from his muscles; he had fulfilled her completely. Everything in Catherine's world now was enhanced by the thought of Trent being in it.

They spent the rest of the day in the hotel room, ordering room service and frequently making love. They had decided that Trent would ride the train back with her to Rosenberg early the next morning and together they would tell the children.

They sat as close as they could to each other after boarding the train, talking, holding hands, and occasionally kissing when they thought no one was watching them.

When they made it back to Catherine's house the children were in the kitchen with the Boudreaux and Sadie. They were all excited and the children were not quite sure what was going on, except Trent was now their father. They got up from their seats and went to him. Trent knelt down so he could be on eye level, grinning at their innocent questions and hugging them. When the children quieted down they sat and had breakfast with everyone.

Catherine and Trent spent the day answering questions the children asked, such as would Trent come to live with them and how long he was going to stay. They laughed and played as any family would and when the children finally went down for their naps, Catherine and Trent went to their bedroom to spend their last couple of hours alone.

"I hope you don't have any regrets. I know the children were rambunctious, but they will settle down once they get used to the idea," she said. Trent pulled her to him and held her.

"No regrets," he said. "And I want you to stop worrying about it. We are going to have a wonderful lifetime together, all of us. I wish I didn't have to leave you. I never told you this, but I've saved just about all the money I've ever made, and since this is my new home, I'll be here whenever I've completed my jobs; but we'll also have the town house for the next three months. Perhaps you could come to Houston occasionally and we could spend a night or two there and return to Rosenberg the next day. You could even bring the children," he suggested.

"I think if you are going to be away weeks at a time, I could manage to be away from the children for one night occasionally," she said.

Weeks turned into months and Catherine often met Trent at their town house when he returned from work, spending time reacquainting themselves with each other. These were the moments they cherished the most. Catherine was in the apartment when Trent returned from one of his trips. She had a wonderful dinner prepared for him and he hungrily kissed her when he came through the door. He always showered and shaved first and Catherine patiently waited for him to come to their bed. She was staring up at the ceiling, listening for the shower to be turned off and wondering how she should give Trent her exciting news. She decided to wait until after they had made love to tell him, as she was afraid he might try to be too gentle with her and she wanted him to have only one thing on his mind; her, and only her.

Their lovemaking had always been a good escape from their tireless work. It was romantic and passionate. She smiled as her naked husband walked over to the bed, and his strong, awesome body sent the usual chills down her spine. She lifted the covers for him as he slid beside her and took her into his arms. These were the moments they cherished. After they made love, Trent put on his robe and followed Catherine over to the table for dinner and noticed only one wine glass.

"Aren't you joining me for a glass of wine?" he asked.

"I'm not sure it would be good for the baby," she replied.

Trent didn't say anything for a few minutes before he broke into a wide grin. "You mean I'm going to be a father?"

She smiled back and shook her head yes. It was at that moment that Catherine knew that she had everything a woman could ask for. Her prayers had been answered and the gentle giant, her loving husband, was sitting in front of her.

She was content and happy now, and she smiled when she thought of having Trent's baby. Nothing from her past was important any more. She didn't have to run away from anything and if she did run, it would be into Trent's loving, strong arms.

CPSIA information can be obtained at www.ICGtesting.com
Printed in the USA
LVOW06s1658250815

451463LV00003B/428/P